FLORIDA

WILDLIFE ENCYCLOPEDIA

FLORIDA
WILDLIFE ENCYCLOPEDIA

AN ILLUSTRATED GUIDE TO BIRDS, FISH, MAMMALS, REPTILES, AND AMPHIBIANS

SCOTT SHUPE

Skyhorse Publishing

Skyhorse Publishing books may be purchased in bulk at special discounts for sales promotion, corporate gifts, fund-raising, or educational purposes. Special editions can also be created to specifications. For details, contact the Special Sales Department, Skyhorse Publishing, 307 West 36th Street, 11th Floor, New York, NY 10018 or info@skyhorsepublishing.com.

Skyhorse® and Skyhorse Publishing® are registered trademarks of Skyhorse Publishing, Inc.®, a Delaware corporation.

Visit our website at www.skyhorsepublishing.com.

10 9 8 7 6 5 4 3 2

Library of Congress Cataloging-in-Publication Data is available on file.

Cover design by Rain Saukas
Cover photos by Scott Shupe

Print ISBN: 978-1-5107-2886-8
Ebook ISBN: 978-1-5107-2891-2

Printed in China

ACKNOWLEDGEMENTS

The author gratefully acknowledges the following individuals who contributed to the completion of this book. In no particular order, those individuals are:

Rob Mottice, senior aquarist at the Tennessee Aquarium in Chattanooga, Tennessee, for help in identifying freshwater fish species photographed at that facility.

David Wilkins, curator at the South Carolina Aquarium in Charleston, South Carolina, for his help in identifying freshwater fish species photographed at his facility.

Larry Warner, North Carolina Aquarium on Roanoke Island, North Carolina, for his help in identifying freshwater fish species photographed at his facility.

The staff of the North Carolina Aquarium at Pine Knoll Shores, North Carolina, for help in identifying freshwater fish species photographed at that facility.

The staff at the Georgia Fish Center for helping identify minnow species photographed at that facility.

The staff at the Texas Freshwater Fisheries Center for help in identifying minnow species photographed at that facility.

Dave Frymire for helping the author secure herp specimens for photography and for allowing me to photograph several snake species in his possession.

John R. MacGregor for providing a number of reptile, amphibian, and mammal photographs used in this book.

Matthew R. Thomas for help in identifying several species of darters and minnows photographed by the author for this book as well as for his technical advice and ichthyological expertise; and for providing a large number of fish photographs used in the book.

Amy Berry, Clay Hill Memorial Forest and Nature Center, for providing fish and amphibian specimens for photography.

Dr. Gordon Weddle, Campbellsville University, for providing fish and amphibian specimens for photography.

Dr. Richard Kessler, Campbellsville University, for help collecting fish specimens for photography.

Jim Harrison and Kristin Wiley of the Kentucky Reptile Zoo for allowing the author to photograph snake species at their facility.

Judy Tipton for allowing me to photograph birds in her yard.

Matt Wagner and John Hardy from the Mississippi Museum of Natural History for helping to ID fishes photographed in aquariums at that facility.

Brainard Palmer-Ball of the Kentucky Ornithological Society for help identifying fall warblers photographed by the author for this book.

Candy McNamee for several photo contributions and for guiding the author on a search for migratory birds along the Texas coast.

Karen Finch for guiding the author in a search for migratory birds in south Florida.

Dr. Tim Spier, Murray State University, for his help in collecting fish specimens for photography.

John Hewlett who accompanied the author in the field and helped locate and collect fish and reptile specimens for photography.

James Kiser for providing several hard-to-get photographs used in this book.

Loren Taylor for help in locating contributing bird photographers.

The Staff of the Appalachicola National Estuarine Reserve for helping to identify fish species photographed at their facility.

The Staff of the Guano Tolomota Matanzas National Estuarine Reserve for helping to identify fish species photographed at their facility.

Jack Richardson for allowing the author to photograph fish at his facility.

Tony Austin and the staff of the Rio Pinar Country Club in Orlando, Florida, for allowing the author to access their properties to photograph Sherman's Fox Squirrels.

Dr. Adam Kaeser, US Fish and Wildlife Service, for his photo contribution.

Frans Vermeulen, www.itrainsfishes.net, for photo contribution.

Don Martin of Don Martin Bird Photography for contributing several of the more excellent bird photos in the book.

T. Travis Brown for his photo contributions

David Speiser, www.lilibirds.com, for several professional quality bird photo contributions.

Jeffrey Offereman for his photo contribution.

Konrad Schmidt of North America Native Fish Association for contributions of several great fish photos.

Brian Zimmerman, www.ZimmermansFish.com, for several quality fish photo contributions.

Cheryl Tanner for her photo contribution.

Chris Crippen for photo contribution.

John Williams for his photo contribution.

Fishing with Pole for photo contributions.

Dr. Edmund Zimmerer, professor emeritus of biology at Murray State University, for his photo contributions.

Tim Johnson for his photo contribution and for his help locating other wildlife photographers.

Aubrey Pawlikowski of the Georgia Department of Natural Resources for her photo contribution.

Kyle S. Shupe for being the author's eyes and ears during wildlife photography excursions across the southeastern United States.

Victor G. Ferenzi for his photo contribution.

Florida Fish and Wildlife Conservation Commission for permission to download and use photos from their Flickr site.

Corey Raimond for his photo contributions.

US Fish and Wildlife Service for photo contribution.

Sandeep Gangadharan for his photo contribution.

Dan Scolaro for his photo contributions.

Greg Schechter for his photo contribution.

Brett Albanese of the Georgia Department of Natural Resources for several fish photo contributions.

Jenifer Wisniewski of the Georgia Department of Natural Resources for assistance in acquiring needed photographs.

Alan Cressler for his photo contributions.

Whit Gibbons, professor emeritus of ecology at University of Georgia, for assistance in locating photos of Florida herpetofauna.

National Oceanic and Atmospheric Admistration/Department of Commerce/NOAH Library and SEFSC Pacagoula Laboratory and collection of Brandi Noble for several fish photos.

Howard Jelks and Noel Burkhead, US Geological Survey, for several fish photo contributions.

J.D. Willson for contributing several reptile and fish photos.

Jake Scott for several outstanding photos of Florida herpetofauna.

W. Mike Howell for providing several important fish photos.

Thanks also to the North American Native Fish Association (NANFA) website, which hosts many of the fish photographers whose photos appear in this book.

Jules Wyman for his photo contribution.

Anthony Terceira for his photo contribution.

Last but certainly not least I would like to thank my publisher Skyhorse Publishing and editor Jason Katzman for patience with and faith in this author. Finally, this book is dedicated to author's three sons. Haydn, Denham, and Kyle Shupe. Though now adults, as youngsters their keen eyes, youthful enthusiasm, and unflinching companionship were responsible for the author getting many of the photographs in this book. More importantly, their presence in this world has consistently provided this author with a unremitting source of love and inspiration.

PHOTOGRAPHERS

Most of the 750-plus wildlife photographs that appear in this book were taken by the author. However, many of the quality photographs were contributed by several other wildlife photographers from across the US and around the world. Those individuals were critical to the completion of this book, and their remarkable photographs add much to its content. The names of those additional photographers and the number of photos each contributed appear below.

Florida Fish and Wildlife Conservation Commission - 19
Brian Zimmerman - 17
Dr. Edmund Zimmerer - 10
Brett Albanese, Georgia Department of Natural Resources - 9
Matthew R. Thomas - 8
John R. MacGregor - 8
Don Martin Bird Photography - 8
J. D. Willson - 7
Candy McNamee - 6
James Kiser - 5
Jake Scott - 5
David Speiser, www.lilibirds.com - 4
Noel Burkhead, USGS - 4
Howard Jelks and Noel Burkhead, USGS - 4
Alan Cressler - 3
Konrad Schmidt - 3
Corey Raimond - 3
W. Mike Howell - 2
NOAH Library and SEFSC Pacagoula Laboratory; collection of Brandi Noble - 2
Fishingwithpole - 2
Dan Scolaro -2
Tim Johnson - 1
Aubrey Pawlikowski - 1
T. Travis Brown - 1
Victor G. Ferenzi- 1
Cheryl Tanner - 1
Jeffrey Offermann, https://www.flickr.com/photos/jeff_offermann - 1
John Williams - 1
Chris Crippen - 1
US Fish and Wildlife Service - 2
Sandeep Gangadharan -1
Greg Schechter - 1
Howard Jelks, USGS - 1
Jules Wyman - 1
Dr. Adam Kaeser - 1
Frans Vermeulen, www.itrainsfishes.net - 1
Anthony Terceira - 1

TABLE OF CONTENTS

FLORIDA

WILDLIFE ENCYCLOPEDIA

INTRODUCTION

Wildlife has always played an important role in the history of human beings inhabiting the state of Florida. Native Americans depended on birds, mammals, and fish for sustenance and used body parts for tools and clothing. The state's first European explorers encountered new and intimidating species like the American Alligator and the Eastern Diamondback Rattlesnake. In later years, "plume hunters" ventured into the Florida wilderness in search of enormous rookeries of herons and egrets, killing an abominable number of birds for feathers that were used to adorn the hats of fashionable ladies. Meanwhile, the American Alligator was hunted to near extinction for its tough, scaly hide that made durable leather for luggage and boots. Although the state's wildlife is still an important resource for human consumption, wildlife is also increasingly important in today's culture for its intrinsic, aesthetic value. For many Floridians, the age-old traditions of hunting and fishing have been replaced by a desire to simply observe wildlife and experience nature. The range of wildlife-related interests and activities has broadened so considerably that the US Fish and Wildlife Service, in its most recent assessment of the economic impact of wildlife in America, lists a broad catagory labeled "Wildlife Watching." In this assessment, the Fish and Wildlife Service further states that the economic impact of wildlife watching in America today far exceeds the impact that hunters and fishermen have on the America economy.

Despite this increased interest in nature and wildlife, most Floridians remain largely unaware of the diversity of species inhabiting their state. This volume is intended to provide an introduction to the state's freshwater fishes, amphibians, reptiles, birds, and mammals.

While a number of excellent books about Florida's birds, reptiles, and fishes exist, there are none that combine all the state's wildlife into a comprehensive, encyclopedic reference. This volume is intended to fill that niche. It is hoped that this book will find favor with school librarians, life science teachers, students in field biology classes, and professional naturalists as well as with the general populace.

As might be expected with such a broad-spectrum publication, intimate details about the natural history of individual species is omitted in favor of a format that provides more basic information. In this sense, this volume is not intended for use as a professional reference, but instead as a handy, usable, layman's guide to the state's wildlife. For those who wish to explore the information regarding the state's wildlife more deeply, a list of references for each chapter appears in the back of the book and includes both print and reliable Internet references.

Embracing the old adage that a picture is worth a thousand words, color photographs are used to depict and identify each species. Below each photograph is a table that provides basic information about the biology of each animal. This table includes a state map with a shaded area showing the species' presumed range in the state, as well as general information such as size, habitat, abundance, etc. The taxonomic classification of each species is also provided, with the animal's Class, Order, and Family appearing as a heading at the top of the page.

The range maps shown in this book are not intended to be regarded as a strictly accurate representation of the range of any given species. Indeed, the phrase "Presumed range in Florida," which accompanies each species range map, should be literally interpreted. The ranges of many species in the state are often not well-documented. The range maps for some species in this book may be regarded as at best an "educated guess." Furthermore, many wide-ranging species are restricted to regions of suitable habitat. Thus an aquatic species like the large, eel-like salamander known as the Two-toed Amphiuma, while found statewide, would not be expected to occur in dry, sandy, upland woods. Additionally, other species that may have once been found throughout a large geographic area may now have disappeared from much of their former range. The Eastern Diamondback Rattlesnake is an example of a species that was once common statewide but has declined significantly in recent decades.

Further complicating the issue of species distribution is the fact that animals like birds and bats, possessed with the ability of flight are capable of traveling great distances. Many species of both birds and bats are migratory and regularly travel hundreds or even thousands of miles annually. It is not uncommon for these migratory species to sometimes appear in areas where they are not typically found.

The mechanisms of migration and dispersal of many animals is still a bit of a mystery and the exact reason why a bird from another portion of the country (or even from another continent) should suddenly appear where it doesn't belong is often speculation. Sometimes these appearances may represent individuals that are simply wandering. Other times it can be a single bird or an entire flock that has been blown off course by a powerful storm or has become otherwise lost and disoriented. Whatever the cause, there are many bird species that have been recorded in the state that are not really a part of Florida's native fauna, and their occasional sightings are regarded as "accidental."

On the other hand, some species may appear somewhere in the state once every few years dependent upon weather conditions or availability of prey in its normal habitat. Although these types of "casual species" could be regarded as belonging among Florida's native bird fauna, their occurrence in the state is so sporadic and unpredictable that deciding which species should be included as a native becomes very subjective. The point is that the reader should be advised that while all the bird species depicted in this volume can be considered to be members of the state's indigenous fauna, *not every bird species that has been seen or recorded in in the state is depicted in this book.*

Finally, because Florida's warm, humid, and subtropical to tropical climates are condusive to the survival of many vertebrate species from around the world, Florida is plagued today with scores of "alien" species that have become established as breeding populations in the state. Although the main thrust of this volume is to depict the state's *native* species, many introduced species are included in this book. Alien species that have become common are included, but each is noted in the Natural History section of the species accounts as being a non-native, introduced species.

For readers who wish to delve into more professional and detailed information about the vertebrate zoology of Florida, the list of references in the back of this book (shown for each chapter) should adequately provide that opportunity.

Scott Shupe, 2019.

CHAPTER 1
THE FACE OF THE LAND

Defining and understanding natural regions is the first step in understanding the natural history of Florida. Man-made political boundaries such as county lines and state borders are meaningless to wildlife, whereas natual features like rivers or upland regions can be important elements in influencing the distribution of wildlife.

The major considerations used in determining and delineating natural regions are factors such as elevation, relief (topography), drainages, geology, and climate. All these are important elements that can determine the limits of distribution for living organisms. It follows then that some knowledge of these factors is essential when involved in the study of the state's natural history. The study of natural regions is known as *Physiography*, which means "physical geography" or literally "the face of the land." While the terms geography and physiography are closely related and sometimes used interchangeably, geography is a broader term which includes such things as human culture, resource use, and man's impact on the land, while physiography deals only with elements of geography created by nature.

The term most often used to define a major natural region is "*Physiographic Division*." There are ten major physiographic divisions across the United States and Canada. Figure 1 below shows the major physiographic divisions affecting the eastern half of the United States.

The **Atlantic Plain Division**, within which all of Florida and much of the southern United States is contained, occurs mostly offshore (the Continental Shelf). The Atlantic Plain Division consists of two smaller subdivisions known

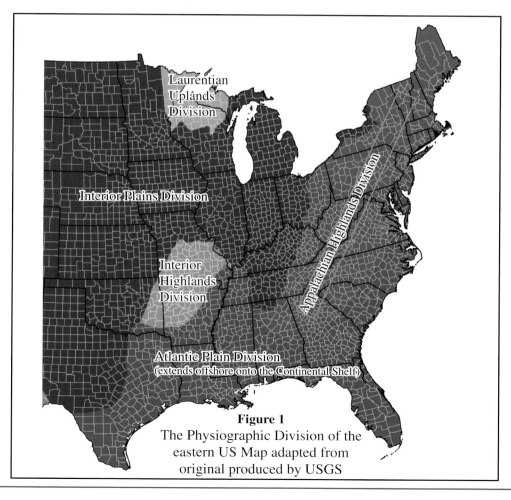

Figure 1
The Physiographic Division of the eastern US Map adapted from original produced by USGS

as provinces, one of which, the **Coastal Plain Province**, affects mainland America (see Figure 2 below).

The Map below shows how the Physiographic divisions of the eastern US are subdivided into smaller units called "*Physiographic Provinces*." Note that the entire state of Florida is contained within the province known as the Coastal Plain. The provinces of the eastern US (shown in Figure 2 below) are subdivided further into

Physiographic Sections (also sometimes call "Natural Regions"). Figure 3 on the following page shows how the Coastal Plain Province is divided into six different Physiographic Sections. Three of those sections—the *Eastern Gulf Coastal Plain Section*, the *Sea Islands Section*, and the *Florida Section*—impact the state of Florida. Figure 4 shows a close-up of Florida with the three physiographic sections of the state.

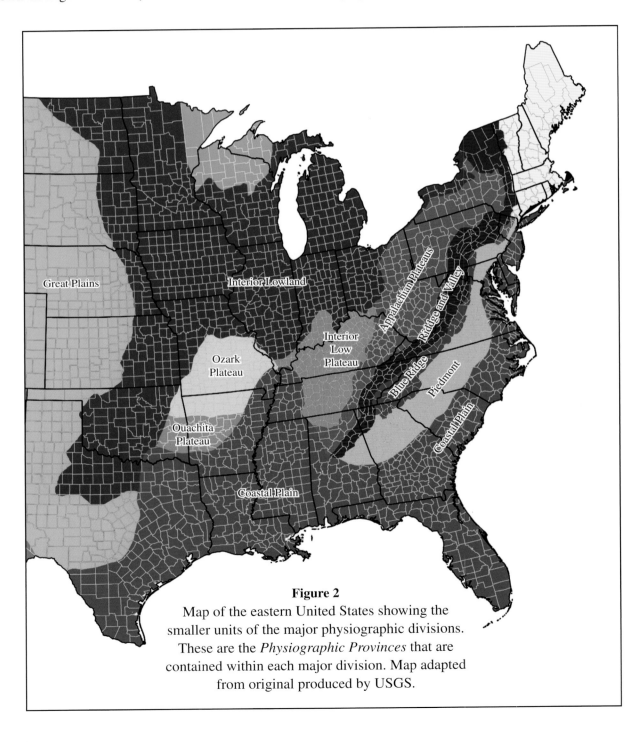

Figure 2
Map of the eastern United States showing the smaller units of the major physiographic divisions. These are the *Physiographic Provinces* that are contained within each major division. Map adapted from original produced by USGS.

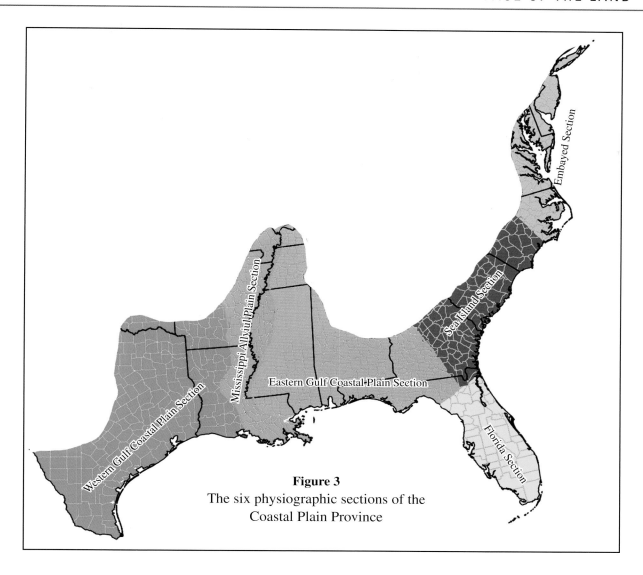

Figure 3
The six physiographic sections of the
Coastal Plain Province

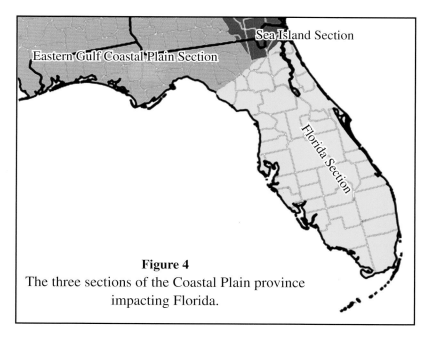

Figure 4
The three sections of the Coastal Plain province
impacting Florida.

CHAPTER 2

ECOREGIONS AND WILDLIFE HABITATS OF FLORIDA

First, it should be noted that in ecology, as in the study of most other scientific disciplines, different opinions exist among experts as to the definition of a particular habitat or ecoregion (such as types of forests). Man's understanding of the earth's ecology continues to evolve and not every ecologist adopts the same model or criteria in describing habitats and ecosystems. Moreover, different models may be used by different researchers based on the needs of that research. The ecological model adopted here is derived from the ecoregions used by the

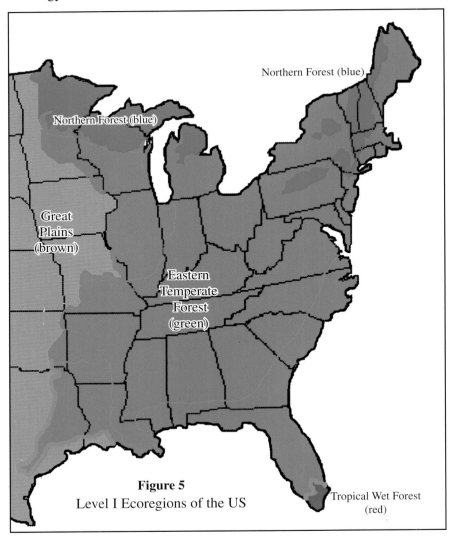

Figure 5
Level I Ecoregions of the US

Environmental Protection Agency (www.epa.gov/ed/ecoregions).

The Environmental Protection Agency recognizes a total of 14 "Level I Ecoregions" in the US and Canada. Most of the state of Florida falls within one of the larger of North America's 14 Level I Ecoregions, known as **Eastern Temperate Forest**. But a small portion of southernmost Florida falls within the ecoregion known as **Tropical Wet Forests**. Figure 5 on page 6 shows the Level I Ecoregions of the eastern US. Ecoregion designations are based upon a number of factors that can include physical considerations such as climate, physiography, and geology. But most important are the biological factors such as the plant and animal species present. The term "ecoregion" is defined by the World Wildlife Fund as "*a*

large unit of land or water containing a geographically distinct assemblage of species, natural communities, and environmental conditions." At the Level I designation, it is apparent that the dominant plant species (or dominant forest type) is a major factor in delineating the region.

Many wildlife species native to Florida are widespread and may occur in more than one major ecoregion. The Eastern Gray Squirrel and the Red Fox for instance are two examples of mammal species that range throughout all the Level I ecoregions of the eastern US. Many birds found in Florida are also wide-rangeing species that for at least a part of the year may be seen throughout the eastern US.

By constrast, some species may be restricted to a single ecoregion. The American Crocodile and the White-crowned Pigeon are two examples of Florida species that

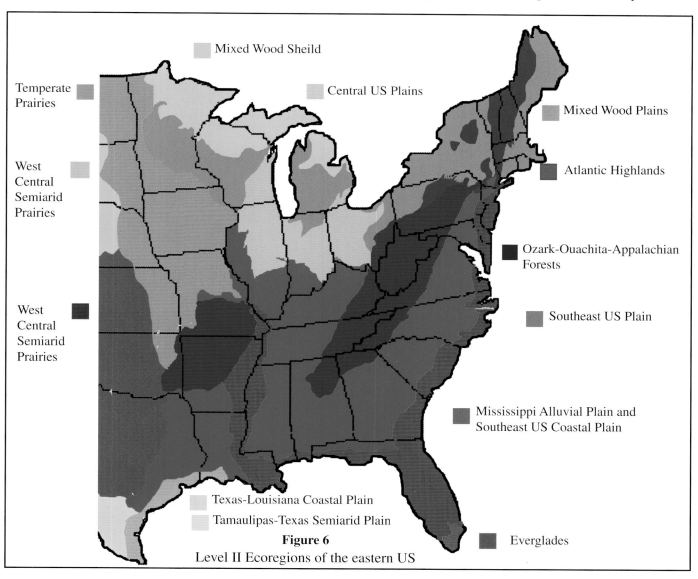

Figure 6
Level II Ecoregions of the eastern US

are endemic to a single Level I ecoregion, the Tropical Wet Forest.

America's Level I ecoregions consist of progressively smaller subunits known as Level II Ecoregions, Level III Ecoregions, and Level IV ecoregions. This hierarchical system with progressively smaller ecoregion units provides a more precise definition of the factors involved in ecoregion designation, i.e. climate, physiography, plant, and animal communities, etc.

When making consideratons of conservation issues related to wildlife populations, natural scientists can find ecoregion designations to be useful. Man-made designations such as state lines or county borders are meaningless to wildlife, whereas ecoregions and habitats may crucial to a species' distribution.

Figure 6 is a map of the eastern US showing the next level of ecoregion designations, the Level II Ecoregions. What is immediately apparent from Figure 6 is that the Level II ecoregions are a much more complex designation than those seen in Figure 5 (the Level I ecoregions). On the map shown in Figure 6, the boundaries of the Tropical Wet Forest (Level I ecoregion) remains unchanged, but the name is changed at Level II to the **Everglades** region. The Eastern Temperate Forest Level I Ecoregion is divided at Level II into 5 smaller ecoregions; but only two of these impact on the state of Florida. The two Level II ecoregions of the Eastern Temperate Forest that occur in Florida are the **Southeast US Plains** and the **Mississippi Alluvial Plain and Southeast Coastal Plain**.

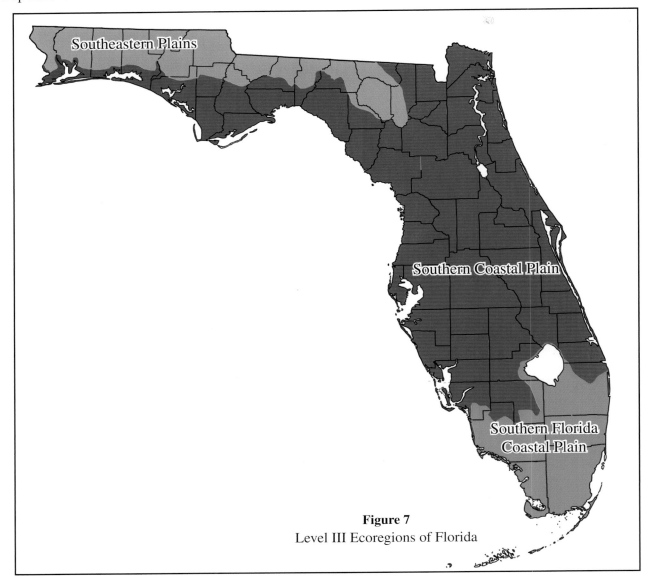

Figure 7
Level III Ecoregions of Florida

The next level of corresponding ecoregions is of course Level III Ecoregions. At this point in the discussion of ecoregions, it becomes appropriate to focus the discussion on the state of Florida only, as three of the five Level II ecoregions of the Mississippi Alluvial Plain and Southeast Coast Plain occur outside the state of Florida.

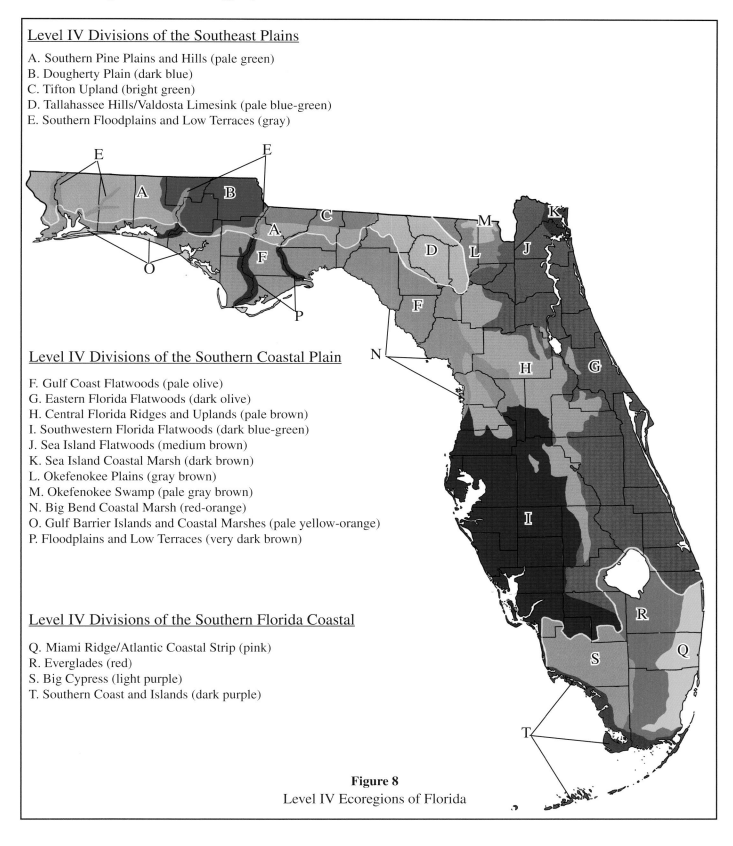

Level IV Divisions of the Southeast Plains

A. Southern Pine Plains and Hills (pale green)
B. Dougherty Plain (dark blue)
C. Tifton Upland (bright green)
D. Tallahassee Hills/Valdosta Limesink (pale blue-green)
E. Southern Floodplains and Low Terraces (gray)

Level IV Divisions of the Southern Coastal Plain

F. Gulf Coast Flatwoods (pale olive)
G. Eastern Florida Flatwoods (dark olive)
H. Central Florida Ridges and Uplands (pale brown)
I. Southwestern Florida Flatwoods (dark blue-green)
J. Sea Island Flatwoods (medium brown)
K. Sea Island Coastal Marsh (dark brown)
L. Okefenokee Plains (gray brown)
M. Okefenokee Swamp (pale gray brown)
N. Big Bend Coastal Marsh (red-orange)
O. Gulf Barrier Islands and Coastal Marshes (pale yellow-orange)
P. Floodplains and Low Terraces (very dark brown)

Level IV Divisions of the Southern Florida Coastal

Q. Miami Ridge/Atlantic Coastal Strip (pink)
R. Everglades (red)
S. Big Cypress (light purple)
T. Southern Coast and Islands (dark purple)

Figure 8
Level IV Ecoregions of Florida

The map in Figure 7 shows the Level III ecoregions of Florida. Note that the boundaries for the Level III ecoregions in Florida are same as those of Level II, but the names are different. For example, the Level III portion of the Mississippi Alluvial and Southeast Coastal Plain (Level II) that occurs in Florida is the **Southeast Plains**. Likewise, the Level III portion of the Southeast US Plains (Level II) that occurs in Florida is known as the **Southern Coastal Plain**. The Everglades region (Level II), at Level III is called the **Southern Florida Coastal Plain**.

Note how closely the Level III ecoregions in Figure 7 below resemble the physiographic sections of the state shown in Figure 4 on page 5. This similarity is due in part to fact that physiography is one of the many factors that are incorporated into the process of delineating ecoregions. The Level III ecoregions shown in Figure 7 are further divided into Level IV Ecoregions, shown below in Figure 8. There are a total of 20 Level IV ecoregions in Florida. The Southeastern Plains Level III ecoregion has 5 Level IV ecoregions in Florida. The Southern Coastal Plain has 11 Level IV ecoregions, and the Southern Florida Coastal Plain has a total of 4.

On the map in Figure 8 the boundaries of Florida's Level III ecoregions are denoted by the bright yellow lines. In this book, as in many discussions about the natural environments of America, the terms *habitat* and *ecoregion* are frequently used interchangeably. But strictly speaking, there are differences between the two. The term "ecoregion," as defined by the World Wildlife Fund, means "a large unit of land or water containing a geographically distinct assemblage of species, natural communities, and environmental conditions." The term ecoregion also usually encompasses some of the regions physiographic features as well. A *habitat* meanwhile is usually defined simply as "where an organism lives." Thus, an area of mesic (moist) forest or xeric (dry) forest are both *habitats* that are contained within a particular *ecoregion*. Each of the 20 Level IV Ecoregions shown in Figure 8 on the previous page can contain a variety of habitats such as wet or dry woodlands, marshes, swamps, prairies, etc. In many publications, the word "biome" is sometimes used synonymously with both the term habitat and the term ecoregion.

The habitats of Florida have been well studied and some experts today recognize well over 50 designated habitat types in mainland Florida. Several more are added when the state's saltwater habitats are included.

A complete discussion of the varied habitats of the state is beyond the scope of this book. However, for those interested in learning more about the habitats of Florida, the following publications are hightly recommended: *Guide to the Natural Communities of Florida* by Florida Natural Areas Inventory and Florida Department of Natural Resources; and *Priceless Florida, Natural Ecosystems and Native Species* from Pineapple Press, Inc., Sarasota, FL.

CHAPTER 3

THE MAMMALS OF FLORIDA

TABLE 1

— THE ORDERS AND FAMILIES OF FLORIDA MAMMALS —

Note: The arrangement below reflects the the order in which the mammals of Florida appear in this chapter. It is not an accurate reflection of the phylogenetic relationship of the mammals.

Class - **Mammalia** (mammals)

Order - **Sirenia**

Family	**Trichechedia** (manatees)

Order - **Artiodactlya** (hoofed mammals)

Family	**Suidae** (pigs)
Family	**Cervidae** (deer family)

Order - **Didelphimorpha** (opossums)

Family	**Didelphidae** (opossum)

Order - **Cingulata** (armadillos, anteaters, and sloths)

Family	**Dasypodidae** (armadillos)

Order - **Carnivora** (carnivores)

Family	**Mustelidae** (weasel family)
Family	**Procyondidae** (raccoon family)
Family	**Ursidae** (bears)
Family	**Felidae** (cat family)
Family	**Canidae** (canines)
Family	**Mephitidae** (skunks)

Order - **Lagamorpha** (rabbits and hares)

Family	**Leporidae** (rabbits)

Order - **Rodentia** (rodents)

Family	**Sciuridae** (squirrel family)
Family	**Castoridae** (beaver)
Family	**Myocastoridae** (nutria)
Family	**Geomyidae** (pocket gophers)
Family	**Muridae** (rats and mice)

Order - **Soricimorpha** (moles and shrews)

Family	**Sorcidae** (shrews)
Family	**Talpidae** (moles)

Order - **Chiroptera** (bats)

Family	**Vespertililionidae** (vesper bats)
Family	**Molossidae** (free-tailed bats)

Class - **Mammalia** (mammals)

Order - **Sirenia**	Order - **Artiodactyla** (hoofed mammals)
Family - **Trichechidae** (manatees)	Family - **Suidae** (pigs)

West Indian Manatee
Trichechus manatus

Size: Can attain a maximum size of 15 feet and over 3,000 pounds.

Abundance: Rare. A federally threatened species.

Variation: No variation in Florida.

Presumed range in Florida

Habitat: Shallow waters of warm, tropical, and subtropical seas along the southeastern coastline of America and throughout the Caribbean. In Florida uses freshwater rivers and spring runs extensively, especially in winter.

Breeding: Manatees have a very low reproductive rate. Females do not breed until nearly 5 years old. Breeding occurs only every 3, 4, or 5 years. A single baby (calf) is born following 13 months of gestation. The young calf will stay with the mother for about 2 years.

Natural History: The Manatee is one of Florida's most unique wild animals. Despite the similarites in lifestyle, they are not closely related to seals, but are more closely related to elephants. They are completely aquatic and totally vegetarian. The list of threats to this placid animal in Florida today is long. Collisions with fast-moving boats in both shallow coastal waters and in freshwater rivers cause many injuries and fatalities. Loss of habitat, pollution, and entanglement in fishing nets or lines are hazards that have caused death and injury. Extreme cold fronts in winter also pose a threat to Manatees caught away from warm water spring runs or in shallow coastal seas. Effluent of warm waters from power plants around the coast have become a new winter refuge for Manatees. These localities have also created new tourist attractions as wildlife lovers flock to boardwalks and viewing platforms see these these gentle giants. The Florida Fish and Wildlife Conservation Commission now has a management plan for the conservation of this magnificent animal in Florida waters.

Feral Hog
Sus scrofa

Size: Males can reach 500 pounds and a length of 6 feet. Females are smaller.

Abundance: Fairly common.

Variation: Highly variable. Typically black or very dark brown but can be reddish or spotted brown and black or black and white.

Presumed range in Florida

Habitat: A real habitat generalist, wild hogs exist throughout Florida in all habitats. They can also be found in the deciduous woodlands of the Appalachians and the xeric plains of Texas.

Breeding: May breed at any time throughout the year. Young are born in a nest of vegetation constructed by the female. Litter size is variable with as many as 16 young recorded. Average litter is probably about 5 or 6. Babies from hogs that have been wild for generations are brown with light stripes and resemble the young of the European Wild Boar. There is some evidence that larger litters occur when ample food is readily available. Female piglets can breed at about 10 months of age.

Natural History: Although not native, Feral Hogs have been a member of Florida's wildlife community for hundreds of years. Some believe they arrived with the very first Spanish explorers. Like most non-native species, they can be detrimental to the overall environment and year-round hunting without a license is allowed on private property in Florida. Some states farther to the north have instituted vigorous eradication programs aimed at preventing the establishment of wild hogs withing their borders. In states like Florida where the species is well established and there is an abundance of cover and nearly impenetrable natural habitats, total eradication of the species is probably not achievable. Anything edible is consumed, including a wide variety of grasses and herbs along with all types of fruits, berries, nuts, seeds, and roots. Ground-dwelling invertebrates and small vertebrates are also eaten, including snakes.

Class - **Mammalia** (mammals)
Order - **Artiodactyla** (hoofed mammals)
Family - **Cervidae** (deer family)
Whitetail Deer - *Odocoileus virginianus*

Buck	Doe	Fawn

Size: Deer from the northernmost regions of America have a larger body size than those in the southern parts of the the US. This is due to a phenomena known as "Bergman's Rule." Larger bodies lose heat less rapidly due to the smaller ratio of body volume to surface area, thus in colder regions mammals with a larger body size tend to survive better. Florida deer are smaller than those found farther north. Males from north Florida may be up to 40 inches high at shoulder. Females are about 20 percent smaller. North Florida males can weigh up to 190 pounds while south Florida bucks can be as small as 80 pounds, as in the case of the Key Deer.

Presumed range in Florida

Abundance: Very common.

Variation: There are as many as 13 different subspecies of Whitetail Deer recognized in mainland North America, plus several more island races. 3 subspecies occur in Florida. Subspecies *osceola* is found in the panhandle, subspecies *seminolis* in peninsula Florida, and *clavium* in the Keys. Young (fawns) exhibit a pattern of white spots that fade with age. Adults have a reddish brown color in the summer and grayish in the fall/winter.

Habitat: Found in virtually every habitat within the state and increasingly common in urban areas. Favorite habitats are a mix of woodland, brushy areas and weedy fields, especially near farmlands. Successional areas, such as regrowth of woodlands after fires or logging, is also a prime habitat. They are least common in mature, unbroken forests and in areas of intensive agriculture or major urbanization.

Breeding: Breeding begins in early fall and may continue into the winter, with the peak breeding season occurring in November. 1 or 2 (rarely 3 or even 4) young are born in the spring or early summer following a 6.5-month gestation. Females (does) usually bear their first offspring at 2 years of age. The first pregnancy typically results in a single fawn, the second pregnancy usually is twins, and the third through fifth twins or triplets (rarely quadruplets). Young lie hidden for the first few weeks and are left alone much of the time. The female will visit the hidden fawn about once every 4 hours to allow nursing, then moves away to avoid attracting predators. At about 1 month of age, the young will begin to follow the mother and stay close through the summer and into the fall.

Natural History: Bucks (males) shed their antlers each year in late winter and regrow a new set by fall. Growing deer antlers are among the fastest growing animal tissue known. While growing, the antlers are covered in a spongy, fuzzy skin called "velvet." Antlers grow larger each year up to about 6 or 7 years of age, when they begin a gradual decline. Whitetail Deer are browsers and they feed on a wide variety of forbs, leaves, twigs, buds, crops, and mast (especially acorns). Although they are sometimes destructive to farm crops like corn or soybeans, they are an important game animal with as many as 100,000 harvested annually for food and sport. The maximum life span is 20 years, but most are dead by age 10. State wildlife agencies are charged with the responsibility of protecting and managing the state's wildlife populations. This means taking into consideration not only the health and well-being of the state's deer herd, but also the cultural aspect of providing food and recreation for the state's hunting population. Additional considerations are such things as crop depredation by deer to the state's farmers and impacts on auto insurance rates by deer-auto collisions. Thus determining how many deer of what sex should be harvested annually involves taking into consideration many factors. Happily, this animal represents one of the world's great wildlife conservation stories. Nearly wiped out by the early 1900s, the Whitetail Deer is today as numerous in America as it was during the time of Daniel Boone. In recent years, these animals have begun to invade urban areas where deer hunting is restricted. In towns and cities, they can become a nuisance as they feed in suburban gardens and devour landscape plants. Still, many urban dwellers enjoy their presence.

Class - **Mammalia** (mammals)

Order - **Didelphimorphia** (opossums)	Order - **Cingulata**
Family - **Didelphidae**	Family - **Dasypodidae** (armadillos)
Virginia Opossum *Didelphis virginiana*	**Nine-banded Armadillo** *Dasypus novemcinctus*

Size: About 2.5 feet from nose to tail tip. Males can weigh up to 14 pounds, females are smaller.	Presumed range in Florida	**Size:** About 30 inches from snout to tail tip. Can weigh up to 17 pounds.	Presumed range in Florida
Abundance: This is one of the most common medium-sized mammals in Florida.		**Abundance:** Very common. One of Florida's most common medium-sized mammals.	

Variation: Opossums are quite variable. All white or all black individuals can occur, along with a cinnamon color.

Variation: There is no significant variation. The sexes look alike but males are somewhat larger than females.

Habitat: Virtually all habitats within the state are utilized except for permanent wetlands. Including suburban and even urban areas where there is enough vegetative cover. Opossums are more common in areas altered by humans, such as farmlands and the vicinity of small, rural communities. They are less common in areas of true wilderness.

Habitat: This wide-ranging animal's habitat includes everything from tropical rain forest to arid semi-desert, grassland, and temperate forests. Moist or sandy soils are preferred as they facilitate easier digging of denning burrows as well as rooting for soil invertebrates. In Florida, this species is common statewide.

Breeding: This is America's only member of the mammalian subclass Marsupialia. Young Opossums are born as embryos only 12 days after conception. The newborn babies are just over 0.5 inches in length. At 1 month, they are about the size of a mouse. Litters are large (up to 13) and 2 litters per year is common.

Breeding: Females always give birth to 4 identical twins, all derived from a single fertilized egg that divides in 2, then divides again to form 4 zygotes before beginning to then develop into individual embryos. The young are well-developed at birth, which reduces mortality among immatures. 1 litter per year is typical.

Natural History: Opossums are one of the most successful medium-sized mammals in America, which is somewhat surprising given that they are slow moving, rather dim-witted animals that rarely survive beyond 2 years in the wild. They are mainly nocturnal and eat mostly any palatable plant matter (seeds, grains, fruits, berries); and any type of meat they can catch or scavenge. They are known to kill and eat venomous snakes and have a strong resistance to pit viper venoms. They are well-known for faking death (playing possum) when stressed. Their greatest enemy today is the automobile. Thousands are killed nightly on highways across America.

Natural History: Armadillos first began their northern expansion into the US from Mexico about 150 years ago. They began to appear in Florida in the 1920s. Today, increasing numbers are being seen farther and farther to the north and they now occur as far north as southern Missouri and southern Illinois. How far north they will spread is unknown. Cold climates may be a limiting factor to their spread. Surprisingly, Armadillos are capable of swimming and they are also known to hold their breath and "bottom walk" short distances across small streams. They are known to sometimes carry the ancient disease of leprosy and have been used in leprosy research.

Class - **Mammalia** (mammals)

Order - **Carnivora** (carnivores)

Family - **Mustelidae** (weasel family)

Mink *Mustela vison*	Long-tailed Weasel *Mustela frenata*	River Otter *Lutra canadensis*

Presumed range in Florida 	Presumed range in Florida 	Presumed range in Florida 
Size: 20 to 27 inches in length. Weighs 2 to 3 pounds.	**Size:** 12 to 15 inches from snout to tail tip. Weighs 6 to 11 ounces,	**Size:** Length 35 to 45 inches. Up to 25 pounds.
Abundance: Uncommon in Florida.	**Abundance:** Uncommon.	**Abundance:** Fairly common.
Variation: Males are twice as large as females. Pelage color varies from light brown to very dark brown. There are 4 subspecies of Mink in Florida.	**Variation:** Males are nearly twice the size of females. Specimens in the far north turn white in winter. No seasonal color variation in Florida populations	**Variation:** As many 7 subspecies range across North America. There is very little variation in Florida specimens, which belong to the subspecies *lataxina*.
Habitat: Swamps and marshes are the primary habitat. Also frequents creeks, rivers and lake shores. Saltmarsh is a prime habitat for mink in Florida.	**Habitat:** Occupies a wide variety of habitats in Florida, including xeric uplands, but usually favors being near stream courses.	**Habitat:** Any freshwater habitat in the state may be suitable for River Otters. They are always in association with rivers, lakes, swamps, or creeks.
Breeding: 3 to 6 young are born in an underground den that is often an old muskrat house.	**Breeding:** Breeding occurs in midsummer but embryo development is delayed until spring. 4 to 5 young.	**Breeding:** 2 or 3 young are born in an underground den often dug in a stream bank.
Natural History: Mink are well-known for their luxurious fur. They are excellent swimmers and will catch fish in stream pools. They are strict carnivores that feed heavily on amphibians and crayfish during the summer. In winter, their diet turns to mammal prey such as rabbits and rodents. As with other members of the Mustelidae family, mink have well-developed musk glands that produce a distinct musky odor that is apparent when agitated or scent marking. The Everglades Mink is threatened.	**Natural History:** Weasels are known for being one of the world's most ferocious predators. Although their prey includes animals as small as insects, they will also take much larger prey. Mice, voles, and other rodents, along with shrews and small birds, make up the bulk of their non-invertebrate diet. They have also been known to scavenge the dead bodies of large animals such as deer. When an animal is killed that is too large to consume at one meal, they will cache the remains.	**Natural History:** River Otters are semi-aquatic mammals that possess fully webbed toes and waterproof fur. They are excellent swimmers that prey on fish, frogs, crayfish, turtles, and small mammals. They are mainly freshwater animals but may sometimes use brackish waters or salt marsh. Their fur is highly valued, a fact that lead to their extirpation from most of the eastern United States by the late 1800s. Although still rare in some states, in Florida populations are stable.

Class - **Mammalia** (mammals)

Order - **Carnivora** (carnivores)

Family - **Procyonidae** (raccoon family)	Family - **Ursidae** (bear family)

Raccoon
Procyon lotor

Size: Up to 2.5 feet in length. Weights of 15 to 30 pounds. Florida Raccoons are small, up to 15 pounds.

Presumed range in Florida

Abundance: Very common. Found in both wilderness and urban areas.

Variation: There is little variation in Florida specimens. A few black individuals occur occasionally. Most resemble the photo above. Females are about a third smaller than males.

Habitat: Found in virtually every habitat in the state, but wetlands, stream courses, and lake shores are favorite haunts. They are also common near swamps and marshes, including salt marshes in coastal regions. Adapts well to urbanization and can be common in small towns and even cities.

Breeding: Breeds in late winter with an average of 4 (maximum of 8) young born 2 months later (April or May). Young begin to accompany the mother on foraging trips at about 2 months. They are on their own by about 5 months. Will breed annually.

Natural History: Raccoons are omnivores that feed on a wide variety of crustaceans, insects, amphibians, reptiles, small mammals, and eggs as well as grains, berries, fruits, acorns, weed seeds, and some vegetables. Although they are mainly nocturnal, they are often active by day, especially in morning and late afternoons. In America, the Raccoon is an important game and fur-bearing animal. Like many other mammals, Raccoons are subject to an interesting phenomena known as "Bergman's Rule." Bergman's rule states that the body size of mammals tends to be larger the farther north the species is found. This phenomena is the result of the fact that larger bodies are capable of retaining more heat. A really big male Raccoon from Canada may top the scale at 40 pounds. Meanwhile, an adult Raccoon in south Florida may weigh only 10 to 12 pounds.

Black Bear
Ursus americanus

Size: 4 to 5 feet in total length. Males can weigh up to 400 pounds. Females are smaller, averaging about 200.

Presumed range in Florida

Abundance: Uncommon. About 4,000 exist in Florida today.

Variation: Despite their name, Black Bears may be black, cinnamon, blond, blue gray, or even white. Florida specimens are invariably black in color.

Habitat: Throughout their range in North America, Black Bears utilize a wide array of habitats. In the Deep South, they use swamplands and woodlands; in the far north they are found in both boreal forests and tundra. In Florida, they may be found in all habitats, but they tend to avoid urban regions.

Breeding: Breeds in summer but development of the embryo is delayed until fall. 1 to 3 cubs are born in January or February. Twins are common. Newborn cubs will weigh only about a pound. Females will typically breed only every other year. Young stay with the female for about a year.

Natural History: Prior to the European invasion of North America, the Black Bear was a common large carnivore. Over-hunting and deforestation led to their complete disappearance in many regions by the 1800s. Young male bears will disperse for sometimes hundreds of miles, and are the first individuals to colonize a new area. A variety of plant and animal matter is eaten. Acorns and nuts are important food items in the fall, along with berries. All types of animal matter is also consumed, including carrion. The home range is quite large, as much as 120 square miles for males, much less for females (about 10 to 20 square miles). The home ranges of several bears may overlap. Bears enjoy a keen sense of smell and rely more on the sense of smell and hearing than on eyesight. Black Bears have been known to live up to 30 years.

Class - **Mammalia** (mammals)

Order - **Carnivora** (carnivores)

Family - **Felidae** (cat family)

Bobcat *Lynx rufus*	Florida Panther *Felis concolor*

Size: Length up to 3 feet. Typically weighs 15 to 45 pounds. Florida specimens tend to be small (about 12 to 20 pounds).

Presumed range in Florida

Size: Males can be 7 feet from nose to tail tip and average 130 pounds. Females are about 30 percent smaller.

Dark gray represents core breeding range. Light gray is disperal range of young males.

Abundance: Fairly common statewide in suitable habitats.

Abundance: Very rare. FWC estimates 120 to 230 individuals.

Variation: Several subspecies occur in America. Some specimens have more pronounced spotting to their fur and males are about one-third larger than females.

Variation: The Florida Panther is 1 of at least 6 (some say up to 32) subspecies of the Cougar. Color can vary from reddish brown to tan or gray brown. Most are tawny brown.

Habitat: Occupies a wide variety of habitats in Florida and is increasingly seen in suburban regions as development encroaches into natural habitats. Favorite haunts are all types of woodlands, swamps, and dense thickets of shrubs and palmetto.

Habitat: Today, the Florida Panther is restricted mainly to the Big Cypress Swamp and the Everglades region in southernmost Florida. They once ranged as far west as Louisiana and Arkansas and as far north as Tennessee and South Carolina.

Breeding: In Florida, Bobcats breed from late summer through early spring. Up to 4 young are born about two months after breeding. Young Bobcats begin to forage with the mother in about 2 months; they may stay with her for up to a year while perfecting hunting skills.

Breeding: Due to a rather long development period for juvenile panthers, females will breed only about every 2 years. 2 young is typical but can be as many as 4. The kittens are marked with thick black spots, which begin to fade as the kitten grows. The spots are gone by 6 months of age.

Natural History: Strictly a meat eater, the Bobcat's food items range from mice to deer. Cottontail Rabbits are a favorite prey as are squirrels, young turkeys, and songbirds. Hunts by ambush or stalking to within close range and making an explosive attack. Although mainly nocturnal, Bobcats can be abroad at any time of day. Their home range can be from one to several square miles and males have larger ranges than females. Scent marking territory with urine and feces is common. In captivity, Bobcats have lived for over 20 years, but the estimate for wild cats is 12 to 14 years. This species has just begun to return to many areas of the Midwest after being extirpated decades ago. In Florida, the species always maintained populations due to the fact that suitable habitat has persisted in the state despite the massive influx of people. Loss of habitat is today becoming a threat, however.

Natural History: The Florida Panther is a distinct population of Northern Cougar and is regarded by many as a distinct subspecies (*coryi*). Some experts list over 30 subspecies of Cougar in the Americas, while others say there are only 6. The latter view regards the Florida Panther as merely a subpopulation of the Northern Cougar. These big cats are strict carnivores. Studies in Florida have revealed the diet of the Florida Panther is mainly raccoons (24 percent), deer (22 percent), and wild hogs (21 percent). Armadillos are also important food items and make up 10 percent of the diet. These large predators have a very large home range and are thus highly vulnerable to habitat loss and development. Highways are a major threat and in fact automobiles are the leading cause of death among adult Florida Panthers. Strenuous efforts to save this magnificent animal are underway, but its future is still in doubt.

Class - **Mammalia** (mammals)		
Order - **Carnivora** (carnivores)		
Family - **Canidae** (canines)		

Gray Fox *Urocyon cinereoargenteus*	**Red Fox** *Vulpes vulpes*	**Coyote** *Canis latrans*

Gray Fox

Size: Length 32 to 45 inches. Weight up to 15 pounds.

Abundance: Fairly common.

Presumed range in Florida

Variation: As many as 6 subspecies range across North America. Only 1 race occurs in Florida with no significant color variation.

Habitat: Primarily a woodland animal that is more common in forested regions of the state. Tends to avoid expansive open regions and is uncommon in permanent wetlands.

Breeding: Dens in a burrow, hollow log or rock cave. 4 pups is usual but up to 7 is known.

Natural History: The Gray Fox is the only American canine with the ability to climb trees. Insects are important food items in summer with mice and rabbits becoming more important in winter. When grapes, persimmons, and other fruits are ripe, they will eat them almost exclusively, and in fact this is the most omnivorous canine in America. Home range can vary from a few hundred acres to over a square mile, depending upon habitat quality. Unlike the Red Fox that can be found as far north as the Arctic Circle, the Gray Fox is a more southerly animal and ranges southward into South America. Gray Foxes have lived for up to 14 years in captivity, but the average life span in the wild is only a few years. Contrary to popular belief, Gray Foxes never interbreed with Red Foxes.

Red Fox

Size: Length 33 to 43 inches. Weight up to 15 pounds.

Abundance: Uncommon in Florida.

Presumed range in Florida

Variation: Red Foxes can occur in several different color phases; the best known are red, silver, and cross fox. Florida specimens are typical red phase.

Habitat: Although habitat generalists, Red Foxes shows a preference for open and semi-open country over deep woods. They are thus uncommon in most of Florida.

Breeding: About 4 to 5 young are born in a den that is often an underground burrow dug by the fox.

Natural History: The Red Fox is one of the world's most widespread mammals and is found in Europe, Asia, North Africa, and Australia (introduced) as well as throughout North America. They are adaptable, opportunistic omnivores that will eat everything from grasshoppers to grapes. Scavenging carrion is also common. Their fur is such a good insulator that they can sleep atop a snow bank without melting the snow beneath their body. These are important fur-bearing animals and are today often reared in captivity on "fur farms." The short, summer coat is paler than the luxurious winter fur. All color phases have a white tail tip. They are relative newcomers to peninsula Florida, but apparently have always been found in the panhandle region.

Coyote

Size: Length up to 49 inches and about 35 pounds.

Abundance: Fairly common and probably increasing.

Presumed range in Florida

Variation: Very dark individuals and reddish specimens are known to occur. Most specimens will resemble the photo above.

Habitat: Coyotes have adapted to all habitats in Florida, but they prefer the more open agricultural areas and large cattle ranches with expansive pasture. Occasionally adapts to urban parks.

Breeding: Coyotes are able to breed before their first birthday. Litter size (2 to 10) varies with availability of prey.

Natural History: The Coyote is a relative newcomer to Florida, having begun their invasion from the west in the 1970s. Today, they range throughout the state. They are a top predator in much of the state, occupying a niche once held by the Red Wolf. They are extremely intelligent, adaptable canines that quickly learn to thrive in almost any environment. In rural areas where hunters abound, they are extremely wary, but in urban areas or protected lands, they may become quite bold around humans. The characteristic yipping and howling of these vocal canines has become a common nighttime sound in rural Florida. Mostly nocturnal, but also active by day. The longevity record is 18 years for a specimen in captivity.

Class - **Mammalia** (mammals)
Order - **Carnivora** (carnivores)
Family - **Mephitidae** (skunks)

Striped Skunk *Mephitus mephitus*	**Spotted Skunk** *Spilogale putorius*

Dark morph

Size: Length 23 to 31 inches. Average weight about 8 to 10 pounds. Males are larger than females.	Presumed range in Florida 	**Size:** Smaller and slimmer than the Striped Skunk. 11 to 24 inches total length. Weighs about 2 pounds as adult.	Presumed range in Florida
Abundance: Fairly common. Occurs statewide except in the Keys.		**Abundance:** Fairly common. Found statewide except the Keys.	

Variation: Varies considerably in the amount of white in the stripes on the back. Sometimes stripes may fuse and create an all-white back. Other times, stripes may be entirely absent.

Variation: There are 2 subspecies known to occur in Florida, but the differences are slight and both are easily recognized and resemble the photo above.

Habitat: Striped Skunks are found in all habitats in Florida except perhaps extensive swamps. They are most common in mixed, semi-open habitats, small woodlands adjoining pastures or grasslands, and edge areas. They can also be common in suburban areas and around rural homesteads.

Habitat: Spotted Skunks are found in a variety of habitats in Florida except permanent wetlands. They like dense cover and tend to avoid expansive open areas, though they will occupy edges of fields near brush or woodland. They can also be seen in suburban areas and around rural homesteads.

Breeding: Breeding usually occurs in late winter, commencing in February. Some breeding may take place as late as April. Litter size averages 3 or 4 but can be as many as 10. Young wean at about 6 weeks and will begin to follow the mother in a single file line as she forages.

Breeding: Averages about 5 young. The den is often a natural cavity or an abandoned burrow of an Armadillo or Gopher Tortoise, but they will also dig their own underground burrow. Young are born blind and with a thin layer of fur. They will wean at about 2 months.

Natural History: The Striped Skunk's distinctive black and white color is almost as well known as its primary defense, which of course is to spray an attacker with its pungent, foul-smelling musk. The musk can burn the eyes and membranes and its odor is remarkably persistant. They can effectively project the musk up to about 15 feet and the odor can be detected hundreds of yards away. Skunks dine mainly on invertbrates and as much as three-fourths of their diet consists of insects and grubs. They possess well-developed front claws for digging and a powerful sense of smell for locating buried grubs, worms, turtle eggs, etc. Baby mice, eggs, and nestlings of ground-nesting birds are also frequently eaten. They are known to sometimes harbor the rabies virus, but the threat they pose is probably overblown. Their greatest enemy today is the automobile.

Natural History: These diminutive little skunks are quite agile and are known for the peculiar behavior of doing a "handstand" on the front feet in preparation for spraying their musk. They are also excellent climbers and sometimes climb trees. They are predominantly nocturnal and feed mostly on small animals like insects, bird eggs, and mice. They are rare in many regions of their range and their exact range within the eastern United States is poorly understood. Although they have a fairly large range in North America, their distribution is spotty and they are not common animals in most regions of their range. They do seem to be a fairly common mammal in much of peninsular Florida, but they can be locally rare in some parts of the state.

Class - **Mammalia** (mammals)
Order - **Lagamorpha** (rabbits and hares)
Family - **Leporidae** (rabbits)

<table>
<tr>
<td colspan="2" align="center">Eastern Cottontail
Sylvilagus floridanus</td>
<td colspan="2" align="center">Marsh Rabbit
Sylvilagus palustris</td>
</tr>
</table>

Size: Adult length up to 17 inches. Weight 2 to 4 pounds.	Presumed range in Florida 	**Size:** Adult length about 17 inches. Weight 3.5 pounds.	Presumed range in Florida 
Abundance: Very common.		**Abundance:** Very common.	
Variation: 4 subspecies are known in Florida, but differences are imperceptible to the average person.		**Variation:** 3 subspecies are found in Florida, but differences are imperceptible to the average person.	

Habitat: May be found in virtually any habitat within the state except for permanent wetlands. Most common in overgrown fields and edge areas. Fond of briers, honeysuckle, and tall weeds. Not uncommon in urban areas, golf courses, parks, and sometimes suburban lawns.	**Habitat:** As its name implies, this species loves marshes. It is especially common in salt and brackish water marshes and estuary regions along the coasts. But can also be found inland in freshwater marshes, wet prairies, and swamps. A semi-aquatic mammal, water is a habitat requirement.
Breeding: This is the most prolific of the several rabbit species in America, producing up to 7 litters per year with as many as 5 young per litter.	**Breeding:** Breeds year-round and averages 3 to 5 young per litter. Young rabbits are sexually mature at about 9 months. They may produce 6 or 7 litters per year.
Natural History: In the spring and summer, Eastern Cottontails feed on a wide variety of grasses, legumes, and herbaceous weeds. Briers, sapling bark, and other woody materials may make up the bulk of the diet in winter. These rabbits are prey for many predators including foxes, coyotes, bobcats, and hawks and owls, especially the Great Horned Owl. The life expectancy for a Cottontail is not high, and only about 1 in 4 will live to see their second birthday. Populations are known to fluctuate and during years when their numbers are highest there may be as many as 9 rabbits per acre in good habitat. In habitats, they are mainly crepuscular and nocturnal, but they may be active in daylight, especially when breeding.	**Natural History:** Highly adapted to a semi-aquatic existence, the Marsh Rabbit is a capable swimmer quite at home in the water. They have been known to escape danger by diving below the surface or hiding submerged with just the top of the nostrils and eyes above the water. As with all rabbits, they are strict vegetarians that will eat a wide variety of plant materials. Marsh grasses and other marsh plants make up the bulk of the diet. They will also eat the twigs and bark of trees, shrubs, and vines. The subspecies which lives in the Florida Keys (*S. p. hefneri*) is regarded as an endangered species. The other 2 subspecies (*S. p. palustris*) of the western panhandle and (*S. p. paludicola*) in peninsular Florida both boast healthy populations.

Class - **Mammalia** (mammals)

Order - **Rodentia** (rodents)

Family - **Sciuridae** (squirrels)

Eastern Chipmunk *Tamias striatus*	**Southern Flying Squirrel** *Glaucomys volans*

	Presumed range in Florida		Presumed range in Florida
Size: About 10 inches in length and weighing about 4.5 ounces.		**Size:** 10 inches or less in length and weighs 2 to 3 ounces.	
Abundance: Very rare in Florida. Found in extreme northwestern panhandle only.		**Abundance:** Common in forested regions throughout the state.	
Variation: Very little variation in Florida specimens.		**Variation:** Very little variation in Florida specimens.	

Habitat: Deciduous forests in upland areas. Avoids wetlands. Fond of rock outcrops, stone fences, etc. Can be common in urban parks and suburbs in many areas of its range. Florida range is restricted to a few counties in the panhandle along the Alabama border.

Habitat: These little squirrels are totally dependent upon trees and make their home in woodlands. Primarily hardwoods but also in mixed pine-hardwood forests. They will live in suburbs and urban areas if sufficient mature trees are present.

Breeding: May breed twice per year, first in February and again in April. Produces 4 to 5 young per litter. Young chipmunks wean at about 6 weeks.

Breeding: Only 1 litter per year with up to 6 young. Nest is usually within a hollow in a tree. Bluebird boxes and other artificial nest sites are also used.

Natural History: While they are excellent climbers, chipmunks are true "ground squirrels," sleeping, rearing young, and wintering in an underground burrow that they dig themselves. They also will use rock crevices or hollow logs. They become less active in winter, and in the northern portions of their range, they will remain below ground, living on stored nuts and seeds for long periods during harsh weather. Although chipmunks are fairly common in much of the eastern United States, they are quite rare in Florida. This is an animal of the deciduous forest, and although they can thrive in mixed deciduous/conifer woodlands, they are not well suited for conifer-dominated forests. Though they feed mostly on nuts and seeds, they will also eat some animal matter including insects, eggs, and baby birds. They will cache food in burrows, especially in the more northerly regions of their range where harsh winters inhibit activity.

Natural History: Lives in tree hollows and old woodpecker holes. Florida's only nocturnal squirrel. Leaps from tree to tree and glides using flaps of skin between front and hind legs like a parachute. Flattened tail serves as a rudder while gliding. Feeds on nuts, seeds, fruits, fungi, lichens, tree buds, insects, bird eggs, and nestling birds as well as mice. Flying Squirrels are gregarious animals and several may share a den. Southern Flying Squirrels can live up to 10 years and will become quite tame in captivity, making reasonable pets. Wild squirrels in rural areas sometimes invade homes and attics where they can become a noisy nuisance as they scramble about in the wee hours. A much larger version, the Northern Flying Squirrel (*Glaucomys sabrinus*), occurs in America in the far north and in the higher elevations of the southern Appalachian Mountains. It can be twice as large as its southern cousin.

Class - **Mammalia** (mammals)

Order - **Rodentia** (rodents)

Family - **Sciuridae** (squirrels)

Eastern Gray Squirrel *Sciurus carolinensis*	**Fox Squirrel** *Sciurus niger*

dark morph *shermani*

typical *shermani*

Size: Size: 19 inches in total length. Weight 18 to 26 ounces.

Presumed range in Florida

Size: Florida specimens can exceed 2 feet and weigh 3 pounds.

Presumed range in Florida

Abundance: Very common.

Abundance: Uncommon.

Variation: 5 subspecies nationwide. 3 occur in Florida. All are very similar in appearance.

Variation: Highly variable. 4 subspecies occur in Florida. See Natural History below for details.

Habitat: Prefers mature deciduous forests but also found in mixed coniferous forests and second growth areas. Can be common in urban parks and lawns.

Habitat: Open pine woodlands, cypress woodlands, and mangroves. Prefers open forests with trees widely spaced and edge areas where forests interface with open pastures.

Breeding: Breeds December through February and again in June/July. 4 to 6 young per litter. Den is usually in a hollow, but will also build nests of leaves in tree forks.

Breeding: Produces 4 to 6 young. Breeds in both winter and summer but in Florida produces only 1 litter per year. Females begin breeding at about 1 year of age.

Natural History: Feeds on nuts, seeds, fungi, tree buds, and the inner bark of trees as well as bird eggs and hatchlings. May sometimes even eat carrion. Like most rodents, they will gnaw bones or shed deer antlers for calcium. Well-known for burying and storing nuts and exhibits a remarkable memory for locating cached food items buried in hundreds of locations within the home range. Frequently calls with a raspy "bark," especially when alarmed. Builds summer nests of leaves in tree crotches. Winter dens are in tree hollows. During severe weather may be inactive for several days. Poor mast years may produce mass migrations. Gray Squirrels are extremely athletic little animals and exhibit remarkable agility in trees. In some parts of their range, albino or melanistic populations occur. A blond population exists in the vicinity of Juniper Springs in Florida's Ocala National Forest. They are strictly a woodland animal. Highly athletic and agile in the treetops, Gray Squirrels posses remarkable climbing and leaping ability.

Natural History: Fox Squirrels wander frequently into open areas and spend more time on the ground than Gray Squirrels. Their home range is much larger. They are generally less common than the Gray, rarely reaching the population densities of their smaller cousins. They feed on many of the same foods of nuts, seeds, buds, berries, etc. But the diet of Fox Squirrels also includes the seeds of pine cones. While they will bark and chatter when disturbed, they are overall less vocal than the smaller Gray Squirrel. Fox Squirrels are highly variable and there are 10 subspecies recognized across the eastern half of America. 4 subspecies occur in Florida. The Upland Fox Squirrel (*S.n. bachmani*) occurs in Florida in the western panhandle. The Eastern Fox Squirrel (*S. n. niger*) is found in north Florida and the eastern panhandle. Sherman's Fox Squirrel (*S.n. shermani*) is widespread in the peninsula but is somewhat rare and regarded as a Species of Special Concern. Finally, the Big Cypress Fox Squirrel (*S.n. avicennia*) is a threatened species from the Everglades.

Class - **Mammalia** (mammals)
Order - **Rodentia** (rodents)
Family - **Castoridae** (beaver family)

Beaver *Castor canadensis*	Beaver dam

Size: Up to 43 inches in total length. Can weigh up to 65 pounds. 35 to 50 pounds is average.

Presumed range in Florida

Abundance: Fairly common.

Variation: The American Society of Mammologists recognizes 24 subspecies in North America. The status of Beavers in the eastern US is difficult to determine due to reintroduction programs using transplanted beavers.

Habitat: Beavers are thoroughly aquatic mammals that to a great extent create their own wetland habitats. To construct their ponds and wetlands, they require the presence of a stream or spring run with constant or near constantly flowing water which can be dammed. Streams that are subject to fierce flooding or with exceptionally powerful flows are avoided in preference for more easily contained water flows.

Breeding: Mating takes place in midwinter with the young being born about 4 months later. There is only 1 litter per year. Baby beavers are quite precocious and are born with well-developed fur and eyes that open immediately. 4 or 5 young, called kits, is typical. In ideal habitats, more young may be produced. Young beavers are usually weaned in just 2 to 3 weeks, but the young Beavers will remain with the family for up to 2 years before striking out on their own to find new territories. Adult beavers may mate for life.

Natural History: Beavers are primarily nocturnal in habits, but they may be active at dawn and dusk. In remote locations where human intrusion is absent, they are observed active during the day as well. They feed mostly on the inner bark of trees, with willow being a dietary mainstay. They will also consume sedges and other aquatic vegetation, but in cold climates in winter they live exclusively on bark. The dorsal-ventrally flattened tail is hairless and scaly and along with the webbed hind feet provide these animals with powerful swimming tools. They also possess enlarged incisors which grow continually throughout life and are used to gnaw through trunks and fallen trees. Most trees cut by Beavers are small saplings which are used as food, but they will also cut large trees up to 2 feet in diameter to open the canopy and promote the growth of new food sources. These largest of the North American rodents are famous for their dam-building abilities and they will also build elaborate living quarters known as "lodges." After many years of use, these lodges may become up to 15 feet across and can house an entire extended family. They have underwater entrances for protection and a hollow "room" that is above the waterline and lined with wood chips or grasses. Other species such as Muskrats and mice may take up residence within these lodges. At one time, Beaver fur was one of the most valuable natural resources in America and the pursuit of Beaver fur led to the exploration of much of the continent. Within a few decades they were nearly exterminated by trappers. They can sometimes be a pest when their dam-building activities flood farmers fields, but their wetland-creating activities benefit many scores of wetland wildlife species. In fact, the Beaver is one of the most significant players in local ecosystems throughout North America and their value to the overall ecology would be hard to overstate. In addition to creating their own habitats, they will use lakes, rivers, swamps, marshes, and large, deep creeks. In rivers and lakes the lodge or den is often a burrow into the bank of the lake or river. In dammed streams or swamps and marshes, a stick lodge is usual.

Class - **Mammalia** (mammals)

Order - **Rodentia** (rodents)

Family - **Myocastoridae** (nutria)	Family - **Geomyidae** (pocket gophers)
Nutria *Myocastor coypus*	**Southeastern Pocket Gopher** *Geomys pinetus*

Size: 3 feet in total length. Maximum of 42 inches and 24 pounds.	Presumed range in Florida 	**Size:** Total length 10 to 12 inches and weighs 5 to 7 ounces.	Presumed range in Florida 
Abundance: Uncommon.		**Abundance:** Common.	
Variation: No known variation in Florida populations. Several subspecies in South America.		**Variation:** Some experts recognize several subspecies. For practical purposes, there is no variation in FL.	

Habitat: Nutria are thoroughly aquatic mammals always found in the immediate vicinity of water. Probably most common in salt and brackish marshes but also in fresh water.

Habitat: Dry uplands with loose and sandy soils are the main habitat requirement for this species. Understory vegetative communities created by frequent fires are favored.

Breeding: Breeds year-round and can produce 2 or 3 litters per year. A maximum of 11 young has been recorded but most litters are about half that amount (5 or 6).

Breeding: May breed year-round and produce 2 litters per year. Fecundity is quite low in this species and only 1 or 2 young per litter is typical.

Natural History: The Nutria is one of many introduced species that has become established in Florida. They were first brought into Louisiana in the early 1900s for fur production. Today they have spread across much of the southeastern United States and have been in Florida since the 1950s. Their exact range in Florida is difficult to determine and the map above is an approximation. Although they are generally an uncommon species in Florida, they can become quite common in certain areas of prime habitat where they are unmolested by humans. Nutria are strict vegetarians and will consume a wide variety of plant materials. Most food is aquatic plant species and includes roots and tubers as well as stems and foliage. They will den in burrows dug into banks or build platforms of vegetation. Muskrat homes are also sometimes used. Most wildlife biologists regard the Nutria as an overall detrimental species in the ecology of Florida. In truth they are probably less harmful than many of the other alien species that have become established in the state.

Natural History: The Geomyidae family of rodents are highly specialized for a subterranean existence. They spend most of their lives in underground burrows which they dig with powerful forelegs and long front claws. They also use their enormous incisors for chewing through roots or patches of hard earth. They possess specialized lips that close behind the front incisors to keep dirt from entering the mouth. The name "Pocket" Gopher comes from their expansive cheek pouches (pockets) within which they store food to be carried into the burrow. They are known to eat a variety of roots and bulbs as well as grasses. Their burrow systems can extend for several hundred feet and excess soil is pushed to the surface periodically, creating the characteristic mounds which indicate their subsurface existence. The burrows leading upward to the mounds of soil are plugged to prevent predators like snakes from being able to easily enter the burrow. Some snake species, such as the Florida Pine Snake, are "gopher specialists," preying on the gophers and hiding in the burrow.

Class - **Mammalia** (mammals)

Order - **Rodentia** (rodents)

Family - **Muridae** (mice and rats)

Round-tailed Muskrat *Neofiber alleni*	Woodland Vole *Microtus pinetorum*	House Mouse *Mus musculus*

Size: Length to 15 inches. Weight up to 10 ounces.	Presumed range in Florida 	**Size:** Length 5 inches. Weight about 1 ounce.	Presumed range in Florida	**Size:** About 6.5 inches and about 0.75 ounces.	Presumed range in Florida 
Abundance: Common in suitable habitats.		**Abundance:** Uncommon to rare in Florida.		**Abundance:** Very common, especially in urban areas.	

Variation: Some experts recognize several subspecies based on small differences in size or color. From a layman's perspective, there is no real variation.	**Variation:** Young exhibit a dark gray color. Adults are more chestnut. 2 nearly identical subspecies are known to occur in Florida.	**Variation:** No variation in wild specimens but the domesticate version, known as laboratory mice, come in a variety of colors and patterns.
Habitat: The primary habitat is freshwater marshes and wet prairies. It also occurs in salt and brackish water marshes. Also known to use flooded sugarcane fields in south Florida.	**Habitat:** Primarily deciduous woodlands but also found in mixed deciduous/conifer woodlands. Prefers mesic upland woods with ample leaf litter or vegetative cover.	**Habitat:** A highly successful rodent that usually associates with human habitations and man-made structures, but can also thrive in wild environments. Probably in all habitats in Florida.
Breeding: May breed year-round and can produce several litters annually. Litter size is 1 to 4 young.	**Breeding:** Breeds spring through fall with up to 4 litters per year. 1 to 4 young per litter.	**Breeding:** Broods can number from 5 to 12. Young females begin breeding at 6 weeks and produce 14 litters per year.
Natural History: Although widely distributed across the state, this species is absent from many areas. However, in ideal habitat it can be a very common species. Builds dome-shaped "houses" made from woven marsh vegetation. Houses are constructed in deeper waters in the marsh and rise well above water level. The houses have hollows within that are above the waterline but have underwater entrances. In addition to these dens where young are born, they also build flat "feeding platforms" just above the waterline. A vegetarian, the Round-tailed Muskrat eats aquatic plants, grasses, and sedges as well as roots and tubers. The Round-tailed Muskrat is a unique species endemic to Florida and the Okefenokee Swamp of southeastern Georgia.	**Natural History:** Woodland Voles create networks of tunnels just below the ground or "runways" that are near the surface but beneath the leaf litter on the forest floor. These tunnel systems are utilized by other small mammals such as shrews. They eat seeds, grasses, and mast and roots, especially roots of grasses. Root crops like potatoes are also eaten. Active both day and night. Their subterranean habits render them less vulnerable to many predators, but they are prey for a wide variety of carnivores, raptors, and especially snakes, which are able to enter the burrow systems. One other vole species has recently been discovered in Florida. The **Florida Salt Marsh Vole** (*M. pennslyvanicus dukecampbelli*) was first discovered in 1979. Less than 50 specimens are known.	**Natural History:** The House Mouse has adapted to living in close proximity to humans and today are found wherever there are people throughout the world. As their name implies, they regularly enter into houses where they can become both a pest and a health hazard. They live both in cities and farmlands. Like the Norway Rat, the House Mouse originated in Eurasia and traveled around the world as a stowaway on sailing ships, eventually populating the entire globe. These mice are primarily nocturnal and their food includes nearly everything eaten by humans plus insects and fungi. Domestic populations of this species are the familiar laboratory mice or "white mice" so called because most are albinos.

Class - **Mammalia** (mammals)

Order - **Rodentia** (rodents)

Family - **Muridae** (mice and rats)

Norway Rat *Rattus norvigicus*	Black Rat *Rattus rattus*	Eastern Woodrat *Neotoma floridana*

Norway Rat

Size: As much as 15 inches and weight up to 12 ounces.

Abundance: Very common in urban areas.

Presumed range in Florida

Variation: None in wild populations. Captives are variable. The well-known Laboratory Rat is an albino form of this species.

Habitat: This highly adaptable rodent can live virtually anywhere, including as a stowaway on ships, which is how it immigrated to America from Europe. Thrives in both cities and wilderness.

Breeding: The fecundity of the Norway Rat is legendary. From 6 to 8 litters per year with up to a dozen young per litter.

Natural History: Also called the Brown Rat, this species has followed man to every corner of the globe. They are responsible for an almost unimaginable degree of human suffering. Throughout the history of human civilization, these rodents have destroyed crops and stored foods while spreading devastating diseases, most notably the Bubonic Plague. Though less of a threat to modern societies, these rats still shadow the human species and are common in both urban and rural settings. The common laboratory rat is a domestic version of this animal that has somewhat redeemed the species for humans, having been used as an experimental animal for medical and scientific research for over a century.

Black Rat

Size: Total length 14 inches. Weighs up to 7 ounces.

Abundance: Common. More so near the coast.

Presumed range in Florida

Variation: Black Rats can be black, gray, or brownish. But generally they are darker than the similar Norway Rat or the Eastern Woodrat.

Habitat: Although found statewide, the Black Rat is more common in the coastal lowlands. This rodent is closely tied to human habitations and invades attics and roof crawl spaces.

Breeding: Probably breeds year-round in Florida. Produces 4 to 8 young and can breed 4 to 6 times annually.

Natural History: This rodent's other common name is "Roof Rat." It is an appropriate moniker as this species is an adept climber. In natural habitats, it shows arboreal tendancies and in urban areas it lives well off the ground in attics, roofs, and walls. Unlike America's other two introduced Eurasian rodents (Norway Rat and House Mouse), this species does not thrive in wilderness and is largely dependent upon human stuctures (or at least human-altered habitats). They do not tolerate cold weather well and are restricted to mostly warmer climates. They also have a strong propensity toward coastal areas and ports. They will invade urban and suburban neighborhoods in coastal areas where they are generally regarded as vermin.

Eastern Woodrat

Size: Adults reach 16 inches and 12 ounces.

Abundance: Fairly common except in the Keys.

Presumed range in Florida

Variation: Although there are 3 subspecies in Florida, are all very similar in appearance and are generally indistinguishable by laypersons.

Habitat: Woodrats from farther north in the Appalachian Mountains love rock outcrops and cliff faces. In Florida, the Eastern Woodrat uses woodlands, swamps, and marshes.

Breeding: 3 to 4 litters per year is possible with 2 young being typical. Litter of up to 6 young have been recorded.

Natural History: The Eastern Woodrat eats both plant and animal matter. Woodrats sometimes go by the name "Packrat," a reference to their tendancy to gather human refuse and use it in the construction of a den that is made mainly from a pile of sticks. In many areas of its range in the Southeastern Coastal Plain, the Eastern Woodrat is in decline. Florida populations are believed to be secure at this time. The subspecies found in the Florida Keys is regarded as an Endangered Species by the USFWS. Woodrats in general seem to never be common animals and loss of habitat is a serious threat. Feral House Cats are also a threat. Sea level rise due to climate change may eventually wipe out the Key Largo subspecies.

Class - **Mammalia** (mammals)
Order - **Rodentia** (rodents)
Family - **Muridae** (mice and rats)

Rice Rat *Oryzomys palustris*	Hispid Cotton Rat *Sigmodon hispidus*	Eastern Harvest Mouse *Reithrodontomys humulis*

Size: Up to 9 inches in length and weighing about 2.5 ounces.

Presumed range in Florida

Abundance: Very common in marshes.

Size: 10 inches in length and about 6 ounces for adults.

Presumed range in Florida

Abundance: Can be very common in ideal habitats.

Size: Length 4.5 inches. Weight 0.5 ounces.

Presumed range in Florida

Abundance: Unknown. Probably uncommon in most of Florida.

Variation: Pelage color variable from gray to gray brown, reddish, or silvery.

Variation: The 6 subspecies in Florida are indistinguishable by laypersons.

Variation: Apparently no significant variation in Florida populations.

Habitat: Prefers to be near water. Wet meadow, marsh, and the edges of swamps. Can also be found in uplands.

Habitat: Old fields, especially in upland areas. Most common in fields dominated by broom sedge.

Habitat: Fallow fields and regenerative areas, especially where broomsedge is dominent.

Breeding: Breeds several times per year. 3 to 5 babies. Young will reach sexual maturity in 2 months.

Breeding: Very prolific. Produces several litters per year (6 to 8 babies) and young are weaned in less than a week!

Breeding: Breeds from early spring through fall. Average litter size is 3 to 4. Several litters per year is possible.

Natural History: The name Rice Rat comes from the prevalence of this species in rice fields throughout the Deep South. These rodents can be quite common in freshwater marshes, but are especially common in coastal marshlands. Though they do sometimes occur in uplands, they are not common there. In addition to rice, they consume several other types of seeds and plants but also eat large amounts of animal matter. In fact, this is one of the most carnivorous rodents in America. The list of animal prey includes insects, crustaceans, fish, and baby birds and bird eggs to name a few. They are accomplished swimmers and will dive and swim underwater to escape a predator. They are also good climbers. They are strictly nocturnal in habits. The Keys subspecies (*O. p. natator*) is federally endangered. Loss of habitat to development in the Keys is the major threat to this subspecies.

Natural History: This is perhaps the most common mammal in much of the southern United States. In Florida, they are common in old fields and flatwoods. An abundance of grasses seems to be a habitat preference. They are active both day and night in their surface runways hidden beneath the grasses and weeds. These are one of the easier to identify of the mouse-like rodents due to the coarse appearance of the fur. Hispid Cotton Rats are a primary prey for a wide variety of predators including snakes, carnivorous mammals, and birds of prey. Their surface runways through overgrown fields are easy to see following a burn, as are the surface nests consisting of a ball of grasses. Populations fluctuate from year to year. Feeds mostly on grasses, herbs, and grass seeds. These rodents are preyed upon by a wide variety of predators and are reported to be a main food item of the Bobcat.

Natural History: The Harvest Mouse is easily confused with several other mice species that are found in Florida. Trained biologists confirm the identity of the Harvest Mouse by examining the upper incisor teeth, which have grooves. These mice are widespread across the southeastern United States but are apparently not common anywhere. Grass seeds and weed seeds are the main food item, but insects may also be eaten. In habitats they are mainly nocturnal. Their nests are usually on the surface of the ground (often at the base of a tuft of grass) and consist of a ball of plant fibers and grass. This is one of Florida's smallest mouse species. Despite the disdain most humans have for small rodents, they play an important role in nature and are food for many predators including hawks, owls, snakes, and mammalian carnivores.

Class - **Mammalia** (mammals)

Order - **Rodentia** (rodents)

Family - **Muridae** (rats and mice)

Cotton Mouse *Peromyscus gossypinus*	**Oldfield Mouse** *Peromyscus polionotus*	**Golden Mouse** *Ochrotomyss nuttalli*

Size: About 8.25 inches and 1.5 ounces.

Presumed range in Florida

Abundance: Probably the most common *Peromyscus* in Florida.

Variation: Several subspecies are recognized but differences between subspecies are not apparent to the lay observer.

Habitat: Generally a lowland mammal that enjoys wetlands, wet woodlands, and bottomland forests. Like other deer mice, may enter both derelict buildings and rural homes.

Breeding: In Florida, breeds throughout the year except in summer. Litters number up to 7 and young mice wean at about 3 to 4 weeks.

Natural History: The *Peromyscus* genus includes several very similar species that collectively range throughout most of North America. In almost every respect the Cotton Mouse is a lowland, southern counterpart of the Deer Mouse and the White-footed Mouse, both of which are widespread and common in North America except for the extreme southeastern US. Most of the range of the Cotton Mouse is in the coastal plain and they range throughout the state of Florida. The name comes from the habit of southern populations to use cotton (pilfered from cotton fields) in the building of their nest. Their diet is omnivorous and consists of seeds, nuts, berries, etc. along with some invertebrates. An endemic subspecies on Key Largo (*P. g. allopaticola*) is endangered.

Size: To 5 inches total length and 0.5 ounces.

Presumed range in Florida

Abundance: Inland forms are fairly common. Beach forms rare.

Variation: At least a dozen subspecies are known in Florida. Many are endemic to a single barrier island.

Habitat: Successional areas. Overgrown pastures, neglected former croplands, sapling pine forests, and edge areas. Old fields dominated by grasses such as broomsedge.

Breeding: Breeds year-round with peak breeding in spring and fall. Up to 8 young per litter with young mice reaching sexual maturity at about 7 weeks.

Natural History: The name "Oldfield" Mouse is derived from their association with "old fields." There are a number of rare subspecies around Florida's coastline which are endemic to coastal sand dunes and barrier islands. Several of these so-called "Beach Mice" are endangered. Florida's beach habitats constitute highly prized real estate and have suffered from extensive development. These coastal forms are also vulnerable to Hurricanes. Among the subspecies listed as imperiled by the Florida Fish and Wildlife Conservation Commission are the St. Andrew's Beach Mouse (*P. p. peninsularis*); the Perdido Key Beach Mouse (*P. p. trissyllepsis*); the Anastasia Island Beach Mouse (*P. p. phasma*); and the Choctahatchee Beach Mouse (*P. p.allophrys*).

Size: About 6.5 inches and 0.75 ounces.

Presumed range in Florida

Abundance: Fairly common in suitable habitats.

Variation: Adults are typically golden brown, orangish, or cinnamon. Young mice are slightly grayer in color.

Habitat: Woodland areas with dense understory cover (especially privet and greenbriar). This mouse is highly arboreal and loves woodlands with thickets, tangles, and vines.

Breeding: Breeds from early spring through fall, producing several litters per year. 2 to 4 young is typical. Nest is often above ground.

Natural History: Mainly nocturnal, Golden Mice have strong arboreal tendencies. They use vines and limbs as highways and will forage for seeds both in the trees and on the ground. The nest is usually in a thicket of vines several feet off the ground. They will also construct small feeding platforms several feet off the ground. Acorns are eaten as are invertebrates and these mice are decidedly omnivorous. These are handsome little mice with fine, golden fur. Unlike many other mice species, the Golden Mouse rarely enters human habitations, preferring a more natural habitat. One captive individual was reported to have lived for 8 years, a very long life span for a mouse. The average life span in the wild is probably less than a year.

Class - **Mammalia** (mammals)

Order - **Rodentia** (rodents)	Order - **Soricimorpha** (moles and shrews)
Family - **Muridae** (rats and mice)	Family - **Talpidae** (moles)

Florida Mouse *Podomys floridanus*	**Eastern Mole** *Scalopus aquaticus*

Size: Total length 7.5 inches and weighs between 1.5 and 1.75 ounces.	Presumed range in Florida 	**Size:** 6 inches total length and weighs up to 3.25 ounces.	Presumed range in Florida 
Abundance: Generally uncommon and patchily distributed. Fairly common in some areas of suitable habitat.		**Abundance:** Common in most of the state but absent from the Everglades and Big Cypress regions.	

Variation: Pelage varies from brown to grayish brown. No subspecies are known.

Variation: Males are slightly larger. Mammologists recognize as many as 5 subspecies in Florida.

Habitat: The habitat of the Florida Mouse is dry, sandy uplands. This species is most common in scrub communities and "sandhill" habitats. Its microhabitat is often within the burrow of the Gopher Tortoise, where it digs it own tunnels within the larger tortoise burrow.

Habitat: Except for wetlands, these moles can be found in any habitat where soils are suitable for burrowing. They can be especially common in coastal regions, barrier islands, and other areas where the soils are mostly loose sands. They can be common in residential lawns and gardens.

Breeding: Most litters are born in the fall and winter months. 2 to 4 young is typical.

Breeding: One litter per year in early spring. 2 to 5 young per litter.

Natural History: The Florida Mouse is endemic to the state of Florida and has one of the smallest ranges of any North American mammal. Although not considered to be endangered or threatened, it is regarded as a vulnerable species by Florida Fish and Wildlife Conservation Commission. Its primary habitat of xeric uplands is also a favorite habitat for developers of suburban communities throughout central Florida. Thus, suitable habitat for this species is continually shrinking. Fire suppression can also negatively impact this species, as it favors plant communities that are shaped by periodic burns. An omnivorous species, the Florida Mouse feeds on seeds, acorns, berries, etc. as well as insects. This species has the unusual habit of digging side tunnels into the burrows of larger animals, especially the Gopher Tortoise. Both the tortoise and mouse have similar habitat requirements and there appears to be a strong link between these two species, with the Florida Mouse being somewhat dependent upon the Gopher Tortoise.

Natural History: The most wide-ranging mole in America. Although considered a pest in suburban lawns and rural gardens, Eastern Moles actually perform some helpful tasks. The tunnels they dig help to aerate the soil and allow rainfall to penetrate more easily. The mounds of soil pushed to the surface from the burrow returns soil nutrients to the surface. They also prey heavily upon destructive grubs such as the Japanese Beetle. The pelage of the Eastern Mole is "reversible" and will lie smoothly against the skin whether mole is moving forward or backward in tight tunnels. The powerful forelegs allow this animal to burrow at an astonishing pace, and the webbed toes help move dirt aside. The eyes are tiny and covered with skin, and there are no external ears. This is an animal that is superbly adapted to a subterrean lifestyle and Eastern Moles will spend 99 percent of their lives below ground. They can be seen above ground when excessive rains flood the burrows and force them to the surface.

Class - **Mammalia** (mammals)
Order - **Soricimorpha** (moles and shrews)
Family - **Sorcidae** (shrews)

Southern Short-tailed Shrew *Blarina carolinensis*	Least Shrew *Cryptotis parva*	Southeastern Shrew *Sorex longirostris*

  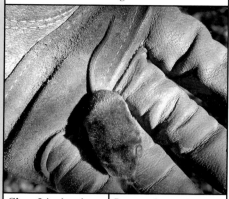

Southern Short-tailed Shrew
Blarina carolinensis

Size: To 4.5 inches and about 0.5 ounces.

Abundance: Common to fairly common in Florida.

Presumed range in Florida

Variation: 2 subspecies in Florida. A third subspecies (**Sherman's Shrew**-subspecies *shermani*) has recently been designated full species status.

Habitat: Fond of damp, deciduous woodlands but a habitat generalist; found in most habitats in the state. Avoids saturated soils, however.

Breeding: Breeds in spring and fall. 2 to 6 young per litter. More than 1 litter per year is common.

Natural History: Short-tailed Shrews are primarily nocturnal animals and have very high metabolic rates. They are hyperactive animals that will eat as much as one-half their body weight daily! The ferocity of shrews is legendary among mammologists. Many have learned the hard way never to place a shrew in a container with a mouse if you want to keep both alive! Food is a variety of insects, snails, earthworms, millipedes, etc. as well as much larger prey including mice that are as large as themselves. They have tiny eyes and their vision is quite poor. Except when breeding and rearing young, they are solitary. They forage in runways and tunnels beneath the leaf litter. Populations occurring in western Lee and Collier counties have been designated full species status (see Variation above).

Least Shrew
Cryptotis parva

Size: Tiny. 3 inches and 0.5 ounces.

Abundance: Probably common but abundance is undetermined.

Presumed range in Florida

Variation: Summer pelage is brownish, turning to slate gray during winter. There are 2 nearly identical subspecies in Florida.

Habitat: Prefers early successional habitats such a grassy areas and overgrown fields, but also found in woodlands.

Breeding: Several litters per year is common averaging 4 to 5 young per litter. Young mature in about 5 weeks.

Natural History: Possessing an extremely high metabolism, this tiny mammal can consume its own weight in food daily. Like many other shrews, they are known to cache food items. Although these shrews are rarely seen due to their diminutive size and reclusive habits, they are probably more common than generally perceived. Owls are a major predator and in fact the presence of these tiny shrews in a given area is often confirmed by examining owl pellets for skeleton remains. Known food items are caterpillars, beetles, other insects, snails, spiders, and earthworms. The local abundance of these small shrews is often difficult to determine because since they are so small, they often fail to trigger the capture mechanism on small mammal traps used to capture small mammals during biological surveys.

Southeastern Shrew
Sorex longirostris

Size: 3 inches in length. About .5 an ounce in weight.

Abundance: Common.

Presumed range in Florida

Variation: 2 subspecies are known in Florida but the differences between the 2 are very slight and noticable only to trained mammologists.

Habitat: Another habitat generalist that may be found in most terrestrial habitats in the state. Probably most common in succesional woodlands.

Breeding: Breeds throughout the summer. At least 2 litters of 4 to 6 young are produced annually.

Natural History: As with most tiny vertebrates, the Southeastern Shrew has a remarkable metabolic rate and must eat almost constantly to survive. Another characteristic of tiny mammals is a short life span. The maximum life span for the Southeastern Shrew is reported to be about 1.5 years. Spiders are reported as the most important food item, but a wide variety of other invertebrates are also eaten. As the name implies, they are found throughout the southeastern United States. Until recently, these shrews were regarded as rare, but increasingly effective trapping/collecting techniques have revealed that they are fairly common in many areas of their range. They can sometimes be discovered hiding beneath cover boards or tins placed in suitable habitats.

Class - **Mammalia** (mammals)
Order - **Chiroptera** (bats)
Family - **Vespertilionidae** (vesper bats)

Tricolored Bat	Southeastern Bat	Gray Bat
Perimyoits subflavus	*Myotis austroriparius*	*Myotis grisescens*

Size: 3.5 inches. Weight about .25 of an ounce.

Presumed range in Florida

Size: 3.5 inches. Weight about 0.25 of an ounce.

Presumed range in Florida

Size: 3.5 inches. Weight about 0.375 of an ounce.

Presumed range in Florida

Abundance: Widespread but uncommon in Florida.

Abundance: Can be common in the panhandle and in north Florida.

Abundance: Very rare. State and federally endangered.

Variation: No significant variation has been noted in this species in Florida.

Variation: No significant variation has been noted in this species in Florida.

Variation: No significant variation has been noted in this species in Florida.

Habitat: Woodlands, stream courses, and edges of fields bordering woodlands are favorite hunting areas.

Habitat: A bat of the Southeastern Coastal Plain of the US. Range extends southward onto the Florida peninsula.

Habitat: Habitats include wooded regions. Always near water (lakes, rivers) in forested areas.

Breeding: Females give birth to 1 or 2 babies (pups) in May or June.

Breeding: Females give birth to 2 babies (pups) in early May.

Breeding: Females produce a single baby born in the spring.

Natural History: Tricolored Bats are widespread and common throughout the eastern United States. In fall, they will migrate short distances to hibernacula. In Florida, they are most common during warmer months, but they sometimes emerge in warm weather during winter. Food is tiny airborne insects. They will leave the roost before dark and are often seen hunting at dusk. Like many bats, the females form maternal colonies where young are reared, often in buildings or sheds. Unlike many other species, however, these maternal colonies are usually small, numbering only 1 or 2 dozen individuals. In northern parts of the state, hibernation begins in late fall and lasts until warm weather returns. Hibernating bats may lose as much as 25 to 30 percent of their body weight before emerging in the spring. This species was formerly known as the Eastern Pipistrelle (*Pipistrellus subflavus*).

Natural History: A colony species that dens in caves, hollow trees, or man-made structures such as bridges, culverts, and buildings. The food is small flying insects with mosquitoes being a major food item. The role that bats play in controlling insect pests like mosquitoes cannot be taken lightly and the demise of so many bat species to the fungal disease known as "White-nose Syndrome" is a cause for alarm. Many bat species are experiencing serious population declines and several are now regarded as threatened or endangered. The Southeastern Bat is still fairly common but it is considered by some conservationists to be a vulnerable species. The Florida Fish and Wildlife Conservation Commission considers it a Species of Greatest Conservation Need. One other member of the *Myotis* genus, The **Gray Bat** (*M. grisecens*), is one of the rarest bats in Florida, being found only in Jackson County.

Natural History: This bat has one of the most restrictive ranges of any bat in Florida. Foraging or migrating Gray Bats might be seen across much of the northern portion of the panhandle, but it can regularly be found in Florida only in a few caves in Jackson County and it is a highly endangered species that is in decline. As much as 95 percent of the world's population of Gray Bats are thought to use only a handful of caves. Several caves that are used as maternity sites for female Gray Bats have been protected from human intrusion by iron grating that allows the bats to move freely in and out while prohibiting the entrance of humans and large animals. This tactic seems to be helping populations to recover. Males reportedly use separate caves while the females are birthing and nursing young. The diet is flying insects of all kinds ranging from moths to beetles and including flies, mosquitoes, etc.

Class - **Mammalia** (mammals)
Order - **Chiroptera** (bats)
Family - **Vespertilionidae** (vesper bats)

Big Brown Bat *Eptisicus fuscus*	**Evening Bat** *Nycticeius humeralis*	**Rafinesque's Big-eared Bat** *Corynorhinus rafinesquii*

Size: 4.5 inches and nearly an ounce.	Presumed range in Florida 	**Size:** 4 inches long. Up to 0.5 an ounce.	Presumed range in Florida 	**Size:** 3.75 inches and 0.4 of an ounce.	Presumed range in Florida
Abundance: Uncommon in north Florida and panhandle. Rare in south Florida.		**Abundance:** Found statewide and probably Florida's most common bat.		**Abundance:** Uncommon in north Florida, rare in south Florida.	

Variation: Possibly 2 very similar subspecies occur in Florida.	**Variation:** 2 nearly identical subspecies occur in Florida.	**Variation:** No significant variation has been noted in this species in Florida.
Habitat: Open fields, vacant lots, rural and urban areas. Sometimes seen hunting insects around suburban streetlights.	**Habitat:** Swamps, stream corridors, and woodlands as well as woods openings and edge areas are used.	**Habitat:** Woods, riparian areas. For roosting uses tree hollows, caves, beneath loose bark, and derelict buildings.
Breeding: Breeds in fall. Delayed fertilization. Twins born in late spring.	**Breeding:** 1 to 3 young are produced in late spring/early summer.	**Breeding:** Breeds in fall and gives birth to a single baby in spring.
Natural History: Summer roosts are usually associated with human structures (buildings, eaves, bridges). Also known to use hollow trees and abandoned mines. The primary food is reported to be beetles. This is perhaps one of the most recognizable bat species in the southeast. They are the large, brown bats that are common around human habitations and they range throughout most of the US and Canada in summer. Roosting bats seen alone during warm weather are nearly always males. Females congregate into "maternity colonies" of up to several dozen adults to rear their young. These bats seem to tolerate cold fairly well and they remain active well into the fall. They can sometimes even be seen flying around on warm days in winter. This bat is useful consumer of insect pests, and beetles are a large percentage of its diet.	**Natural History:** Evening Bats are summer residents throughout the eastern half of the US but winter farther south where hibernation is not necessary. Most leave northern states by early fall, but some may stay into late fall. Summer roosts include hollow trees as well as buildings, and they do not seem to utilize caves as is the habit of many bat species. A wide variety of small insects are eaten, including species that are injurious to farm crops. The Evening Bat is a threatened species in its summer range in some northern states, but appears secure in Florida. Though widespread across much of the southeast, these are lowland and low plateau animals that avoid the higher elevations of the Appalachian Mountains. Most of these bats found in the northern portions of their range in summer are females, with the males apparently staying farther to the south.	**Natural History:** Rafinesque's Big-eared Bat is found in Florida year-round. It may roost communally or singly, and like many bats it will sometimes roost among other species. Northern populations use caves, but in Florida it uses hollows in trees or under loose bark. Food is mostly moths (as much as 90 percent). More nocturnal than many bats, these bats do not fly at twilight, instead waiting for full darkness. Females congregate in "nursery roosts" in the spring to give birth. Young bats can fly at about 3 weeks and may live more than 10 years. This bat occurs rather sporadically throughout its range and it is a rare to uncommon species in Florida. It is most common in the panhandle and the northern third of the peninsula. It is quite rare in the southern half of the state. Regarded as a Species of Greatest Conservation Need by the FWC.

Class - **Mammalia** (mammals)
Order - **Chiroptera** (bats)
Family - **Vespertilionidae** (vesper bats)

Seminole Bat *Lasiurus seminolus*	**Northern Yellow Bat** *Lasiurus intermedius*	**Hoary Bat** *Lasiurus cinereus*

Seminole Bat — *Lasiurus seminolus*

Size: 4.25 inches and 0.5 of an ounce.

Presumed range in Florida

Abundance: Common statewide except in Everglades where it is uncommon.

Variation: Some individuals show a "frosted" appearance to the fur.

Habitat: Found statewide in a variety of forested habitats. Often uses clumps of Spanish moss as a roosting site.

Breeding: Large litters for a bat with 1 to 4 pups born in May or June.

Natural History: Found statewide except for the Keys, this is one of the more common bat species in Florida. They are widespread across the southern United States but populations in more northerly regions migrate south in winter and swell the local populations in Florida. As with most other bats they feed on the wing, eating flying insects of all variety. They are commonly seen around street lights catching insects drawn to the light. As with other *Lasiurus* bats, they are mostly solitary animals that roost and forage singly. Their populations are regarded as secure, due in part to the fact that they are solitary animals that do not congregate in large colonies where the spread of disease can become a problem. They also avoid caves where the fungal disease "White-nose Syndrome" thrives and decimates so many cave dwelling bat species.

Northern Yellow Bat — *Lasiurus intermedius*

Size: 5.25 inches and 0.75 of an ounce.

Presumed range in Florida

Abundance: Common throughout the state except for the Keys.

Variation: Fur color varies from yellowish to grayish brown.

Habitat: Forest edges and forest openings. Shows a preference for dead palm fronds as a roosting site.

Breeding: Capable of producing up to 4 pups per litter, born in May or June.

Natural History: A large bat with a wingspan of up to 16 inches. The range of this species is across the Lower Coastal Plain from South Carolina into Texas, mostly within a few dozen miles of the coast. This range closely coincides with the range of Spanish moss, which along with palm fronds is one of this bat's favored microhabitats is for roosting. Like all Florida bats, this bat is strictly an insectivore. Collectively bats consume prodigeous amounts of flying insects nightly and their role in controlling pests like mosquitoes, gnats, biting midges, etc., would be hard to overstate. Florida residents should be encouraged to recognize the presence of bats in the neighborhood as a blessing rather than pests. Land owners can help the state's bats by erecting bat houses and refraining from trimming dead palm fronds or clearing Spanish moss from tree branches.

Hoary Bat — *Lasiurus cinereus*

Size: Maximum 5.5 inches. Weight 1 ounce.

Presumed range in Florida

Abundance: Very rare in northern Florida. Absent from southern Florida.

Variation: Females are on average slightly heavier than males.

Habitat: Another forest species that is seen in both rural and urban areas. Roosts are in edges of woodlands.

Breeding: Averages 2 pups born in mid-May to mid-June.

Natural History: This is the second largest bat species in Florida. The wingspan of the Hoary Bat can be up to 16 inches. Its name comes from the white-tipped hairs of the fur on its back. Despite being very rare in Florida, Hoary Bats have the greatest distribution of any American Bat. They summer as far north as Canada and winter in the coastal plain of the southeastern United States. They are apparently migrants that merely pass through Florida and are very rare in the state. They are most likely to be seen in Florida in October and November and again in February through May (Zinn and Baker, 1979). Oddly, the sexes segregate themselves following breeding and most of those seen in the eastern US in summer are females. Males summer farther west in the Great Plains, Rocky Mountains, or West Coast.

Class - **Mammalia** (mammals)

Order - **Chiroptera** (bats)

Family - **Vespertilionidae** (vesper bats)	Family - **Molossidae** (free-tailed bats)	
Eastern Red Bat *Lasiurus borealis*	**Florida Bonneted Bat** *Eumops floridanus*	**Brazilian Free-tailed Bat** *Tarida brasiliensis*

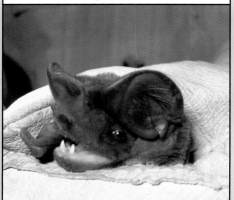

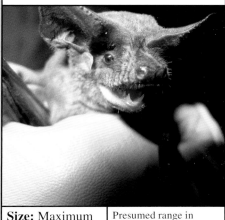

Eastern Red Bat	**Florida Bonneted Bat**	**Brazilian Free-tailed Bat**
Size: Maximum 5 inches. Up to 0.5 ounces.  Presumed range in Florida	**Size:** To 6.5 inches and weighs up to 2 ounces.  Presumed range in Florida	**Size:** Maximum 3.75 inches. Up to 0.5 ounces.  Presumed range in Florida
Abundance: Common in north Florida. Uncommon on the peninsula.	**Abundance:** Very rare and endangered. Found in southern Florida only.	**Abundance:** Very common. Maybe Florida's most common bat species.
Variation: Males conspicuously red, females chestnut frosted with white.	**Variation:** No significant variation has been noted in this species in Florida.	**Variation:** Several subspecies are known but no variation in Florida.
Habitat: Woodlands and edge areas in both rural and urban regions. Shows a preference for deciduous woodlands.	**Habitat:** Little is known about the habitat requirements, but it is believed they favor open lands for foraging.	**Habitat:** Found statewide in a wide variety of habitats. Readily uses man-made bat boxes for roosting.
Breeding: Litter size is 1 to 4 with the pups born in late May or early June.	**Breeding:** Females give birth to a single pup. May have 2 broods annually.	**Breeding:** Females give birth to a single pup in late spring.
Natural History: In summer this species usually roosts in trees by hanging from a limb. Usually solitary but sometimes more than one bat will roost together. Roosting bats resemble dead leaves. Trees chosen for roosting are often at the edge of a woodland bordering an open field. This is a migratory species that summers in the northern US and winters farther to the south. The range is quite large and includes most of the United States east of the Rocky Mountains and much of southeastern Canada. Hibernation takes place in hollow trees or beneath leaf litter on the forest floor, a very unusual tactic for a bat! Though mainly nocturnal, this species often flies in daylight, especially in late afternoon or early evening. This bat and the other *Lasiurus* bats are among the more handsomely colored bat species in America.	**Natural History:** Florida's largest and rarest bat. Formerly regarded as a subspecies of Mastiff Bat and not recognized as a distinct species until 2004. Being residents of southern Florida allows these bats to remain active year-round. Like other bats they feed on flying insects, but the Bonneted Bat can take much larger prey such as beetles and stinkbugs. They are known to use tree hollows, bat boxes, and in at least some instances, roofing tiles on occupied homes as roost sites. Because they are so rare and because they live in southern Florida, they may be vulnerable to natural disasters such as hurricanes. The current population estimate for this species puts it at only about 1,000 individuals, making this perhaps the world's rarest bat. The Florida Wildlife Commision, working with other agencies and organizations, is currently exploring conservation needs for this species.	**Natural History:** Unlike the vesper bats, Free-tailed Bats actually have a distinctly visible tail. The Brazilian Free-tailed bat is a widespread species that ranges across the southern half of North America from coast to coast. In most areas of its range, it uses caves both for roosting and hibernating. In Florida, they don't hibernate and caves are scarce, so they often use cracks in bridges or Spanish Tile on building's roofs. These bats have a distinctive musky odor and biologists familiar with the species can often detect the presence of large colonies just by using their nose. They are known to travel over 25 miles a night on their feeding forays. Another species of Free-tailed Bat, the **Velvety Free-tailed Bat** (*Molossus molossus*) is an uncommon resident of the Florida Keys.

CHAPTER 4

THE BIRDS OF FLORIDA

TABLE 2

THE ORDERS AND FAMILIES OF FLORIDA BIRDS

Note: The arrangement below reflects the the order in which the birds of Florida appear in this chapter. It is not an accurate reflection of the phylogenetic relationship of the birds.

Class - **Aves** (birds)

Order - **Passeriformes** (songbirds)

Family	**Tyrannidae** (flycatchers)
Family	**Turdidae** (thrushes)
Family	**Lanidae** (shrikes)
Family	**Aluidae** (larks)
Family	**Mimidae** (thrashers)
Family	**Bombycillidae** (waxwings)
Family	**Motacillidae** (waxwings)
Family	**Certhidae** (creepers)
Family	**Paridae** (chickadee family)
Family	**Polioptilidae** (gnatcatchers)
Family	**Regulidae** (kinglets)
Family	**Sittidae** (nuthatches)
Family	**Troglodytidae** (wrens)
Family	**Pycnonotidae** (bulbuls)
Family	**Hirunidae** (swallows)
Family	**Corvidae** (crows and jays)
Family	**Vironidae** (vireos)
Family	**Parulidae** (warblers)
Family	**Passerellidae** (sparrows)
Family	**Passeridae** (weaver finches)
Family	**Icteriidae** (chat)
Family	**Thraupidae** (tanagers)
Family	**Cardinalidae** (grosbeaks)
Family	**Icturidae** (blackbirds)
Family	**Fringillidae** (finches)

Order - **Cuculiformes**

Family	**Cuculidae** (cuckoos)

Order - **Apodiformes** (swifts and hummingbirds)

Family	**Apodidae** (swifts)
Family	**Trochylidae** (hummingbirds)

Order - **Coraciiformes**

Family	**Alcedinidae** (kingfishers)

Order - **Piciformes**

Family	**Picidae** (woodpeckers)

Order - **Columbiformes**

Family	**Columbidae** (doves)

Order - **Galliformes** (chicken-like birds)

Family	**Phasianidae** (grouse)
Family	**Odontophoridae** (quail)

Order - **Psittaciformes**

Family	**Psittacidae** (parrots and parakeets)

Order - **Caprimulgiformes**

Family	**Caprimulgidae** (nightjars)

Order - **Strigiformes** (owls)

Family	**Strigidae** (typical owls)
Family	**Tytonidae** (barn owl)

Order - **Falconiformes** (falcons)

Family	**Falconidae** (falcons)

Order - **Cathartiiformes** (vultures)

Family	**Cathartidae** (vultures)

Order - **Acciptridiformes** (diurnal raptors)

Family	**Pandionidae** (osprey)
Family	**Accipitridae** (hawks, eagles, and kites)

Order - **Gruiformes** (rails and cranes)

Family	**Rallidae** (rails)
Family	**Aramamidae** (limpkin)
Family	**Gruidae** (cranes)

Order - **Pelecaniformes**

Family	**Threskiornithidae** (ibis)
Family	**Ardeidae** (herons)
Family	**Pelecanidae** (pelicans)

Order - **Ciconiformes**

Family	**Ciconidae** (storks)

Order - **Suliformes**

Family	**Anhigidae** (anhinga)
Family	**Phalacrocoracidae** (cormorants)
Family	**Sulidae** (boobys)
Family	**Frigatidae** (frigatebirds)

Order - **Gaviiformes**

Family	**Gaviidae** (loons)

Order - **Podicipediformes**

Family	**Podicipedidae** (grebes)

Order - **Chariidriformes** (shorebirds)

Family	**Haematopodidae** (oystercatchers)
Family	**Recurvirostridae** (stilts)
Family	**Charadriidae** (plovers)
Family	**Scolapacidae** (sandpipers)
Family	**Laridae** (gulls and terns)

Order - **Anseriiformes** (waterfowl)

Family	**Anatidae** (ducks, geese, and swans)

Class - **Aves** (birds)

Order - **Passeriformes** (songbirds)

Family - **Tyrannidae** (flycatchers)

Eastern Wood Pewee *Contopus virens*	Acadian Flycatcher *Empidonax virescens*	Least Flycatcher *Empidonax minimus*

Size: 6.5 inches.	Presumed range in Florida	**Size:** 5.75 inches.	Presumed range in Florida	**Size:** 5.25 inches.	Presumed range in Florida
Abundance: Fairly common.		**Abundance:** Uncommon.		**Abundance:** Rare in Florida.	
Variation: No significant variation. Sexes alike.		**Variation:** No significant variation. Sexes alike.		**Variation:** No significant variation. Sexes alike.	

Migratory Status: Summer resident in the panhandle. Seasonal migrant elsewhere in the state.	**Migratory Status:** Summer resident in northern Florida. Seasonal migrant in peninsula Florida.	**Migratory Status:** Mainly a seasonal migrant but has been recorded in the state from late August through May.
Habitat: Wood Pewees are forest birds but they favor small openings in the woods or edge areas where marshes or fields border woodlands.	**Habitat:** A woodland species that prefers mature forests. Fond of stream-side habitats and can be common in swamps and marshes.	**Habitat:** Least Flycatchers prefer regenerative woodlands and edge areas. Migrants passing through Florida may be seen in a variety of habitats.
Breeding: Nests are usually built high in trees in a terminal fork. Nest material consists of grasses and lichens. 2 to 4 eggs are laid.	**Breeding:** The Acadian Flycatcher weaves a flimsy nest of grass on a low branch and lays 2 to 4 eggs. Breeding in Florida restricted to northern Florida.	**Breeding:** Nesting occurs in northern US, Canada, and in the higher elevations of the Appalachians. 3 to 5 eggs in nest woven into forked branch.
Natural History: These nondescript little brown birds often go unnoticed except for the distinctive call from which they derive their name. Their "pee-a-weee" song is a common summer sound in the woodlands throughout the eastern half of America. Like other members of the flycatcher family, they hunt flying insects from high perches, swooping out to catch their food on the wing. Very similar to Eastern Phoebe, but note orange lower bill and pale wing bars on the Wood Pewee. These birds can be fairly common summer residents in rural yards that are surrounded by woodlands. They will often become quite tame in those situations. The range of Eastern Wood Pewee in America coincides closely with the Eastern Temperate Forest Level I Ecoregion.	**Natural History:** The Acadian Flycatcher may be less numerous in many areas of the southeastern US today due to the decline of mature forested habitats. These flycatchers like to be near water and are often associated with swamps or wooded, lowland floodplains. The *Empidonax* genus contains several very similar species. Many are almost impossible to differentiate from one another in the field except by their songs. The Acadian Flycatcher is quite similar to the next species (Least Flycatcher), from which it can be told by its slightly larger size. Although they may be seen statewide, this is a rather uncommon species in Florida. Their numbers peak in the state in late summer and early fall when young of the year fledge and migrants pass through that are headed south.	**Natural History:** These flycatchers appear to have a strong social instinct when it comes to nesting and nests are clustered fairly close to each other in small groups. Males and females migrate at different times during spring migration, and fall migration begins fairly early. The winter range is mostly in southern Mexico and Central America but some fall migrants pass through Florida and a few will winter in the southern tip of the state. They appear to be vulnerable to logging and some regions of the country have seen declines in nesting. Strangely, one study in Pennslyvania indicated a decline in nesting in areas of intensive understory browsing by overpopulated White-tailed Deer (DeCalesta, 1994).

Class - **Aves** (birds)

Order - **Passeriformes** (songbirds)

Family - **Tyrannidae** (flycatchers)

Eastern Phoebe *Sayornis phoebe*	Vermilion Flycatcher *Pyrocephalus rubinus*	Great Crested Flycatcher *Myiarchus crinitus*

Male / Female

Size: About 7 inches.

Presumed range in Florida

Abundance: Common.

Variation: No significant variation. Sexes alike.

Migratory Status: Winter resident. A few are seen in spring and fall.

Habitat: Woodlands and woods openings. Also in rural yards or parks in wooded regions. Can be common around rural homesteads.

Breeding: Phoebes are early nesters. Nesting can occur by early April and there will often be a second nesting later in the summer. 2 to 5 eggs are laid.

Natural History: The Eastern Phoebe is most easily told from other flycatchers by its habit of constantly wagging its tail down and up. Its nests are also distinctive, being constructed of mud and lined with mosses. Nests are placed beneath some form of overhang, most often the eaves of buildings. The cup-shaped nest is plastered to the surface in the manner of many swallows. Natural nest sites are built on cliff faces and steep banks with overhanging rocks or tree roots. Man-made structures like bridges and buildings have provided a bonanza of nest sites for the Phoebe and may have helped them increase their range and populations. These are normally tame little birds that may nest on the back porch and allow humans to approach to within a few yards before flying off only a short distance.

Size: About 6 inches.

Presumed range in Florida

Abundance: Very rare in Florida.

Variation: Sexualy dimorphic. See photos above.

Migratory Status: Winter migrant and winter resident. October to March.

Habitat: In Florida this species is most likely to be seen along the Gulf Coast, but has also been seen inland on the peninsula and in the Everglades region.

Breeding: Males perform a singing flight display to attract females. Nesting occurs in the arid Southwest. 4 eggs is typical.

Natural History: Winter visitors to Florida are from a northern population that ranges from Belize through Mexico to the southwestern US. Southern populations are common residents of Central America and northern South America. They are very rare winter visitors to Florida. A few are seen every year in the Sunshine State and vigilant birdwatchers are always on the lookout for a chance to add this handsome species to their life lists. Like other flycatchers, they chase airborne insects from a perch that affords a good vantage point for watching for airborne prey. They will also catch terrestrial invertebrates such as spiders by swooping down on them. The range for this species in Florida is problematic, but it does seem to be limited to the western side of the state. Juvenile males resemble females.

Size: 8.75 inches.

Presumed range in Florida

Abundance: Common.

Variation: None. No sexual dimorphism.

Migratory Status: Summer resident and year-round in south Florida.

Habitat: Deciduous and mixed woodlands. Favors small woods openings and edge areas. Usually with some large trees present.

Breeding: Unlike most flycatchers, this bird is a cavity nester, often using old woodpecker holes. 3 to 5 eggs, laid in mid-May, is typical.

Natural History: The name comes from the "crested" look of the head, which may not be readily apparent. Reddish underside of the tail and wing primaries along with the distinctly yellowish belly contrasting with gray breast is readily apparent, however. These features plus large size make it one of the more recognizable members of the flycatcher family. Feeds on large insects captured in flight from its perch, which is often high in the canopy. In Florida, this species is most common from April though June. Most will have retreated south by the end of September. Forages for insects in treetops and catches flying insects on the wing. A similar species, the **Ash-throated Flycatcher** (*M. cinerascens*) is a very rare winter migrant that sometimes appears in Florida.

Class - **Aves** (birds)

Order - **Passeriformes** (songbirds)

Family - **Tyrannidae** (flycatchers)

Eastern Kingbird *Tyrannus tyrannus*	Western Kingbird *Tyrannus verticalis*	Scissortail Flycatcher *Tyrannus forificatus*

Eastern Kingbird	Western Kingbird	Scissortail Flycatcher
Size: 8.5 inches. **Abundance:** Fairly common. **Variation:** No significant variation. Sexes alike.  Presumed range in Florida	**Size:** 9.5 inches. **Abundance:** Rare in Florida. **Variation:** No significant variation. Sexes alike.  Presumed range in Florida	**Size:** Up to 14.5 inches. **Abundance:** Rare in Florida. **Variation:** Males have longer tails. Presumed range in Florida
Migratory Status: Summer resident.	**Migratory Status:** Winter resident.	**Migratory Status:** Winter resident.
Habitat: Prefers open fields and pastures in rural areas. In urban settings it likes open parks and large empty lots. Commonly seen perched on fences.	**Habitat:** Prefers open habitats such as prairies, arid grasslands, and desert. In Florida, the primary habitat is open grasslands in southern Florida.	**Habitat:** On breeding range the habitat is grassland, pastures, prairies, scrublands, semi-desert, and desert. In Florida it uses the Everglades.
Breeding: Sturdy nest is built of twigs and grass and is placed on limb near the top of large tree. The average clutch size is 3 to 5 eggs. 1 clutch per year.	**Breeding:** Nest is woven from vines and lined with feathers and down. 4 eggs is typical. Does not nest in Florida. Nesting range is in the western US.	**Breeding:** Breeds throughout the southern Great Plains region. Nest is fairly low in small trees and bushes. 5 eggs is a typical clutch.
Natural History: The name "Kingbird" is derived from its aggressive defense of territory against other birds, including even large hawks! "Hunts" flying insects from an open perch, which is frequently a fence or power line. When flying insect prey is spotted, they will launch themselves into an attack that often results in an aerial "dogfight" between bird and insect. These are conspicuous birds. Their charcoal gray upper parts contrast strongly with a whitish breast and belly. The bright reddish-orange blaze on the top of the head is usually not visible to the casual observer. A very similar and closely related species common in the West Indies known as the **Gray Kingbird** (*T. dominicensis)* nests in most of the coastal regions of Florida. It is best described as a paler, slightly larger (9.5 inches) version of the Eastern Kingbird.	**Natural History:** In many ways this bird is the western counterpart of the preceding species. Feeds in the same manner of other flycatchers using both in-flight pursuit of airborne insects and perch to ground attacks on terrestrial invertebrates. Like its eastern cousin, this flycatcher is an agressive defender of its nesting territory and they will attack and harass much larger hawks and owls that venture to close the the nest. eBird records for Florida show that the Western Kingbird is seen in Florida mostly from late October through March. Some studies suggest this species is increasing in population in many western states. A nearly identical species known as the **Cassin's Kingbird** (*T. vociferans*) has been recorded in Florida but that species is very rare in the state and most birds seen in Florida that resemble the photo above will be the Western Kingbird.	**Natural History:** The Scissortail Flycatcher is a common summer resident of the southern plains of North America. Most will winter in Mexico and Central America but some will winter in Florida's Everglades. With its long, deeply forked tail, this is one of America's most recognizable birds. The length of the tail can vary with both sex and age, with older males having the longest tails. A fairly common to common summer resident from the Big Bend region of Texas eastward to central Louisiana. Summer range extends north to southwest Missouri and extreme southern Nebraska. They are known to wander widely and because they are such extravagantly beautiful birds, they rarely go unnoticed. Vagrant specimens have been recorded in every state in the southeast. They have been seen as far north as New Jersey in the east and as far as California in the west.

Class - **Aves** (birds)		
Order - **Passeriformes** (songbirds)		
Family - **Turdidae** (thrush family)		

Eastern Bluebird *Sialia sialis*	**Robin** *Turdus migratorius*	**Wood Thrush** *Hylocichla mustela*
 Male / Female		 

Size: 7 inches.	Presumed range in Florida	**Size:** 10 inches.	Presumed range in Florida	**Size:** 7.75 inches.	Presumed range in Florida
Abundance: Fairly common.		**Abundance:** Very common.		**Abundance:** Uncommon.	
Variation: Sexually dimorphic. See photos above.		**Variation:** Females are less brightly colored.		**Variation:** No variation. Sexes alike.	

Migratory Status: Year-round resident.	**Migratory Status:** Winter resident on the peninsula. Year-round in panhandle.	**Migratory Status:** Summer resident in the panhandle. Migrant on peninsula.
Habitat: Field edges, woods openings, open fields, marshes, and pastures. Savanna-like habitats, i.e. open spaces interspersed with large trees, are a favorite habitat.	**Habitat:** Virtually all habitats in the state may be utilized. Most common in areas of human disturbance, especially older suburbs. They are fond of hunting earthworms in suburban lawns.	**Habitat:** Woodlands. May be found in both mature forests and successional areas. In both, it likes thick undergrowth. Recent population declines are blamed on habitat loss.
Breeding: Bluebirds are cavity nesters that readily take to man-made nest boxes. 2 broods per summer is common in the south. 3 to 6 eggs per clutch.	**Breeding:** The 3 to 4 "sky blue" eggs are laid in a nest constructed of mud and grass, often in the crotch of a tree in an urban yard.	**Breeding:** Nest is mud, twigs, and grass similar to that of the Robin. Nest may be in under story or at mid-level. Lays 2 to 5 blue-green eggs.
Natural History: The Eastern Bluebird's habit of readily adapting to artificial nest boxes has helped bring them back from alarmingly low numbers decades ago, when rampant logging of eastern forests depleted nest cavities. They are primarily insect eaters and in the northern portions of their range thay are vulnerable to exceptionally harsh winters. In winter, Bluebirds eat many types of berries and will readily eat raisins from feeders. Their popularity among humans has lead to the establishment of The North American Bluebird Society. This organization, dedicated to bluebird conservation, encourages the placement of artificial nest boxes and promotes the study of bluebird biology. Ratsnakes are a major predator of nestlings and eggs.	**Natural History:** Despite the fact that the Robin is a migratory species, individuals are seen in Florida year-round. In winter they are sometimes seen in large migratory flocks numbering over 100 birds. In fact, winter is when they are most numerous in Florida, as their ranks are swelled by migrant birds that have summered father to the north. Perhaps the best known of America's bird species, Robins are commonly seen on both urban and rural lawns throughout the state. They feed heavily on earthworms, but will also eat insects and in winter they will take berries or fruits such as crabapples. Robins are a North American endemic and their combined summer and winter ranges coincide with the North American continent, ranging from southern Mexico to the Arctic.	**Natural History:** The Wood Thrush feeds on insects, spiders, earthworms, and other invertebrates found by foraging beneath leaf mold on the forest floor. They will also feed on berries, which can be an important food during fall migration. Like many songbirds, this species is threatened by the fragmentation of forest habitats throughout North America. Smaller forest tracts make it easier for Cowbirds to find Wood Thrush nests. Consequently, nest predation by Cowbirds has increased dramatically in the last few decades. Most Wood Thrushes merely pass through Florida on their way to and from summer/winter habitats, with population peaks in Florida occuring in April and October. Some nesting occurs in the Florida panhandle.

Class - **Aves** (birds)

Order - **Passeriformes** (songbirds)

Family - **Turdidae** (thrush family)

Hermit Thrush *Catharus guttatus*	**Veery** *Catharus fuscescens*	**Swainson's Thrush** *Catharus ustulatus*

Size: 7 inches.	Presumed range in Florida	**Size:** 7 inches.	Presumed range in Florida	**Size:** 7 inches.	Presumed range in Florida
Abundance: Uncommon.		**Abundance:** Uncommon.		**Abundance:** Uncommon.	
Variation: No significant variation. Sexes alike.		**Variation:** No variation in Florida birds.		**Variation:** No variation in Florida birds.	

Migratory Status: Winter resident.	**Migratory Status:** Seasonal migrant.	**Migratory Status:** Seasonal migrant.
Habitat: Damp woodlands, thickets, and successional areas with heavy undergrowth.	**Habitat:** Understory of deciduous woodlands. Most common in second growth forest with thick undergrowth.	**Habitat:** Moist to wet woodlands and swamps with heavy underbrush and cool, heavily shaded woods.
Breeding: 3 to 5 blueish-green eggs are laid in a nest built just above ground level. Birds seen in Florida in winter nest in the boreal forests of Canada.	**Breeding:** Breeds well to the north of Florida. Nest is hidden in thickets on or near the ground. From 3 to 5 eggs are laid.	**Breeding:** Builds its moss-lined nest in a coniferous tree in boreal forest far to the north of Florida. Lays 3 to 5 eggs that are blue with brown spots.
Natural History: Any Thrush seen in Florida during the winter will be this species. They are rather shy but less so than other *Catharus* and they will sometimes visit feeders for suet or raisins. They feed mainly on insects found on the forest floor and beneath leaf mold, but berries are also an important element in the diet, especially in winter. The song of the Hermit Thrush is regarded by many as one of the more beautiful summer sounds in the northern forests. Although secretive, their presence during winter makes them more conspicuous than they would be at other times of the year, especially when in deciduous forests. Unlike most other thrush species that have experienced population declines in recent decades, populations of the Hermit Thrush appear stable. Other thrushes winter in tropical forest and many tropical forests habitats are shrinking rapidly.	**Natural History:** Although the Veery is widespread during migration, they are hard to observe in Florida since they are usually just passing through and they migrate mostly at night. One of the more secretive of the thrushes, they stay mostly in thick undergrowth where they feed on a variety of insects, earthworms, spiders, and berries. Birdwatchers often confirm this bird's presence by recognizing its distinctive call, which has been described as "hauntingly beautiful." Most thrushes present an identification problem for the lay observer, but the Veery can usually be identified by the fact that its overall coloration tends to be much more reddish than the other members of its genus. Veerys winter in the tropical forests of South America. Birds that pass through Florida in the spring likely come across the Caribbean. Others may cross the Gulf of Mexico to make landfall in Texas, Louisiana, etc.	**Natural History:** Another secretive, difficult-to-observe thrush that in migration flies by night and spends its days resting and feeding in heavy undergrowth. As with many of the thrushes, positive identification can be difficult. This species and the Gray-cheeked Thrush are easily confused. The buff-colored cheeks are a good identification character. Like others of its kind, the Swainson's Thrush feeds on insects and invertebrates as well as berries. Unlike others of its genus, however, this thrush is known to feed higher in trees (most other thrushes feed mostly on the ground). As is the case with many of America's neotropical migrant songbirds, this species has been declining in numbers for several years. The exact reason for the decline is not known but habitat alterations that have occurred on both American continents may play a role.

Class - **Aves** (birds)		
Order - **Passeriformes** (songbirds)		
Family - **Turdidae** (thrush family)	Family - **Lanidae** (shrikes)	Family - **Alauidae** (larks)

Gray-cheeked Thrush *Catharus minimus*	**Loggerhead Shrike** *Lanius ludovicianus*	**Horned Lark** *Eremophila alpestris*

Size: 7.25 inches.	Presumed range in Florida	**Size:** 9 inches.	Presumed range in Florida	**Size:** 7.5 inches.	Presumed range in Florida 
Abundance: Uncommon.		**Abundance:** Fairly common.		**Abundance:** Very rare in FL.	
Variation: Variable shades of brown.		**Variation:** No variation. Sexes alike.		**Variation:** Male is slightly more vividly colored.	

Migratory Status: Seasonal migrant.	**Migratory Status:** Year-round resident.	**Migratory Status:** Winter migrant.
Habitat: Summer habitats are boreal forests. Winters in South America. May be seen in woodlands throughout the state during migration.	**Habitat:** Open to semi-open habitats are preferred. In Florida, this species utilizes coastal areas, pastures, open fields, and edge areas.	**Habitat:** This is mainly a prairie species that is seen in expansive, open fields. Large, harvested crop fields are a primary habitat for this bird in the east.
Breeding: Breeds in remote tundra and taiga in northern Canada and Alaska. Lays 3 to 6 eggs.	**Breeding:** Shrikes build a bulky nest of sticks in a thick bush or small tree. Lays up to 7 eggs.	**Breeding:** Nests on barren ground and well concealed amid grasses. Lays 3 to 5 eggs. Does not breed in Florida.
Natural History: A secretive spring and fall nighttime migrant that is easily missed. Spends the summer as far north as Alaska and Siberia. Because it is both secretive and uncommon, the biology of the Gray-cheeked Thrush is poorly known. Its summer habitats are dense spruce forests and willow-alder thickets in the far north. Breeding range extends well into the Arctic Circle and winter range is at least as far south as northern South America. Differentiating between the various thrush species can be challenging. The Gray-cheeked Thrush is easily confused with both the Swainson's Thrush and the Hermit Thrush but it can be told from those species by the gray color of the cheek. The very similar **Bicknell's Thrush** (*C. bicknelli)* was once regarded as a subspecies of the Gray-Cheeked. Bicknell's migrates through Florida but it is extremely rare.	**Natural History:** These fierce little birds are much like a miniature raptor. They hunt mostly insects, but will also attack and kill lizards, mice, small snakes, and birds as large as themselves. Sometimes called "Butcher Bird," they kill with a powerful beak and have the unusual habit of caching food items by impaling the bodies of prey onto a thorn or fence barb. They will form permanent territories which they defend from other shrikes. An endemic North American bird, Loggerhead Shrikes range from south-central Canada to southern Mexico. Sadly, this unique species is declining throughout much of the northern portions of its range. Most experts blame modern agricultural practices that create expansive fields of monoculture crops. The shrikes are mainly Old World in distribution and there are only 2 members of this family found in North America.	**Natural History:** This prairie species needs open ground and has probably moved eastward from its core range in the western plains as a result of human habitat alterations. Closely cropped pastures, tilled lands, or sand dunes are used by the few birds that stray into the northern portion of the state in winter. Except during nesting, these are gregarious birds that are nearly always seen in flocks. They feed on small seeds and tiny arthropods gleaned from what may appear to be nearly barren ground. This species is Holarctic in distribution and can be found in Scandinavia, Siberia, and much of Eurasia. In the Old World, it goes by the name "Shore Lark." The Horned Lark is the only representative of its family found in North America. Professional orinothologists recognize 21 subspecies of this widespread bird. The differences between subspecies are very subtle.

Class - **Aves** (birds)

Order - **Passeriformes** (songbirds)

Family - **Mimidae** (thrashers)

Brown Thrasher *Toxostoma rufum*	Gray Catbird *Dumetella carolinensis*	Northern Mockingbird *Mimus polyglottis*

Size: 11.5 inches.

Abundance: Common.

Variation: No significant variation. Sexes alike.

Presumed range in Florida

Migratory Status: Year-round resident.

Habitat: Edges of woods, thickets, fence rows, overgrown fields, and successional areas. Suburban lawns that have adequate cover in the form of bushes and shrubs may also be used. Avoids deep woods.

Breeding: Builds a stick nest in the heart of a dense shrub, usually within a few feet of the ground. Lays 2 to 5 eggs. 2 broods per year is common.

Natural History: During warm weather, the Brown Thrasher feeds on insects and small invertebrates of all types. It uses its long bill to overturn leaves and debris beneath trees and shrubs and also actively hunts in the grass of urban lawns. In winter, they will eat berries and sometimes come to feeders for raisins or suet. During the breeding season, males perch atop bushes or small trees and serenade all within earshot with their song. Though the Brown Thrasher lacks the repertoire of its cousin the Mockingbird, it does possess one of the most varied song collections of any bird in America. Florida birds are year-round residents but many northern populations are migratory. Migrates at night.

Size: 8.5 inches.

Abundance: Common.

Variation: No significant variation. Sexes alike.

Presumed range in Florida

Migratory Status: Year-round in north Florida. Winter resident on peninsula.

Habitat: Edge areas, thickets, and overgrown fence rows are this bird's preferred habitat. In urban areas, it is often found in older neighborhoods containing landscapes overgrown with large bushes and shrubs.

Breeding: The loosely constructed nest is made of sticks, vines, and leaves placed in dense bushes. 3 to 4 eggs is common. Double broods.

Natural History: The Gray Catbird is much more secretive than its relative the Mockingbird. Food includes all manner of insects, spiders, larva, and berries. Feeds both in the trees and on the ground. When feeding on the ground will use the bill to flip over dead leaves. Named for their call which sounds remarkably like a meowing cat, these shy birds are often heard but unseen as they "meow" from beneath a dense shrub. Like their cousins the Mockingbirds, Gray Catbirds have a large repertoire of songs and they are accomplished mimics of other bird species. They winter along the Lower Coastal Plain of the US, the Caribbean, Mexico, Central America, and throughout the state of Florida.

Size: 10.5 inches.

Abundance: Very common.

Variation: No significant variation. Sexes alike.

Presumed range in Florida

Migratory Status: Year-round resident.

Habitat: Prefers semi-open habitats with some cover in the form of bushes and shrubs. Found in both rural and urban environments. During colder months, they are usually found in the vicinity of berry-producing plants.

Breeding: The nest is made of sticks and is usually in a thick bush or small tree. 3 to 4 eggs are laid and more than 1 nesting per season is usual.

Natural History: The name "Mocking Bird" is derived from this bird's habit of mimicking the calls of other birds. They have a huge repertoire of songs. They are known to mimic the calls of everything from warblers to blue jays and even large hawks. New songs are learned throughout their life and the number of different songs recorded by this species is up to 150. They feed largely on insects, but in the winter will switch to berries and fruits. Mockingbirds have a reputation among rural folk as a useful bird that will chase away other pesky birds such as blackbirds and other species that can be garden pests. There are 2 other very similar species of Mockingbirds from the Caribbean that sometimes show up in south Florida.

Class - **Aves** (birds)

Order - **Passeriformes** (songbirds)

Family - **Bombycillidae** (waxwings)	Family - **Motacillidae** (wagtails)	Family - **Certhiidae** (creepers)
Cedar Waxwing *Bombycilla cedrorum*	**American Pipit** *Anthus rubescens*	**Brown Creeper** *Certhia americana*

Size: 7 inches.

Abundance: Fairly common.

Migratory Status: Winter resident.

Presumed range in Florida

Variation: No significant variation. Sexes are alike.

Habitat: Found both in forests and semi-open country including overgrown fields, orchards, etc. May be seen in both rural and urban settings.

Breeding: Builds a nest of grasses. Nest site is typically high on a tree branch. Nesting occurs well to the north of Florida.

Natural History: Waxwings are named for the peculiar red-colored waxy feathers on their wings. The name "Cedar" Waxwing comes from their propensity for Eastern Red Cedar trees where they consume large quantities of cedar berries. These birds are highly social and are usually seen in large flocks. They feed mostly on berries and wander relentlessly in search of this favored food item. In summer insects, mulberries and serviceberries are important food items. Crabapples and other fruiting trees are also favored. They are highly irregular in occurrence but are frequently seen across the state as they rove around in search of food sources. Large flocks are known to descend on a fruiting bush and consume every berry. Rarely seen singly or in pairs.

Size: 6.5 inches.

Abundance: Rare in Florida.

Migratory Status: Winter resident.

Presumed range in Florida

Variation: Seasonally variable. Breeding plumage is not seen in Florida.

Habitat: In migration and wintering grounds, the American Pipit is usually seen in expansive open areas such as harvested croplands or mud flats.

Breeding: Breeds in tundra areas and southward into the higher altitudes of the Rocky Mountains. Lays 3 to 7 eggs in a nest on the ground.

Natural History: The American Pipit is a hardy species that nests in America's coldest climates. They move south in the winter where they are easily overlooked. Their mottled brown winter plumage is highly cryptic, especially where they usually reside in expansive, open fields or mud flats. During migration and in winter, they may be seen in the company of flocks of Horned Larks and other winter migrants from the far north. This species characteristically wags its tail up and down, a trait that aids in identification. Despite being widespread (their range includes all of North America), they are relatively unknown birds to many. Another similar species, the **Sprague's Pipit** (*Anthus spragueii*), has very rarely been observed in Florida in winter.

Size: 5.25 inches.

Abundance: Very rare in FL.

Migratory Status: Winter resident.

Presumed range in Florida

Variation: No significant variation. Sexes are alike.

Habitat: This is a forest species that prefers mature woodlands with large trees for breeding. In winter, they are seen in a variety of wooded habitats.

Breeding: The nest is nearly always built behind a piece of loose bark on the trunk of a large dead tree. 5 or 6 eggs is typical. No nesting in Florida.

Natural History: Brown Creepers feed on small insects, spiders, etc., found in tree-trunk bark crevices. They have the peculiar foraging habit of landing on the trunk at the base of the tree and "creeping" upward, spiraling around the tree as they go. When they reach a certain height, they fly down to the base of another nearby tree and begin again. In winter, the Brown Creeper is a bit of a loner, and it is rare to see more than 1 or 2 in any one area. This is the only representative of the creeper family (Certhidae) found in North America. Several other species occur in Eurasia and Africa. Population declines in regions where mature forests have been reduced suggests a dependence upon that habitat type. Has probably declined in America since European settlement.

Class - **Aves** (birds)

Order - **Passeriformes** (songbirds)

Family - **Paridae** (chickadee family)		Family- **Poliptilidae** (gnatcatchers)

Carolina Chickadee
Poecile carolinensis

Tufted Titmouse
Baeolophus bicolor

Blue-gray Gnatcatcher
Polioptila caerulea

Size: 4.75 inches.

Presumed range in Florida

Abundance: Common.

Migratory Status: Year-round resident.

Size: 6 inches.

Presumed range in Florida

Abundance: Very common.

Migratory Status: Year-round resident.

Size: 4.5 inches.

Presumed range in Florida

Abundance: Very common.

Migratory Status: Year-round resident.

Variation: No significant variation. Sexes are alike.

Variation: No significant variation. Sexes are alike.

Variation: No significant variation. Sexes are alike.

Habitat: Primarily a woodland species but may be found anywhere so long as at least a few trees are present. Prefers edge areas in both urban and rural areas.

Habitat: All types of forests in the state. Small woodlots and successional areas. Favors edge habitats. Common in both rural and urban habitats.

Habitat: Occupies a wide variety of forested or successional habitats. Most common along wooded streams and bottoms. Prefers deciduous woodlands.

Breeding: Cavity nesters that will use hollows in limbs, rotted fence posts, etc., or very often, old woodpecker holes. Man-made nest boxes may also be used. Clutch size 4 to 6 eggs.

Breeding: This species is a cavity nester that will utilize natural cavities as well as old woodpecker holes. Will also use man-made nest boxes. Average of 5 eggs.

Breeding: Nest is a cuplike structure built with lichens and plant fibers glued together with spider web. Nest usually placed at mid-level near the terminus of a branch. 4 to 5 eggs is average.

Natural History: Among our smallest songbirds, Chickadees are a familiar bird at feeders throughout America. They will become quite acclimated to people and with some patient coaxing they may be induced to land upon an outstretched hand containing sunflower seeds. An acrobatic little bird when searching for insect prey, they can dangle upside down from tiny branches. Their whistling song and their "chick-a-dee-dee-dee" call is distinctive and they can be quite noisy at times, but most people find them to be endearing little birds. In winter, they will form mixed flocks with other small birds. They are hyperactive, tiny birds that have high energy requirements. Winter mortality can be high among populations that winter farther to the north.

Natural History: Primarily a seed eater in winter, the Tufted Titmouse is one of the first birds to find a new bird feeder. Sunflower seeds are favored, but they also love peanuts. Like Chickadees, they are sometimes quite bold around humans servicing feeders. In warm months, they forage for small insects and spiders among the foliage of trees. They can sometimes be seen hanging upside down on a small branch or leaf as they search for prey. Their familiar song is a melodic "birdy-birdy-birdy." In winter, they mix readily with Chickadees and other small birds. Their range corresponds closely to the Eastern Temperate Forest Level I Ecoregion. Recently this species appears to be expanding its range farther to the north.

Natural History: As their name implies, gnatcatchers feed on tiny prey. Any type of small arthropod is probable food item. They hunt the tips of tree branches and sometimes pick off prey while hovering. Despite their small size, they will chase away larger birds and will mob predators such as hawks, snakes, or house cats. The gnatcatchers are a unique family that is probably most closely related to the wrens. Like many small songbird species, the Blue-gray Gnatcatcher is often the victim of nest parasitism by the Brown-headed Cowbird, which lays its eggs in other birds' nests. Despite cowbirds, they seem to be a thriving species and their range has been expanding northward in recent times.

Class - **Aves** (birds)
Order - **Passeriformes** (songbirds)
Family - **Regulidae** (kinglets)

Ruby-crowned Kinglet *Regulus calendula*	**Golden-crowned Kinglet** *Regulus satrapa*

Size: 4.25 inches.

Abundance: Fairly common.

Variation: Male has red stripe on head that is most visible when the male is excited. Females lack this red stripe on the crown. Otherwise sexes are very similar. Spring birds and juveniles are grayer above and less yellowish below.

Presumed range in Florida

Migratory Status: Winter resident that arrives as early as October in north Florida after summering well to the north. Numbers peak in south Florida in November, December, and January and slowly taper off in late February and March.

Habitat: Summer habitat is undisturbed boreal forest across all of Canada from the Atlantic to the Pacific and well into Alaska. Also summers in the higher elevations of the Rocky Mountains. Winter habitats much more generalized to include deciduous and mixed woodlands as well as swamps and lowlands.

Breeding: Breeds in old growth conifers in the far north. Produces enormous clutches of up to 12 eggs. Nest is built near the tops of spruce trees or fir trees. Nest is constructed of a wide variety of materials including mosses, lichens, blades of grass, and conifer needles. Fur, feathers, or animal hair are used to line the nest.

Natural History: This is one of America's smallest songbird species, smaller even than the Chickadee. The bright red blaze on the top of the male's head is usually not visible unless the feathers of the crown are erected. Males most often display the red feathers on the crown when issuing a challenge to other males, displaying to females, or singing their territorial song. Otherwise their bright red crown feathers will remain hidden from view. In summer, they prey on arthropods and their eggs. In winter, they will also feed on berries and some seeds. They are hyperactive little birds that forage throughout the canopy as well as along lower branches. Clumps of dead leaves hanging from a tree limb are like magnets to these tiny hunters who will find small spiders, insects, and other diminutive arthropods hiding within the clumps. They are constantly in motion and regularly flick the wings open as they hop quickly from tiny branch to tiny branch at the terminal end of boughs of trees and bushes. Hunts mostly along the tips of smaller branches. Some studies suggest this species may be declining in the eastern United States. Some suggest this decline may be due to logging and forest fragmentation in the breeding range. Birds that winter in Florida are true latitudinal (north-south) migrants. Populations living in the Rocky Mountains of the western United States migrate from high elevations to lower elevations (altitudinal migration).

Size: 4 inches.

Abundance: Uncommon.

Variation: Male has orange crown, female yellow.

Presumed range in Florida

Migratory Status: A winter resident that usually arrives in Florida in October or November.

Habitat: This is a forest species that prefers mature woodlands with large trees for breeding. In winter, they are seen in a variety of wooded habitats.

Breeding: Builds its nest in the top of a spruce or fir in northern woodlands. Lays a large clutch of up to 11 eggs and may produce 2 broods per year.

Natural History: Even smaller than its cousin the Ruby-crowned Kinglet, the Golden-crowned is a hardier bird that can tolerate colder winter weather. However, severe winter conditions can lead to near 100 percent mortality in localized areas. Amazingly, this little carnivore manages to find arthropod prey throughout the winter and does not switch to seeds and berries in colder weather. Hyperactive and always in motion. They often feed by "leaf hawking" (hovering while picking tiny insects from beneath leaves). In winter, they are often seen in small groups or mixed flocks. This is a northern species that in winter sometimes moves as far south as northern Florida.

Class - **Aves** (birds)

Order - **Passeriformes** (songbirds)

Family - **Sittidae** (nuthatches)

White-breasted Nuthatch	Red-breasted Nuthatch	Brown-headed Nuthatch
Sitta carolinensis	*Sitta canadensis*	*Sitta pusilla*

Size: 5.75 inches.	**Size:** 4.5 inches.	**Size:** 4.5 inches.
Abundance: Uncommon in Florida.	**Abundance:** Very rare in Florida.	**Abundance:** Fairly common.
Migratory Status: Year-round resident.	**Migratory Status:** Winter resident.	**Migratory Status:** Winter resident.

Presumed range in Florida

Variation: No significant variation. Sexes are alike.

Variation: No significant variation. Sexes are alike.

Variation: No significant variation in Florida. Sexes are alike.

Habitat: This is a bird of deciduous and mixed woodlands. Mature forests are preferred.

Habitat: Summers in the coniferous forests of the north and west. Occupies a variety of woodland habitats in Florida.

Habitat: A species of the classic southern pine forests. Favors mature woodlands with natural fire cycles.

Breeding: Nests in natural tree cavities or woodpecker holes. Averages 6 eggs per clutch.

Breeding: Cavity nesters that excavate their own nest holes in the manner of woodpeckers. Average of 6 eggs.

Breeding: Cavity nester that usually excavates its own nest hole in a dead snag. May use an existing cavity.

Natural History: Nuthatches are famous for foraging tree trunks in an upside down position. This behavior gives them the opportunity to occupy a different feeding niche from woodpeckers and other bark hunting birds that may miss insects hidden in crevices visible only from an above perspective. In addition to insects, they also eat seeds and are regulars at most bird feeders in the state. They will cache seeds in bark crevices and they tend to be quite territorial. Pairs will stake out a territory and typically live within that area throughout the year. The White-breasted Nuthatch is 1 of 4 species of nuthatch found in North America and the only one that is a full-time inhabitant of deciduous woodlands. Other species occupy boreal forests (Red-breasted), southern pine forests (Brown-headed), and western pine forests (Pygmy Nuthatch).

Natural History: These birds usually appear in the southern US in significant numbers only every second or third winter and the exact mechanism of their irruptive movements remains something of a mystery. It is believed to be related to cone production in northern coniferous forests where this species usually lives. Northern Florida represents the southernmost extension of their winter range and they are usually quite rare in the state. During the spring and summer, the Red-breasted Nuthatch feeds entirely on small arthropods. Seeds are the staple food during winter and Sunflower seeds are a favorite item at bird feeders. They will wedge seeds into bark crevices to hold them fast while using the beak to hammer open the shell in characteristic "nuthatch" fashion. They will glean insects from bark in the same upside down manner as their larger cousin the White-breasted Nuthatch.

Natural History: In the mature pine woodlands of the Deep South where this species lives, it can be difficult to observe. Clear cutting of old growth pine forests along with fire suppression tactics lead to a significant decline in populations of this species. It is so dependent upon mature pine forests and the cyclical wild fires which suppress hardwoods that this species is regarded as an indicator of a healthy southern forest. Insects are the major food in warm months and pine seeds are eaten in winter. Pine cones are hammered open for their seeds in a typical nuthatch fashion. Foraging is generally high up in the trees, making observation of this species under natural conditions difficult. However, they do readily come to feeders for sunflower seeds and suet and are not hard to see for residents of the southern pine forests who feed birds.

Class - **Aves** (birds)

Order - **Passeriformes** (songbirds)

Family - **Troglodytidae** (wrens)

Carolina Wren *Thryothorus ludovicianus*	**Marsh Wren** *Cistothorus palustris*	**Sedge Wren** *Cistothorus platensis*

Size: 5.5 inches.	**Size:** 5 inches.	**Size:** 4.5 inches
Abundance: Common.	**Abundance:** Uncommon.	**Abundance:** Uncommon.
Migratory Status: Year-round resident.	**Migratory Status:** Year-round but rare in summer.	**Migratory Status:** Seen in Florida October through April.
Presumed range in Florida 	Presumed range in Florida	Presumed range in Florida 

Variation: No significant variation in Florida, sexes alike.

Habitat: Carolina Wrens are very flexible in habitat choices. They can be seen in remote wilderness or in suburban backyards.

Breeding: A nest of fine twigs and grass is built in a sheltered place, often provided by man. Eggs number 3 to 6. Will produce at least 2 clutches per year.

Natural History: The most common wren in Florida, the Carolina Wren is well-known for building its nest in an old pair of boots or in an vase of flowers left on the back porch for a few days. They will become quite tame around yards and porches and frequently endear themselves to their human neighbors. They are voracious consumers of insects, spiders, and caterpillars and help control insect pests around the home. Homeowners using pest control *outside the home* risk poisoning these natural insect controllers. These are incessant singers whose musical song serves as a dawn alarm for many residents throughout the state. Although vulnerable to harsh winters, Carolina Wrens are expanding their range northward, perhaps in response to climate change.

Variation: No significant variation in Florida, sexes alike.

Habitat: Pastures, marshes, and lowland meadows as well as open, grassy edges of wetlands or ponds. Coastal salt marshes are widely used in winter.

Breeding: Nest is low in grasses or small bush. Nest is built of grasses woven into a ball with an entrance hole in the side. Several unused "decoy" nests are built. 7 eggs is typical.

Natural History: Marsh Wrens summer mostly to the north of Florida but they can be seen statewide from early fall through spring. Nesting does occur in the gulf coastal bend and in the panhandle of Florida, but most will move far to the north to nest. Known food items are insects and spiders. These are secretive birds that can be very difficult to observe, even in areas where they are common. They spend most of their time hidden in thick stands of cattails or other vegetation deep in the marsh. Like most wrens, they will sing continuously in the breeding season and most birdwatchers confirm their presence by learning to recognize their song. They will build one or more "decoy" nests that are never used and they are also known to destroy the eggs in other nearby nests.

Variation: No significant variation in Florida, sexes alike.

Habitat: This is a wetland species that enjoys marshes and wet meadows. Unlike the Marsh Wren, it does not occupy cattail marsh but prefers grassy areas.

Breeding: Nest is built low to the ground, often in a clump of sedges or a small bush. 6 or 7 eggs is typical and some may produce 2 broods per year. Does not nest in Florida.

Natural History: This is another secretive species that is difficult to observe. The natural history of this species is poorly known, but it is known that nesting dates vary considerably from one region of the country to another. Nesting is well to the north of Florida and can occur from May to as late as September. Some birds may produce 2 broods per year in 2 different regions. The diet is spiders and insects. Sedge Wrens winter in the coastal plain of the southeastern United States from the Carolinas all the way to northwestern Mexico and they can be seen throughout Florida in winter. Spring migration begins in April and most birds are usually gone from Florida by the end of May. They will begin to return in September or October.

Class - **Aves** (birds)

Order - **Passeriformes** (songbirds)

Family - **Troglodytidae** (wrens)		Family - **Pycnonotidae** (bulbuls)

House Wren
Troglodytes aedon

Winter Wren
Troglodytes hiemalis

Red-whiskered Bulbul
Pycnonototus jocosus

Size: 4.75 inches.

Presumed range in Florida

Abundance: Fairly common.

Migratory Status: Winter resident from September through May.

Size: 4 inches.

Presumed range in Florida

Abundance: Rare in Florida.

Migratory Status: Winter resident from October through April.

Size: 7 inches.

Presumed range in Florida

Abundance: Very rare.

Migratory Status: Year-round resident of the greater Miami area.

Variation: Color may vary from grayish brown to reddish brown.

Variation: No significant variation in Florida, sexes alike.

Variation: Juvenile lacks characteristic red "whiskers" on face.

Habitat: Prefers open and semi-open habitats. These wrens readily associate with humans and are most common in small towns and suburbs. They can also be common in more natural habitats.

Habitat: Mature, old growth forests are the primary summer habitat, often near a stream or bog. Deciduous and mixed woodlands are utilized in winter, but conifers are preferred.

Habitat: Suburban neighborhoods and urban parks in the immediate vicinity of Miami are where this bird can be seen in Florida. Natural habitats are in tropical southern Asia.

Breeding: A cavity nester, the House Wren readily takes to artificial nest boxes. In fact, this species may owe its increase in population to man-made "bird houses." Lays up to 8 eggs.

Breeding: Breeds well to the north of Florida, mainly in the boreal forests of Canada. Nest is often constructed in the root wad of an upturned tree. Lays 5 to 9 eggs.

Breeding: Nest is usually low to the ground in a dense shrub. In Florida, nest occurs in suburban neighborhoods or urban parks. 2 to 3 eggs is typical but can be as many as 5.

Natural History: House Wrens are probably more common today than in historical times, as they favor open and semi-open habitats over dense forests. They also have a strong affinity for human-altered habitats and settlements, and they respond positively to the erection of artificial nest boxes by urban residents. They feed on a wide variety of insects, spiders, snails, caterpillars, etc. When feeding large broods of young, they catch huge quantities daily. In this regard, they are a useful assest to the homeowner in Florida. House Wrens range from coast to coast across America and northward into the prairie provinces of Canada.

Natural History: Much shyer and more secretive than other wrens, the Winter Wren skulks about under dense bushes and shrubs where it tends to stay close to the ground. Like other wrens, these birds are strictly carnivorous and feed on a wide variety of small insects, larva, arachnids, amphipoda, etc. As with many other invertivorous birds, they are vulnerable to exceptionally harsh winters. Their stubby, upturned tail makes identification easy, but they are more often heard than seen as they are persistent, loud singers. Winter Wrens are Holarctic in distribution, being found in Europe and northern Asia as well as North America.

Natural History: The Red-whiskered Bulbul joins a long list of exotic species that have become established in Florida. They first appeared in the Miami area around 1960 when several birds escaped from captivity. They have since become established as a breeding population but they have not spread far and their range remains restricted to the immediate vicinity of Miami. These birds eat a great deal of fruit and if they ever did become common, they could be a problem for Florida's agriculture community. In addition to fruit, they will eat berries, flowers, and some insects. They seem to thrive in human-altered habitats both in Florida and in their native lands.

Class - **Aves** (birds)

Order - **Passeriformes** (songbirds)

Family - **Hirunidae** (swallows)

Bank Swallow *Riparia riparia*	**Barn Swallow** *Hirundo rustica*	**Cliff Swallow** *Petrochelidon pyrrhonota*

Size: 5.25 inches.	Presumed range in Florida 	**Size:** 7 inches.	Presumed range in Florida	**Size:** 5.5 inches.	Presumed range in Florida
Abundance: Uncommon in Florida.		**Abundance:** Common.		**Abundance:** Uncommon.	
Variation: No variation. Sexes alike.		**Variation:** Males are slightly more vivid.		**Variation:** No variation. Sexes alike.	

Migratory Status: Migrant. Most commonly seen in spring and fall.	**Migratory Status:** Most common in Florida from March to November.	**Migratory Status:** Migrant. Most common in Florida in spring and fall.
Habitat: Open country near large rivers. In migration may be seen in a wide variety of habitats but most often observed near water, lakes, etc.	**Habitat:** Open and semi-open habitats. Most common in agricultural areas but seen virtually everywhere in the state. Least common in forested areas.	**Habitat:** Open areas near large bodies of water are the preferred habitat for this species. Breeding habitat was historically limited to regions with cliffs.
Breeding: Nest hole in banks is dug by the parents and may be as much as 2 to 3 feet deep. 4 to 6 eggs.	**Breeding:** Nest is bowl-shaped and made of mud and grasses plastered to roof joists of a barn or building eaves.	**Breeding:** Conical mud nests are plastered beneath sheltered overhangs of concrete structures such as bridges.
Natural History: Although widespread across America during migration, this species is rather uncommon in Florida. Like many swallows, the Bank Swallow nests in large communities. Nest colonies are usually associated with large river systems with exposed cliff faces. Despite being somewhat uncommon in Florida, these birds are found throughout the world. In fact they are one of the most widespread bird species on earth. The natural nesting habitat has always been riverbanks and bluffs, but today they utilize the banks created by man-made quarries or road cuts through hillsides. They do not nest in Florida but pass through in migration. During migration they can be seen in the company of other species of migrating swallows. Food is exclusively flying insects caught on the wing. Mostly flies, flying ants, small beetles, and mayflies.	**Natural History:** A familiar bird to all who grew up on rural farmsteads. Barn Swallows are common throughout most of North America in summer. They summer in the US and winter mostly in Central and North America. In peninsular Florida, they are mostly migrants. European breeders winter in the Mediterranean, Africa, and the Middle East while Asian breeding birds winter throughout southeast Asia to Australia. Thus this is one of the most widespread bird species in the world. Its long association with humans throughout the world has led to the invention of many legends. Barn Swallows nesting in your barn was considered by pioneers as good luck, while destroying a nest in the barn would cause the milk cow to go dry. Flying insects are the main food including pesky flies and even wasps. This is the world's most common swallow species.	**Natural History:** The Cliff Swallow is primarily a western species that nested historically on cliff faces in the Rocky Mountains. They are more numerous today than even a few decades ago. Man-made structures such as dams and bridges have likely helped this species expand its range in the eastern United States. These birds are colony animals that seem to always nest in groups. A source of mud for building nests is required and there seems to be a preference for nesting near water. Colony size varies from a few dozen to a few hundred nests. In the far west, where the species is more common and widespread, colonies consisting of several thousand nests are known. Like other swallows, they feed almost entirely upon airborne insects, and they are adept at locating swarms of airborne prey. Does not nest in Florida.

Class - **Aves** (birds)

Order - **Passeriformes** (songbirds)

Family - **Hirunidae** (swallows)

Northern Rough-winged Swallow *Stelgidopteryx serripennis*	**Tree Swallow** *Tachycineta bicolor*	**Purple Martin** *Progne subis*

Northern Rough-winged Swallow
Stelgidopteryx serripennis

Size: 5.5 inches.

Abundance: Fairly common.

Variation: No variation, sexes alike.

Presumed range in Florida

Migratory Status: Year-round along Gulf Coast. Summer resident elsewhere in the state.

Habitat: Mainly open and semi-open areas. In Florida uses agricultural fields and open marshlands, prairies, etc. Fond of being near lakes and rivers.

Breeding: Nest is in rock faces and crevices. Today often uses man-made situations such as road cuts, quarries, etc. Not a colony nester. Lays 4 to 8 eggs.

Natural History: As with other swallows, the Rough-winged Swallow feeds by catching flying insects in midair. All swallows in America are diurnal hunters whose predatory role is replaced at dusk by the bats. Although this swallow is found from coast to coast across America, it is not extremely common anywhere. Unlike the similar Bank Swallow, Rough-winged Swallows are not known to dig their own burrow and availability of nest burrows may be one reason why these swallows tend to be solitary nesters. They will use burrows dug by other species of birds or small mammals as well as natural cavities in cliff faces or fissure spaces in man-made concrete structures. Some will winter in the Everglades region or along the Gulf.

Tree Swallow
Tachycineta bicolor

Size: 5.75 inches.

Abundance: Common.

Variation: Sexes alike. Immatures are gray.

Presumed range in Florida

Migratory Status: Winter resident throughout the state. Most common from October to April.

Habitat: Open and semi-open habitats. Fond of being near water, including small ponds and Beaver swamps. Also likes marshes and wet prairies.

Breeding: A cavity nester, Tree Swallows will use old woodpecker holes or tree hollows. They also use artificial nest boxes and sometimes nest in close proximity to Purple Martins.

Natural History: Tree Swallows are more numerous today than in historical times and are increasing in numbers. Human activities have benefited this species by creating more open lands and also by creating more ponds and lakes throughout the landscape. The proliferation of artificial nest boxes has also helped (they take readily to Bluebird Boxes). The resurgence of Beaver populations is also credited with helping this species. Flying insects are the primary food items, but they also eat bayberries during the winter. They are known to eat snails during the breeding season to obtain calcium for eggshell production. The Tree Swallow winters along the southeastern coastline of the US, Florida, Mexico, and the Caribbean.

Purple Martin
Progne subis

Female   Male

Size: 8 inches.

Abundance: Uncommon.

Variation: Sexually dimorphic (see photo).

Presumed range in Florida

Migratory Status: Summer resident. The first arriving birds are males and they may arrive as early as late winter.

Habitat: Inhabits both rural areas and suburbs. Artificial nest boxes near water in open areas are major attractants. Strongly associated with humans.

Breeding: Originally nested in natural cavities but today nearly all use artificial nest sites. 3 to 6 eggs is typical but may lay as many as 7 or 8. Purple Martins are colony nesters.

Natural History: Our largest swallow and perhaps the most beloved bird in America. Many people anxiously await the return of Purple Martins each spring to nest boxes erected in their yard. This is especially true in notherly regions where their arrival signals the end of winter. Their relationship with humans extends at least as far back as the eighteenth century and today there are 2 national organizations dedicated to Purple Martin enthusiasts. A warm weather species that is dependent upon flying insect prey, Purple Martins are vulnerable to spring cold fronts in the more northern reaches of the summer range. This species is so adapted to nesting in man-made nest boxes that today it is rare to find one nesting in natural cavities.

Class - **Aves** (birds)		
Order - **Passeriformes** (songbirds)		
Family - **Corvidae** (crows and jays)		

American Crow *Corvus brachyrhynchos*	**Fish Crow** *Corvus ossifragus*	**Blue Jay** *Cyanocitta cristata*
		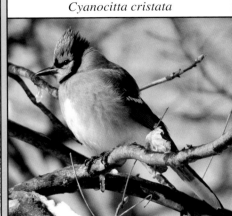

Size: 19 inches. **Abundance:** Fairly common. **Variation:** No significant variation. Sexes alike.	Presumed range in Florida 	**Size:** 17 inches. **Abundance:** Common. **Variation:** No significant variation. Sexes alike	Presumed range in Florida	**Size:** 11 inches. **Abundance:** Very common. **Variation:** No significant variation. Sexes alike.	Presumed range in Florida 

Migratory Status: Year-round resident.	**Migratory Status:** Year-round resident.	**Migratory Status:** Year-round resident.
Habitat: Occurs in virtually all habitats including urban areas. Most common where there is a patchwork of woods and open spaces.	**Habitat:** Occurs in virtually all habitats including urban areas. Probably most common in areas near the coast, but can be seen anywhere in the state.	**Habitat:** Statewide from dense woodlands to semi-open farmlands. Also suburban and urban neighborhoods. Woodlands are the favored habitat.
Breeding: Crows build a bulky stick nest high in the fork of a tree, well hidden by thick foliage. 4 eggs is typical.	**Breeding:** Large stick nest is placed in a tree crotch. Averages about 4 eggs. A single clutch is produced annually.	**Breeding:** Builds a stick nest fairly high up on a branch or in a fork. Lays an average of 4 eggs.
Natural History: Crows are omnivores that will eat virtually anything, including the young and eggs of other birds. They are among the most intelligent and resourceful of birds. They may be seen in pairs, small groups, or large flocks numbering in the hundreds. Highly adaptable, crows have fared well in human-altered habitats and the species is more common today than prior to European settlement. It is almost certain to remain a common species. As a testament to the crow's intelligence, in rural areas where hunting is commonplace, they are extremely wary of humans; while in protected parks and urban regions they will become quite accepting of the presence of humans. In such environments they will boldly raid suburban yards for pet food and garbage. Longevity record for a wild bird is 17.5 years.	**Natural History:** Identical to the America Crow but smaller (17-inch), the Fish Crow occurs throughout America's Coastal Plain. They are often seen in the company of their larger cousin and when seen together the Fish Crow can be distinguished by its smaller size. Expert birdwatchers can identify this species by its call, which is higher pitched than that of the American Crow. A southern species that historically was found in coastal areas and lowlands of the Lower Coastal Plain, the Fish Crow has expanded its range northward over the last few decades. Today they range well up into the Mississippi River Valley, appearing as far north as St. Louis. They can be extremely common in Florida around esturaries and coastal areas, and they will become very tolerant of humans in parks or popular fishing sites.	**Natural History:** The Blue Jay's handsome blue, black, and white feathers and distinctive crest make it one of the most recognizable birds in the state. They mainly eat insects, acorns, and grains, but also eat eggs and young of other songbirds. They will aggressively mob much larger birds like hawks and owls, as well as snakes and house cats. Members of this family are relatively long-lived. The record life span for a wild Blue Jay is 18 years, but a captive specimen was reported to have lived for 26 years. An endemic American bird, Blue Jays are found throughout the eastern half of the United States from about the Rocky Mountains eastward. They also range northward into Canada but well below the Arctic Circle. They have adapted well to human impacts on the land and they can be common in suburbs with large trees.

Class - **Aves** (birds)

Order - **Passeriformes** (songbirds)

Family - **Corvidae** (crows and jays)	Family - **Vironidae** (vireos)	

Florida Scrub Jay
Aphelocoma coerulescens

Size: 11.5 inches.	Presumed range in Florida
Abundance: Uncommon.	
Variation: No significant variation. Sexes alike.	

Migratory Status: Year-round resident.

Habitat: Restricted to "scrub habitats" in central Florida. These habitats occur on dry, sandy, upland locales that were once beach dunes.

Breeding: Breeds in early spring. Nest is relatively low in a dense shrub. Clutch size is typically 2 or 3 eggs.

Natural History: This is the only species of bird in Florida that is endemic to the state. They are native to the habitat usually referred to as Florida's "Central Florida Scrub." Their range in the state today is rather fragmented as much of their habitat has been converted to orange groves or urban and suburban use. The US Fish and Wildlife Service lists them as a Threatened Species and some reports indicate that their populations may have declined by as much as 50 percent from historical times (Stith, *et al*, 1996). Diet is varied and consists of a variety of arthropod prey as well as berries and acorns. They are also known to eat small vertebrates such as treefrogs and *Anolis* lizards. Unlike many bird species that use the power of flight to travel great distances, the Florida Scrub Jay tends to remain within the area where it was hatched.

White-eyed Vireo
Vireo griseus

Size: 5 inches.	Presumed range in Florida
Abundance: Common.	
Variation: No variation, sexes alike.	

Migratory Status: Year-round resident throughout the state.

Habitat: Dense thickets and early successional deciduous woodlands are favored. Also in overgrown fields with small saplings and thickets. Mangroves.

Breeding: Nest is a woven, hanging basket held together with silk from caterpillars or spiders. 3 to 5 eggs.

Natural History: This is the only vireo with a white iris, making identification easy. Nest parasitism by Brown-headed Cowbirds is estimated to be as high as 50 percent, with no young surviving in parasitized nests. Highly insectivorous. Caterpillars are a favorite food item. Will also eat fruit. White-eyed Vireos are seen year-round in Florida. Many breed in the state and Florida birds probably don't migrate. Birds summering farther to north do migrate south in winter, some as far as Central America. Nest parasitism by Brown-headed Cowbirds possess a constant threat and deforestation contributes to the problem. Brown-headed Cowbirds tend to avoid deep woods in favor of more open habitats. Loss of large tracts of woodland makes life easier for the cowbirds and more difficult for the species which they parasitize.

Yellow-throated Vireo
Vireo flavifrons

Size: 6.5 inches.	Presumed range in Florida
Abundance: Uncommon.	
Variation: No variation, sexes alike.	

Migratory Status: Mainly March through October in Florida.

Habitat: A woodland bird that will inhabit a wide variety of forest types. Likes edges of more mature, larger tracts of woodlands.

Breeding: The nest is a woven basket suspended from the fork of a small branch. 4 eggs is typical.

Natural History: The nest is usually located in a branch overhanging a forest opening such as a lane or a stream. Feeds on a wide variety of arthropods with caterpillars being a mainstay. Also eats small amount of berries and seeds in the fall. The biology of this species is not as well understood as with many other vireos, but it is known that it has decreased in numbers in areas of deforestation. As with many small woodland songbirds, the nest of the Yellow-throated Vireo is subject to parasitism by cowbirds. The summer range of this species coincides closely with the Eastern Temperate Forest Level I ecoregion. Although a few may linger in Florida into the winter, most will winter in the Carribean or from southern Mexico to northern South America. Migrants regularly cross the Gulf of Mexico.

Class - **Aves** (birds)
Order - **Passeriformes** (songbirds)
Family - **Vironidae** (vireos)

Blue-headed Vireo *Vireo solitarius*	**Red-eyed Vireo** *Vireo olivaceus*	**Black-whiskered Vireo** *Vireo altiloquus*

Blue-headed Vireo	Red-eyed Vireo	Black-whiskered Vireo
Size: 5.5 inches.	**Size:** 6 inches.	**Size:** 6.25 inches.
Abundance: Fairly common.	**Abundance:** Common.	**Abundance:** Rare in Florida.
Variation: No significant variation. Sexes alike. Presumed range in Florida	**Variation:** Sexes alike but males are slightly larger. Presumed range in Florida	**Variation:** No significant variation. Sexes alike. Presumed range in Florida
Migratory Status: Winter resident.	**Migratory Status:** Summer resident.	**Migratory Status:** Summer resident.
Habitat: This vireo summers in the boreal forests of the far north and high Appalachians. In winter in Florida, it uses swamps, thickets, and woodlands.	**Habitat:** Although a woodland species, the Red-eyed Vireo is very generalized in its habitat requirements. Mature forests and regenerative woodlans are used.	**Habitat:** In Florida this species uses coastal mangroves, especially on the Gulf Coast. Also uses hammocks in the Everglades region.
Breeding: Nest construction is similar to other vireos. A tightly woven cup is suspended from a horizontal fork. 4 eggs is typical.	**Breeding:** 2 to 4 eggs are laid in May. May have 2 broods per summer with second brood fledging as late as late August.	**Breeding:** In Florida often nests in mangrove swamps. Nest is a woven cuplike structure suspended from forked branches. 3 eggs is typical.
Natural History: Also known as the Solitary Vireo. Blue-headed Vireos summer well to the north of Florida in Canada and in the higher elevations of the Appalachian Mountains. They winter from the Lower Coastal Plain of the southeastern US all the way to Central America. They are quite common in peninsular Florida throughout the winter. Food is mostly insects, with moths and butterflies and their larva being a major portion of the diet. Most foraging is done in trees well above the forest floor. As is the case with many of America's migrant songbirds, the Blue-headed Vireo is highly dependent upon large tracts of forest. Deforestation negatively impacts local populations; but forest regeneration in many areas of its summer range has helped this species in recent years.	**Natural History:** This is one of the most common summer songbirds in American forests and woodlots and it can be especially common in deciduous woodlands. It is not readily observed due to its habit of staying high in the forest canopy. It is, however, regularly heard as it sings incessantly throughout the spring. While on their breeding grounds, they are primarily insectivorous feeders, but they do consume some fruits while wintering in the tropics. The population health of the Red-eyed Vireo may be due to its less stringent dependence upon large tracts of forest. This species can subsist happily in small woodlands and regenerative areas. However, in these habitats it is more susceptible to the parasitic nesting of the Brown-headed Cowbird. Their red eye color is unique among vireos.	**Natural History:** This is mainly a Caribbean bird that ranges northward onto both coasts of the southern half of the Florida peninsula. They superficially resemble the Red-eyed Vireo, but have the characteristic black "mustache" marking on the throat. Eats both insects and fruits. Birds that breed and summer in Florida spend the winter in South America. Like the similar Red-eyed Vireo, this species sings constantly and trained birdwatchers can usually locate it by ear. Seeing it amid the tangle of mangroves is not as easy. As is the case with other vireos and most neotropical migrant songbirds, nest parasitism by cowbirds is a threat. Loss of mangrove habitat may also pose problems for this species unless protection of these habitats is continued.

Class - **Aves** (birds)
Order - **Passeriformes** (songbirds)
Family - **Parulidae** (warblers)

Ovenbird *Seiurus aurocapilla*	**Worm-eating Warbler** *Helmitheros vermivorus*	**Louisiana Waterthrush** *Parkesia motacilla*

Size: 6 inches.

Presumed range in Florida

Abundance: Fairly common.

Variation: Fall and female plumages more greenish overall.

Migratory Status: Winter resident.

Habitat: Mature, contiguous forests. Seems to prefer upland woods. A substrate of abundant leaf litter is an important element to this bird's habitat.

Breeding: Nests is on the ground and is constructed of leaves and grass. Nest is unique in that it has a domed roof with an opening in front. 3 to 6 eggs. Does not nest in Florida.

Natural History: This large warbler is a ground dweller, and is usually observed on the ground or in low foliage. Food is a wide variety of insects and arthropods taken mostly on the ground among the leaf litter. The song of the Ovenbird is distinctive and has been variously described as "emphatic" and "effervescent." Often 2 nearby birds will sing at once, with their overlapping songs sounding like a single bird. This species has experienced a decline in the last few decades. Forest fragmentation and Brown-headed Cowbird nest parasitism may be to blame. Winter range includes West Indies and Cuba as well as Mexico, Central America, and all of peninsula Florida. Summer range is in woodlands north of the Coastal Plain.

Size: 6 inches.

Presumed range in Florida

Abundance: Uncommon.

Variation: No significant variation and the sexes are alike.

Migratory Status: Seasonal migrant.

Habitat: This is a woodland species, but it seems to avoid lowland forests. Uses low shrubs and bushes in dense undergrowth in Florida.

Breeding: Nests are built on the ground in deep woods and are often hidden beneath overhanging vegetation. 4 to 5 eggs is typical. Does not breed in Florida.

Natural History: This is a species that specializes in feeding amid low bushes searching the dead leaf clusters and low-hanging foliage for insects, spiders, and primarily, caterpillars. Like many of America's neotropical migrant songbirds, the Worm-eating Warbler is highly dependent upon deciduous forests for breeding habitat. Winters in Mexico, Central America, and the West Indies. This species is the world's only member of its genus. Its closest relative may be the Swainson's Warbler. They are most commonly seen in Florida from late March through early May, and again in the fall from August through October. Breeds widely in the Ozark-Ouachita-Appalachian Forests and the Southeast US Plains. It winters in the Caribbean and Central America.

Size: 5.5 inches.

Presumed range of both species in Florida

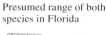

Abundance: Uncommon.

Variation: 2 nearly identical species (see below).

Migratory Status: Seasonal migrants.

Habitat: Forested streams are the preferred habitat. In migration they may also be seen along the edges of swamps or small woodland ponds.

Breeding: Nesting occurs as early as May in the Louisiana Waterthrush. 4 to 6 eggs are laid in a nest placed in tree roots along the banks of a stream. Northern Waterthrush nests in June.

Natural History: This species is famous for its incessant "tail bobbing" behavior. The entire rear half of the body constantly wags up and down when foraging in stream side habitats. There are 2 nearly identical species of waterthrush in America. The **Northern Waterthrush** (*P. noveboracensis*) is so similar to the Louisiana Waterthrush that most casual observers will not be able to tell them apart. Both are mainly seasonal migrants that passs through Florida but a few may be seen in the state in winter. The Louisiana breeds in most of the Eastern Temperate Forest (but not in Peninsular Florida). Meanwhile, the Northern breeds farther north in boreal forests. Both associate with water and both are usually seen near streams or wetlands.

Class - **Aves** (birds)

Order - **Passeriformes** (songbirds)

Family - **Parulidae** (warblers)

Blue-winged Warbler	Golden-winged Warbler	Black-and-white Warbler
Vermivora cyanoptera	*Vermivora chrysoptera*	*Mniotilta varia*

Size: 4.75 inches.	**Size:** 4.75 inches.	**Size:** 5.25 inches.

Presumed range in Florida

Presumed range in Florida

Presumed range in Florida

Abundance: Uncommon in FL.

Migratory Status: Seasonal migrant. A few may winter in FL.

Abundance: Rare in Florida.

Migratory Status: Seen in Florida mostly in fall.

Abundance: Fairly common.

Migratory Status: Seen year-round except in summer.

Variation: Seasonal and sexual plumage changes are slight. Females may be slightly duller.

Variation: Females and immatures have gray rather than black on face; gold color on crown and wings reduced.

Variation: Female very similar but has more white on the face and breast. Male is more heavily streaked.

Habitat: Overgrown weed fields with ample brushy undergrowth and early successional woodlands constitute this bird's habitat in summer. Least common in areas of intensive agriculture.

Habitat: Second growth woodlands and overgrown fields. Most of summer range is in boreal forest; a few summer in the higher elevations of the Appalachian Highlands.

Habitat: Found in a wide variety of forest types, but mature and second-growth deciduous forests are the primary habitat. Mixed conifer-hardwood forests are also used.

Breeding: Nest is near the ground in or under a low bush. From 4 to 6 eggs are laid in May.

Breeding: Nests on the ground near the ground at the base of a bush, hidden in thick grass and weeds. 4 to 5 eggs.

Breeding: Nest is placed in a depression on the ground at the base of tree or stump. Lays 3 to 5 eggs.

Natural History: A shrub-land specialist, the Blue-winged Warbler has experienced an upswing in populations as a result of deforestation by pioneering Europeans settlers of eastern North America. In recent years, there has been a decline in their numbers in the northeast as forests have begun recovering from the rampant logging of the last century. These birds sometimes hybridize with the similar Golden-winged Warbler and produce at least 2 additional forms of difficult-to-identify hybrid birds. The 2 hybrid morphs are known as "Brewster's Warbler" and "Lawrence's Warbler." Some ornitholgists fear that hybridization could possibly lead to the disappearance of the declining Golden-wing Warbler as a species.

Natural History: Sightings of migrant birds in Florida are very rare in the spring, but they are presumed to pass through most of the state. They are more commonly seen in Florida during fall migration. This is a species in decline throughout its range. Hybridization with Blue-winged Warblers, loss of winter habitat, and nest parasitism by the Brown-headed Cowbird are possible reasons for a recent population decline. Winters in a variety of forest habitats in Mexico, Central America, and northern South America from sea level to 7,000 feet. Like many warblers, this species migrates across the Gulf of Mexico. This crossing can become perilous if migrants encounter strong headwinds, heavy downpours, and hail associated with spring thunderstoms.

Natural History: Feeds by plucking tiny creatures from tree bark and branches. Its feeding habits are more similar to that of woodpeckers, nuthatches, and creepers than to most warblers. This species is dependent upon deciduous and mixed conifer forests, but apparently it has not been significantly impacted by deforestation. Black-and-white Warblers can be seen throughout the state during winter and they can be common in spring and fall. About the only time they cannot be seen in the state is during late May through June. This is an unsual warbler and it is the only member of the *Mniotilta*. The unusual name translates from Latin to English as "moss plucker" and is a reference to the bird's habit of feeding in clumps of Spanish moss.

Class - **Aves** (birds)

Order - **Passeriformes** (songbirds)

Family - **Parulidae** (warblers)

Prothonotary Warbler *Protonotaria citrea*	Swainson's Warbler *Limnothlypis swainsonii*	Tennessee Warbler *Oreothlypis peregrina*

Size: 5.5 inches.	**Size:** 5.5 inches.	**Size:** 4.75 inches.
Abundance: Uncommon.	**Abundance:** Rare.	**Abundance:** Fairly common.
Migratory Status: Summer resident and seasonal migrant.	**Migratory Status:** Summer resident and seasonal migrant.	**Migratory Status:** Seasonal migrant. April/ May and September/ October.

Presumed range in Florida

Variation: Sexes nearly identical. Female slightly less vivid.

Variation: No variation. Sexes are alike in this species.

Variation: Females less gray and more greenish overall. Fall plumage similar.

Habitat: Prothonotary Warblers always nest near water. They are most common in swamps and marshes but can also be seen along lake shores, riparian areas, and in the vicinity of small ponds.

Habitat: Swainson's Warblers are known to associate with stands of giant cane in the southern US. In the Appalachians they frequent Rhododendren thickets. Winter habitat is tropical forest.

Habitat: Summer habitat is the boreal forest of Canada. Winter habitat in Central America is semi-open forest and forest edges. In migration, it may be seen anywhere.

Breeding: Unlike other warblers that build a nest, the Prothonotary Warbler nests in tree cavities. Lays 4 or 5 eggs.

Breeding: The nest is built on the ground and is made of dead leaves, rendering difficult to locate. Lays 3 to 4 eggs.

Breeding: Nest is on the ground at the base of a tree or among upturned roots. Clutch size ranges from 3 to 8.

Natural History: The dredging and draining of swamplands in the southeastern United States significantly reduced breeding habitat for this warbler in the first half of the twentieth century. Loss of wetlands in the US has stabilized somewhat in the last few decades, but the species now faces threats from habitat loss on its wintering grounds in northern South America. In Florida, this warbler breeds in the northern half of the state and is a spring/fall migrant in the southern half. In summer, it feeds on aquatic insects, snails, and tiny crustaceans. In winter in tropical forests of Central America and northern South America, they will also eat fruits and nectar. During spring migration, they are attracted to the nectar-producing flowers of some shrubs commonly planted as ornamentals in the South.

Natural History: Very few Americans ever see this rare and secretive warbler. It has a reputation for being both rare and exceedingly secretive and even seasoned birdwatchers may go their entire lives and not see this species. It is very similar in appearance to the Worm-eating Warbler, but the Swainson's Warbler is primarily a ground dweller and the Worm-eating Warbler is more of a lowbush species. In thick cover, it moves mouse-like quietly along on the ground, foraging for food among the leaf litter. Although it ranges across much of the southeastern US in summer, it is nowhere common. They are known to nest in the panhandle of Florida but elsewhere in the state they are seasonal migrants. Wintering grounds are the Caribbean, Cuba, and the Yucatan Peninsula.

Natural History: The numbers of this species passing through Florida each spring and fall fluctuates depending upon the previous year's abundance of its primary summer food, the Spruce Budworm. In the northern forests of Canada in good budworm years, this is one of the most common bird species. In years of diminished budworm populations, the population of these birds also crashes. This relationship provides a valuable insight into the intricate interdependencies of unrelated organisms. Though they are fairly common most years, they are inconspicuous birds as they feed high in trees during spring migration. Despite the name, they merely pass through the state of Tennessee. The original description of the species was made from a specimen from Tennessee, hence the name.

Class - **Aves** (birds)

Order - **Passeriformes** (songbirds)

Family - **Parulidae** (warblers)

Orange-crowned Warbler *Oreothlypis celata*	Nashville Warbler *Oreothlypis ruficapilla*	Connecticut Warbler *Oporonis agilis*

	Presumed range in Florida		Presumed range in Florida		Presumed range in Florida
Size: 5 inches. **Abundance:** Fairly common. **Migratory Status:** Winter resident. November to April.		**Size:** 4.75 inches. **Abundance:** Rare in Florida. **Migratory Status:** Migrant. Mostly seen in fall.		**Size:** 5.75 inches. **Abundance:** Very rare. **Migratory Status:** Seasonal migrant. Moves through quickly.	

Variation: Sexes very similar. Female slightly duller gray above and slightly less yellow below. Varies regionally.	**Variation:** An eastern and western subspecies. Eastern birds show very little variation and the sexes are alike.	**Variation:** Females are duller and lack the conspicuously gray head of the male.
Habitat: Summers in northern woodlands (Canada and Rocky Mountains) where it prefers habitats with significant understory. Also found old weedy fields, brier thickets, etc. during migration.	**Habitat:** Summer habitat includes tamarack bogs and boreal forests. Prefers second growth and open woodlands with shrubby undergrowth. Avoids the deep woods.	**Habitat:** Summer/breeding habitat is boreal forest. There it prefers wetland habitats like tamarack bogs and muskeg. Winter habitat is forests in Central and South America.
Breeding: Breeds in northern Canada and as far north as Alaska and well into the Arctic Circle. Western subspecies breeds along West Coast. Lays 4 to 5 eggs.	**Breeding:** Nests on the ground under bushes or in hummocks of grasses or sphagnum moss. Clutch size ranges from 3 to 6.	**Breeding:** Nest is hidden in thick undergrowth on or near the ground. 3 to 5 eggs are laid. Nests in boreal bogs and mesic northern forests.
Natural History: Like most warblers, this species is highly insectivorous, but in winter it also eats some fruit and is known to feed at the sap wells created by sapsucker woodpeckers. Feeds deliberately in the lower branches of trees and in bushes. These can be very common birds on their northern breeding grounds. They are seen in Florida during winter months only. The orange streak on the crown from which this species derives its name is not typically visible in the field. A fairly hardy warbler, it winters across the southern US from the Carolinas to California (including all of Florida), and south to northernmost Central America. They are generally more common in the western US than in the east.	**Natural History:** This warbler species has benefited from human alterations to the American landscape (they prefer logged over, second growth habitats). However, some human alterations have also had a very negative effect. As with many other migrant songbirds, they are vulnerable to towers, power lines, and antennas. No one knows exactly how many birds are killed during migration each year by flying into these obstacles, but some estimates are in the millions. Insects are eaten almost exclusively by this warbler. Despite its name, it merely passes through the state of Tennessee. Most of these birds migrate to the west of Florida, but a few can be seen in the western panhandle of the state. Fall migrants may be farther east.	**Natural History:** This shy warbler is rarely observed in Florida (or anywhere else for that matter!). In part due to its secretive nature (migrating birds are typically observed low to the ground in dense undergrowth). But also due to the fact that it is a rare bird. In addition, it occurs in Florida only briefly during the migration. Fall migrants follow the Atlantic Coast southward. Despite its name, this species is quite rare in Connecticut, where it may only occasionally be seen during fall migration. Due to its secretive nature and relative rarity, this is one of the least understood and least commonly observed of America's warbler species. It is a highly sought species among birdwatchers.

Class - **Aves** (birds)

Order - **Passeriformes** (songbirds)

Family - **Parulidae** (warblers)

Kentucky Warbler *Geothlypis formosus*	Common Yellowthroat *Geothlypis trichas*	Hooded Warbler *Setophaga citrina*
	 Male	 Male  Female

Size: 5.25 inches.	Presumed range in Florida	**Size:** 5 inches.	Presumed range in Florida	**Size:** 5.25 inches.	Presumed range in Florida
Abundance: Rare in Florida.		**Abundance:** Common.		**Abundance:** Uncommon.	
Migratory Status: Spring and fall migrant.		**Migratory Status:** Year-round resident.		**Migratory Status:** Migrant and summer resident.	

Variation: Sexes very similar. Female has black on face reduced a bit.

Variation: Sexes very similar. Female lacks prominent black mask of the male.

Variation: Prominent black hood of male reduced on female and immature.

Habitat: Throughout its summer range the Eastern US, this warbler enjoys deciduous bottomland forests and wooded riparian habitats. Within this macrohabitat it requires a microhabitat of dense undergrowth.

Habitat: Likes thick vegetation in wetland areas. Cattails and sedges in marshes and swamp edges are especially favored. Avoids deep woods but may be seen around edges of woods, especially near streams.

Habitat: A forest species. Most common in the mountains of the eastern portion of the state but can be found anywhere that there is significant woodlands with dense understory.

Breeding: A ground nester. The nest is constructed of dead leaves and grasses and is usually well hidden. 4 to 5 eggs are laid by mid-May.

Breeding: The nest is woven from wetland grasses among cattails or sedges. 4 to 6 eggs are laid in late May or early June.

Breeding: Cup-shaped nest of grasses, bark, and dead leaves is woven into 2 or more upright limbs of a small bush near the ground. 4 eggs.

Natural History: Kentucky's namesake warbler is an abundant and widespread bird in suitable habitats throughout the "Bluegrass State" during summer. But it also ranges across most of the Eastern Temperate Forest Level I Ecoregion. In Florida, however, it is a transient migrant that merely passes through. The Cornell Laboratory of Ornithology website reports that this species appears to be in decline. Destruction of mature tropical forests may be to blame. It is also possible that fragmentation of large forests tracts in North America could be a threat. Unlike many warblers whose habitat is high in the canopy, this species feeds low to the ground. It eats a wide variety of invertebrates.

Natural History: The Common Yellowthroat is one of the more abundant warblers in America and their summer range includes most of North America south of the Arctic. They do avoid the desert Southwest and dry Southern Plains. Not surprising since they are mainly a wetland-loving species. They feed low to the ground on almost any type of tiny invertebrate. Their behavior when foraging is rather "wren-like" as they negotiate dense stands of cattails, reeds, and tall grasses. They tend to stick to heavy cover and when flushed make short flights into deep cover. Cowbird parasitism is a problem for this species. The baby cowbird will be larger than the adult Common Yellowthroat well before leaving the nest.

Natural History: Like many small, woodland birds, the Hooded Warbler is more likely to be heard than seen. On their breeding grounds in the eastern US they require large tracts of woodlands, and they have declined in areas where intensive agriculture or development has resulted in the loss of this habitat. This handsome little warbler is a good example of why the protection of extensive tracts of forest can be so important in the conservation of neotropical migrant songbirds. This is a summer resident of the panhandle region of Florida where it will nest in forest openings or regenerative areas. It is a transient migrant on the Florida Peninsula.

Class - **Aves** (birds)

Order - **Passeriformes** (songbirds)

Family - **Parulidae** (warblers)

American Redstart *Setophaga ruticilla*	Cape May Warbler *Setophaga tigrina*	Cerulean Warbler *Setophaga cerulea*

Size: 5.75 inches.	Presumed range in Florida	**Size:** 5 inches.	Presumed range in Florida	**Size:** 4.75 inches.	Presumed range in Florida
Abundance: Fairly common.		**Abundance:** Fairly common.		**Abundance:** Rare in Florida.	
Migratory Status: Mostly a seasonal migrant. A few in winter.		**Migratory Status:** Seasonal migrant, mostly seen in spring.		**Migratory Status:** Fall migrant mostly.	

American Redstart	Cape May Warbler	Cerulean Warbler
Variation: Male black, and orange, female gray and yellow and lacks color on wings and flank. Immature like female.	**Variation:** Females and immatures lack chestnut cheek patch and have less yellow on belly.	**Variation:** Male is pale blue above with black streaks on sides, female is blueish green with faded gray streaks.
Habitat: Prefers deciduous woodlands over conifers. More common in second growth areas and riparian thickets.	**Habitat:** Another species that summers in boreal forests, primarily in the vicinity of spruce bogs and other forest openings. Winters mostly in West Indies.	**Habitat:** Summer habitat is primarily deciduous forests. Both bottomland forest and moist mountain slopes.
Breeding: The nest is woven of thin fibers of grass or bark strips and placed in the crotch of an upright branch or trunk. Usually 4 eggs.	**Breeding:** Nest is near the trunk in the top of a spruce or fir. 5 or 6 eggs are laid in early to mid-June. 1 clutch per year.	**Breeding:** Nest is a tight cup woven around forked branches in the mid to upper canopy level. Average clutch size is 3 or 4 to as many as 5.
Natural History: The striking bright orange-on-black colors of the male flash like neon in the heavily shaded forests where this species makes its home. They are active little birds that display their bright colors by regularly spreading their tail feathers and drooping their wings. They hunt tiny insects among the foliage and often catch flying insects in midair. Summer breeding range includes much of the eastern and northern US. In Canada, they breed virtually from coast to coast. Small numbers winter in coastal Louisiana, the lower Rio Grande Valley, and the Everglades region of south Florida. Most winter from northwest Mexico to northern South America, but a few will linger throughout the winter in the southern tip of Florida.	**Natural History:** On summer breeding grounds, the Cape May Warbler feeds heavily on Spruce Budworm caterpillars. Their breeding cycle corresponds to the timing of maximum availability of budworm caterpillars and the population density of this species is known to be closely tied to the presence of this food source. In years of heavy budworm infestations, they will rear large broods. On wintering grounds they are known to feed heavily upon nectar and fruits and they have a specialized tubular tongue for extracting nectar from flowers and juices from fruit. Most birds seen in Florida will be spring/fall migrants but they may be seen all winter in the Florida Keys. Fall migration through Florida is mostly along the East Coast.	**Natural History:** The Cerulean Warbler hunts high in the canopy, gleaning tiny invertebrates from small branches and leaves. Searches both upper and lower surface of leaves for food. Like many species dependent upon forests, this warbler experienced significant population declines following the European settlement of America. Historically it was common in the Mississippi Valley, but it is now rare there and Cerulean Warbler populations have declined significantly throughout their range. In fact, this is one of the more threatened of our neotropical migrant songbirds. The migration route for this species is mostly to west of Florida, but a few can be seen in the panhandle region. Like many warblers, the Cerulean is a trans-gulf migrant.

Class - **Aves** (birds)

Order - **Passeriformes** (songbirds)

Family - **Parulidae** (warblers)

Northern Parula *Setophaga americana*	**Magnolia Warbler** *Setophaga magnolia*	**Bay-breasted Warbler** *Setophaga castenea*

Northern Parula		Magnolia Warbler		Bay-breasted Warbler	
Size: 4.5 inches. **Abundance:** Common. **Migratory Status:** March through October on peninsula.	Presumed range in Florida 	**Size:** 5 inches. **Abundance:** Fairly common. **Migratory Status:** Spring and fall migrant. Mostly fall.	Presumed range in Florida	**Size:** 5.5 inches. **Abundance:** Uncommon. **Migratory Status:** Spring and fall migrant. Mostly fall.	Presumed range in Florida

Variation: Females lack black on breast but otherwise sexes are similar.	**Variation:** Female has dark gray mask (male black); immature head plain gray.	**Variation:** Pronounced seasonal variation. Females typically less vivid.
Habitat: Habitat is forest. Mostly bottomland woods or swamps or along streams and rivers in Florida. Also mesic woods and moist ravines in its summer range.	**Habitat:** Summer habitat is spruce forests of Canada. Can be seen anywhere during migration. Winters in Mexico, Central America, and Caribbean. Often forages in low bushes and shrubs.	**Habitat:** Summer habitat is spruce/fir woodlands of Canada. Very little information is available regarding habitat preference while migrating through Florida. Probably quite variable.
Breeding: Nests high in trees. Sycamores, Baldcypress, and Hemlocks are reported as favorite nest trees. In the Deep South, nests are often built in Spanish moss. 4 or 5 eggs.	**Breeding:** Does not nest in Florida. Nests in evergreen trees. The nest is usually well concealed amid dense vegetation. 4 eggs laid. Hemlock groves are a favorite nesting habitat.	**Breeding:** Nests in dense conifer trees on horizontal limb. Nest is cup-shaped and made of woven twigs, pine needles, and grasses. Average clutch size is 5 or 6 eggs.
Natural History: The Northern Parula feeds by gleaning tiny arthropods from tree branches. They tend to feed and spend much time in the middle and upper story of the forest. This habit couple with their small size make sometimes difficult to observe. These handsome little warblers are most common on their summer range in the deep forests of the Appalachian Mountains and in the swamps and bottom lands of the southeastern United States. Their summer range is roughly the eastern half of America. Some will winter in the Everglades region of Florida, while many others winter across the Caribbean and in southern Mexico or northern Central America. Some will fly across the Gulf, some up the FL peninsula.	**Natural History:** Feeds on insects (including large numbers of caterpillars) that are caught near the ends of branches in dense conifer trees. Known to feed on the Spruce Budworm and may enjoy greater survival of offspring during years of budworm outbreaks. This is an abundant species that appears to be stable in population numbers. Leaves Central American wintering grounds in February and passes through Florida in April and May and again in September and October. Fall migration routes generally more easterly than spring. They are thus probably more common migrants through the state in the fall than they are in the spring. Fall migration begins in September and may last into early November.	**Natural History:** This long-distance migrant is not commonly seen by residents of Florida, as they pass through rather quickly. Their primary food in summer is the Spruce Budworm caterpillar, and their populations may rise and fall with the availability of this insect. Populations have declined possibly due to spraying of Canadian forests to control spruce budworms. These birds are less common today than decades ago. They winter from southern Central America to northwestern South America. In winter they are known to eat fruit, a stable food source that is more readily available in tropical forests than in temperate regions, where availability would be much more seasonal.

Class - **Aves** (birds)

Order - **Passeriformes** (songbirds)

Family - **Parulidae** (warblers)

Blackburnian Warbler *Setophaga fusca*	Yellow Warbler *Setophaga petechia*	Chestnut-sided Warbler *Mniotilta varia*

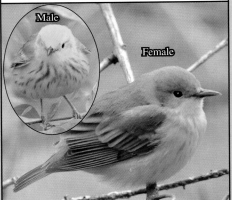

Size: 5 inches.	**Size:** 5 inches.	**Size:** 5 inches.
Abundance: Uncommon.	**Abundance:** Fairly common.	**Abundance:** Uncommon.
Migratory Status: Spring and fall migrant in Florida.	**Migratory Status:** Seasonal migrant and year-round resident.	**Migratory Status:** Spring and fall migrant in Florida.

Presumed range in Florida

Variation: Females and immature males are duller.

Variation: Female lacks chestnut streaks present on breast of male.

Variation: Yellow crown and chestnut flanks reduced on female and young.

Habitat: Summers mostly in mature coniferous and mixed forests. Migration habitat is highly variable. Birds in the Appalachians favor hemlocks.

Habitat: Thickets of willow or buttonbush in wet lowlands are the classic habitat for this species. Western populations favor riparian habitats.

Habitat: The Chestnut-sided Warbler is a bird of successional areas and shrubby, second-growth. In Florida, it uses a variety of woods, shrubby areas,.

Breeding: Does not nest in Florida. Elsewhere nest is usually in a conifer and well concealed amid foliage. Average of 4 to 5 eggs.

Breeding: Nest is built in the upright fork of a sapling and averages 4 eggs. Yellow Warbler nests are often victimized by Brown-headed Cowbirds.

Breeding: Does not breed in Florida. Nests fairly low to the ground in thick cover of dense sapling growth. 3 or 4 eggs are laid.

Natural History: The beautiful blaze orange coloration on the head, throat, and breast of the Blackburnian Warbler is unmistakable. However, this is a difficult species to observe due to the fact that it is primarily a treetop dweller. It feeds mostly on caterpillars. Blackburnian Warblers seen in Florida are merely passing through en route to and from breeding grounds in the boreal forests far to the north. Winter habitats are in northern South America. Some of these warblers will nest in the southern Appalachians as far south as Alabama, but most nesting takes place in Canada and New England. Insects (especially caterpillars) are primary food. Forest fragmentation on wintering grounds in South America may pose a threat.

Natural History: This is one of the most wide-ranging of the warblers. In fact, some nest north of the Arctic Circle. Their summer breeding range encompasses the entire northern two-thirds of North America, from the Atlantic to the Pacific and over 3 dozen subspecies are recognized. One subspecies of Yellow Warbler known as "Golden Warbler" will breed in the Everglades region. Throughout the rest of Florida, the Yellow Warbler is mostly a transient migrant. Feeds on a variety of insects and other arthropods and uses a variety of foraging techniques including gleaning of leaves and branches, flying from perch to seize airborne prey, and picking insects from leaves and branches while hovering.

Natural History: This is one of the few warbler species that has benefited from deforestation. These birds are more common now than they were in the days prior to the European settlement of America. Despite their overall increase in population, they are negatively impacted by modern agricultural practices. The clearing of fence rows and overgrown field corners, and conversion of successional habitats into cropland is a threat. As with many other warbler species that travel through Florida, the Chestnut-sided warbler breeds mostly far to the north in the boreal forests of Canada and New England. Its spring migration is mostly along the western Gulf Coast. More likely to be seen in Florida in fall migration. Winter range is in Central America.

Class - **Aves** (birds)

Order - **Passeriformes** (songbirds)

Family - **Parulidae** (warblers)

Blackpoll Warbler *Setophaga striata*	Black-throated Blue Warbler *Setophaga caerulescens*	Palm Warbler *Setophaga palmarum*

Size: 5.5 inches.

Abundance: Fairly common.

Migratory Status: Migrant. Seen in Florida mostly in spring.

Presumed range in Florida

Variation: Sexual, ontogenetic, and seasonal variation. Fall male resembles female.

Habitat: Summer breeding habitat is taiga and tundra-taiga transition zones; often well above the Arctic Circle. Winter habitat is South American forests.

Breeding: Nest is an open cup built on a branch near the tree trunk, usually in a spruce. Eggs number 3 to 5. Does not nest in Florida.

Natural History: This is one of the great long-distance migrants among America's songbird species. In fall migration, some may travel nonstop over the Atlantic Ocean from Newfoundland (Canada) all the way to South America. Considering that this is a bird that weighs less than 0.5 ounces, that is a remarkable feat of endurance. Following this long flight, many birds will arrive at their wintering grounds in South America in an emaciated condition. Although a fairly common migrant in Florida during the spring, they are rarely seen in the state during fall migration as their migration route is apparently offshore. At all times they tend to stay hidden high in the forest canopy, and even during spring migration this species is easily missed.

Size: 5.25 inches.

Abundance: Fairly common.

Migratory Status: Seasonal migrant and winter resident.

Presumed range in Florida

Variation: Strongly sexually dimorphic. Female is olive brown above, drab olive-yellow below.

Habitat: Mature forests with large tracts of unbroken woodlands. Both hardwood and mixed forest. Winter habitat is tropical forests.

Breeding: Nest is strips of bark lined with finer materials such as moss. Usually placed in an upright fork of dense shrub. Clutch size typically 4.

Natural History: This warblers summer/breeding habitat is well to the north of Florida. These birds spend their summers mostly in the high Appalachians, the northeastern US and eastern Canada. In Florida they are seen only as a migrant in much of the state, but a few will linger throughout the winter in the southern tip of Florida in the state's Tropical Wet Forests Level I Ecoregion. The core winter range is on the Caribbean islands of Cuba, Jamaica and Puerto Rico. This species forages mostly in shrubs and branches at the mid-story level for caterpillars and other small arthropod prey. As this species requires large tracts of woodlands as both a breeding and wintering habitat, deforestation and forest fragmentation are the greatest threats to the species.

Size: 5.5 inches.

Abundance: Common.

Migratory Status: Winter resident in Florida.

Presumed range in Florida

Variation: Winter plumage is drabber and the crown of the head is gray-brown rather than bright chestnut.

Habitat: Summer habitat consists of bogs in boreal forests. Transient in a variety of habitats during migration. Winter habitat is mostly open woods.

Breeding: Nests of moss is on the ground in a northern bog, usually at the base of a conifer tree. Clutch size is 4 or 5.

Natural History: This species nests in the boreal forests of Canada and winters along the southeastern US coast (including all of Florida). Unlike most warblers that spend most of their time high in the canopy, the Palm Warbler is a decidedly terrestrial species that hunts primarily on the ground or in low shrubs. It is one of the most northerly wintering of the warblers, with many staying in the southeast US or Florida (thus the name Palm Warbler). Some winter in the Caribbean. Summer habitats are far to the north, well into northern Canada. Food is mainly insects caught on the ground (grasshoppers, crickets, flies, butterflies, etc.) Though a nondescript bird in winter plumage, its habit of bobbing the tail while foraging on the ground make it easy to recognize.

Class - **Aves** (birds)

Order - **Passeriformes** (songbirds)

Family - **Parulidae** (warblers)

Pine Warbler *Setophaga pinus*	Yellow-rumped Warbler *Setophaga coronata*	Yellow-throated Warbler *Setophaga dominca*

Pine Warbler

Size: 5.5 inches.

Abundance: Fairly common.

Migratory Status: Year-round resident in Florida.

Presumed range in Florida

Variation: Males are brighter greenish-yellow. Females and immatures are drabber, more brownish.

Habitat: Pine forests are the primary habitat, but they are also seen in deciduous and mixed woodlands, especially during migration.

Breeding: Builds its nest high in pine trees. This is one of the earliest nesting warblers with 3 or 4 eggs laid by early April. Breeding range is limited to regions where pines occur.

Natural History: As its name implies, this species is nearly always found in association with pine trees. This is the only warbler whose range is contained entirely within the US and Canada. It is found year-round in most of Florida but is largely absent from the South Florida Coastal Plain. It is also the only warbler to regularly change its diet from insects to seeds in the winter, thus it is one of the few warblers that may be seen at bird feeders. These birds can reach high densities in winter in the southern pine forests, when resident populations are supplemented by northern migrants. They are hardy birds for a warbler and those that migrate are among the first warblers to appear in northern regions in the spring.

Yellow-rumped Warbler

Size: 5.5 inches.

Abundance: Very common.

Migratory Status: Winter resident in Florida.

Presumed range in Florida

Variation: Sexual and seasonal plumage variations (see above). Winter males, females, and immatures similar.

Habitat: Outside its breeding range, this warbler is a habitat generalist. It can be seen virtually anywhere in the state from late fall through spring.

Breeding: Breeds in the boreal forest of Canada and Alaska. Nest is built on the branch of a conifer. Clutch size is usually 4 or 5 eggs. Does not nest in Florida.

Natural History: There are 2 morphologically distinct forms of this common warbler, one in the eastern US and one in the western US. The form seen in Florida is sometimes called the "Myrtle Warbler." In summer it feeds mainly on insects, but if bad weather necessitates, it is capable of surviving on berries during the winter. Unlike most warblers that winter in the tropics, the Yellow-rumped is a hardy species and in mild winters can be seen as far north as southern Illinois, Indiana, and Ohio in the Midwest and New Jersey on the East Coast. Large numbers will winter in Florida and in fact this is one the most common warblers in Florida. Populations seem fairly stable and it is probably in less jeopardy than many other warbler species.

Yellow-throated Warbler

Size: 5.25 inches.

Abundance: Common.

Migratory Status: Year-round resident in Florida.

Presumed range in Florida

Variation: Sexes similar. No significant variation.

Habitat: Found in bottomland forests and cypress swamps as well as upland woods. Uses both deciduous and conifer woodland but favors pine forests.

Breeding: Nesting in Florida begins as early as late March or early April. Nest is high in the canopy. 4 or 5 eggs is typical. Spanish moss is often used in nest construction in the southern US.

Natural History: This warbler species can be seen year-round in the northern half of the state. It winters in south Florida and the Caribbean. This is another "treetop" species that spends most of its time high in the canopy. It feeds on diminutive arthropods gleaned in a very deliberate fashion from branches, bark, leaves, and petioles. This species retreated from the northern portions of its breeding range several decades ago, but is now showing a resurgence back into those areas. The cause of this population fluctuation is unknown, but possibly relates to habitat alterations by man, and a subsequent recovery of those habitats. Reportedly has an affinity to Sycamore trees in the eastern deciduous woodlands.

Class - **Aves** (birds)

Order - **Passeriformes** (songbirds)

Family - **Parulidae** (warblers)

Prairie Warbler *Setophaga discolor*	Black-throated Green Warbler *Setophaga virens*	Canada Warbler *Cardellina canadensis*

Size: 4.75 inches.

Abundance: Fairly common.

Migratory Status: Summer in north FL, winter on peninsula.

Presumed range in Florida

Size: 5 inches.

Abundance: Uncommon in FL.

Migratory Status: Mostly a seasonal migrant.

Presumed range in Florida

Size: 5.25 inches.

Abundance: Very rare in FL.

Migratory Status: Seasonal migrant. Seen mostly in fall.

Presumed range in Florida

Variation: Sexes similar, but females are less vividly marked, immatures are paler.

Variation: Sexes similar, but females have less black and more yellow on the throat (see photos above).

Variation: On females and juveniles, the black streaks on the breast are gray and the black on the face is absent.

Habitat: Semi-open habitats. Old overgrown fields, shrubby successional areas. Uses coastal dunes during winter.

Habitat: This warbler requires significant tracts of unbroken forests. Except for migration, it is an inhabitant of conifer and mixed conifer/deciduous forests.

Habitat: Breeding habitat is moist, high mountain forests with understory shrubs such as rhododendron. Farther north it uses mixed woodlands.

Breeding: Breeds in extreme north Florida. An average of 4 eggs (3 to 5) are laid May to June. Sometimes produces 2 broods.

Breeding: Most nests are in conifers such as hemlock or pine. Only the female incubates the 4 or 5 eggs. Nesting occurs well to the north of Florida.

Breeding: Nest is on the ground and hidden amid dense vegetation. In Canada the nest is often placed amid carpet of moss. 4 or 5 eggs is typical.

Natural History: Insects, spiders, slugs, and other soft-bodied arthropods are listed as food items. Feeds from the ground all the way up to treetops, but mainly gleans lower bushes and shrubs. Tail-bobbing is a common behavior in this species. The Prairie Warbler winters farther north than many warbler species. While some fly as far as the Yucatan Peninsula, others stay in the northern Caribbean or peninsular Florida. They can be fairly common in the Florida Everglades during winter. Despite having benefited from clearing of forests the last century, there are unexplained declines in some populations in recent years. Although it is fairly common on the peninsula in winter, the highest frequency of occurrence in Florida is in April and September.

Natural History: Like others of its kind, this small, handsome warbler faces many threats. Red Squirrels are reportedly an important nest predator in the boreal forests of Canada and New England. In other regions, the major threat may come from other birds like the Blue Jay and from the common and widespread Woodland Rat Snake. Sharp-shinned Hawks are always a threat to the adults, while Brown-headed Cowbirds parasitize the nest. Human activities such as forest fragmentation threaten populations as a whole. Despite all these hazards, the population appears stable. This species is mostly a seasonal migrant in Florida, but it can be a winter resident in the extreme southern tip of the state in the Everglades region, and also in the Keys.

Natural History: Some of these birds will nest in the higher elevations in the Appalachians, but the bulk of the population summers in the boreal forests of Canada from the Atlantic all the way to northeastern British Columbia. Although they do migrate through most of the Florida, they do so mostly at night and pass through quickly en route to breeding grounds far to the north. Returning migrants in the fall are probably more common than spring migrants, that take a more westerly route north. The Canada Warbler has been in decline for several decades. Loss of breeding habitat in North America as well as loss of wintering habitat in South America is probably to blame. Until recently, this species was placed in the genus *Wilsonia*.

Class - **Aves** (birds)

Order - **Passeriformes** (songbirds)

Family - **Parulidae** (warblers)

Family - **Passerellidae** (sparrows)

Wilson's Warbler	Bachman's Sparrow	Henslow's Sparrow
Cardellina pusilla	*Peucaea aestivalis*	*Ammodramus henslowii*

Female

Size: 4.75 inches.

Abundance: Rare in Florida.

Migratory Status: Migrant and very rare winter resident.

Presumed range in Florida

Size: 6 inches.

Abundance: Uncommon.

Migratory Status: Year-round resident in Florida.

Presumed range in Florida

Size: 5 inches.

Abundance: Very rare in FL.

Migratory Status: Winter resident. October to May.

Presumed range in Florida

Variation: Male has prominent black cap on top of head. In females, the top of the head is usually olive green.

Variation: There are 2 subspecies, but they are very similar in appearance. No sexual dimorphism in this species.

Variation: Sexes are alike and juveniles are very similar to adults but less heavily streaked.

Habitat: Summer breeding habitat is in the boreal forests of Canada, the Pacific northwest, the Northern Rockies, and Alaska. Winter habitat is tropical forests.

Habitat: The Bachman's Sparrow is endemic to the southern pine forests. It is probably most most numerous in pine/wiregrass habitats where fire keeps down dense undergrowth.

Habitat: In Florida, this species seems to be more common in fire-maintained pine savannas including Longleaf/Wiregrass habitats. Also in moist pine flatwoods with abundant grasses.

Breeding: Nest is on the ground. Uniquely, the nest of this warbler is usually placed in a small depression. 2 to 7 eggs may be laid.

Breeding: Nest is on the ground. Woven from grasses and concealed at the base of a shrub or clump of grass. About 5 eggs. 2 broods is common.

Breeding: Breeds in grassland habitats across the Midwest. Nest is on the ground in thick grass and well concealed. 2 to 5 eggs are laid in May.

Natural History: Wilson's Warbler is quite rare in Florida. The bulk of the population ranges well to the west of Florida, although they may migrate through any part of the state and they have been recorded in Florida throughout the winter months. Most sightings of this bird in Florida appear to be in the fall (September and October). Some studies indicate that they are declining in their core range in the western US. Due perhaps to loss of riparian habitat. They range as far north as the Arctic Ocean in summer and as far south as Panama in winter. The name is in honor of naturalist Alexander Wilson, who was the first to describe the species to science.

Natural History: The Bachman's Sparrow is one of the least known bird species to most Floridians. They live deep in the pine forests and tend to be rather shy and secretive and they thus are easily overlooked. This species is often found sympatrically with the Red-cockaded Woodpecker. The favorite habitat is Long-leaf Pine/Wiregrass woodlands. Almost none of this habitat remains in Florida in a virgin state, but state and federal forest agencies today manage many thousand of acres to help regenerate this unique and important habitat throughout the state. Bachman's Sparrow can be found in suitable habitats throughout Florida except for the South Florida Coastal Plain.

Natural History: The Henslow's Sparrow has declined significantly since the European invasion of North America. They once were found across the Midwest in summer where they inhabited open and semi-open grassland/savanna habitats. All but a tiny fraction of those native habitats have been lost to agriculture and development. Their winter habitats of pine savanna in the Coastal Plain of the southeastern US have also been radically diminished by logging and agriculture. Attempts to restore these habitats may be helpful, but restored habitats are highly fragmented. Although not yet listed as threatened or endangered by USFWS, the future of this species is in doubt.

Class - **Aves** (birds)

Order - **Passeriformes** (songbirds)

Family - **Paserellidae** (sparrows)

Le Conte's Sparrow *Ammodramus leconteii*	Grasshopper Sparrow *Ammodramus savannarum*	Nelson's Sparrow *Ammodramus nelsoni*

Le Conte's Sparrow

Size: 5 inches.

Abundance: Very rare in FL.

Migratory Status: Winter resident. November to May.

Presumed range in Florida

Variation: Sexes are alike and juveniles are very similar to adults but buff-colored areas are more faded.

Habitat: Wet meadows, damp hayfields, and marshy areas as well as grassy, upland fields. Summer habitat is prairie of northern US and Canada.

Breeding: 4 to 5 eggs are laid in a nest woven from grass and placed in a clump of grass. Nests widely across south central Canada and western Great Lakes.

Natural History: This is a small and secretive sparrow that eludes attempts to study it closely. Little is known about many aspects of its biology. For instance, only a small number of nests have ever been found. Usually remains hidden from view in dense grasses, and when flushed flies only a short distance before diving back into cover. Food items listed include small grass seeds and arthropods. There is even less information available regarding the habits of birds that winter in Florida. The bulk of this species range is west of the Mississippi River, but its winter range includes the extreme western end of the the Florida Panhandle. Both rare and secretive, this is a bird that few Floridians will be fortunate enough to glimpse.

Grasshopper Sparrow

Size: 5 inches.

Abundance: Rare in Florida.

Migratory Status: Winter resident. November to April.

Presumed range in Florida

Variation: Sexes are alike. Slight geographic variation exists, but differences are insignificant to the laymen.

Habitat: A grassland species, the Grasshopper sparrow likes short and midgrass prairie. In Florida, it uses heavily grazed pastures or native prairie.

Breeding: Nest is on the ground and well hidden beneath overhanging grass. 2 broods per summer is usual with 4 to 5 eggs per clutch.

Natural History: In many ways similar to the preceding species, but much more common. Its name is derived from the sound of its song which mimics the buzzing sound made by some types of orthopteran insects. Throughout its range (which includes most of the US east of the Rocky Mountains), it is a rather inconspicuous bird. Though unfamiliar to most Floridians, in the High Plains region of the north-central US it is commonly seen (and heard). Feeds entirely on the ground. Food is mostly grasshoppers and other insects in summer. In winter, it eats both insects and seeds, especially tiny grass seeds. Most range maps show the entire state within Grasshopper Sparrow's winter range, but they are much less common in Florida than farther to the west.

Nelson's Sparrow

Size: 5 inches.

Abundance: Rare in Florida.

Migratory Status: Winter resident on coast. Migrant inland.

Presumed range in Florida

Variation: Nelson's Sparrow shows very little variation and the sexes are also alike.

Habitat: Primary habitat is marshes, both fresh (in summer) and brackish/salt marshes (winter). Also may use grassy fields during migration.

Breeding: Nest is a cuplike structure placed amid and supported by upright grass stems. 3 to 5 eggs is typical, with a minimum of 2 and maximum of 6.

Natural History: Nelson's Sparrow winters along the southeastern coastline of the US from the Chesapeake Bay to Texas. Most spend the summer in the Canadian Plains or along the southern shore of Hudson Bay. They can be found along both coasts of Florida in winter, but are absent from regions of the coast lacking in extensive marshes. Until recently this species was considered conspecific with the Salt Marsh Sparrow. This species requires large tracts of undisturbed marshland or grassland habitat and both habitats have experienced significant alteration or outright destruction. Subsequently, loss of grassland habitat in central Canada and loss of coastal marshes poses a significant threat to this species.

Class - **Aves** (birds)		
Order - **Passeriformes** (songbirds)		
Family - **Passerellidae** (sparrows)		

Seaside Sparrow *Ammodramus maritimus*	**Saltmarsh Sparrow** *Ammodramus caudacutus*	**Chipping Sparrow** *Spizella passerina*

Size: 6 inches.	Presumed range in Florida 	**Size:** 5 inches.	Presumed range in Florida 	**Size:** 5.5 inches.	Presumed range in Florida 
Abundance: Rare.		**Abundance:** Very rare.		**Abundance:** Failry common.	
Migratory Status: Non-migratory year-round resident.		**Migratory Status:** A winter resident of north Florida coast.		**Migratory Status:** Mostly a winter resident.	

Variation: Several subspecies with different color morphs. See below.	**Variation:** No significant variation among adults.	**Variation:** No sexual dimorphism, but winter plumage is much more subdued.
Habitat: Lives in salt and brackish water marshes along the eastern coastline of North America. Ranges from southern New England to Mexico. Range restricted to coastal regions.	**Habitat:** The Saltmarsh Sparrow is an endemic bird of the salt marshes of the eastern United States. It lives exclusively in tidal-influenced marshes from Maine to Florida.	**Habitat:** Edge areas and woods openings. Thrives in human-altered habitats including farmsteads, suburban yards and parks. A wide-ranging species seen across America.
Breeding: Nest is a cup woven from blades of dried grass. Coarse grass stems make up the outer nest with finer grasses used as liner. 2 to 5 eggs.	**Breeding:** Nest is a woven cup of coarse grasses placed amid upright stems of marsh grasses. 4 eggs is typical and 2 broods per year is common.	**Breeding:** Breeds earlier than most other songbirds. Nests may be complete and eggs can being laid as early as mid-April.
Natural History: Several subspecies of the Seaside Sparrow are recognized. 5 occur in Florida and 2 of those subspecies are now probably extinct. Another, the Cape Sable Seaside Sparrow of the Everglades region, is endangered. The coastlines of North America have been subjected to two centuries of man-made alterations. Harvesting of salt grass hay, draining projects aimed at creating cattle pasture or filling marshes for development have had major impacts. Ditching to drain marshes as part of mosquito control is another serious threat, along with the widespread spraying of insecticides to kill mosquitos. Future threats may be loss of marshes to coastal erosion as climate change brings sea level rise and more frequent storms.	**Natural History:** The Saltmarsh Sparrow and the Nelson's Sparrow are very similar and the 2 were once considered to be the same species. Saltmarsh Sparrows in Florida are winter residents that summer in coastal marshes farther to the north, from North Carolina to Maine. Female Saltmarsh Sparrows may mate with several males resulting in a clutch of eggs with more than one father. Apparently only the female cares for and feeds the young. Flooding is an inherent threat to nesting in tidal marshes and exceptional tides or storm surges can destroy nests. Renesting is common if nest is destroyed. Adults feed on both invertebrates and seeds, but the young are reared on animal foods only. Mostly insects, spiders, amphipods, and snails.	**Natural History:** Most Chipping Sparrows move to the Deep South in winter after summering throughout most of the continent. In most winters, they can be seen throughout the winter in the Coastal Plain of the southeastern US, including all of Florida. Nesting has been recorded in the western panhandle, but most breed and spend the summer in regions well to the north of Florida. They adapt well to human disturbance of natural habitats and they are undoubtedly more common today than prior to settlement. The Chipping Sparrow feeds mostly on the seeds of grasses and forbs, and does most of its foraging on the ground. Insects are eaten during the breeding season and are fed to the young. They can be a common bird at feeders.

Class - **Aves** (birds)
Order - **Passeriformes** (songbirds)
Family - **Passerellidae** (sparrows)

Field Sparrow *Spizella pusilla*	Fox Sparrow *Passerella iliaca*	Dark-eyed Junco *Junco hyemalis*

Size: 5.75 inches.

Abundance: Rare in Florida.

Migratory Status: Mostly a winter resident.

Presumed range in Florida

Variation: Sexes alike. No seasonal plumage changes but immature birds have dark streaks on the breast.

Habitat: Open and semi-open areas with good cover in the form of weeds and taller grasses. Also shrubby, early regenerative woodland areas.

Breeding: Nest is on the ground usually at the base of a clump of grass or in a low bush. 2 broods per year is common. 2 to 5 eggs.

Natural History: Another species that has adapted well to man-made changes in natural landscapes, the Field Sparrow is probably more numerous today than in historical times. Unlike many sparrows, however, the Field Sparrow is a "country" sparrow that prefers rural regions over towns and suburbs. Food is mostly grass seeds; insects are also eaten, especially during the breeding season. This sparrow can be seen year-round in northernmost Florida but is a winter resident in most areas of its range in the state. The sparrows can present an identification challenge for most laypersons, but this species can be recognized by its pink legs and pinkish bill. Although a very common bird across the eastern US, they are not commonly seen in Florida.

Size: 7 inches.

Abundance: Very rare in FL.

Migratory Status: Winter migrant.

Presumed range in Florida

Variation: This is a highly variable species and includes reddish, grayish, and sooty brown morphs.

Habitat: The Fox Sparrow is a lover of dense cover and thickets. Thick weeds and shrubs bordering woodlands or thickets of brier, saplings, weeds, etc.

Breeding: Nests are low to the ground or even on the ground. Nests in northern Canada and the northwestern Rocky Mountains. Usually 4 eggs.

Natural History: The Fox Sparrow is widespread across the North American Continent, summering in the far north (Canada, Alaska, and the Northern Rockies) and wintering across much of the southern United States. Several distinct subspecies are recognized. They feed on a variety of insects and other arthropods in summer and subsist mainly on seeds in winter. Their appearance in Florida is always in winter and usually only during extremely harsh winter weather. Even then they are seen only in the northernmost portion of the state. They can be an occasional to regular visitor at bird feeders during winter, especially during periods of snowy weather farther to the north. Unlike many other sparrows, the Fox Sparrow is never seen in large flocks.

Size: 6.25 inches.

Abundance: Rare in Florida.

Migratory Status: Winter migrant.

Presumed range in Florida

Variation: Highly variable. Most birds seen in Florida are the typical "Slate-colored" morph shown above.

Habitat: Occupies a wide variety of habitats in winter, but is most fond of semi-open areas or woods openings. Summer habitat is boreal forests.

Breeding: Nest is on the ground. 4 eggs is usual. Compact nest is made of dead leaves and grasses with finer grasses as an inside liner.

Natural History: Juncos are a familiar wintertime bird at feeders throughout the continental US. They arrive with the colder weather fronts and are often associated with snowstorms. In fact, a common nickname in America is "Snowbird." They may arrive in northern Florida as early as November and most are gone by mid-March. Those that summer in the southern United States do so only at the highest elevations in the Appalachian Mountains (above 3,500 feet). The combined summer, winter, and migratory ranges of the Dark-eyed Junco includes nearly all of the North American continent except peninsula Florida. There are several geographic color morphs that are so different that at one time they were regarded as up to 5 distinct species.

Class - **Aves** (birds)

Order - **Passeriformes** (songbirds)

Family - **Passerellidae** (sparrows)

White-crowned Sparrow *Zonotrichia leucophrys*	White-throated Sparrow *Zonotrichia albicollis*	Vesper Sparrow *Pooecetes gramineus*

Size: 7.75 inches.	**Size:** 6.75 inches.	**Size:** 6.25 inches.
Abundance: Rare in Florida.	**Abundance:** Uncommon in FL.	**Abundance:** Uncommon.
Migratory Status: Winter migrant and winter resident.	**Migratory Status:** Winter migrant and winter resident.	**Migratory Status:** Winter migrant and winter resident.
Presumed range in Florida	Presumed range in Florida	Presumed range in Florida

Variation: First-year birds have chestnut and beige head stripe as opposed to black and white (see photos above). Sexes alike.

Variation: 2 adult morphs. One has bright white eye stripe, other has tan. Immatures have striped breasts. No sexual dimorphism.

Variation: No sexual dimorphism and no significant variation in specimens seen in Florida.

Habitat: White-crowned Sparrows prefer areas where there are weeds, grasses, or brush in sufficient amount to provide good cover for roosting and escape from predators. Woodland edges and overgrown fence rows are best.

Habitat: Brushy thickets, fence rows, weedy fields, edges areas, and regenerative woodlands. Both in upland and lowland areas. Can be seen in both rural and urban areas but always near weeds and/or shrubs.

Habitat: This is a bird of open country. Its natural habitats are grasslands and today it also uses agricultural fields. Prefers dry areas. Though found throughout Florida in winter, its core range is in the Plains and Southwest.

Breeding: Breeds in boreal regions, tundra, and mountain meadows. Nest is in a low bush with about 4 eggs. Breeds very far to the north in northern Canada and Alaska.

Breeding: Breeds in a broad band across Canada and the northeastern US, as well as northern Great Lakes states (Michigan, Wisconsin, and Minnesota). Nest is on the ground in open areas, forest edges, etc.

Breeding: Nest is on the ground in open fields, sometimes concealed by grass tussock. 3 to 5 eggs. May to produce 2 broods per year.

Natural History: White-crowned Sparrows produce multiple broods (as many as 4 per season in some western populations). Most will have at least 2 broods annually. Some summer well into the Arctic Tundra and make annual migrations of over 4,000 miles up and down the continent. Eats insects and seeds in summer, mostly seeds in winter. Forages on the ground near cover. Less common than the related White-Throated Sparrow, but still a familiar bird at winter feeders in most of the continental US. This is one of the most highly studied songbirds in America.

Natural History: In early spring just before flying north to summer breeding grounds, the White-throated Sparrow serenades the fields and woodlands with its distinctive whistling song. As these birds are ground foragers, snow cover is one of the most important conditions that influence migratory patterns. Feeds mostly on insects in summer and switches to seeds in winter. When feeding uses both feet with a backward thrusting motion to clear away leaf litter. They are well represented at bird feeders throughout the eastern US in winter. A short-distance migrant, this species winters mostly within the United States.

Natural History: The Vesper Sparrow is much more common in the western region of North America, but they are widespread in Florida in winter. They are declining in the eastern portions of their range which includes much of the Midwest and Great Lakes region. They winter across the southern US and southward to northern Central America. A preference for open regions means it is uncommon, rare, or absent in much of the more heavily wooded regions of the state, although it may occur in large woods openings. This species is probably more common in the eastern US today than before European settlement.

Class - **Aves** (birds)

Order - **Passeriformes** (songbirds)

Family - **Passerellidae** (sparrows)

Savannah Sparrow	Song Sparrow	Lincoln's Sparrow
Passerculus sandwichensis	*Melospiza melodia*	*Melospiza lincolnii*

Size: 5.5 inches.	Presumed range in Florida	**Size:** 5.5 inches.	Presumed range in Florida	**Size:** 5.5 inches.	Presumed range in Florida
Abundance: Fairly common.		**Abundance:** Fairly common.		**Abundance:** Very rare in FL.	
Migratory Status: Widespread winter resident.		**Migratory Status:** Widespread winter resident.		**Migratory Status:** Winter resident and winter migrant.	

Variation: Highly variable with as many as 28 subspecies.

Habitat: Pastures, grasslands, mowed areas, cultivated fields, and vacant lots in urban areas are all used in Florida. Also inhabits salt marsh, tundra, and bogs habitats.

Breeding: Nests on the ground beneath overhanging vegetation. 4 to 5 eggs is typical. Does not breed in Florida. Nests in northern US and Canada.

Natural History: This is one of the most widespread sparrow species in America. Between breeding range, winter range, and migration routes, the Savannah Sparrow may be seen anywhere on the continent. In Florida, they are a winter resident and winter migrant that may be seen from October through April. They occur statewide. They feed on arthropods in summer and seeds in winter. The name comes from the Georgia town of Savannah (where the first specimen was described) rather than from the habitat type. As with many grassland animals, the Savannah Sparrow has experienced population declines in areas of intensive agriculture or urbanization. Delaying cutting of hayfields benefits by allowing young time to fledge.

Variation: Many subspecies nationwide with light and dark morphs.

Habitat: Overgrown fields, dense underbrush, and rank weeds are the preferred habitat of the Song Sparrow throughout their range. They are especially common in edge habitats.

Breeding: Nests are built low to the ground in weeds or shrubs. 4 eggs is typical. Nesting occurs well to the north of Florida.

Natural History: Both the common and scientific names of the Song Sparrow are references to its distinct and melodic song. Primarily seed eaters, these sparrows migrate in response to heavy snow cover, and they are common at bird feeders throughout the southern United States each winter. Sharp-shinned and Cooper's Hawks are major predators of adults, and the young and eggs are vulnerable to a variety of snake predators. However, they remain a thriving species. There are dozens of subspecies nationwide with light and dark color morphs. Most Florida specimens will probably resemble the photo above. One of the earliest and most comprehensive studies of bird biology was conducted on this species.

Variation: No significant variation between sexes or juveniles.

Habitat: Summer habitat is boreal regions of Canada and Northern Rockies where it occupies damp woodlands with dense brush such as willow. Most winter west of the Mississippi River.

Breeding: Nests on the ground amid sedges or at the base of willow in boreal wetlands. Lays 3 to 5 eggs.

Natural History: Lincoln's Sparrows are more common west of the Mississippi and are rather rare in Florida. In addition, it is shy and secretive and tends to stick to heavy cover. Add to this the fact that it is a winter-only species in Florida and sightings are uncommon. During winter migrations, they are believed to be fairly widespread across the state. When excited, they will raise the feathers on the back of the head, giving them a "crested" look. Due to their secretive habits, the biology of these sparrows is not well understood. Feeds on insects in summer and seeds in winter. Unlike many sparrows, they rarely visit feeders except during periods of harsh winter weather. Very similar to the Song Sparrow, but has finer streaking.

Class - **Aves** (birds)

Order - **Passeriformes** (songbirds)

Family - **Passerellidae** (sparrows)		Family - **Passeridae** (weaver finches)

Swamp Sparrow
Melospiza georgiana

Size: 5.75 inches.

Abundance: Fairly common.

Migratory Status: Winter resident and seasonal migrant.

Presumed range in Florida

Variation: Breeding males are richer in color with a reddish crown.

Habitat: Summers in wetlands. Swamps, marshes (including salt marsh), and wet meadows. More diverse habitats may be used in winter, including upland fields.

Breeding: Nest is made of grasses and placed in cattails, grasses, or low bush. 3 to 6 eggs, 4 on average.

Natural History: Secretive and elusive, the Swamp Sparrow is less familiar to Americans than most of its kin. They will visit feeders during the winter, but they are rarely a commonly seen bird at feeders. These birds are highly dependent upon wetlands for breeding, and they may be negatively impacted by loss of wetlands. At this time, however, populations appear stable. Grassy fields are also heavily used and can be an important winter refuge. Although they can be quite common in summer habitats and in the bayous of the Deep South in winter, they do not typically flock during the breeding season and are nearly always seen singly or in pairs. There are 3 distinct subspecies of Swamp Sparrow recognized by professional orinithologists.

Eastern Towhee
Pipilo erythrophthalmus

Male

Female

Size: 8 inches.

Abundance: Fairly common.

Migratory Status: A nonmigratory resident.

Presumed range in Florida

Variation: Sexually dimorphic. See photos above.

Habitat: Succesional woodlands, overgrown fields/fence rows, edges of stream courses, and woodlots where honeysuckle, briers, weeds, and saplings are predominate.

Breeding: Nests are low to the ground or even on the ground, but it always well hidden. Usually 4 eggs.

Natural History: Our largest member of the sparrow family. Sometimes called "Rufous-sided Towhee." Its "tow-wheee" song is a familiar sound beginning as early as March. The widespread range of the Eastern Towhee corresponds closely to the Eastern Temperate Forest Level I Ecoregion, but they normally do not occur in dense populations. Most bird feeders in rural areas of the eastern US will have a pair for the winter, but rarely more than 2 pairs. Populations of this large sparrow in the Midwest, Great Lakes, and New England will migrate southward in winter, some perhaps wintering in Florida. Florida populations do not migrate. The similar Spotted Towhee (*P. maculatus*) replaces the Eastern Towhee in the western half of America.

House Sparrow
Passer domesticus

Male

Female

Size: 6.25 inches.

Abundance: Very common.

Migratory Status: Seen year-round except in summer.

Presumed range in Florida

Variation: Sexually dimorphic. See photos above.

Habitat: The House Sparrow's name comes from its affinity for human habitations. These are mostly urban birds and when they do occur in rural areas it is always near farms and homesteads.

Breeding: House Sparrows build bulky nests of grass, feathers, paper strips, etc. 5 to 6 eggs on average.

Natural History: A European immigrant, the House Sparrow was released into the United States about 150 years ago. They have spread across the continent and they are now perhaps the most familiar bird species in America. They roost communally in dense vegetation. Roosting sites are often in yards or foundation plantings next to houses. They are common scavengers around outdoor restaurants and fast food parking lots. They are often considered to be a nuisance bird, but their tame demeanor endears them to many. Despite being extremely common in urban areas, they are quite rare in wilderness. These highly successful birds may nest up to 4 times in a season. Despite their common name, House "Sparrow," they are not closely related to sparrows.

Class - **Aves** (birds)

Order - **Passeriformes** (songbirds)

Family - **Icteriidae**	Family - **Sturnidae** (mynas)	

Yellow-breasted Chat
Icteria virens

European Starling
Sturnis vulgaris

Common Myna
Acridotheres tristis

Size: 7.5 inches.	**Size:** 8.5 inches.	**Size:** 8.75 inches.
Abundance: Uncommon.	**Abundance:** Very common.	**Abundance:** Uncommon.
Migratory Status: Migrant and summer resident.	**Migratory Status:** Non-migratory year-round resident.	**Migratory Status:** Non-migratory year-round resident.

Presumed range in Florida

Presumed range in Florida

Presumed range in Florida

Variation: No significant variation. No sexual dimorphism.

Variation: Non-breeding plumage has white speckles. Juveniles drab brown.

Variation: No significant variation. Males average slightly larger.

Habitat: This species likes overgrown fields, second growth areas, and early successional regenerating woodlands. It avoids the deep woods.

Habitat: Urban and suburban areas as well as farms and ranches. Starlings are closely tied to human activity and are rarely seen in true wilderness.

Habitat: Seems to favor open and semi-open habitats and apparently avoids forested regions. Usually found in association with humans.

Breeding: Cuplike nests low to the ground in brier thickets or a dense shrub such as a multiflora rose. Lays 2 to 5 eggs. Nests in northern Florida.

Breeding: Nest is made of grass, leaves, etc., stuffed into a cavity. Often uses cracks or holes in man-made structures. Clutch size is typically 5 eggs.

Breeding: Nesting behavior is similar to the Starling. Mainly uses cavities and crevices but may nest in palm fronds. 3 to 5 eggs is usual.

Natural History: The Yellow-breasted Chat was once regarded as America's largest wood warbler (family Parulidae). But its status in the warbler family was questioned by many experts. It has recently been reclassified and assigned its own family (Icteriidae). They are fairly common in suitable habitats in summer months but are not easily observed due to their secretive nature and preference for dense vegetation. Foods are a wide variety of arthropods with a preference for crickets, grasshoppers, caterpillars, and spiders. They are also known to eat some fruits and berries. These birds are probably more numerous today than prior to deforestation. Their breeding range in eastern North America corresponds closely to the Eastern Temperate Forest Level I Ecoregion.

Natural History: The Starling is one of the most familiar birds in America, but ironically it is a non-native species. All the Starlings in America are descendant from a handful of birds released in New York City in the 1890s. Contrary to popular belief, the Starling is not related to the blackbirds. Instead, they belong to the same family as the Old World mynas. These birds have enjoyed remarkable success since being introduced to North America and they are now found throughout the continent. They represent a real threat to many of our native species, especially those that nest in cavities. They are well-known for taking over Bluebird Boxes and Martin Houses. In winter, they often join grackles and blackbirds in large mixed flocks that can become a messy nuisance in urban and suburban areas.

Natural History: Like its relative the Starling, the Common Myna is an invasive exotic. Also like the Starling, it may be negatively impacting some native bird species. Common Mynas are originally from central and southern Asia. Today they are much more widespread around the globe and they are a common bird in the Hawaiian Islands. Hawaii's Mynas were intentionally released. Florida populations are believed to have originated from escaped or released cage birds in the early 1980s. The food of the Common Myna can include almost anything eaten by a bird. Seeds and grain, fruit, berries, nectar from flowers, insects and their larva, crustaceans, eggs of other birds, and even some small vertebrates such as *Anolis* lizards. Human food garbage and French fries are also on their menu.

Class - **Aves** (birds)
Order - **Passeriformes** (songbirds)
Family - **Thraupidae** (tanagers)

Scarlet Tanager *Piranga ludoviciana*	**Summer Tanager** *Piranga rubra*

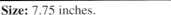

Size: 7 inches.

Abundance: Fairly common seasonal migrant.

Presumed range in Florida

Migratory Status: A seasonal migrant that passes through Florida in April and May and again in September and October. A few may linger in south Florida into December.

Variation: Sexual and ontogenic plumage variations. Juvenile males resemble females for the first year of their lives. See photos above.

Habitat: The summer habitat for the Scarlet Tanager closely coincides with the Eastern Temperate Forest Level I ecoregion. It prefers large tracts of unbroken woodlands.

Breeding: The thin, saucerlike nest of the Scarlet Tanager is placed on the fork of an outer branch. 4 eggs is typical. Only 1 brood is produced.

Natural History: The Scarlet Tanager is one of the most strikingly colored birds in America. Unfortunately, this species' dependence upon larger tracts of forested land means that its future is uncertain. Forest fragmentation leads to vulnerability to cowbird nest parasitism. Throughout much of the Midwest, where deforestation and fragmentation of forests has been rampant, this species is in decline. In the Midwest it has become an uncommon to rare species except where large tracts of deciduous woodlands remain. Food in summer is mostly insects, including wasps and hornets, a habit that makes them a valuable bird to have around the rural homestead. Add to that their gaudy black and red plumage and you have a bird that all Americans should strive to protect. Winter range is from Panama to northwestern South America.

Size: 7.75 inches.

Abundance: Fairly common. Numbers peak in spring/fall.

Presumed range in Florida

Migratory Status: Well named, this bird is seen in most of America only during summer. Some will winter in the Tropical Wet Forests Level I Ecoregion of Florida.

Variation: Sexual and ontogenic dimorphism. See photos above. The mottled yellow-green and bright red of the juvenile male entering its second year can be seen in early spring.

Habitat: Like their Scarlet Tanager cousins, Summer Tanagers are birds of the eastern forests. However, this species is more likely to occupy fragmented forests and edge areas.

Breeding: The rather flimsy nest is on a terminal fork of a branch that is usually low over an opening such as a creek bed. The typical clutch size is 3 to 4.

Natural History: Summer Tanagers feed on a variety of woodland insects and larva, but they also eat some berries and fruits. One of their primary food items, however, is bees and wasps, a fact that makes them an attractive species to have around the rural homestead. Immature males resemble females their first summer. By the following spring, they begin transformation into the bright red plumage of the adult male. During this transformation, they are one of the most colorful birds in America's woodlands (see photos above). Breeding bird surveys in recent years have detected a slight decline in populations of this species. Landscape changes in their wintering grounds may be the reason. They will winter from southern Mexico to northern South America, as well as in southern Florida. Like many migratory songbirds, they often migrate at night.

Class - **Aves** (birds)

Order - **Passeriformes** (songbirds)

Family - **Cardinalidae** (grosbeaks)

Northern Cardinal	Rose-breasted Grosbeak	Dickcissel
Cardinalis cardinalis	*Pheucticus ludovicianus*	*Spiza americana*

Female / Male

Male / Female

Female / Male

Size: 8.75 inches.

Abundance: Very common.

Migratory Status: Non-migratory year-round resident.

Presumed range in Florida

Size: 8 inches.

Abundance: Fairly common.

Migratory Status: Seasonal migrant. April/May and September/October.

Presumed range in Florida

Size: 6.25 inches.

Abundance: Rare in Florida.

Migratory Status: Migrant. Early fall to late spring.

Presumed range in Florida

Variation: Pronounced sexual dimorphism. See photos above.

Variation: Sexually dimorphic. See photos above.

Variation: Females are duller and lack the black "bib" of the male.

Habitat: From undisturbed natural areas to suburbs, the Northern Cardinal favors edge areas with shrubs and brush. Avoids areas of extensive forests in favor of successional habitats.

Habitat: A forest species primarily, but enjoys edge areas and regenerative woodlands with thick shrubby cover. May be fairly common in suburbs with adequate cover in the form of bushes.

Habitat: Fallow lands with weeds, saplings, and grasses. Weedy fields in open areas are the preferred habitat. Original range was probably natural prairie regions.

Breeding: Nest is usually in a thick shrub or bush. About 4 eggs on average. Most nesting is from mid-April to August. 2 broods per year.

Breeding: 3 to 5 eggs are laid in a nest of twigs, grass, and plant fibers. Nesting begins in late May. May rarely produce 2 broods per year.

Breeding: Does not breed in Florida. Produces only 1 brood per year. Nest is in a shrub low to ground. 4 eggs is usual but may be as many as 6.

Natural History: Conspicuous and highly recognizable, the Northern Cardinal enjoys the distinction of being the state bird for a total of 7 states. They are mainly seed and berry/fruit eaters, but they will eat insects and feed insects to the young. They are common birds at feeders throughout their range, especially during winter, and they are equally abundant in rural and urban regions. In the last century, they have expanded their range farther to the north into the Great Lakes region and New England. Today they are seen throughout much of the United States east of the Rockies. The southern extent of their range is northern Central America. Throughout their range, they are often known by the name "Redbird."

Natural History: Rose-breasted Grosbeaks seen in Florida are passage migrants that nest farther to the north. They will pass through the state in spring (April and May) and again in the fall (September and October) en route to wintering habitats in Central and South America. Food in summer is about 50/50 insects and plant material such as seeds, fruits, flowers, and buds. During migration they are readily attracted to bird feeders where sunflower seeds are a favorite food. Birdwatchers throughout the eastern US enthusiastically await the return of migrant songbirds each spring, and the bright pink breast and striking black and white plumage of the male Rose-breasted Grosbeak makes this species a favorite. By contrast, the female is a cryptic, drab brown.

Natural History: The bulk of the Dickcissel's summer range is in the central Great Plains. It probably always ranged eastward into natural prairies but today has expanded its range farther east into suitable habitats created by deforestation and subsequent conversion of woodlands to cropland and pasture. Outside their core breeding range, they are distributed sporadically and they are also known to wander well outside their core range. Flocks numbering in the thousands have been recorded during migration. Eats seeds almost exclusively during migration and on winter range. During breeding is more omnivorous, consuming both insects and seeds. An open country bird, the Dickcissel avoids the more heavily forested regions of the state.

Class - **Aves** (birds)

Order - **Passeriformes** (songbirds)

Family - **Cardinalidae** (grosbeaks)

Blue Grosbeak *Passerina caerulea*	Indigo Bunting *Passerina cyanea*	Painted Bunting *Passerina cirris*

Size: 6 inches. **Abundance:** Uncommon. **Migratory Status:** Summer resident.	Presumed range in Florida	**Size:** 5.5 inches. **Abundance:** Fairly common. **Migratory Status:** Summer in north Florida, winter in south.	Presumed range in Florida	**Size:** 5.25 inches. **Abundance:** Fairly common. **Migratory Status:** Summer in north Florida, winter in south.	Presumed range in Florida

Blue Grosbeak	Indigo Bunting	Painted Bunting
Variation: Sexually dimorphic. Female is chestnut brown.	**Variation:** Sexually dimorphic. See photos above.	**Variation:** Sexual and ontogenetic plumage variations. See photos above.
Habitat: On summer range the Blue Grosbeak enjoys overgrown fields dominated by forbs and saplings. Also uses fence rows, thickets, brambles, etc.	**Habitat:** Edge areas, fence rows, rural roadsides with substantial brushy/weedy cover, and overgrown fields or early successional woodlands.	**Habitat:** Breeding habitat is mostly in the southern Great Plains and the western Gulf Coastal Plain of Louisiana and Texas.
Breeding: Nest is a tightly woven cup placed in a low bush or tangle of vines, brush. About 4 eggs. Double brooding is known in the southern part of range.	**Breeding:** 2 broods are common. Lays 2 to 4 eggs in a nest of woven grasses that is usually placed in thick cover only a few feet above the ground.	**Breeding:** Nest is usually built low to the ground in a bush. Grasses are tightly woven and attached to stems. Nesting does occur in northeastern Florida.
Natural History: The Blue Grosbeak can be seen in most of the Florida Peninsula but it avoids the South Florida Coastal Plain as a breeding ground. It is also rather rare in the western panhandle region except as a transient migrant. Recent breeding bird surveys suggest that this species is expanding its range northward and they may soon become more common in more northern regions of the US. During summer they feed mostly on crickets, grasshoppers, and other insects, but eat mostly seeds in the early spring and fall. They often will visit bird feeders at these times. These birds are more common in the eastern United States today than they were in historic times, but they are still uncommon birds compared to some of the other members of the Cardinalidae family.	**Natural History:** Indigo Buntings are common in summer throughout the eastern half of America. Probably more so today than in historical times when forests dominated the region's habitats. The neon blue color of the male makes it one of the most striking of North American birds. These birds are found throughout the eastern United States in summer, generally ranging from the short grass plains eastward to the Atlantic and as far north as southern Canada. They are most common in the southeastern US. Their annual migration may encompass up to 2,500 miles and many make the long flight across the Gulf of Mexico. Seeds and berries are the primary food with insects eaten during the breeding season.	**Natural History:** The plumage of the male Painted Bunting is one the most colorful of any North American bird and they are a favorite of American birdwatchers. Males don't acquire their characteristic coloration until their second spring. Juvenile males resemble females. Painted Buntings that nest in Florida represent an eastern population that is disjunct from the larger populations that occupy the Southern Plains and Western Gulf Coastal Plain. The Cornell University website "Birds of North America" state that this is a species in decline, especially the eastern population which ranges into Florida. Loss of habitat is probably the main threat. Athough they may be seen statewide as migrators, in winter they are found only in the South Florida Coastal Plain.

Class - **Aves** (birds)

Order - **Passeriformes** (songbirds)

Family - **Icturidae** (blackbirds)

Baltimore Oriole *Icturus galbula*	Orchard Oriole *Icturus spurius*

Presumed range in Florida

Presumed range in Florida

Size: 8.75 inches.

Size: 7 inches

Abundance: Fairly common.

Abundance: Fairly common.

Migratory Status: A winter resident in most of Florida. In the panhandle, they occur as a seasonal migrant. Throughout the peninsula, they are most common from the end of September through early May.

Migratory Status: Summer resident in the northern half of Florida and a seasonal migrant elsewhere in the state. Peak numbers in the state are from late March through early September.

Variation: Significant sexual- and age-related dimorphism (see photos above). Immature male less vividly colored.

Variation: Significant sexual and ontogenic plumage variation. Immature males resemble female (see photos).

Habitat: Savanna-like habitats are preferred. Pastures with scattered large trees, parks and lawns in urban areas, or farms and ranches in rural areas. During migration, they may be seen in a variety of habitats.

Habitat: This species shows a preference for semi-open habitats and narrow strips of woodland bordering rivers and streams. Their name comes from the fact that they are fond of orchards and they will often nest fruit trees.

Breeding: The nest is an easily recognizable "hanging basket" woven from grasses and suspended from a tree limb. 4 to 6 eggs is typical.

Breeding: The nest is a rounded basket woven from grasses and suspended from a forked tree branch. 4 eggs is typical, but can be as many as 6.

Natural History: These handsome orange and black birds are a favorite with backyard birdwatchers. They will come to nectar feeders and fruits such as oranges, and they relish grape jelly. In addition to nectar and fruit, they feed heavily on insects. In some areas of their range, they have adapted well to human activities. Small town neighborhoods with large trees and city parks are among their habitats today. A similar species known as the **Spot-breasted Oriole** (*I. pectoralis*) is an exotic species native to Mexico and Central America that has become established along Florida's southern Atlantic Coast.

Natural History: Like the larger Baltimore Oriole, Orchard Orioles will eat fruit. They also feed on a wide variety of arthropods gleaned from tree branches and leaves, as well as from weedy fields. Immature males resemble females but have a large black throat patch. These birds are somewhat gregarious and they often occur in flocks on tropical wintering grounds. They are also known to nest in small colonies where ideal habitat exists. Spraying for insects in orchards can be dangerous for these insect and fruit eaters as it can be for other bird species, many of which are highly susceptible to insecticides.

Class - **Aves** (birds)		
Order - **Passeriformes** (songbirds)		
Family - **Icteridae** (blackbirds)		

Bobolink *Dolichonyx oryzivorus*	**Eastern Meadowlark** *Sturnella magna*	**Red-winged Blackbird** *Agelaius phoeniceus*

Size: 7 inches.	Presumed range in Florida 	**Size:** 9.5 inches.	Presumed range in Florida 	**Size:** 9 inches.	Presumed range in Florida 
Abundance: Uncommon.		**Abundance:** Fairly common.		**Abundance:** Common.	
Migratory Status: Seasonal migrant seen in spring and fall.		**Migratory Status:** Non-migratory year-round resident.		**Migratory Status:** Non-migratory year-round resident.	

Variation: Females and winter males are sparrow-like in color.	**Variation:** Breeding adults exhibit slightly brighter plumage colors.	**Variation:** Sexual and seasonal plumage variations.
Habitat: Bobolinks are open country birds usually seen in pastures and hayfields. Their original habitats in the state were probably tallgrass prairies, which no longer exist in any significant amount.	**Habitat:** Open, treeless pastures and fields that are kept closely grazed or mowed. They like short grasses and avoid overgrown areas. In winter, they are often seen in harvested croplands or emerging wheat fields.	**Habitat:** The Red-wing Blackbird's favorite breeding habitat is marsh or wet meadows. They are also found along roadside ditches and the edges of ponds, lakes, or other lentic waters in open areas.
Breeding: Females breed with a number of males and a clutch of 5 eggs may have several fathers. Nest is woven of grasses and placed on the ground.	**Breeding:** Nest is on the ground and well hidden beneath overhanging grasses or under the edge of a grass tussock. 3 to 5 eggs.	**Breeding:** The nest of the Red-winged Blackbird is a woven basket usually suspended from 2 or 3 cattail blades and often positioned over water.
Natural History: Bobolinks are one of the greatest migrators of any bird. They will nest in the northern US and Canada and winter in southern South America in the open grasslands of the Pampas region of Uruguay and Argentina. Thats a round trip of nearly 20,000 miles! In Florida they are most likely to be seen in late April or early May during spring migration. Fall migration is longer, from late August through October. This species has experienced population declines in the last half century, but has recently benefited from CRP programs. Food items include seeds, grains, and many invertebrates during breeding. Many people are surprised to learn that these handsome birds are in the blackbird family.	**Natural History:** As might be expected of a bird that loves open spaces, the Eastern Meadowlark is least common in forested regions of the state. Even in the heavily wooded regions, however, this bird can be found in areas of open habitat. They feed mostly on insects in warmer months, with grasshoppers and crickets being a dietary mainstay in the summer. During winter, they will eat seeds and grain. They tend to occur in small flocks during the winter, but pair off and scatter in the breeding season. In the western United States, this bird is replaced by the nearly identical Western Meadowlark. They are so similar in appearance that where the ranges overlap experts rely on listening to the bird's songs to make a positive identification.	**Natural History:** In winter, Red-winged Blackbirds often join large mixed flocks that can include grackles, cowbirds, and starlings. Altogether the blackbirds are probably the most numerous birds in America in winter. Males sing conspicuously in spring. Like the other blackbirds, the Red-winged has benefited from human alterations to America's natural habitats, thriving in open land and agricultural areas. Food is almost entirely insects and the along with the Common Grackle this species plays an important role in insect control. The bright red and yellow "epaulets" on the wing of the male are greatly reduced in winter, but some color is still visible on the wing.

Class - **Aves** (birds)

Order - **Passeriformes** (songbirds)

Family - **Icteridae** (blackbirds)

Rusty Blackbird *Euphagus carolinus*	Brewer's Blackbird *Euphagus cyanocephalus*	Brown-headed Cowbird *Molothrus ater*
 Winter plumage	  Female / Male	  Male / Female

Size: 9 inches.	Presumed range in Florida	**Size:** 9.5 inches.	Presumed range in Florida	**Size:** 5.25 inches.	Presumed range in Florida
Abundance: Rare in Florida.		**Abundance:** Very rare in FL.		**Abundance:** Fairly common.	
Migratory Status: Winter migrant and rare winter resident.		**Migratory Status:** Winter migrant and rare winter resident.		**Migratory Status:** Seen year-round except in summer.	

Variation: Significant seasonal plumage variations (not seen in Florida).	**Variation:** Sexually dimorphic. See photos above.	**Variation:** Sexually dimorphic. See photos above.
Habitat: Wintering Rusty Blackbirds favor wetland habitats. Floodplain forests, edges of swamps, and woods bordering marshes make up the bulk of this bird's winter habitat. Summers in wet boreal woodlands and tundra edges.	**Habitat:** Favors open country. It is usually seen in harvested or plowed agricultural fields, pastures, etc. It may also frequent feedlots where it feeds on waste grain. In the bulk of its range out west, it inhabits grasslands.	**Habitat:** Open fields and agricultural areas primarily, but can also be common in towns and suburbs. Inhabits edge areas and woods openings but avoids deep forest. Lives year-round in north Florida. In southern Florida in winter.
Breeding: Breeding occurs far to the north (as far as the Arctic). An average of four eggs are laid in a bulky nest of twigs, lichens and grass.	**Breeding:** As many as 8 eggs may be laid, but 5 or 6 is probably average. Nests on the ground. Does not nest in Florida.	**Breeding:** Female cowbirds lay their eggs in the nest of other bird species, a unique nesting strategy known as "brood parasitism" (see below).
Natural History: In the last few years, Rusty Blackbirds have garnered the attention of birdwatchers and conservationists concerned about an apparently significant decline in the population of this species. The loss of wet woodlands to agriculture throughout much of their wintering grounds in the southern US may be partly to blame. Unlike many blackbirds that regularly intermingle with other species, the Rusty Blackbird seems to remain mostly segregated from the large winter flocks of grackles, cowbirds, starlings, and Red-wingeds. These birds summer far to the north and are seen in Florida only in winter. They will migrate farther to the south if the winter weather gets harsh. Food is insects, seeds, grains, etc.	**Natural History:** The Brewer's Blackbird is a western species that historically inhabited the Great Plains and Rocky Mountain Regions all the way to the Pacific Ocean. With the clearing of land brought on by human activities, the Brewer's Blackbird began to invade the Eastern Temperate Forest Level I Ecoregion in the early 1900s. Although they are still uncommon in Florida compared to our other blackbirds, birdwatchers report sightings nearly every winter. Feeds mostly on grains and seeds of grasses or weeds in winter. Summer diet is largely insects. The stomach of one bird reportedly contain over 50 tiny grasshoppers! This is a very common blackbird in the western half of North America.	**Natural History:** The cowbirds are unique among American birds in that the adults play no role in rearing their young. Instead the female lays an egg in another species' nest and the adoptive parents rear the young cowbird, usually to the detriment of their own offspring. The disappearance of extensive forest tracts has allowed the cowbird to parasitize many more woodland songbirds than was possible prior to settlement. As a result, this species now poses a real threat to many smaller songbird species, especially the warblers. The **Bronze Cowbird** (*M. aeneus*) and the **Shiny Cowbird** (*M. bonariensis*) are 2 other cowbird species native to the tropics that have recently begun to appear in southern Florida.

Class - **Aves** (birds)

Order - **Passeriformes** (songbirds)

Family - **Icteridae** (blackbirds)

Family - **Fringillidae** (finches)

Boat-tailed Grackle *Quiscalus major*	**Common Grackle** *Quiscalus quiscula*	**House Finch** *Haemorhous mexicanus*

Size: 16 inches.

Abundance: Common.

Migratory Status: Year-round resident of Florida.

Presumed range in Florida

Size: 12 inches.

Abundance: Common.

Migratory Status: Year-round resident of Florida.

Presumed range in Florida

Size: 6 inches.

Abundance: Fairly common.

Migratory Status: Year-round resident in north Florida.

Presumed range in Florida

Variation: Significant sexual dimorphism.

Variation: 2 color morphs, "bronze" and "purple."

Variation: Significant sexual dimorphism. See photos above.

Habitat: Open and semi-open habitats throughout Florida, including urban and suburban areas. Common on lawns and in parks and shopping mall parking lots.

Habitat: Grackles favor open areas. They are common in urban areas where they inhabit lawns, parks, etc. In winter, it roosts in large flocks in small woodlots.

Habitat: As implied by the name, House Finches are usually associated with human habitation. Found both in cities and rural areas.

Breeding: Often nests near water. May nest as early as late February or early March in Florida. Nests in loose colonies. 2 broods per year is common in Florida. 4 eggs is typical.

Breeding: Often nests in groups that may consist of a dozen or more pairs. The nest is built in the upper branches of medium-sized trees and several nests can be in the same tree.

Breeding: Typical nest of woven grasses is usually placed in dense evergreen shrub, cedar, or conifer tree. Lays 3 to 5 eggs and multiple broods are common.

Natural History: The Boat-tailed Grackle owes its name to its long, deeply V-shaped tail. This species has a strong affinity to human habitation and it can be quite common in the vicinity of fast food restuarants, dumpsters, and parking lots in urban and suburban regions. Human refuse has become an important part of its diet. In wilder, more natural habitats, it feeds on insects and some small vertebrates such as small frogs, lizards, or crabs. Although they are widespread in Florida, they are probably most common in areas of human habitation along the coasts and near inland lakes and rivers. They are very similar to the Common Grackle and at times the 2 species may be seen in close proximity. The Boat-tailed is larger and has a longer, V-shaped tail.

Natural History: Common Grackles are known for forming large flocks during the winter that will roost communally and can number in the thousands. When these large congregations move into a town or neighborhood, they can become a messy nuisance, but their reputation for spreading disease is exaggerated. Throughout most of the year, they are busy consuming millions of injurious insect pests. In harsh winter weather, they may descend on backyard bird feeders in large flocks that overwhelm the regular residents, creating consternation among backyard birdwatchers. The 2 color morphs known as "bronze" and "purple" reflect the color of the iridescence of the plumage. Florida birds are typically bronze morphs.

Natural History: House Finches have extended their range into the eastern United States over the last few decades. Originally native to the southwestern United States, the first House Finches appeared in the Midwest in the 1960s. Today they are found throughout the United States except for the southern half of Florida. Primarily a seed eater, these birds can be very common at urban feeders. Weed seeds, fruit, buds, and flowers are also reported to be eaten. Birds seen at feeders sometimes exhibit signs of a disease (mycoplasmal conjuctivitis) that causes swelling of the eyes with occasional blindness or death. Similar to and easily confused with the less common Purple Finch, which has a larger head and lacks dark streaking on the belly of the males.

Class - **Aves** (birds)

Order - **Passeriformes** (songbirds)

Family - **Fringillidae** (finches)

Purple Finch *Haemorhous purpureus*	**Pine Siskin** *Spinus pinus*	**Goldfinch** *Spinus tristis*
	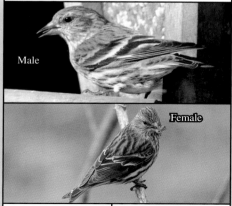	

Purple Finch	**Pine Siskin**	**Goldfinch**
Size: 6 inches.	**Size:** 5 inches.	**Size:** 5 inches.
Abundance: Rare in Florida.	**Abundance:** Very rare in FL.	**Abundance:** Uncommon.
Migratory Status: Winter migrant and rare winter resident.	**Migratory Status:** Very rare winter migrant in January to March.	**Migratory Status:** Winter resident throughout Florida.
Presumed range in Florida	Presumed range in Florida	Presumed range in Florida
Variation: Significant sexual dimorphism. See photos above.	**Variation:** Mildly sexually dimorphic. See photos above.	**Variation:** Exhibits sexual and seasonal plumage variations. See above.
Habitat: Summer habitat is moist coniferous forests. In winter, they are seen in almost all habitats across the eastern half of the United States.	**Habitat:** Pine Siskins prefer coniferous woodlands but in winter they are often seen in mixed or even pure hardwood forests.	**Habitat:** Edge areas and successional habitats, fence rows, overgrown fields, and floodplains in open and semi-open areas.
Breeding: Nest of twigs, roots, and grasses is built in a fork on the outer portion of a branch of a conifer. 3 to 6 eggs per clutch. 2 broods per year. Does not nest in Florida.	**Breeding:** Nest is woven of grasses, twigs, rootlets, etc. and lined with mosses or fur. 3 to 4 eggs is typical. May nest in loose colonies. Does not nest in Florida.	**Breeding:** 4 to 6 uniformly white eggs are laid. Nest is a tightly woven cup of grasses usually wrapped around a triad of upright branches. Does not nest in Florida.
Natural History: The Purple Finch seems to a be declining species in the eastern United States. Competition with the House Finch may be to blame. Although Purple Finches are quite rare in Florida, they may move well south in some winters, all the way to the Gulf Coast in years of poor cone production. Seeds are the major food item, including seeds of deciduous trees (elm, maples, ash) and seeds of fruits. Buds are also eaten. Insects are also consumed in summer. As with most other seed eaters, they will frequent bird feeders in winter. It may be fairly common at feeders one year, but rare or absent the next. Most likely to be seen during extremely harsh winter weather. Easily confused with the House Finch, but has a larger head and a heavier bill.	**Natural History:** The Pine Siskin is a coniferous forest species. Although it is also found in mixed deciduous/coniferous woodlands and in pure deciduous woods during winter irruptions, it is mostly a bird of the far north and the Rocky Mountains. However, they do exhibit erratic north/south movements in winter and sometimes range as far south as the Gulf Coast of North America. In Florida they are seen only in the northern part of the state, but their erratic movement means they may be common in one area and rare in another. Feeds on seeds of coniferous trees, grass seeds, and weed seeds and will regularly visit feeders in winter and where thistle seeds are favored. Insects are also eaten during breeding. They are often seen in the company of Goldfinches.	**Natural History:** The transition of the male Goldfinch into its strikingly yellow breeding plumage in spring is a profound example of a condition that is common in male birds in which they acquire bright colors. The Goldfinch is a common visitor to bird feeders and is especially attracted to thistle seeds. Unlike many other species that eat seeds in winter and insects in summer, the Goldfinch is mainly a seed eater. Weed seeds, grass seeds, and especially seeds from forbs like thistles, sunflowers, and coneflowers are consumed. This species is apparently immune to parasitism by the Brown-headed Cowbird, as young cowbirds cannot develop on a diet that contains no insects. Female Goldfinches resemble the winter male (see photos above).

Class - **Aves** (birds)		
Order - **Cuculiformes** (cuckoos, anis, and roadrunner)		
Family - **Cuculidae**		
Black-billed Cuckoo *Coccyzus erythropthalmus*	**Yellow-billed Cuckoo** *Coccyzus americanus*	**Smooth-billed Ani** *Crotophaga ani*

Size: 12 inches. **Abundance:** Rare in Florida. **Migratory Status:** Seasonal migrant. April/May to September/October.	**Size:** 12 inches. **Abundance:** Fairly common. **Migratory Status:** Summer resident and seasonal migrant.	**Size:** 14 inches. **Abundance:** Rare. **Migratory Status:** Year-round resident in southern Florida.
Presumed range in Florida 	Presumed range in Florida	Presumed range in Florida 
Variation: Sexes alike. No significant variation.	**Variation:** Sexes alike. No significant variation.	**Variation:** Sexes alike. No significant variation.
Habitat: Successional areas, thickets, and mature woodlands with some open areas. Shows a preference for being near water (riparian areas, lakes, etc).	**Habitat:** Open woodlands, edge areas, regenerative woodlands near open fields, overgrown fence rows, etc. Uses similar habitats on winter range.	**Habitat:** Open and semi-open savanna-like habitats. Frequent around suburbs and parks in urban areas and cattle pastures in rural regions.
Breeding: Does not breed in Florida. Nests in northern portions of the eastern US and throughout the Appalachians. Clutch size averages 2 to 4 eggs.	**Breeding:** Breeds from early June through the summer. Nest is flimsy and placed in thick vegetation. 2 to 4 eggs. Will nest in most of Florida.	**Breeding:** Often nests in communal groups. Typically lays 4 eggs and multiple (2 or even 3) broods per year is not uncommon.
Natural History: Although once common, the Black-billed Cuckoo has declined in abundance over the past several decades. Widespread use of pesticides may be to blame. Caterpillars are a primary food and pesticide-depleted caterpillar numbers results in a scarce food source for the birds. Ironically, large flocks of these handsome birds once acted as a natural control of caterpillars and historical observers reported seeing flocks of Black-billed Cuckoos descend on a tree full of caterpillars and eat every caterpillar on the tree! Today it is rare to see more than 1 or 2 of these birds at a time. Cicadas are another important insect food, and in years of cicada outbreaks, cuckoos (along with many other birds species) will produce larger clutches and successfully rear more young.	**Natural History:** The Yellow-billed Cuckoo is one of the latest arriving of America's neotropical migrant songbirds. They often go by the nickname "Raincrow" and folklore states that they call right before a rain. Although much more common than the Black-billed Cuckoo, Yellow-billed Cuckoos are not abundant birds today. Like our other cuckoo, their numbers have diminished significantly in modern times. Caterpillars are an important food and widespread pesticide use is likely the major contributing factor in their decline. These are secretive birds that are heard more often than seen. Their call is quite distinctive and is heard most frequently during the "dog days" of mid to late summer. A similar species, the **Mangrove Cuckoo** (*C. minor*), is a year-round resident in southernmost Florida.	**Natural History:** The members of this genus (*Crotophaga*) are mainly birds of the American tropics. A total of 3 species live in the Carribean, Mexico, and Central/South America. One (the Groove-billed Ani) ranges into southern Texas. The Smooth-billed Ani has occured in Florida on a regular basis, but is very rare. The Groove-billed has been recorded in panhandle on rare occasions. The population of these birds in Florida is known to fluctuate over long periods of time and they were once more common than today. Southern Florida represents the northernmost extension of their range and they are more common in the Carribean and in South America. Anis feed mainly on insects and do most of their foraging on the ground. Snails and some fruits are also included in its diet.

Class - **Aves** (birds)
Order - **Apodiformes** (swifts and hummingbirds)

Family - **Trochylidae** (hummingbirds)		Family - **Apodidae** (swifts)

Ruby-throated Hummingbird
Archilochus colubris

Male

Female

Rufous Hummingbird
Selasphorus rufus

Chimney Swift
Chaetura pelagica

Size: 3.75 inches.	**Size:** 3.75 inches.	**Size:** 5.5 inches.
Presumed range in Florida	Presumed range in Florida	Presumed range in Florida
Abundance: Common.	**Abundance:** Rare in Florida.	**Abundance:** Fairly common.
Migratory Status: Year-round and seasonal migrant.	**Migratory Status:** Rare winter migrant.	**Migratory Status:** Summer resident and seasonal migrant.

Variation: Female lacks ruby throat patch. See photos above.

Variation: Females has less red on sides and belly and has a greenish back.

Variation: No sexual dimorphism. Immatures slightly lighter.

Habitat: Woodlands. Both deciduous and mixed forests are utilized. Edge areas and open fields are used for feeding.

Habitat: Mostly a western species that wanders widely across the southeastern US in winter. May appear anywhere.

Habitat: Mainly seen in open and semi-open country and in urban/suburban areas.

Breeding: Nest is a tiny cup of fine plant fibers and lichens glued together with spider webs. 2 eggs is typical.

Breeding: Breeds in the Pacific Northwest. An early breeding that arrives on breeding grounds in early spring.

Breeding: Nest is a flimsy cup plastered to the inside of a chimney. 2 to 5 eggs are laid.

Natural History: The tiny hummingbirds are ounce for ounce one of the world's greatest travelers. Many fly across the Gulf of Mexico each year during migration! Considering that they weigh barely more than 1/10 of an ounce, that is a remarkable feat of endurance. The range of the Ruby-throated Hummingbird includes all of the Eastern Deciduous Forest Level 1 Ecoregion, as well as portions of the Boreal Forest and Great Plains Ecoregions. Nectar is the major food item for hummingbirds and they show a preference for red, tubular flowers. They possess a highly specialized beak and tongue for reaching nectar deep within flowers. They will also eat some small flying insects caught on the wing, and are known to pluck tiny invertebrates from foliage or small spiders from their webs. These birds will readily use artificial nectar feeders containing a 1 to 4 mix of sugar water.

Natural History: Hummingbirds are generally regarded as tropical birds that move northward into temperate regions in summer. The Rufous is known for being the world's most northerly ranging hummingbird, nesting as far north as southern Alaska. This hardy bird also winters farther north than others of its kin, sometimes spending the winter in the southeastern United States, including Florida. The migration routes of this species have been well studied. Spring migration is typically along the West Coast and fall migration is along the spine of the Rockies. Winter migrants fan out across the lower Gulf Coastal Plain with a few moving as far east as Florida. It is these wide-ranging winter migrants that often surprise and delight birdwatchers across the southeastern United States in winter. More and more winter records are obtained as more birders begin to look for this species.

Natural History: This is a species that has benefited from human population expansion. Historically, the Chimney Swift nested mainly in hollow trees. These birds require a vertical surface within a sheltered place for nesting. When people began to build houses and large structures like schools, churches, and factories equipped with chimneys, their populations exploded. Today they are perhaps less common than a few decades ago when most dwellings and other buildings had chimneys. Some nesting in natural hollows still occurs. Swifts have long, narrow, pointed wings that allow for extreme maneuverability and these birds feed entirely on the wing. Small flying insects are their prey. During migration, they are sometimes seen in large flocks that can contain over 1,000 birds. Today, the greatest population densities occur in the vicinity of urban centers.

Class - **Aves** (birds)

Order - **Coraciiformes** (kingfishers)	Order - **Piciformes** (woodpeckers)	
Family - **Alcedinidae** (kingfisher)	Family - **Picidae** (woodpeckers)	

Belted Kingfisher
Megaceryle alcyon

Size: 13 inches.

Abundance: Fairly common.

Migratory Status: Mostly a spring, fall, and winter bird in FL.

Presumed range in Florida

Variation: Female has a rust-colored band across belly.

Habitat: Kingfishers require water and they thus haunt creeks, rivers, lakes, swamps, and farm ponds. Likes the presence of a convenient perch over the water; limb, snag, pole, or wire.

Breeding: Kingfishers nest in burrows they excavate into vertical banks of dirt or sand that are at least 8 feet high.

Natural History: The Belted Kingfisher is one of the most widely distributed birds in North America. In fact, they range throughout the continent from Alaska and northern Canada south to Panama. Although widespread, they are usually widely dispersed and unlike many bird species they do not form flocks. The presence of suitable nesting habitat in the form of vertical earthen cliffs may be a limiting factor in their abundance. Human activities such as digging of quarries and road cuts through hills and mountains may have helped this species in modern times by providing the requisite vertical banks for nest sites. Small fish are the primary food item. They are known for diving headfirst into the water from either a perch or while hovering to catch fish near the surface.

Pileated Woodpecker
Dryocopus pileatus

Size: 16.5 inches

Abundance: Fairly common.

Migratory Status: Year-round resident of Florida.

Presumed range in Florida

Variation: Male has a red cheek patch and more extensive red on the head.

Habitat: A forest species, the Pileated Woodpecker prefers mature woodlands. It is also seen in semi-open areas where large tracts of woods occur nearby. Floodplain forests are a favorite habitat.

Breeding: Nest is a hollow cavity excavated into the trunk of a tree. Nests are usually fairly high up. 4 eggs.

Natural History: By far America's largest woodpecker, Pileated Woodpeckers play an important role in the mature forest ecosytem. Their large nest cavities are utilized as a refuge by many other woodland species including small owls, Wood Ducks, bluebirds, and squirrels. In the boreal forests of Canada the Pine Marten is reported to use their holes. Using their powerful, chisel-like beaks to break apart dead snags and logs, they also help accelerate decomposition of large dead trees. In addition to mast and fruit such as wild cherries, they eat insects, mainly Carpenter Ants and beetle larva. In Florida they occur statewide in regions where ample forests exist. Successional forest are used but they do need some mature trees and especially large, dead trees and fallen logs.

Northern Flicker
Colaptes auratus

Size: 12.5 inches

Abundance: Fairly common.

Migratory Status: Year-round resident of Florida.

Presumed range in Florida

Variation: Male has black "mustache." 2 color morphs, only 1 in Florida.

Habitat: Semi-open areas and open lands with at least a few large trees. Farmlands, older urban neighborhoods, and parks are also used. Least common in dense, mature woodlands.

Breeding: Nest is usually excavated in a fairly large-diameter dead tree. Also uses natural hollows. 6 to 8 eggs.

Natural History: In addition to feeding on insects (mainly ants) usually caught on the ground, the Flicker also eats berries and in winter, grains (including corn). 2 distinct subspecies of Northern Flicker occur in North America. The "Yellow-shafted Flicker" is native to Florida and the rest of the eastern US. In the Rocky Mountains west the "Red-shafted Flicker" occurs. The 2 are distinguished by the dominant color on the underneath side of the wing, which is visible only in flight. As with Florida's other large woodpecker (Pileated), the Northern Flicker is regarded as a "keystone" species that is important to other species which use its excavations for shelter and nesting. Thus recent unexplained declines in the population of this species is a cause for concern.

Class - **Aves** (birds)

Order - **Piciformes** (woodpeckers)

Family - **Picidae** (woodpeckers)

Red-headed Woodpecker *Melanerpes erythrocephalus*	Red-bellied Woodpecker *Melanerpes carolinus*	Yellow-bellied Sapsucker *Sphyrapicus varius*

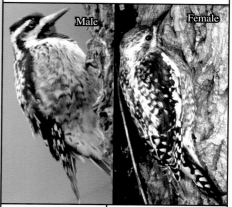

Size: 9.25 inches.

Abundance: Uncommon.

Migratory Status: Year-round resident of Florida.

Presumed range in Florida

Size: 9.75 inches.

Abundance: Very common.

Migratory Status: Year-round resident of Florida.

Presumed range in Florida

Size: 8.5 inches.

Abundance: Fairly common.

Migratory Status: Winter migrant and winter resident.

Presumed range in Florida

Variation: No sexual variation. Juveniles have gray-brown heads and brown wings.

Variation: Female has gray crown. Juvenile lacks all head markings and head is uniformly gray.

Variation: Male has red patch on throat, female's throat is white. Juveniles lack red markings on head/throat.

Habitat: Savanna-like habitats with widely spaced, large trees are the preferred habitat of the Red-headed Woodpecker. They seem to show a preference for areas near lakes or rivers.

Habitat: A woodland species that inhabits all forest types in the eastern United States. Uses both mature woodlands and successional forests and shows a preference for edge areas.

Habitat: In winter, this woodpecker occupies a wide variety of woodland habitats. Birds that winter in Florida use mixed woodlands, but usually prefer at least some hardwoods.

Breeding: Nest hole is usually in a dead tree but it is also fond of using utility poles. 5 eggs is typical and some may produce 2 broods per summer.

Breeding: Nests in holes excavated by the adults. 4 to 5 eggs are laid in mid-April to early June. Most nest cavities are in dead trees, but may use live.

Breeding: Nest is an excavated hole in dead tree or a living tree with heart rot. Clutch size ranges from 2 to 7 eggs. Does not breed in Florida.

Natural History: Once regarded as very common, this handsome woodpecker has declined significantly in the last century. It eats large amounts of acorns and other mast, especially in fall and winter, and may move about in fall and winter in search of areas with good mast crops. Insects are regularly eaten in warmer months and some may be caught on the wing, but they also commonly forage on the ground. Although they may be found throughout the state they seem to be relatively uncommon, and overall this species has experienced a nationwide population decline. The Red-headed Woodpecker was apparently well-known to many Native Americans, and was a war symbol of the Cherokee.

Natural History: Feeds on all types of tree-dwelling arthropods as well as seeds, nuts, fruit, and berries. Widespread and common throughout the eastern half of the US, generally east of the Rocky Mountains. These woodpeckers are known to take over the nest holes of the endangered Red-cockaded Woodpecker where their ranges overlap in the southern United States. Conversely, the introduced Starling sometimes takes over the nest hole of the Red-bellied Woodpecker. Due to its fairly large size and its tendency to be quite vocal year-round, the Red-bellied Woodpecker is a fairly conspicuous bird in both rural and urban areas. Like other woodpeckers, they will come to bird feeders for suet or sunflower seeds.

Natural History: The Yellow-bellied Sapsucker is unique among Florida woodpeckers in that it creates feeding opportunities by drilling small holes into the bark of trees. These holes, called "sap wells," fill with sap which the sapsucker then drinks. Sapsuckers regularly visit the "sap wells" to maintain them and defend them from other sapsuckers. Many other bird species benefit from the Sapsucker's activities, especially the Ruby-throated Hummingbird, which will drink sap from the woodpecker's holes. The sap also attracts insects which in turn feed many species of insectivorous birds. In addition, the nest holes excavated by the sapsucker may be used other birds, flying squirrels, etc.

Class - **Aves** (birds)
Order - **Piciformes** (woodpeckers)
Family - **Picidae** (woodpeckers)

Hairy Woodpecker *Picoides villosus*	**Downy Woodpecker** *Picoides pubescens*	**Red-cockaded Woodpecker** *Picoides borealis*

Hairy Woodpecker	Downy Woodpecker	Red-cockaded Woodpecker
Size: 9.25 inches.	**Size:** 6.75 inches.	**Size:** 8.5 inches.
Abundance: Uncommon.	**Abundance:** Common.	**Abundance:** Rare.
Migratory Status: Mostly a winter resident in Florida.	**Migratory Status:** Year-round resident of Florida.	**Migratory Status:** Year-round resident of Florida.

Presumed range in Florida (Hairy)
Presumed range in Florida (Downy)
Presumed range in Florida (Red-cockaded)

Variation: Male has red spot on nape.	**Variation:** Male has red spot on nape.	**Variation:** Female lacks red "cockade."
Habitat: A forest species that likes woodlands with large, mature trees.	**Habitat:** Occupies a wide variety of woodland habitats throughout the state.	**Habitat:** Old growth pine forests and mature pine savannas.
Breeding: Nest hole may be in dead snags or living trees with heart rot. 4 eggs is typical.	**Breeding:** Nests is usually excavated in a dead limb. Eggs range from 3 to as many as 8. Eggs hatch in 12 days.	**Breeding:** Nest is excavated into the trunk of a mature, living pine tree, usually infected with heartwood fungus.

Natural History: The range of the Hairy Woodpecker closely coincides with that of the smaller Downy Woodpecker and they occur sympatrically in Florida. The 2 are often confused but the Hairy is a much larger bird and has a heavier, longer bill. Like the Downy, this woodpecker excavates nest holes that may be used by a variety of other species, making it an important species in forest ecosystems. A wide variety of insects and other arthropods are eaten along with seeds and fruits. This species can be seen at feeders and although it is less common than its smaller cousin, it can often be seen in the company of the Downy Woodpecker. When both are seen together, size differences become more apparent. The Hairy Woodpecker varies somewhat geographically in both size and coloration. Western specimens have few white spots on the wings. Specimens shown above are typical for the eastern United States.

Natural History: Ranging across all of North America except the far North and the desert Southwest, the Downy is one of the most widespread woodpeckers in American and is one of the most common woodpeckers in Florida. These appealing little woodpeckers are well-known and frequent visitors to bird feeders where they eat suet and seeds. Arthropods are the most important food item, making up as much as 75 percent of the diet. Fruit and sap is also eaten. Like other woodpeckers, the Downy's nest holes in dead limbs and trunks may be utilized by a wide array of other species as a home and shelter. Many small cavity nesting birds may use old woodpecker holes, and mice, lizards, snakes, treefrogs, spiders, and insects can often be found using their abandoned nests. The Downy Woodpecker is very similar to the Hairy Woodpecker but is smaller and has a thinner beak. It is also much more common.

Natural History: Very similar to the 2 preceding species but much rarer. The name comes from the presence of a tiny red spot on each side of the nape of the male (often very hard to see in the field). This woodpecker is an endemic of the southern pine forests and pine savannas that were once common across the southeast. It is a specialist of the habitat known as "Longleaf Pine/Wiregrass Habitat." As much as 90 percent of this habitat is now gone from the Southeast (nearly 100 percent of the virgin Longleaf Pines are gone). As a result, the Red-cockaded Woodpecker is today listed as a federally endangered animal. Attempts to restore mature Longleaf/Pine Wiregrass habitats are being undertaken by both state and federal forest management agencies in the southeast and the Red-cockaded Woodpecker has begun to recover. Nesting colonies are closely monitored and protected.

Class - **Aves** (birds)

Order - **Columbiformes** (doves)

Family - **Columbidae** (doves)

White-winged Dove *Zenaida asiatica*	**Mourning Dove** *Zenaida macroura*	**Eurasian Collared-Dove** *Zenaida decaocto*

White-winged Dove	Mourning Dove	Eurasian Collared-Dove
Size: 11.5 inches.  Presumed range in Florida	**Size:** 12 inches.  Presumed range in Florida	**Size:** 13 inches.  Presumed range in Florida
Abundance: Uncommon.	**Abundance:** Very common.	**Abundance:** Fairly common.
Migratory Status: Year-round resident and winter migrant.	**Migratory Status:** Year-round resident of Florida.	**Migratory Status:** Year-round resident of Florida.
Variation: None, sexes alike.	**Variation:** None, sexes alike.	**Variation:** None, sexes alike.
Habitat: Original habitat was arid and semi-arid country. Deserts, arid grasslands, and xeric woodlands. Today they can be seen in suburbs.	**Habitat:** Agricultural areas and open lands with short grass or areas of bare ground. Also common in parks and suburbs in urban areas.	**Habitat:** Open and semi-open lands. Agricultural areas and small towns are favored. Common around small towns and in suburbs.
Breeding: The nest is a flimsy platform of sticks containing 2 eggs. Will sometimes nest in colonies. 2 eggs.	**Breeding:** Builds a flimsy nest of small sticks in sapling or low branch usually from 6 to 15 feet above ground. 2 eggs.	**Breeding:** Usually nests in trees or bushes near human habitation. Lays 2 eggs per clutch with multiple broods.
Natural History: The White-winged Dove is a southwestern species originally native to the American deserts, Mexico, and Central America. In the last few decades it has begun to expand its range eastward. It is spreading rapidly across the southeast and it may already occupy most or all of Florida (the range map above is an approximation). Along with the Mouring Dove, this species is regarded as game bird and is widely hunted in Texas and in Mexico. Although similar in size to the Mourning Dove, the White-winged appears a bit stockier. Food is mostly seeds and mast but they also eat the fruits of cacti and shrubs such as privet. The population of these birds in Texas plummated in the early 1900s, probably due to loss of habitat. They appear to have recovered there and as previously mentioned are now thriving and expanding across the southeastern United States.	**Natural History:** Mourning Doves are regarded as a game species throughout much of the United States, including Florida. The US Fish and Wildlife Service estimates that as many as 20 million doves are killed each fall during America's dove season. While that seems an appallingly high number, the Mourning Dove is actually one of the most numerous bird species in America and the total population is estimated at around 350 million birds! Seeds are the chief food item. They will eat everything from the tiniest grass seeds to every type of seed crop produced by man, including corn, wheat, sorghum, millet, and sunflower as well as peanuts and soybeans. They can be frequent at bird feeders. This abundant species may be facing competition from the invasive Eurasian Collard Dove, which occupies a similar ecological niche and which is becoming increasingly more common.	**Natural History:** Originally native to Eurasia, the Collared-Dove has colonized much of the southern United States since its release in the Bahamas in the 1970s. Since then, they have rapidly expanded their range north and west. Today they have colonized nearly all of the United States except for the northeast and the northern Atlantic states. In food habits and other aspects of its biology, the Collard-Dove is similar to the Mourning Dove. Young Collard-Doves disperse widely and this species continues to increase across North America. Cold weather does not seem to be a limiting factor but food availability may limit range expansion. How far this species will extend its range in North America is still unknown. As with all other members of the Columbidae family, young birds are fed a semi-liquid "crop milk" regurgitated from the adults' crop.

Class - **Aves** (birds)

Order - **Columbiformes** (doves)

Family - **Columbidae** (doves)

Common Ground Dove *Columbina passerina*	**White-crowned Pigeon** *Patagioenas leucocephala*	**Rock Pigeon** *Columba livia*

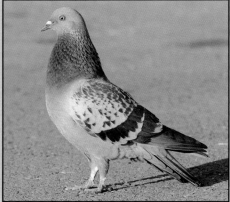

Size: 6.5 inches.	**Size:** 13.5 inches.	**Size:** 13 inches.
Abundance: Uncommon.	**Abundance:** Uncommon.	**Abundance:** Very common.
Migratory Status: Year-round resident of Florida.	**Migratory Status:** Summer resident in southernmost Florida.	**Migratory Status:** Year-round resident of Florida.

Presumed range in Florida

Presumed range in Florida

Presumed range in Florida

Variation: Males are more reddish.	**Variation:** No significant variation.	**Variation:** Highly variable (see below).
Habitat: Uses xeric woodlands, dry, sandy savanna, dunes, and sandy scrub. Likes bare ground and open habitats.	**Habitat:** Mangroves are widely used along the coasts and on islands. Also uses hardwood hammocks.	**Habitat:** Farms and ranches in rural areas and parks and streets, parks, and shopping malls in urban environments.
Breeding: Nest is a slightly concave platform woven of grasses and twigs and placed in a low bush. Sometimes nest on the ground. 2 eggs is typical.	**Breeding:** Most nesting in Florida takes place in mangroves in Florida Bay (often over water) or in the Keys. 2 eggs is typical but may be only 1.	**Breeding:** Nests on man-made ledges and beneath overhangs in cities. Bridges and barns are used in rural areas. Multiple nesting with 2 eggs per clutch.

Natural History: This is the smallest member of the Columbridae family. Unlike other doves, this species is not seen in large flocks but rather in mated pairs. These small doves were fairly common in Florida just a few decades ago and can still be fairly common in the Citrus Groves of central Florida. But overall, the species appears to be in decline in the state. The cause of this decline is unknown. Most members of the genus Columbina are tropical birds and this is the most northerly ranging species of the genus. They occur throughout the southern US from the Carolinas to southern California. They range southward through Mexico and Central America into northern South America, and they are well distributed throughout the Caribbean. Their diet includes a wide variety of seeds and berries as well as some insects. In flight, it shows bright reddish brown wings.

Natural History: The White-crowned Pigeon is mainly a tropical bird that ranges as far north as the southern tip of the Florida peninsula in summer. It is most common in Florida in the Keys and it is fairly common and wide-ranging across the Caribbean, being found on most islands having a cover of trees. The diet of this species seems to consist mostly of fruits and berries and it is thus dependent upon the presence of fruit and berry-bearing plants. Loss of habitat and overhunting has reduced the population in many areas of the Caribbean, and today it is regarded as Threatened Species. Although restricted mostly to the Everglades region of southern Florida, a few individuals may wander northward up the peninsula in summer. A few individuals may stay year-round in the state in the extreme southern tip of Florida and especially in the Keys, but most move south in winter.

Natural History: Although the Rock Pigeon is about the same overall length as the Mourning Dove and Collard Dove, the pigeon is a much stockier, heavier bird that weighs over twice as much as the Mourning Dove. Despite the fact that this familiar bird ranges from coast to coast across North America, the Rock Pigeon is not a native species. It was introduced into North America by the earliest European settlers in the 1600s. Pigeons followed the first settlers into America (including Florida), colonizing towns and settlements and living in close proximity to rural farms and livestock. Today, they are one of the most familiar urban birds in America and are also common around farms and ranches. Young pigeons known as "Squab" are eaten in many places throughout the world. Rock Pigeons are incredibly variable and can exhibit almost any color or pattern.

Class - **Aves** (birds)	
Order - **Galliformes** (chicken-like birds)	
Family - **Phasianidae** (grouse)	Family - **Odontophoridae** (quail)
Wild Turkey *Meleagris gallopavo*	**Bobwhite** *Colinus virginianus*

Size: Males to 47 inches.	Presumed range in Florida	**Size:** 10 inches.	Presumed range in Florida
Abundance: Fairly common.		**Abundance:** Fairly common.	
Migratory Status: Year-round resident of Florida.		**Migratory Status:** Year-round resident of Florida.	
Variation: Females are smaller, duller, have less red on head and neck, and lack the "beard."		**Variation:** Sexually dimorphic. As with all ground nesting birds, females are drabber.	

Habitat: Inhabits all major habitats in the state except for extensive wetlands and urban areas. Most common in mixture of woods and farms.

Habitat: Small woodlands, edge areas, and Pine Savanna. Overgrown fields bordering agricultural land are one of its favorite habitats.

Breeding: Nests on the ground in thick cover such as thickets, honeysuckle, Multiflora Rose, or tall grasses. Lays up to 14 eggs.

Breeding: Ground nester. Clutch size averages about 15 eggs but nest failure due to predation is high. Multiple nestings are common.

Natural History: There are several subspecies of Wild Turkey in the United States. The race known as the Osceola Turkey is found in Peninsular Florida, while the Eastern Wild Turkey occupies most of the panhandle. The courtship of the male Wild Turkey includes a "strutting" display that involves spreading the tail feathers, drooping the wings, and producing a low frequency "drumming" sound. When attempting to attract females in the spring breeding season, males become quite vocal and regularly emit a loud "gobble" that can be heard for a mile. The saga of the disappearance and resurgence of the Wild Turkey in America is one of wildlife managements greatest success stories. In pioneer days, turkeys were found throughout the eastern half of America but by the early 1900s they had disappeared from many regions. Re-stocking efforts by the state wildlife agencies, aided by sportsmen groups, has been highly successful and Wild Turkeys are now found in suitable habitats throughout the state. The National Wild Turkey Federation is an organization dedicated to conservation of the species.

Natural History: Bobwhite have always been an important game bird in the United States. In recent decades, however, the species has experienced significant population declines, especially in the northern portions of its range (including all the Midwest and much of the mid-South). Some blame a resurgence in predators for the decline, and that is undoubtably a part of the problem. But the real culprit is modern agricultural practices that have eliminated fence rows and created expansive crop fields with no ground cover. This is the main factor contributing to the decline of the Bobwhite. A large crop field of a single plant species is typically devoid of wildlife in any significant amount. Bobwhite will feed along the edges of crop fields if there is sufficient cover nearby, but modern row crop practices are ecologically detrimental. Through fall and winter, Bobwhite stick together in family groups known as a "covey." In spring, adults pair off for breeding with the resultant offspring and their parents producing the next fall's covey. Mortality through the winter is high and survivors from more than one covey will often join together as winter wanes.

Class - **Aves** (birds)		
Order - **Psittaciformes** (parrots)		
Family - **Psittacidae**		

Monk Parakeet *Myiopsitta monachus*	**Budgerigar** *Melopsittacus undulatus*	**Nanday Parakeet** *Nandayus nenday*

Size 11.5 inches.	Presumed range in Florida 	Size: 7 inches.	Presumed range in Florida	Size: 12 inches.	Presumed range in Florida 
Abundance: Fairly common.		**Abundance:** Uncommon.		**Abundance:** Uncommon.	
Migratory Status: Non-migratory, year-round resident.		**Migratory Status:** Non-migratory, year-round resident.		**Migratory Status:** Non-migratory, year-round resident.	

Variation: No significant variation among adults.	**Variation:** Selective breeding by man has produced many color variants.	**Variation:** No significant variation among adults.
Habitat: Native to South America where it uses forests and savannas. In the US, it has adapted well to urban parks and can be found as far north as Chicago and New England.	**Habitat:** Native to Australia. In Florida, it is restricted to urban environments. Not known to thrive in Florida's wild environments. May possibly be seen anywhere in the state in towns an cities.	**Habitat:** Native to South America in Peru, Brazil, Paraguay, and Argentina. Known from at least 14 counties in Florida where it uses both urban habitats and natural pinelands.
Breeding: Nest is built of sticks and is large and bulky. 4 to 6 eggs.	**Breeding:** A cavity nester but may use man-made nest boxes. Up to 12 eggs.	**Breeding:** Known to nest on cliffs and in cavities in native range.

Natural History: Introduced. Shown above are 3 of the Florida's psittacine birds. All are introduced along with as many as 6 dozen other species of parrots and parakeets that have been observed living in the wild in Florida (source: Florida Wildlife Conservation Commission website). The Florida eBird "Illustrated Checklist" webpage lists 26 species that are regularly to rarely sighted in the state. Some are very rare and restricted to a small area, while at least 1 (Monk Parakeet) is fairly widespread and expanding its range. Many others are only occasionally seen as escaped or intentionally released pets. The Monk Parakeet often nests in colonies and may construct a huge, heavy nest of sticks. Their habit of commonly using man-made structures such as utility poles and towers sometimes causes short-circuit fires and power outages. The Budgerigar was for a time fairly common and widespread in Florida as a breeding bird but has apparently declined significantly in recent years. Its popularity as a caged species will likely insure that escapees and intentionally released birds will continue to repopulate urban and surburban areas in the state. Nanday Parakeets (also called Black-hooded Parakeets) have been reported in the state since the late 1960s but are apparently restricted to southeastern Florida and the Tampa Bay area. The species is native to South America. Ironically, America's only native psittacine bird, the **Carolina Parakeet** (*Conuropsis carolinensis*), became extinct in the early 1930s. The reason for their disappearance is not completely understood, but they apparently began to decline with the European invasion of America. The last of these birds seen in the wild were living in central Florida.

Class - **Aves** (birds)

Order - **Caprimulgiformes**

Family - **Caprimulgidae** (nightjars)

Common Nighthawk *Chordeiles minor*	**Whip-poor-will** *Antrostomus. vociferus*

Size: 9.5 inches.

Abundance: Fairly common to uncommon.

Migratory Status: A summer resident and a seasonal migrant. Many will spend the summer in Florida while others merely pass through the state en route to breeding grounds farther north.

Presumed range in Florida

Variation: Sexes alike. No significant variation.

Habitat: Open and semi-open areas. Can be common around cities and towns but also in rural areas. Open forests, large forest openings, recently logged, very early regenerative woodlands, and dunes may be used in Florida.

Breeding: No nest is constructed and 2 eggs are laid on bare gravel. Most nests are on flat, gravel-covered rooftops.

Natural History: These birds sometimes go by the nickname "Bullbat." They are can be quite common in urban areas in summer but they are also seen in open and semi-open rural areas. Like our other nightjars, the Common Nighthawk feeds on the wing, catching moths and other flying insects. But unlike the others, this bird is active both at night and at dawn and dusk, or sometimes on cloudy days. Around towns and cities they chase airborne insects attracted to streetlights at night. This is one of the great travelers of the bird world, wintering in South America. Their summer range includes nearly all of North America south of the Arctic. Nighthawks are usually seen in flight, but they will occasionally be spotted resting atop a fence post in open country. They often migrate in large flocks, sometimes numbering over 1,000 birds. Along with other members of the Caprimulgidae family, these birds have experienced a precipitous decline in recent years. Seen in Florida from April through September.

Size: 12 inches.

Abundance: Uncommon to rare.

Migratory Status: Fairly common to uncommon as a seasonal migrant and uncommon to rare as a winter resident. Population peaks in March with spring migration.

Presumed range in Florida

Variation: Sexes alike. No significant variation.

Habitat: Forest edge, power-line cuts through wooded areas, and xeric woods. Show a preference for deciduous and mixed forest over pure conifers. Favors thickets for daytime roosting.

Breeding: Nests on the ground amid leaf litter. No nest is built and the eggs (usually 2) are laid on the ground.

Natural History: Few animals exhibit a more cryptic color and pattern than this species. When resting on the forest floor during the day, they are nearly invisible. A very similar species, the **Chuck-wills-widow** (*A. carolinensis*) is an uncommon summer resident in most of the state and a winter resident in the southern tip. It is smaller (9.75 inches) and browner than the Whip-poor-will. The two are easily differentiated by the their songs, usually described as *whip-prrr-weel* for the Whip-poor-will and as *chuk-wills wee-dow* for the Chuck-will's-widow. Both calls are usually repeated rapidly and at times incessantly. Equipped with a very large mouths for feeding on moths and other large flying insects, both species are nocturnal and catch most of their food in midair. Both species have experienced an unexplained decline in populations over the last decade. It has been suggested that a decline in large moths and other flying insect prey may be to blame.

Class - **Aves** (birds)

Order - **Strigiformes** (owls)

Family - **Strigidae** (typical owls)

Eastern Screech Owl *Megascops asio*	**Burrowing Owl** *Athene cunicularia*	**Barred Owl** *Strix varia*

Red morph

Gray morph

Size: 8.5 inches.	**Size:** 9.5 inches.	**Size:** 21 inches.
Abundance: Failry common.	**Abundance:** Uncommon.	**Abundance:** Fairly common.
Migratory Status: Year-round resident of Florida.	**Migratory Status:** Year-round resident of Florida.	**Migratory Status:** Year-round resident of Florida.

Presumed range in Florida

Presumed range in Florida

Variation: 2 distinct color morphs. See photos above.

Variation: Juveniles have unspotted, buff-colored breast and belly.

Variation: No sexual variation. 3 subspecies are known in America.

Habitat: All types of habitats within the state may be used, including suburban areas and in the vicinity of farms. Favors edge areas, fence rows, etc.

Habitat: Open country. In Florida most likely to be seen in dry prairies and upland pastures in the southern two-thirds of the peninsula.

Habitat: Woodlands primarily. Especially in swampy areas and riparian corridors, but also in upland woods. May occur woodlots within urban areas.

Breeding: Nest is in tree hollows and old woodpecker holes. 4 to 6 eggs are laid and young fledge in June.

Breeding: Nest is in an old Armadillo or Gopher Tortoise burrow or in a burrow dug by the owls. 4 to 6 eggs.

Breeding: Nest is usually in tree cavities but known to nest tree crotches or old hawk nests. Usually 2 eggs are laid.

Natural History: The eerie call of the Screech Owl is often described as "haunting and tremulous." Despite being at times vocal birds, these small owls often go unnoticed. They may even live in suburban yards and small towns, especially if older, large trees with hollow limbs and trunks are present. They feed on insects such as crickets and grasshoppers and on a wide variety of small vertebrate prey including mice, voles, and songbirds that are plucked from their roosts at night. These wide-ranging birds are found throughout the eastern United States as from the Atlantic to the Rocky Mountains and from southern Canada to Florida and Mexico. Birds in the northern portions of their range can be negatively impacted by severe winters. They will take up residence in man-made nest boxes.

Natural History: Burrowing Owls that live in Florida are a distinct subspecies from those that live in the American west. The food of the Burrowing Owl in Florida includes almost any animal small enough to be killed and swallowed. Insects and other invertebrates are a major part of the diet but lizards, small snakes, frogs, rodents, and a few birds are also eaten. These small owls have always captured the interest of Floridians. A few live in urban parks in southeastern Florida where they share the park with recreating humans. Park personnel place ropes around the burrows and both owls and humans curiously watch each other from a safe distance during the day. At night, the owls prowl the park and hunt nearby lawns. Despite their seeming adaptability to human activities, they are in decline and are a Threatened Species in Florida.

Natural History: The Barred Owl ranges throughout the eastern half of the United States from the eastern edge of the Great Plains eastward. The 8-noted call of the Barred Owl is described as "Hoo-hoo-hoo-hoo, hoo-hoo-hooaahh." In addition, the species is capable of a wide array of hoots, screeches, and coarse whistles. Small vertebrates are the main prey, especially rodents like voles, mice, and flying squirrels. Birds, lizards, small snakes, and amphibians are also eaten. In the eastern United States, the range of the Barred Owl closely coincides with that of the Red-shouldered Hawk and the 2 predators are often regarded as ecological counterparts occupying the same niche at different times. This is a woodland species that favors lowland areas and can be common in swamps and river bottoms in Florida.

Class - **Aves** (birds)

Order - **Strigiformes** (owls)

Family - **Strigidae** (typical owls) | Family - **Tytonidae** (barn owl)

Great Horned Owl *Bubo virginianus*	Short-eared Owl *Asio flammeus*	Barn Owl *Tyto alba*

Size: 23 inches.	Presumed range in Florida 	**Size:** 15 inches.	Presumed range in Florida 	**Size:** 16 inches.	Presumed range in Florida 
Abundance: Fairly common.		**Abundance:** Very rare in FL.		**Abundance:** Rare in Florida.	
Migratory Status: Year-round resident of Florida.		**Migratory Status:** Very rare winter migrant in Florida.		**Migratory Status:** Year-round resident of Florida.	

Great Horned Owl	Short-eared Owl	Barn Owl
Variation: Males are slightly smaller and have a larger white patch on throat.	**Variation:** Females tend to be slightly darker.	**Variation:** Females have more buff on breast and sides, more spots on belly.
Habitat: Woodlands, semi-open, and open habitats are all utilized, but most common in mosiac of upland woods and fields.	**Habitat:** These are open country birds and the primary habitat is prairie, marsh, and tundra. They steadfastly avoid wooded areas.	**Habitat:** Prefers open and semi-open habitats. Short grass pastures are a favorite hunting ground. Probably more common around farms and small towns.
Breeding: One of the earliest nesting birds in America. Horned Owls may be sitting on eggs by late January (even earlier in Florida). Nest is often an old hawk nest. 2 eggs is usual.	**Breeding:** Nest is on the ground. A slight depression is scraped out by the owl and lined with grasses. 5 or 6 eggs is typical. Nest is usually amid grasslands. Does not nest in Florida.	**Breeding:** Nested in hollow in trees or in caves historically. Now uses old buildings or barns. Up to 11 eggs hatch days apart producing owlets of many sizes and ages.
Natural History: There are 10 subspecies of Great Horned Owl in North America. Occurs throughout the Americas from Alaska to southern South America. In the US, specimens from the western portions of the country are much paler than those seen in the east. In the eastern United States, Red Cedars and other evergreen trees are a favorite roosting site. The Great Horned Owl is the ecological counterpart of the Red-tailed Hawk, hunting much the same prey in the same regions, with the hawk hunting by day and the owl at night. These powerful predators eat a wide variety of small animals. Rabbits are a favorite food item. They are also known to eat larger mammals like muskrats, groundhogs, and even skunks or rarely, domestic cats!	**Natural History:** In Florida, the Short-eared Owl is most likely to be seen in open regions during winter, often in coastal dunes. A few birds from the far north rarely will wander into the state in winter and an individual from the Cuban or Puerto Rican population sometimes shows up in southern Florida. The food is mostly small rodents. Voles are the most significant item in their diet. Rodent prey is located mostly by sound while flying low and slow over open, grassy fields. Most hunting is done at night or dusk and dawn, but these owls are more diurnal than most and may hunt during the day. The erectile feathers on the face that form the "ears" are not usually visible unless the owl is agitated or defensive. They appear to be in decline in much of America.	**Natural History:** The Barn Owl is one of the most widespread owl species in the world, being found throughout most of North America, south of Canada, all of Central and South America, most of Europe and sub-Saharan Africa, parts of southern Asia, and all of Australia. In spite of its wide range, they are usually not common anywhere. Small rodents are the primary prey, especially mice and voles. When feeding a large brood of young, a pair of Barn Owls may catch over 2 dozen mice in a single night. Like other owls, their hearing is so acute they can catch mice unseen beneath leaves by homing in rustling sounds. Ironically, man's attempts to control rodents with poisoned baits may be in part responsible for the demise of rodent-eating species like the Barn Owl.

Class - **Aves** (birds)
Order - **Falconiformes**
Family - **Falconidae** (falcon family)

Peregrine Falcon *Falco peregrinus*	**Merlin** *Falco columbarius*	**American Kestrel** *Falco sparverius*
		 Female · Male
Size: 17 inches.  Presumed range in Florida **Abundance:** Uncommon. **Migratory Status:** Winter resident and winter migrant.	**Size:** 11 inches.  Presumed range in Florida **Abundance:** Uncommon. **Migratory Status:** Winter resident and winter migrant.	**Size:** 10 inches.  Presumed range in Florida **Abundance:** Fairly common. **Migratory Status:** Seen year-round except in summer.
Variation: Juvenile birds have dark streaks on the breast rather than bars.	**Variation:** Male has blue-gray back, female and immatures have brown back.	**Variation:** Sexually dimorphic. Male has gray wings, female brown.
Habitat: Prefers cliffs in remote wilderness areas but has adapted to living among skyscrapers in many cities.	**Habitat:** Habitat is open regions. In Florida, it is most common in coastal marshes and dunes in winter.	**Habitat:** Throughout its range the Kestrel is seen in open country. Least common in forested regions.
Breeding: Nests on ledges of cliff faces and on man-made structures like skyscrapers and bridges. 4 eggs is typical, sometimes up to 6.	**Breeding:** Breeds far to the north in Canada, Alaska, and parts of the north-central Rockies and plains. Uses old crow or hawk nests as well as cliffs.	**Breeding:** Usually nests in tree cavities or old woodpecker holes within trees situated in open fields. May also nest in man-made structures. 4 to 5 eggs.
Natural History: Falcons are fast flying birds and the Peregrine is among the fastest. Hunts pigeons, waterfowl, shorebirds, grouse, etc. Hunting technique usually involves soaring high above and diving in on birds in flight, or diving toward resting birds and panicking them into flight. Once airborne, no other bird can match the Peregrine's speed. Diving Peregrines may reach speeds approaching 200 mph, making them perhaps the fastest animal on earth. This species has recently been reintroduced into many areas of the eastern United States after being extirpated as a breeding bird many decades ago. The name "peregrine" means "wanderer," and these birds may be seen almost anywhere in North America, although they are still quite rare in the eastern interior of the continent. Widespread in Florida in winter.	**Natural History:** The Merlin is seen in Florida mainly in winter (or as an occasional wandering bird). These small falcons are only slightly larger than the Kestrel and they are easily confused with that species. The facial markings of the Merlin are less distinct than the Kestrels, and they appear somewhat stockier in build. Summering mostly far to the north and wintering along coastlines, their migration routes are mostly in the western United States or along the Atlantic Coast. Like most falcons, however, these birds are prone to wander widely. Although they may occur almost anywhere in the state, they are most common in coastal regions and in expansive marshes, prairies, or pastures. Food is mostly small birds, especially shorebirds. In urban areas, they may focus on common species like house sparrows. Insects are also food items.	**Natural History:** While the Kestrel is a fairly common bird in open regions throughout America, there has been some decline in populations in the eastern United States in recent years. But they remain America's most common falcon species. Though they are sometimes called "Sparrow Hawk," these are true falcons. The Kestrel is widespread throughout North and Central America and as many as 17 subspecies are recognized. They are often seen perched on power lines and poles along roadways in rural farmlands throughout the country, but they are uncommon in the heavily forested regions. Insects are the major food in summer (especially grasshoppers). In winter they eat small mammals and rarely, small birds. Hunts both from a perch and by hovering over open fields. Availability of suitable nest cavities may limit distribution in places.

Class - **Aves** (birds)

Order - **Falconiformes**	Order - **Cathartiformes**	
Family - **Falconidae** (falcon family)	Family - **Cathartidae** (vultures)	

Crested Caracara *Caracara cheriway*	**Turkey Vulture** *Catharus aura*	**Black Vulture** *Coragyps atratus*

Size: 23 inches.

Abundance: Uncommon.

Migratory Status: Year-round resident in Florida.

Presumed range in Florida

Variation: Juveniles have buffy rather than whitish-colored throat.

Habitat: In Florida, this species is found mostly in the dry prairie habitats of the southern peninsula.

Breeding: Nest is made of sticks and place in the top of a tree. Nests may be reused and be quite bulky. 2 to 4 eggs.

Natural History: In appearance the Caracara looks like a hybrid between a vulture and an eagle. In habits they are also bimodal, feeding both on carrion and hunting down small animals ranging from insects to small mammals and snakes. Extreme opportunists, they will eat virtually any type of small animal they can catch and kill. They will also raid the nest of other birds and steal the eggs (or the fledglings) and they have even been known to scratch open turtle nests for eggs. This is strictly a warm climate species. They range from south Texas through Mexico and Central America as well as much of South America. In North America they are restricted to semitropical environments and the Florida population is disjunct from other North American populations. They also occur on the island of Cuba. In Texas they often go by the name "Mexican Buzzard."

Size: 26 inches.

Abundance: Common.

Migratory Status: Year-round resident in Florida.

Presumed range in Florida

Variation: Skin on face is pinkish gray on immature birds, bright pink on adult.

Habitat: Seen in all habitats throughout the state. Less common in urban areas and expansive swamps.

Breeding: Nests in large tree hollows or on the ground in hollow logs. Almost always lays 2 eggs.

Natural History: The absence of feathers on the head and neck of vultures is an adaptation for feeding on carrion. Vultures may stick the head deep inside a rotting carcass and feathers would become matted with filth. The bare skin on the neck and face on the other hand is constantly exposed to the sterilizing effects of sunlight. Turkey Vultures are one of the few birds with a well-developed sense of smell, and food is often located by detecting the odor of rotting flesh. Sight is also important and they become quite familiar with the landscape of their territory. They are quick to notice a fresh carcass on a roadway within their territory. Newly mowed fields and other disturbed areas within their range are closely scanned for small animal victims. Highly social, they roost communally, sometimes with Black Vultures. Vultures have benefited from a constant supply of road-killed animals.

Size: 25 inches

Abundance: Very common.

Migratory Status: Year-round resident in Florida.

Presumed range in Florida

Variation: Older birds have lighter gray heads with more wrinkles.

Habitat: Found in a wide variety of habitats throughout the state. Can be very common around cattle ranches.

Breeding: No nest is built and the 2 eggs are laid on a bare surface. The nest site is often in a derelict building.

Natural History: America's vultures are named for the color of the skin on the face. Turkey Vultures have reddish skin (like a turkey). Black Vulture has dark gray or black facial skin. Black Vultures also have shorter tails and lesser wing span, giving them a much "stubbier" look than the Turkey Vulture. Vultures were once regarded as a threat to livestock by spreading disease. In fact, the powerful digestive juices of the gut of vultures destroys bacteria. They may actually help control diseases. Both the Turkey Vulture and the Black Vulture have the unappealing habit of defecating on the legs and feet as a way of disinfecting the feet (which can become quite nasty and the birds feed on rotted carcasses). Black Vultures lack the well-developed sense of smell of Turkey Vultures, but they do have keen eyesight. Although smaller than the Turkey Vulture, they are more aggresive.

Class - **Aves** (birds)

Order - **Acciptridiformes**

Family - **Pandionidae** (osprey)	Family - **Accipitridae** (eagles, hawks, and kites)	
Osprey *Pandion haliaetus*	**Bald Eagle** *Haliaeetus leucophalus*	**Northern Harrier** *Circus cyaneus*

Osprey	Bald Eagle	Northern Harrier
Size: 30 inches.	**Size:** 31 inches.	**Size:** 24 inches.
Abundance: Fairly common.	**Abundance:** Uncommon.	**Abundance:** Fairly common.
Migratory Status: Year-round resident in Florida.	**Migratory Status:** Year-round resident in Florida.	**Migratory Status:** Winter resident and migrant.

Presumed range in Florida (for each species)

Variation: No significant variation. Females are slightly larger than males.	**Variation:** Juvenile lacks the characteristic white head and tail.	**Variation:** Strongly sexually dimorphic. See photos above.
Habitat: Typically seen in the vicinity of large lakes and rivers inland and along coastlines. Always near water.	**Habitat:** Like Ospreys, Bald Eagles are associated with water. Large rivers, lakes, wet prairies, and marshes.	**Habitat:** Open country. Pastures, marshes, agricultural fields, wet prairies and grasslands.
Breeding: Bulky stick nest is often built on man-made structures like bridges and power line towers. 2 to 4 eggs.	**Breeding:** Extremely bulky stick nest is reused and gets larger each year. Usually only 2 eggs per clutch.	**Breeding:** Nests on the ground in thick grass. Builds a nest of grasses and weed stems. Lays 4 to 6 eggs.
Natural History: Subsists mainly on fish. No other raptor is as specialized for piscivorous lifestyle. Hunting tactics consist of a steep dive that ends with the Osprey plunging feet first into the water, allowing them to catch fish up to 3 feet below the surface. Most fish caught in fresh water are nongame species, thus they have little to no impact on sport fisheries. Like the Bald Eagle, Osprey populations in the mid-United States plummeted dramatically in the first half of the twentieth century. The same types of conservation efforts that restored the Bald Eagle (including reintroduction programs) have brought Osprey numbers back to respectable levels. Once regarded as an endangered species, the Osprey has recovered enough to have recently been delisted. Most states now boast healthy populations of nesting Ospreys and they continue to increase across the country.	**Natural History:** One of the great conservation success stories, Bald Eagles were highly endangered just a few decades ago. Strigent protection, banning of the pesticide DDT, and a widespread education campaign has lead to a remarkable recovery. They first began to recover as a breeding species in most of the country in the 1980s following years of strict protection and banning of DDT, but Florida's wild waterways were always a stronghold. Bald Eagles feed largely on fish and carrion but are also capable hunters. Some birds specialize in hunting migratory waterfowl in winter, picking off birds wounded by hunters. Bald Eagles wander widely in the winter and may be seen virtually anywhere in the state, but they are nowhere numerous. Most nesting is around large rivers, lakes or expansive wetlands. The national emblem of the United States of America since 1782.	**Natural History:** The range of the Northern Harrier is Holarctic and includes Europe and northern Asia as well as North America. Unlike most diurnal raptors that hunt entirely by sight, the Northern Harrier mimics the technique used by owls and hunts partly by sound. A special "parabola" of feathers surround the face and direct sound waves to the ears. It hunts by flying low to the ground with a slow, buoyant flight that resembles a giant butterfly. Food is mostly small mammals and birds, but reptiles and amphibians are also listed as food items. Roosting and nesting on the ground and hunting as much by sound as by sight, the Northern Harrier is unique among America's diurnal raptors. In historical times before the draining of America's marshes, this was a more common species. Loss of habitat on prairie breeding grounds is also a problem for this species.

Class - **Aves** (birds)

Order - **Acciptridiformes**

Family - **Accipitridae** (eagles, hawks, and kites)

Sharp-shinned Hawk *Accipiter striatus*	**Cooper's Hawk** *Accipiter cooperi*	**Mississippi Kite** *Ictina mississippiensis*

Size: 9 to 13 inches. **Abundance:** Uncommon. **Migratory Status:** Winter resident and winter migrant.	**Size:** 19 inches. **Abundance:** Fairly common. **Migratory Status:** Year-round resident in Florida.	**Size:** 14 inches. **Abundance:** Uncommon. **Migratory Status:** Summer resident in the panhandle.

Presumed range in Florida (all three columns)

Variation: Females are larger. Juveniles are heavily streaked with dark brown.

Variation: Ontogenetic plumage variation (see photos). Females can be 30 percent larger than males.

Variation: Juveniles are streaked with brown on the breast. Adults very similar but males have lighter gray heads.

Habitat: Forests and thickets. Found in both rural and urban areas where vegetative cover is present.

Habitat: Woodlands, regenerative areas, and edge habitats are favored. Can also be seen in tree-lined urban yards.

Habitat: In Florida, the Mississippi Kite mostly frequents mature hardwood forests along major rivers.

Breeding: Pine trees are a favored locale for placing the nest. Lays as many as 8 eggs, with 5 to 6 being the average.

Breeding: Stick nest is built high in tree and eggs are laid in April or May. Clutch size averages 4 to 6.

Breeding: Builds a stick nest high up in a large tree. Nests across the panhandle and into the Big Bend. Lays 2 eggs.

Natural History: A relentless hunter of small songbirds, the Sharp-shinned Hawk is sometimes seen raiding backyard bird feeders and they are known to pluck baby songbirds from nests. These small raptors are capable of rapid, twisting flight while pursuing their small songbird prey through woodlands and thickets. In Florida, they are seen from late September through April when birds that summer farther north move southward. No nesting occurs in Florida and many will nest far to north, some as far north as Alaska and the Yukon Territory. The Sharp-shinned Hawk is a widely distributed species that ranges across all of North America south of the Arctic region and southward all the way to southern Central America. These small hawks are easily overlooked since they favor dense thickets and woodland habitats.

Natural History: Feeds almost exclusively on birds and is known to haunt backyard bird feeders. These hawks are a major predator of the Bobwhite, an important game species that is in decline throughout most of its range. Cooper's Hawks are fierce hunters that will fearlessly attack birds as large or larger than themselves, including grouse, waterfowl, and domestic chickens. Although quite widespread and fairly common, they are not as observable as the Buteo hawks. Cooper's Hawks tend to stay in wooded areas and thickets with heavier cover than their bulkier cousins. These birds are fast fliers and capable of great maneuverability, an adaptation to hunting in forest and thickets. They have adapted well to human activities and they sometimes exist in urban areas, especially in parks and heavily wooded neighborhoods.

Natural History: With their small beaks and feet, the Mississippi Kite appears somewhat delicate-looking compared to other raptors. In flight they are one of the most graceful. The several species that make up the raptor group known as kites are mainly tropical birds. The Mississippi Kite is the most northerly ranging of the kites, and can be seen as far north as southern Illinois in summer months. Long distance migrants, they arrive in Florida by early May and leave for South America by mid-September. These are gregarious birds that may nest communally and in some parts of their range it is not uncommon to see several nests in close proximity or see groups of birds soaring together. They feed on insects and small vertebrates. Flying insects are taken on the wing, and lizards may be plucked from tree limbs.

Class - **Aves** (birds)
Order - **Acciptridiformes**
Family - **Accipitridae** (eagles, hawks, and kites)

Swallow-tailed Kite *Elanoides forficatus*	White-tailed Kite *Elanus leucurus*	Snail Kite *Rostrhamus sociabilis*

Size: 22 inches.	**Size:** 15 inches.	**Size:** 17 inches.
Abundance: Uncommon.	**Abundance:** Very rare in FL.	**Abundance:** Rare.
Migratory Status: Summer resident and seasonal migrant.  Presumed range in Florida	**Migratory Status:** Very rare year-round resident.  Presumed range in Florida	**Migratory Status:** Rare year-round resident in south Florida.  Presumed range in Florida
Variation: Adults have longer tails.	**Variation:** Juvenile has mottled wings.	**Variation:** See Natural History below.
Habitat: A tropical species that in Florida uses a wide variety of habitats. Requires large trees for nesting.	**Habitat:** Open country. Likes grasslands and prairies, both wet and dry. Also uses savanna-like habitats.	**Habitat:** Freshwater marshes. Also uses canals and lake shores. Mainly in the Everglades and the Kissimmee Valley.
Breeding: In Florida the nest is built of sticks and Spanish moss and is usually near the crown of a very tall Pine tree. 2 eggs is usual.	**Breeding:** Very little information is available on nesting for this species in Florida. Nest is made of twigs and grass and placed in a tree. 4 eggs is usual.	**Breeding:** Nest is usually over water in a shrub or small tree. Sometimes several nests in the same vicinity. Lays 2 to 3 eggs on average.
Natural History: Among the many unique and beautiful birds of Florida, the Swallow-tailed Kite stands out for its striking black and white color, long, forked tail, and gracefulness in flight. Add to that a delicate, almost fragile appearance and you have a bird that never fails to elicit appreciation from both avid birdwatchers and typical residents throughout the state. Almost never seen perched, the Swallow-tailed Kite is seemingly always aloft. Its graceful command of invisible air currents gives the impression of effortlessness in flight. It feeds mostly on the wing and will pluck prey from treetops or out of the air. It usually then eats while in flight. In addition to insects, it will eat lizards, frogs, small snakes, and nestling birds. These birds once ranged much farther north in summer, as far as southern Minnesota in the Mississippi Valley and southwestern Ohio in the Ohio Valley.	**Natural History:** Another primarily tropical kite that ranges into southern Texas and is a very rare resident in the Everglades region of Florida. They are a fairly common bird along the western coastline of America as far north as southern Washington. The bulk of the range is in Mexico, Central America, and down into South America. When not breeding, these birds are quite gregarious and will roost communally. Hunts by soaring and hovering as well as from a perch. In food preference this kite is a small mammal specialist and it feeds almost entirely on small mammals. This is a rather rare situation for a predator. Since every meal must first be hunted down and killed, most predators are consumate opportunists and will take a wide variety of prey species. Like other kites, this bird has a graceful countenance in the air. The name "kite" is appropriate for these aerodynamic birds.	**Natural History:** Snail Kites exhibit sexual dimorphism. Males are slate gray while females and juveniles are a mottled brown with light splotches. The core range of this tropical species is in southern Mexico and Central/South America. Florida populations are endemic to the once great "river of grass" that flowed from the upper Kissimmee River to Florida Bay. Thanks to the changes wrought upon this important ecosystem by man, the Snail Kite in Florida is now an Endangered Species. The aptly named Snail Kite is a true dietary specialist that feeds entirely upon freshwater snails, mostly Apple Snails (genus *Pomacea*). The deeply hooked upper mandible of the Snail Kite is an adaptation for deftly removing snails from their shell. Hunts by soaring and gliding over expansive marshes, plucking snails from the stems of emergent marsh grasses.

Class - **Aves** (birds)
Order - **Acciptridiformes**
Family - **Accipitridae** (eagles, hawks, and kites)

Short-tailed Hawk *Buteo brachyurus*	Broad-winged Hawk *Buteo platypterus*	Red-shouldered Hawk *Buteo lineatus*

Light morph

Adult

Juvenile

Size: 16 inches.

Abundance: Very rare in FL.

Migratory Status: Rare year-round resident in south FL.

Presumed range in Florida

Size: 16 inches.

Abundance: Fairly common.

Migratory Status: Summer in panhandle, winter in south.

Presumed range in Florida

Size: 17 inches.

Abundance: Common.

Migratory Status: Year-round resident in Florida.

Presumed range in Florida

Variation: 2 color morphs, light and dark. See Natural History below.

Variation: First-year plumage is mottled brown (see juvenile Red-shouldered).

Variation: Female is larger. Ontogenetic variation (see above).

Habitat: In Florida, this species inhabits open lands adjacent to woodlands. Pasture and prairie with nearby woods.

Habitat: Favors large tracts of unbroken deciduous woodlands or mixed deciduous/conifer woods in upland areas.

Habitat: Woodlands of all kinds, but especially woods bordering swamps, rivers, or along wooded creek-sides.

Breeding: Bulky nest of sticks and Spanish moss is placed high up in trees. Nests as early as February. 2 eggs.

Breeding: Stick nest is in a tree crotch, usually in deep woods. Lays 2 to 3 eggs on average.

Breeding: Bulky stick nest is in the fork of a tree about 20 to 40 feet high and often near water. 2 to 4 eggs in April.

Natural History: Another primarily tropical species that ranges northward onto the Florida peninsula. The bulk of this species range is from southern Mexico south to southern South America. It can be found year-round in southernmost Florida and the keys and as far north as the Big Bend region in summer. Two distinct color morphs occur. The dark morph appears nearly solid black from a distance, while the light morph shows an all-white breast, throat, and belly. White morphs have a distinctive dark "hood" that covers the head and side of the face. The 2 color morphs regularly interbreed. This species has never been common in the state, and today the total population is estimated to be no more than 500 individuals, making it perhaps the rarest bird in Florida. Despite being very rare in Florida, it is common and widespread in Central and South America.

Natural History: A decidedly woodland raptor whose breeding range in North America closely mimics the Eastern Temperate Forests Level I ecoregion. This species is more common in the Appalachian Highlands and in interior regions where expansive forest remain (such as the Ozarks). They may be seen as a migrant throughout Florida. They do nest in the panhandle region and will winter in the Everglades. Elsewhere in the state they are seen as seasonal migrants in spring and fall. They are less conspicuous than most hawks except during the fall migration when they band together in large flocks known as "kettles." Extremely large flocks that may contain 200 birds can be seen during fall migrations. Food includes insects, but consists mostly of small vertebrates like rodents as well as a large amount of reptile and amphibian prey.

Natural History: The Red-shouldered Hawk is the daytime counterpart of the Barred Owl, and the 2 species often occur in the same territory. These are vocal birds. Their call, described as "kee-ah, kee-ah, kee-ah," is rapidly repeated about a dozen times. They can be fairly tame if unmolested and their raucous calling will not go unnoticed when the nest is nearby. They feed on a wide variety of small vertebrates but mostly eat reptiles, amphibians, and rodents. The range of the Red-shouldered Hawk coincides closely with the Level 1 ecoregion known as the Eastern Temperate Forest. However, a disjunct population (subspecies *elegans*) is found on the West Coast of North America in the Mediterranean California Ecoregion. In America, this hawk is most common in portions of the country that are more heavily forested and shows a preference for bottomland forests.

Class - **Aves** (birds)

Order - **Acciptridiformes**

Family - **Accipitridae** (eagles, hawks, and kites)

Red-tailed Hawk *Buteo jamiacensis*	**Swainson's Hawk** *Buteo swainsoni*

Typical

Dark-morph

Light-morph Adult

Juvenile

Size: 19 inches.

Abundance: Common.

Migratory Status: Year-round resident.

Variation: Highly variable. Can vary from nearly solid dark brown to very pale (almost white). Most adult birds are like the typical adult specimen pictured on top left above. Light and dark morphs are mostly winter migrants in Florida. Females are about 20 percent larger than males. Juveniles have brownish tails with dark crossbars. Some experts recognize as many as 16 subspecies throughout North America.

Light-morph

Size: 19 inches.

Abundance: Rare in Florida.

Migratory Status: Rare winter resident in southernmost Florida.

Presumed range in Florida

Variation: Shows significant age-related variation (see inset photo) as well as light and dark color morphs.

Habitat: Swainson's Hawk is a prairie/grassland obligate that spends the summer on North America's prairies and desert grasslands. Most winter in the Pampas region of Argentina and make an annual migration of 10,000 miles. One of the greatest migrations of any raptor. A few winter in the grasslands of southern Florida each year.

Habitat: Found in virtually all habitats within the state except perhaps extensive swamps. Likes open and semi-open areas and is uncommon in continuous forest, although they do occur there. Favors a mosaic of woodlands, farmland, fencerows, overgrown fields, etc.

Presumed range in Florida

Breeding: In Florida, the large stick nest is built high in trees. Nest is usually situated in place that is remote from human activities. Lays 2 to 4 eggs. Young fledge at 6 weeks.

Breeding: Stick nest is built in isolated trees on the open plains, usually in a Cottonwood. Nests on native prairie and on pastures/rangelands. Lays 2 to 4 eggs, rarely 5.

Natural History: This is the most common and widespread large *Buteo* hawk in America. Their range includes all of North America south of the Arctic and much of the Caribbean and Central America. The Red-tailed Hawk is generally regarded as the daytime counterpart of the Great Horned Owl, hunting by day many of the same species in the same habitats utilized by the owl at night. "Red-tails" prey mostly on rodents (mice, voles, and ground squirrels). Much larger prey like rabbits may also be taken on occasion. In some areas, ground-dwelling birds like quail are taken and they have been known to attack large flocks of blackbirds. They also take large snakes such as the Rat Snake (*Pantherophis*) or Pine Snake (*Pituophis*). Large examples of these snakes (which are strong constrictors) have been known to turn the tables and end up killing a hungry hawk. Though accomplished predators, these large hawks are not above eating carrion and they may be seen feeding on road kills.

Natural History: Feeds on a variety of small vertebrates, mostly rodents, but also small snakes, lizards, birds, and large insects. Will hunt both from a perch and by soaring. These raptors are quite common on the high northern plains of the Dakotas in summer. In fall, they often migrate in huge flocks known as "kettles" that can contain hundreds of hawks. The hawks circle upward in rising thermals to great height, then soar horizontally to the next updraft.

Class - **Aves** (birds)
Order - **Gruiformes** (rails and cranes)
Family - **Rallidae** (rails)

King Rail *Rallus elegans*	**Virginia Rail** *Rallus limicola*	**Clapper Rail** *Rallus crepitans*

King Rail

Size: 16 inches.

Abundance: Uncommon.

Migratory Status: Year-round resident in Florida.

Presumed range in Florida

Variation: Juvenile is dusky gray.

Habitat: Marshes. Found throughout the state in freshwater marshes and along the coast in brackish water. Some move inland into central US in summer.

Breeding: Builds a loosely woven cup from marsh vegetation. Breeding takes place on summer range well to the north of Florida.

Natural History: Rails are well adapted to life in the marsh. They move with ease through thick grasses and rarely fly except when migrating. They can run quite fast through the grass and rarely offer more than a glimpse. They can also swim and dive beneath the surface, using the wings to swim underwater. Despite the fact that rails are listed as a game bird by most state wildlife agencies, almost no one hunts them, due probably to their scarcity and secretiveness. They feed mostly on aquatic insects and their larva, spiders, and other invertebrates. Some plant material is also eaten. The species has declined from its historical breeding range in the central United States and is today quite rare except in the Lower Coastal Plain from Texas to the Carolinas. Probably can be found statewide in Florida where suitable habitat exists.

Virginia Rail

Size: 9.5 inches.

Abundance: Uncommon.

Migratory Status: Winter resident in Florida.

Presumed range in Florida

Variation: Juvenile is darker.

Habitat: Primarily a marsh dweller. In migration may visit ponds, swamps, or wet meadows. Uses fresh, brackish, and salt marshes in Florida.

Breeding: Builds a nest platform of aquatic vegetation a few inches above water level. Nest is usually well hidden among vegetation. Lays 8 or 9 eggs.

Natural History: The Virginia Rail is more common than the larger King Rail, but this is not a common bird in the state and this fact coupled with its secretive nature means that it is a species that remains unfamiliar to most Floridians. Historically, this species was much more common in America, but today very little of the wetland habitats that once occurred in the eastern United States remain. As a result, this species along with its larger cousin the King Rail are both species being monitored by many state wildlife agencies in their former breeding range in the Midwest. One other rail species, much rarer and even more secretive, is the **Black Rail** (*Laterallus jamiacensis*). It has been observed in the state, but sightings in Florida of the species are extremely rare. Trained birders locate it hidden deep within the marsh by listening for its call.

Clapper Rail

Size: 14.5 inches.

Abundance: Fairly common.

Migratory Status: Year-round resident in Florida.

Presumed range in Florida

Variation: Juvenile is grayer.

Habitat: An obligate of salt marsh that ranges along America's coastlines from Massachusetts to northern Mexico. Found in salt marsh along state's coasts.

Breeding: Nest is built in the marsh amid emergent vegetation. Some nests may be inundated by high tides. Clutch size can range from 4 to 16 eggs.

Natural History: Despite the fact that the Clapper Rail is listed as a game bird by Florida Game and Fish Commision, almost no one hunts them, due probably to their secretiveness and the difficulty of accessing their habitats within expansive salt marshes. Rail hunters must pole throught the marsh at high tide to flush birds for gunning. Few people not actively seeking this secretive bird will ever see one as they typically remain hidden in thick marsh grasses. At low tide, they can sometimes be glimpsed as they emerge onto bare mud flats. They can, however, easily be heard calling within the marsh. They feed mostly on aquatic insects and their larva, spiders, and other invertebrates. Some plant material is also eaten. In the northern potions of their range along the Atlantic Coast they may be migratory, but Florida birds are sedentary.

Class - **Aves** (birds)

Order - **Gruiformes** (rails and cranes)

Family - **Rallidae** (rails)

Sora *Porzana carolina*	**American Coot** *Fulica americana*	**Common Gallinule** *Gallinula galeata*

Size: 9 inches. **Abundance:** Uncommon. **Migratory Status:** Winter resident in Florida. Presumed range in Florida 	**Size:** 15 inches. **Abundance:** Fairly common. **Migratory Status:** Year-round resident in Florida. Presumed range in Florida 	**Size:** 14 inches. **Abundance:** Common. **Migratory Status:** Year-round resident in Florida. Presumed range in Florida 
Variation: Juvenile lacks black on face and throat. Sexes are alike.	**Variation:** Sexes alike. Juvenile paler gray with yellowish beak.	**Variation:** Sexes alike. Juvenile is paler gray without red bill and forehead.
Habitat: Primarily a marsh dweller. Favors heavily vegetated wetlands.	**Habitat:** Rivers, lakes, large ponds, marshes, and wetlands.	**Habitat:** Freshwater wetlands and lake shores with abundant vegetation.
Breeding: Builds a nest platform of aquatic vegetation a few inches above water level. Nest is well hidden in dense upright plants. Does not breed in Florida. Lays 8 to 11 eggs.	**Breeding:** Breeds mostly to the north and to the west of Florida, but does nest sporadically in Florida. Nest is a platform built amid emergent vegetation. About 6 eggs are laid.	**Breeding:** Nest is a platform of vegetation slightly above the waterline and usually well concealed. Nests throughout the state. Will lay as many as 10 eggs.
Natural History: The Sora is one of the more observable of America's rails. Still, it is fairly secretive, especially during fall migration. They are usually observable on both breeding and wintering grounds, but catching a glimpse of this species can be difficult. They are vocal birds, however, and their whinnying call can be heard for a long distance. They feed on a variety of aquatic invertebrates but also eat seeds of aquatic plants, particularly wild rice. Soras have exceptionally long toes, an adaptation that allows for walking across floating vegetation. Although the Sora is one of the most common and widespread rail species in America, their dependence upon wetlands renders them vulnerable. America's wetlands remain under a constant assault from land developers and agricultural interests.	**Natural History:** During migration and in winter, American Coots gather in large flocks on open water and behave more like ducks than rails. During the breeding season, they act more like rails and live among cattails and reeds in freshwater marshes. But they are not as elusive as the rails and are usually easily observed even in summer. They are considered a game species, but rarely hunted as most waterfowl hunters regard them as a "trash" species. They sometimes go by the nickname "Mud Hen." Although the feet are not webbed as with ducks and geese, their long toes are equipped with lateral lobes which flare out when swimming and create an ample surface for pushing against the water. They feed both on land (on grasses) and in the water (aquatic plants, algae, and aquatic invertebrates). Small fish and small amphibians are also food.	**Natural History:** Sometimes known as the Common Moorhen, but that name is properly reserved for a very similar bird that lives in Europe. Although these birds may be seen in suitable habitat throughout they rather secretive. In the Deep South and in Florida they can be quite common and usually more observable than they are in more northerly portions of their range. They feed largely on seeds of aquatic plants but also eat animal matter, most predominantly snails and insects. Although similar to the American Coot in size and appearance, the Common Gallinule is rarely seen in the open and prefers to stay close to heavy cover. Additionally, they don't form large flocks as do American Coots. However, they can be quite tame and approachable within the heart of their range in Florida and the Lower Coastal Plain.

Class - **Aves** (birds)

Order - **Gruiformes** (rails and cranes)

Family - **Rallidae** (rails)	Family - **Aramidae** (limpkin)	Family - **Gruidae** (cranes)

Purple Gallinule
Porphyrio martinica

Limpkin
Aramus guaruana

Young

Sandhill Crane
Antigone candensis

Size: 13 inches.

Abundance: Fairly common.

Migratory Status: Year-round resident in Florida.

Presumed range in Florida

Size: 26 inches.

Abundance: Uncommon.

Migratory Status: Year-round resident in Florida.

Presumed range in Florida

Size: 42 inches.

Abundance: Failry common.

Migratory Status: Year-round resident and migrant.

Presumed range in Florida

Variation: Juveniles are a dull olive green with buff-colored breast and belly.

Variation: White spots on juveniles appear more streaked rather than spotted.

Variation: Juvenile has brownish head (see bird on right above).

Habitat: Favors freshwater marshes. Also uses edges of lakes. Requires ample floating aquatic vegetation.

Habitat: Riparian areas, marshes, swamps, canals, edges lakes, and other shallow water areas.

Habitat: Open lands, pastures, mudflats, marshes, and shallow water areas. In migration uses harvested crop fields.

Breeding: Nest is usually over water and often a platform built on floating vegetation. Clutch size varies but can be at least as high as 6 eggs.

Breeding: Nesting can occur from early winter (south) to early spring (north). Nest may be a mat of floating vegetaion or above water. 5 or 6 eggs is average.

Breeding: Typically lays 2 eggs on a platform nest built of vegetation. There are breeding populations in Florida.

Natural History: Neon blue and purple plumage with a bright red cere and long yellow legs make this an almost gaudy bird. Although definitely tropical in appearance and mostly restricted in range to the Deep South, this species is known for rare individual birds that have wandered far to the north. There is one record of nesting in southern Ohio! By contrast, the species ranges as far south as South America. Summer birds can be seen northward into the Carolinas, southern Georgia, and southern Alabama, but these birds retreat southward into peninsula Florida in winter, swelling the ranks of those that live year-round in the state. A similar-looking species from the Middle East and Asia known as the **Gray-headed Swamp Hen** (*P. poliocephalus*) has become established in the Everglades region.

Natural History: In the United States the Limpkin is a species that is found only in Florida. It also ranges from southern Mexico southward though South America. The food of the Limpkin is almost exclusively snails and the long decurved bill is used to deftly remove snails from their shell. These unusual birds are the only members of their family (Aramidae) and while they resemble many of the rails, they are generally considered to be most closely related to the cranes. Once quite common throughout most of the peninsula, their populations have declined very significantly since the begining of the twentieth century. Development and loss of wetlands are a perennial threat to many of Florida's unique and special wildlife species and the Limpkin is one of those species.

Natural History: Standing over 3 feet tall, the Sandhill Crane is one of the largest birds seen in America. Populations were seriously depleted by the beginning of the twentieth century, but the species has recovered dramatically in the last few decades. The largest populations are seen west of the Mississippi River and number tens of thousands. Eastern populations have been slower to recover but are now reasonably healthy. Some states now allowing hunting seasons on this species. America's other crane species, the **Whooping Crane** (*Grus americana*), is the nation's rarest bird with less than 500 indviduals remaining in the wild. It is both a winter migrant and a year-round resident in a few areas of the south-central peninsula of Florida. It stands nearly 5 feet tall with a 7-foot wingspan.

Class - **Aves** (birds)

Order - **Pelecaniformes** (herons, pelicans, ibis, and spoonbill)

Family - **Threskiornithidea** (ibis and spoonbill)

Roseatte Spoonbill *Platalea ajaja*	**Glossy Ibis** *Plegadis falcinellus*	**White Ibis** *Eucocimus albus*

Juvenile
Adult

Size: 32 inches.

Presumed range in Florida

Abundance: Uncommon.

Migratory Status: Year-round resident in Florida.

Variation: No sexual dimorphism. Juvenile birds are much paler.

Habitat: Found in all types of shallow aquatic habitats in the state. Swamps, marshes (fresh and salt), shallow lakes, mangroves, canals, etc.

Breeding: Breeds colonially. Nest is built in trees or shrubs over water or on an island. 3 to 4 eggs is average.

Natural History: Feeds by feel. The unique "spoon"-shaped bill is swept back and forth through the water in a semi-open position and snaps shut when aquatic organisms are touched. Small fish, crayfish, crabs, and insects are known food items. Spoonbill populations are today recovering from a very low ebb at the beginning of the twentieth century. They are still not as numerous as they were historically, and given the pressures being exerted on Florida's natural environments by a large and still growing human population, this species will likely never again be as common as it was prior to the European invasion of America. Florida's other large, pinkish bird is the **Greater Flamingo** (*Phoenicopterus ruber*) which exists as a very rare, semi-tame bird in parks and suburbs in the southern tip of the state.

Size: 23 inches.

Presumed range in Florida

Abundance: Fairly common.

Migratory Status: Year-round resident in Florida.

Variation: Seasonally variable, breeding plumage is more iridescent.

Habitat: Fresh and saltwater marshes, estuaries, swamps, flooded fields, and pastures. Almost any shallow water habitat may be used.

Breeding: Nests in low trees, shrubs, mangroves usually over water. 3 or 4 eggs is usual.

Natural History: These are birds mostly of the Lower Coastal Plain of the Atlantic and Gulf Coasts. They winter along the Coastal Plain from east Texas to South Carolina. In summer some move northward along the coast as far as Maine, occupying marshes and estuaries all along the way. A few will move into inland areas in summer, mostly along major river valleys like the Mississippi and Ohio, but they are rare away from the Coastal Plain. Food is mainly crayfish, but they will eat a wide variety of small aquatic vertebrate and invertebrate prey. The long, decurved bill is used to "feel" for food in mud, muck, and shallow water. In contrast to many bird species native to Florida, the Glossy Ibis seems to be thriving and expanding its range farther and farther to the north.

Size: 25 inches.

Presumed range in Florida

Abundance: Common.

Migratory Status: Year-round resident in Florida.

Variation: Juvenile has brown on wings, back, neck, and head.

Habitat: Fresh and saltwater marshes, estuaries, swamps, flooded fields, pastures, and rice fields. Almost any shallow water habitat may be used.

Breeding: Nest is in a low tree or bush. Often nests in colonies, including rookeries with herons or egrets. 2 to 5 eggs.

Natural History: Like the preceding species feeds by tactile sense with the decurved bill but also hunts by sight. Crustaceans are the main prey but many types of aquatic organism are eaten. These birds can be seen both in Florida's remote wilderness and in the midst of urban sprawl. They usually associated with water (marshes, swamps, canals, etc.) but they are also commonly seen in suburban lawns and around retention ponds within shopping malls. Like many other wading birds, White Ibis are colony birds that roost and nest in large groups. While this species has adapted admirably to mankind's changes to Florida's ecosystems, it is much less numerous than it once was, and loss of freshwater wetland habitats throughout its range poses a real threat to its ability to maintain a healthy population.

Class - **Aves** (birds)

Order - **Pelecaniformes** (herons, pelicans, ibis, and spoonbill)

Family - **Ardeidae** (herons)

American Bittern *Botaurus lentiginosus*	**Least Bittern** *Ixobrychus exilis*	**Great Blue Heron** *Ardea herodias*

Size: 26 inches.	**Size:** 13 inches.	**Size:** 47 inches.
Abundance: Uncommon.	**Abundance:** Uncommon.	**Abundance:** Common.
Migratory Status: Winter resident, September through April.	**Migratory Status:** Year-round resident in Florida.	**Migratory Status:** Year-round resident in Florida.
Presumed range in Florida	Presumed range in Florida	Presumed range in Florida

Variation: None. Sexes alike. | **Variation:** See both sexes above. | **Variation:** 2 color morphs.

Habitat: Large freshwater marshes are used in summer, coastal marshlands in winter. | **Habitat:** Favors marshes with dense growths of tall grasses and sedges. Uses both fresh and brackish marshes. | **Habitat:** Along rivers and streams, swamps, marshes, ponds, and wet meadows and floodplains.

Breeding: Nest is in dense emergent vegetation of the marsh and is well hidden. 3 to 5 eggs is typical. Breeds far to the north of Florida. | **Breeding:** Nest is a well concealed platform built amid dense growth of cattails or other sedges/grasses. Up to 6 eggs are laid. | **Breeding:** Nests in colonies. Nest is a platform of sticks in tree or bush above water. Nest is a bulky platform of sticks. 3 to 4 eggs is typical.

Natural History: The biology of this species is not well-known. Presumably they may be seen anywhere in suitable habitats in the state, and they are frequent in Everglades National Park in winter. But few visitors to the park will ever see one, as they are usually quite secretive and remain hidden among thick stands of cattails. Hunts by stealth and may remain motionless for long periods of time. The eyes of this heron are situated with a downward slant, better facilitating the bird's ability to see into the water. When startled, they will throw the head back and point the beak straight up. The streaked brown pattern of the neck and breast is remarkably cryptic amid vertical stalks of marsh grasses and sedges, and an individual in "frozen" posture becomes almost invisible. Like most herons, an opportunistic feeder. Eats fish, amphibians, crayfish, small mammals, and some insects.

Natural History: This smallest of American herons is also a secretive bird that often stays hidden in dense marsh grasses and sedges. When alarmed, they point their bill skyward and freeze, mimicking the vertical vegetation of their habitat. These small herons move with ease through thick stands of marsh vegetation. When flushed, they fly only a short distance just above the vegetation before dropping back down. Despite their seemingly weak flying abilities, some will migrate great distances from wintering areas in south Florida and the Caribbean to summer breeding grounds that may be as far north as northern Minnesota. They have very long toes for grasping stems of grass and sedge. Feeds on small fish, insects, crayfish, and amphibians. This species has declined significantly over the last century. In some areas of its summer range it is now threatened.

Natural History: The largest heron in North America, the Great Blue Heron will eat almost anything it can swallow. Fish and frogs are major foods, but it also eats snakes, salamanders, small mammals, and even small turtles. Birds are sometimes eaten, including other smaller heron species. All food items are swallowed whole. Large prey is killed by stabbing repeatedly with the beak or by bashing against a hard object. Smaller prey is often swallowed alive. Hunts both day and night and reportedly has good night vision. Great Blue Herons are found throughout most of the United States and much of Canada, including in riparian habitats in desert regions. Sexes are alike but juveniles will have streaked breast and neck and are duskier overall than adults. A solid white subspecies is found in parts of southern Florida (see inset photo above).

Class - **Aves** (birds)

Order - **Pelecaniformes** (herons, pelicans, ibis, and spoonbill)

Family - **Ardeidae** (herons)

Great Egret *Ardea alba*	Snowy Egret *Egretta thula*	Little Blue Heron *Egretta cearulea*

Great Egret — *Ardea alba*

Size: 39 inches.

Presumed range in Florida

Abundance: Very common.

Migratory Status: Year-round resident in Florida.

Variation: Breeders acquire plumes.

Habitat: Along major streams, lakes, swamps, and marshes. Also wet meadows, low-lying areas, and open fields.

Breeding: Nests in colonies, often with other wading bird species. Nest is a platform of sticks in tree or bush above water. Lays 3 or 4 eggs.

Natural History: This heron species (along with the Snowy Egret and several other herons) was nearly hunted to extinction during the last half of the nineteenth century. The long, wispy feathers of breeding birds (known as "plumes") were once used to adorn the hats of fashionable ladies. The plumes are most pronounced during the breeding season. Thus the catastrophic impact of the plume hunters was magnified as hunters killed birds at their nesting colonies. Killing of parent birds doomed nestlings as well. Efforts to save this and other plume bird species lead to some of America's earliest laws to protect wildlife. Today this species is still a symbol of conservation efforts and is the logo of the National Audubon Society. It is also known by the names Common Egret or Great White Egret. As with many other herons, it often nests in large colonies.

Snowy Egret — *Egretta thula*

Size: 24 inches.

Presumed range in Florida

Abundance: Common.

Migratory Status: Year-round resident in Florida.

Variation: Breeders acquire plumes.

Habitat: In the vicinity of streams, lakes, swamps, and marshes. Also low-lying area, roadside ditches, etc.

Breeding: Like other herons, they will nest in colonies with different heron species. Nest is made of sticks and twigs. 3 to 5 eggs is average.

Natural History: As with several other heron species, the Snowy Egret during breeding season sports long "plume" feathers on the back. The plumes of the Snowy Egret were the most highly valued and their value once exceeded that of gold on an ounce-for-ounce basis. As with other plume bird species the Snowy Egret was nearly wiped out by the feather trade of the late 1800s. Today, the species has recovered to healthy numbers but remains under threat due to its dependence upon coastal wetlands. This species feeds on smaller prey such as worms, insects, crustaceans, amphibians, and small fish. It is an active feeder that often chases prey through the shallows rather than using the stealth method employed by its larger cousins. It also often feeds by swishing its feet in the mud to disturb benthic organisms. Similar to the Great Egret but smaller and has black bill and bright yellow feet.

Little Blue Heron — *Egretta cearulea*

Juvenile

Size: 24 inches.

Presumed range in Florida

Abundance: Common.

Migratory Status: Year-round resident in Florida.

Variation: See Natural History below.

Habitat: Wetlands. Inhabits swamps, marshes, lake shores, etc. May be seen in roadside ditches and small ponds.

Breeding: Builds a stick nest platform in bushes and low trees in wetlands. Lays 2 to 5 eggs. Most breeding in Florida is on the Peninsula.

Natural History: Even within the heart of its range along the Lower Coastal Plain of the southeastern US, the Little Blue Heron is generally less common that other heron species. In Florida, however is can be quite common. The dark plumage of adults and its rather secretive nature make it one of the least observable of our herons. Like most herons, it is an opportunistic feeder that eats almost anything it can swallow. Food is mostly frogs, fish, crustaceans and insects. It is a daytime hunter that hunts by stalking slowly through wetland habitats. First-year birds are solid white transforming to blue at one year of age. The transitional plumage of the juvenile is unique, and produces for a brief time a white bird with blue splotches. Blue increases throughout the molt, ending in a solid blue adult.

Class - **Aves** (birds)

Order -Pelecaniformes (herons, pelicans, ibis, and spoonbill)

Family - **Ardeidae** (herons)

Tri-colored Heron *Egretta tricolor*	**Reddish Egret** *Egretta rufescens*	**Cattle Egret** *Bulbulcus ibis*

Size: 26 inches.	**Size:** 30 inches.	**Size:** 19 inches.
Abundance: Fairly common.	**Abundance:** Uncommon.	**Abundance:** Very common.
Migratory Status: Year-round resident in Florida.	**Migratory Status:** Year-round resident in Florida.	**Migratory Status:** Year-round resident in Florida.
Presumed range in Florida 	Presumed range in Florida	Presumed range in Florida
Variation: None. Sexes alike.	**Variation:** 2 color morphs occur.	**Variation:** See Natural History below.
Habitat: Shows a distinct preference for estuaries and salt and brackish marshes in coastal regions, but it may use freshwater habitats as well.	**Habitat:** More tied to salt water than any other American heron. Mainly restricts itself to coastal lagoons, shallow bays, and salt marsh.	**Habitat:** Unlike other herons, these birds are less tied to aquatic situations and are usually seen in open pastures and fields in association with cattle.
Breeding: Will nest in colonies with other heron species. Nest is a flimsy platform of sticks built above water. 3 to 4 eggs is usual. Maximum of 5.	**Breeding:** Nest is built of sticks and often placed in a fork of a mangrove over water. 3 or 4 eggs is typical but could be as many as 7.	**Breeding:** Stick nest built in trees or bushes. Nests are usually over water. Nests in large colonies. 3 or 4 eggs is average.
Natural History: Although it is found throughout the Caribbean and in southern Mexico and Central America, the range of the Tri-colored Heron in the US is restricted to the Lower Coastal Plain from Texas to the Florida Peninsula. Its food consists mostly of small fishes. The Tri-colored Heron is less likely to be seen in large flocks than many other herons, and they are usually seen singly or in pairs. At one time this was a very common bird along America's Gulf Coast. But there is some evidence that this species is now declining in its range in North America. No definitive explanation for the decline is known. Loss of habitat and contamination by chemicals in the food chain are possible explanations. Its status elsewhere in its range is not known. This species is also commonly called "Louisiana Heron."	**Natural History:** This is the least common heron species in America. In Florida it is regarded as a Threatened Species. The Reddish Egret is widespread along America's southern coastlines and can be found from Florida to southern California. But in the US it is nowhere a common species. This is strictly a coastal species and although some rare wanderers have been recorded well inland in the US, it is very rare to see this bird away from saltwater habitats. As with many other of its relatives, the Reddish Egret was hard hit by plume hunters in the late 1800s and the species was all but wiped out in many areas of its range. An all white color morph (see inset photo above) is rather rare in Florida, but occurs much more commonly in other regions such as in the Caribbean, Mexico, and Central America.	**Natural History:** The Cattle Egret is one of our most interesting heron species. Originally native to Africa, Cattle Egrets began an inexplicable range expansion in the early 1800s. They first migrated across the Atlantic to South America and then appeared in North America around 1950. The species continues to expand its range and is today an uncommon summer migrant as far north as the Great Lakes. Their name is derived from their habit of associating with cattle herds in pastures. Before expanding their range out of Africa they associated with herds of Cape Buffalo, Hippopotamus, and wild ungulates. They feed mostly on insects that are disturbed by the large grazers they follow through pastures and grasslands. Develops orange highlights on throat and crown during breeding (see photo above).

Class - **Aves** (birds)
Order - **Pelecaniformes** (herons, ibis, pelicans, and spoonbill)
Family - **Ardeidae** (herons)

Green Heron *Butorides virescens*	**Yellow-crowned Night Heron** *Nyctanassa violacea*	**Black-crowned Night Heron** *Nycticorax nycticorax*

Size: 19 inches. **Abundance:** Fairly common. **Migratory Status:** A year-round resident in all of Florida.	Presumed range in Florida 	**Size:** 25 inches. **Abundance:** Fairly common. **Migratory Status:** A year-round resident in all of Florida.	Presumed range in Florida 	**Size:** 25 inches. **Abundance:** Fairly common. **Migratory Status:** A year-round resident in all of Florida.	Presumed range in Florida 

Green Heron:

Variation: Juvenile birds are browner above and have streaked throat.

Habitat: Usually seen in the vicinity of water. Swamps, marshes, ditches, streams, lakes, and small ponds.

Breeding: Usually nests singly rather than in colonies. Nest is a stick platform in a tree fork. Lays 3 to 5 eggs

Natural History: In many areas the Green Heron often goes by the name "Shy-poke." This is one of our most familiar herons and its range encompasses all of the eastern United States as well as the West Coast. It also ranges southward throughout Central America. When flushed it nearly always emits a loud "squawking" alarm call. Feeds mostly in shallow water and often feeds from a perch on a floating log or a limb just above the water's surface. Hunts by stealth and may remain frozen for long periods as it watches and waits for prey. Fish is the primary food item with small frogs probably being the next most common prey. Amazingly, this species has been reported to catch insects and worms to use as bait for luring in fish. While the Green Heron is one of our most common wading birds, it is dependent upon wetlands and loss of wetland habitats is a threat.

Yellow-crowned Night Heron:

Variation: Juveniles are brown with white streaks.

Habitat: Swamps and marshes mostly, but may be seen in most aquatic habitat. Favors heavier cover than many herons.

Breeding: Flimsy stick nest is fairly high in tree, usually over water. 3 to 5 eggs. Breeds throughout Florida.

Natural History: These birds are often active at night, hence the name "night heron." Food is mostly crustaceans. Crabs are important foods in coastal regions, while crayfish are eaten in freshwater areas. A classical ambush predator, the Yellow-crowned Night Heron does most foraging from a stationery position, sitting like a statue and waiting for prey to wander into striking range. They will also stalk slowly and methodically with slow, deliberate movements that are largely undetectable to prey. Diet may be supplemented with fish and invertebrates, but this heron is mainly a crustacean specialist. Has recovered nicely from low numbers decades ago and now seems to be expanding its range farther to the north. Today, they range well into the Midwest in summer with a few isolated breeding colonies as far north as Minnesota and Pennslyvania.

Black-crowned Night Heron:

Variation: Juveniles are heavily streaked with brown and white.

Habitat: Utilizes all types of aquatic habitats in the state, with fresh and saltwater marshes being most widely used.

Breeding: Nests in large colonies that are often situated on an island. 3 or 4 eggs per nest.

Natural History: Although the Black-crowned Night Heron may be locally common near breeding colonies, it is not a commonly seen bird. Surprisingly, this is a widespread species that is found not only in much of the US, but in fact throughout most of the world. They can be found on every continent except Australia and Antarctica. As its name implies this species is often active at night. The food is primarily fish. However, the list of known foods is quite long and includes, insects, leeches, earthworms, crustaceans, gastropods, amphibians, snakes, small turtles, small mammals, and even birds! Prefers to feed in shallow water along the margins of weedy ponds, marshes, and swamps. This species has been widely studied as an apex predator that can accumulate toxins and it may be considered a barometer of environmental contamination.

Class - **Aves** (birds)

Order - **Pelecaniformes** (herons, ibis, pelicans, and spoonbill)

Family - **Pelecanidae** (pelicans)

Order - **Ciconiiformes** (storks)

Family - **Ciconiidae** (wood stork)

White Pelican *Pelecanus erythrorhynchos*	Brown Pelican *Pelicanus occidentalis*	Wood Stork *Mycteria american*

Size: 62 inches.

Abundance: Uncommon.

Migratory Status: Winter resident, a few year-round.

Presumed range in Florida

Size: 51 inches.

Abundance: Common.

Migratory Status: Year-round resident in Florida.

Presumed range in Florida

Size: 40 inches.

Abundance: Uncommon.

Migratory Status: Year-round resident in Florida.

Presumed range in Florida

Variation: Develops a hornlike plate on the upper bill during breeding. Juvenile resembles nonbreeding adult.

Variation: Juvenile has neck the same color as the body. Breeding adults develop dark chocolate brown on neck.

Variation: Juvenile birds have downy feathers on the head and neck and a yellowish bill.

Habitat: Summer habitat is inland freshwater marshes and lakes. Winter habitat is coastal marshes and estuaries.

Habitat: Coastlines. Beaches, estuaries, islands, marshes, mangroves, and all other shallow marine habitats.

Habitat: Mostly freshwater swamps but also in marine esturaries. In Florida may be seen in any aquatic habitat.

Breeding: Nests in colonies in protected areas such as islands on large lakes. Does not nest in Florida. Nesting occurs on large lakes and marshes in the northern plains. Lays 2 eggs.

Breeding: Nest is a stick platform placed in the top of a small tree or bush. Mangroves are a favorite nest site in Florida. Sometimes nest on the ground. Usually lays 3 eggs.

Breeding: Bulky stick nest is built in trees such as cypress or oaks, usually over water or on islands. Clutch size can be as many as 5 eggs. Young Wood Storks fledge at about 8 to 10 weeks.

Natural History: Most commonly seen in Florida along coastlines and in estuaries and salt marshes. They are mostly winter residents in Florida but a few birds may linger throughout the summer. Unlike their cousin the Brown Pelican, which feeds by plunging into the water, White Pelicans feed in a more placid manner. Flocks of feeding White Pelicans corral fish by swimming in a coordinated group and dipping the head beneath the surface in perfect unison. The appearance of a feeding flock is that of a perfectly choreographed ballet. Competition between baby White Pelicans in the nest is fierce, and the strongest nestling often kills its sibling. Primarily a bird of the southern coasts in winter and the Great Plains region in summer.

Natural History: The Brown Pelican is marine species that is closely tied to coastal regions and rarely seen more than a few miles inland. Groups of Brown Pelicans flying in formation is a common sight along America's coastlines. They make spectacular head-first plunges into the sea to capture fish near the surface. As with the other pelican species, they have an expandable pouch on the lower bill that is capable of "vacuuming" large quantities of water into the mouth, pulling in with it nearby fishes. Pelicans are awkward and ungainly on land but in flight they are quite graceful. Brown Pelicans are renown for their ability to skim the surface just inches above the water. They may even sometimes disappear in troughs between the waves.

Natural History: This is North America's only stork species. In addition to Florida and much of the southeast, they can also be found on both coasts of Mexico, throughout the Yucatan Peninsula, and across the Caribbean. They also occur in South America. These huge wading birds feed on all types of aquatic vertebrates which they usually capture by feel. Feeding storks swish their thick bills back and forth in the shallow waters of drying pools and snap the beak shut on anything touched. Fish are the main prey but all types of vertebrates have been recorded in the diet, as well as invertebrates such as crustaceans and insects. Adults have an all black head and black bill with wrinkled skin on the head and neck. They resemble large beaked vultures.

Class - **Aves** (birds)

Order - **Suliformes** (anhinga, cormorants, gannet, and frigatebird)

Family - **Anhingidae** (anhinga)	Family - **Phalacrocoracidae** (cormorants)	Family - **Sulidae** (boobys)
Anhinga *Anhinga anhinga*	**Double-crested Cormorant** *Phalacrocorax auritus*	**Northern Gannet** *Morus bassanus*

Size: 35 inches.	**Size:** 33 inches.	**Size:** 37 inches.
Abundance: Fairly common.	**Abundance:** Common.	**Abundance:** Rare in Florida.
Migratory Status: A year-round resident in Florida.	**Migratory Status:** A year-round resident in Florida.	**Migratory Status:** Winter resident off both coasts of Florida.

Presumed range in Florida (all three)

Variation: Females have brown head, neck and breast. Male is all black.	**Variation:** Juveniles are browner with whitish throat and breast.	**Variation:** Juveniles are gray-black above with scattered white spots.
Habitat: Totally aquatic and always seen near water except when migrating. Most types of freshwater habitats are used, with slow moving rivers being a favorite habitat.	**Habitat:** Lakes, rivers, estuaries, marshes, and swamplands. Use both fresh and saltwater habitats. Tends to favor saltwater habitats in winter, moving inland to fresh waters in summer.	**Habitat:** Closely tied to the sea, Northern Gannets ply the waters of the continental shelf. They come to land only to breed on cliffs or remote islands. Breeding occurs far to the north.
Breeding: Stick nest is always built over water. Clutch size is 3 to 5 eggs.	**Breeding:** Large colonies nest on islands. Bulky nest of sticks. 2 to 4 eggs.	**Breeding:** Breeding colonies are usually situated on a cliff. Lays a single egg.
Natural History: The local nickname "Snakebird" comes from the way this bird sometimes swims with the body beneath the water and just the head and long, snake-like neck sticking above the surface. The feathers of the Anhinga are not waterproof as is the case with some aquatic birds such as ducks. As a result, immediately after emerging from the water the water-logged feathers render them flightless. After emerging from a swim they can be seen perched in the sun with the wings spread, attempting to dry their feathers. Their swimming ability is remarkable and they are quite adept at catching fish while underwater. The Long, stiletto-like bill, coupled with the long neck which can be withdrawn and then plunged forward with blinding speed, creates a great "spear-fishing" technique for capturing fishes.	**Natural History:** Cormorants are rarely seen far from water. They are thoroughly aquatic birds that have webbed feet and frequently submerge and swim underwater in search of fish. Their exclusive diet of fish and their uncanny aquatic abilities have caused these birds to come into conflict with man. Occurring in large flocks, they will concentrate in areas where food is most readily available. Under natural conditions, they catch a wide variety of fish species and thus do not impact significantly upon fisheries. However, around fish farms or hatcheries they can become quite a nuisance. Nearly wiped out by the pesticide DDT a half century ago, they have made an incredible comeback. In some regions they have come to be seen as an ecological problem by crowding out other colonial nesting bird species and impacting negatively on fish stocks.	**Natural History:** Though mainly a marine species, the Northern Gannet sometimes shows up far inland. These birds are native to both sides of the North Atlantic, and are found from France to Norway on the European side of the Atlantic. In North America, they summer in maritime provinces of Canada and winter along the coast as far south as Florida and Texas. They are rather rare in Florida and are only seen in marine environments. Although they may range many miles out into the ocean, they are not a true pelagic (open ocean) bird. They feed by diving from height of up to 120 feet and may reach speeds of over 100 mph in a dive. A variety of marine organisms may be eaten opportunistically but the main food is fish and squid. Among the most common fish eaten are mackeral and herring.

Class - **Aves** (birds)

Order - **Suliformes**

Family - **Frigatidae** (frigatebirds)

Magnificent Frigatebird
Fregata magnifiscens

Size: 40 inches.

Abundance: Uncommon.

Migratory Status: Summer migrant in keys and along coasts.

Presumed range in Florida

Variation: Female has white breast. Male is all black. Juvenile has white head and breast.

Habitat: Mainly a tropical species that uses warm, shallow water habitats. Common near islands, mangroves, lagoons, etc. Also uses pelagic waters.

Breeding: Breeds on mangrove islands. Nest is built on the leeward side of island. Lays a single egg.

Natural History: This is a tropical bird that ranges northward along Florida's coastlines in summer. Although they can be seen along all Florida's coast from June through August, they are most common in the Keys and in the Florida Bay. They are masters of the air and can soar almost indefinitely without flapping their wings. They feed mainly on small fish and squid plucked from the surface. They will also follow shrimp and fishing boats to scavenge whatever is discarded. They are well-known for stealing food from other sea-going birds such as gulls, terns, Pelicans, etc., and this habit has earned them the nickname of "Man-of-War Bird," a reference to the pirate ships of old. Morphologically their body is mostly wings. Their small feet are used only for perching and they never walk.

Order - **Gaviiformes** (loons)

Family - **Gaviidae**

Common Loon
Gavia immer

Summer

Winter

Size: 32 inches.

Abundance: Rare in Florida.

Migratory Status: Winter resident and seasonal migrant.

Presumed range in Florida

Variation: Sexes are alike but exhibits significant seasonal plumage changes. See photos above.

Habitat: Highly aquatic. In inland areas such the Common Loon lives on lakes but in Florida they are usually seen along the coasts in winter.

Breeding: Nests is built on small islands in northern lakes. Usually lays 2 eggs. Chicks often ride on adult's back.

Natural History: On lakes and marshes in the far north the call of the Common Loon echoes through the wilderness. The sound is so distinctive and unique that it has inspired many poetic depictions. "Haunting," "ethereal," and "lonely" are words that are often used in conjunction with describing its yodeling cry that can carry for a great distance. They call both day and night on the breeding grounds in the northern half of the continent, but they are rarely heard calling on their winter range. Remarkable swimmers, they dive beneath the surface and propel themselves through the water with their powerful webbed feet. Fish caught in this manner are the main food item. In Florida, they are winter residents along the coasts. Migrants may be seen statewide on rivers and lakes.

Red-throated Loon
Gavia stellata

Winter

Size: 35 inches.

Abundance: Very rare in Florida.

Migratory Status: Winter migrant along coast of north Florida.

Presumed range in Florida

Variation: Exhibits seasonal plumage changes but birds seen in Florida will be in winter plumage (see above).

Habitat: Thoroughly aquatic. In inland areas in summer or on migration they may be seen on lakes and rivers. In winter they use mostly coastlines.

Breeding: Breeds in small ponds in remote tundra. Nest is a large mound of aquatic vegetation. 2 eggs.

Natural History: These are birds of the High Arctic. In summer they live as far north as the Arctic Ocean. They will move to North America's coastlines in winter. They typically winter well to the north of Florida and they are extremely rare in the state. But in most winters a few will make it as far south as the Jacksonville area. In winter, they are very similar to the Common Loon but are smaller and have white spots on the back. They are circumpolar in distribution and occur throughout Scandinavia. The legs of loons are situated very far back on the body which works well for propelling through water, but makes movement on land very difficult. This species appears to be in decline in North America. No explanation for this decline is known at this time.

Class - **Aves** (birds)

Order - **Podicipediformes** (grebes)		Order - **Charadriiformes** (shorebirds)
Family - **Podicipedidae**		Family - **Haematopodidae** (oystercatchers)

Pied-billed Grebe *Podilymbus podiceps*	**Horned Grebe** *Podiceps auritus*	**American Oystercatcher** *Haematopus palliatus*

Size: 13 inches.	Presumed range in Florida 	**Size:** 14 inches.	Presumed range in Florida	**Size:** 17 inches.	Presumed range in Florida 
Abundance: Fairly common.		**Abundance:** Uncommon.		**Abundance:** Uncommon.	
Migratory Status: A year-round resident in Florida.		**Migratory Status:** A winter only resident in Florida.		**Migratory Status:** A year-round resident in Florida.	

Variation: Winter birds are grayer and lack the prominent dark ring on bill.

Variation: Winter plumage (shown) is always seen in Florida.

Variation: On young chicks the bill is not fully developed until about 6 weeks.

Habitat: Completely aquatic, the Pied-billed Grebe uses everything from large lakes to small farm ponds. Also open water areas of swamps and marshes.

Habitat: In Florida this species uses the larger lakes as well as large marshes with open water and also coastal areas. Not usually seen on small ponds.

Habitat: Habitat is beaches and dunes primarily. Barrier Islands are a favorite habitat. Winter habitat includes mud flats and salt marshes.

Breeding: Nests on floating platform among emergent vegetation. 4 to 8 eggs.

Breeding: Nests on floating platform among emergent vegetation. 5 to 7 eggs.

Breeding: Nest is a scrape on bare sand, gravel or shell. Lays 3 eggs.

Natural History: This little grebe evades potential threats by submerging and they sometimes swim with just the head sticking out the water. They feed on a wide variety of small fish and other aquatic vertebrates as well as crustaceans and insects. This is the most widespread and common grebe in North America and they range from coast to coast. They may be seen year-round in Florida but their numbers increase in winter with migrants from farther north. They can be seen all winter across the southern half of the US, but tend to concentrate along the Gulf Coast in winter. Their summer range extends well into Canada. These little grebes are almost never seen in flight as they escape threats by diving and swimming. When threatened, they can swim for long distances underwater and resurface hundreds of yards away. All grebes are almost helpless on land.

Natural History: As is the case with other grebes (and loons), their adaptations for an aquatic lifestyle include the legs being positioned far back on the body. The legs can also be flared outward to a remarkable degree to facilitate underwater swimming maneuvers. As a result of this adaptation, these birds are very clumsy on land and walk with difficulty. Breeding birds (not seen in Florida) are handsomely marked with chestnut neck and flanks and golden brown head stripe that flares out to form "horns." The specimen shown above is in winter plumage and is typical of fall migrants and winter residents. Food is small fish, crustaceans, insects, etc. Their summer range is to the west and north of Florda (all the way to Alaska), but their winter range includes both coastal and inland regions of the northern half of the state.

Natural History: The common name Oystercatcher aptly describes the feeding habits of this unusual species. The laterally flattened bill is adapted for prying open the shells of mollusks like oysters and mussels. The technique involves stalking through shallows in search of mollusks with shells open and quickly inserting the blade-like bill into the open bivalve. It then stabs with the bill until the abducter muscle is severed allowing the shell to be pried open and the contents extracted. This species is completely dependent upon beaches and coastal dunes as habitat. Human encroachment and coastal development have ravage these habitats for decades and today this is one of America's most threatened natural habitats. In the year 2000 a population census revealed the entire population of American Oystercatchers to be only around 10,000 birds. A Threatened Species in Florida.

Class - **Aves** (birds)

Order - **Charadriiformes** (shorebirds)

Family - **Recurvirostridae** (stilts and avocet)		Family - **Charadriidae** (plovers)

American Avocet
Recurvirostra americana

Size: 18 inches	Presumed range in Florida
Abundance: Rare in Florida.	
Migratory Status: A winter only resident in Florida.	

Variation: Breeding birds have bright rusty-orange head and neck.

Habitat: Marshes, shallow lakes, and wetlands. Especially fond of saline wetlands and alkaline lakes of the west.

Breeding: Nests on the ground in a shallow scrape lined with grass. Does not nest in Florida. 4 eggs.

Natural History: Few people will be lucky enough to see the American Avocet in Florida, but those who do will not easily forget it. With its dramatic coloration, long legs and long, upturned bill it is one of the most striking birds in America. Avocets feed by sweeping the upturned bill back forth through the water. Feeds mostly on small aquatic insects (especially midges) and eats both adult insects and their aquatic larva. They also feed on brine shrimp and brine flies in saline wetlands and akaline lakes in the Great Basin region of the western US. Along the coastal marshes where they spend the winter amphipods and marine worms are important foods. Their breeding habitat is in the prairies and intermountain basins of the western United States, where they utilize marshes and wetlands. These habitats have been greatly reduced in recent times.

Black-necked Stilt
Himantopus mexicanus

Size: 14 inches	Presumed range in Florida
Abundance: Uncommon.	
Migratory Status: A year-round resident in parats of Florida.	

Variation: Sexes alike. Juvenile birds are dark brown above rather than black.

Habitat: Marshes and flooded fields, especially flooded pastures or grassy roadside ditches filled with rainwater.

Breeding: Nests in or adjacent to wetlands in clumps of vegetation. 4 eggs. A rare nester on Florida's southwest coast.

Natural History: Common names for birds are usually descriptive. None more so than this species with its black neck and long, stilt-like legs. With their exceptionally long legs, Black-necked Stilts can feed in fairly deep waters. They thus take advantage of foods not available to many of the shorter-legged shorebirds that may share their habitat. Their food is mostly aquatic invertebrates, but a few small fishes are also taken. They winter along southern coastlines of North America and in Mexico and Central America, where many are residents that will breed on these wintering grounds. But some move inland to breed and summer on marshlands in the western United States. Some breeding by this species occurs in the southwestern portion of Florida, but most specimens seen in the state are migrants summer only residents that winter in the Caribbean.

Killdeer
Charadrius vociferus

Size: 10 inches.	Presumed range in Florida
Abundance: Failry common.	
Migratory Status: A year-round resident in Florida.	

Variation: None. Sexes are alike and older juveniles resemble adults.

Habitat: Open lands. Mudflats, agricultural fields, lake shores, sandbars, and even gravel parking lots.

Breeding: Lays 4 eggs directly on the ground. Nest is often in gravelly or sandy situations in wide-open spaces.

Natural History: Although the Killdeer is found statewide, they are much more common in areas of the state where open habitats are more widespread. This is a species that has likely benefited significantly from human alterations of natural habitats. The creation of open spaces where there was once grassland or forest has resulted in a habitat boom the Killdeer. They will use man-made habitats such as golf courses, airports, baseball fields, and heavily grazed, short grass pastures. They are found all over North America south of the Arctic Circle. They were once hunted for food and their populations suffered a serious decline in the days of "market hunting." They feed on the ground and earthworms are a major food source along with grasshoppers, beetles, and snails. A few seeds are also consumed. Highly precocious young can walk/run within hours of hatching.

Class - **Aves** (birds)

Order - **Charadriiformes** (shorebirds)

Family - **Charadriidae** (plovers)

Black-bellied Plover *Pluvialis squatarola*	**Golden Plover** *Pluvialis dominica*	**Wilson's Plover** *Pluvialis wilsonia*

Size: 11.5 inches.	**Size:** 10.5 inches.	**Size:** 8 inches.
Abundance: Uncommon.	**Abundance:** Very rare in FL.	**Abundance:** Uncommon.
Migratory Status: Seasonal migrant. Rare in summer months.	**Migratory Status:** Seasonal migrant. Mostly spring and fall.	**Migratory Status:** A year-round resident in Florida.

Presumed range in Florida *(three maps shown)*

Variation: Seasonal plumage variations (see above).

Variation: Seasonal plumage variations (see above).

Variation: Non-breeders are drabber and lack black on breast.

Habitat: Beaches are the preferred winter habitat. Inland migrants will use shorelines, mudflats, and bare fields.

Habitat: Beaches are the preferred winter habitat. Inland migrants will use shorelines, mudflats, and bare fields.

Habitat: Beaches mainly. Also mud flats in tidal areas and coastal lagoons. Ranges well down into South America.

Breeding: Nest is a shallow cup scraped into the Arctic tundra and lined with lichens. 4 eggs are laid.

Breeding: Nest is a scrape on tundra soil. 4 eggs are laid and young are highly precocial, able to walk immediately.

Breeding: Nests all along Florida's coastline on dunes and sandy islands. 3 eggs are laid in a shallow scrap.

Natural History: Black-bellied Plovers occur in both the New and Old Worlds and in fact they are one of the most widespread shorebirds in the world. North American birds winter along both coastlines from just south of Canada to South America, including the Caribbean. Summers are spent within the Arctic Circle of Alaska and Canada. During migration they are seen mostly along America's coastlines and in the Great Plains region. Unlike many shorebirds, the Black-bellied Plover exhibits nocturnal tendencies and will often feed at night. Food items are marine worms and small clams and mussels plucked from the mud at low tide. On the breeding grounds in the far north they will eat insects, small freshwater crustaceans, and berries. Climate change may be a threat if tundra nesting habitat undergoes transformation.

Natural History: Like the similar Black-bellied Plover, the American Golden Plover is a long distance traveler that nests in the Arctic and spends its winters in southeastern South America. Its epic migrations sometimes include extensive flights over vast expanses of open ocean. Many migrate through inland regions and they are known for their propensity to appear almost anywhere during migrations. Food items include some plant material (berries, seeds, foliage) as well as a wide variety of invertebrate prey. Like many shorebirds the American Golden Plover was hunted relentlessly during the days "market hunting" throughout the 1800s. Tens to perhaps hundreds of thousands were killed annually. Today, they are still legally hunted hunted in some South American countries. Habitat loss remains an ever present threat as is climate change.

Natural History: Differing from all other American plovers, the Wilson's Plover does not travel inland. Instead this plover stays close to the sea. A few may be seen on salt lakes a few miles inland, but in Florida this is chiefly a coastal species. Fiddler crabs are reported to be a favorite food item along with other crustaceans and insects, worms, and other benthic invertebrates. Large, hard-shelled prey like fiddler crabs are reduced to managable swallowing size by removing the legs and large claw, then swallowing the body. The name "Wilson's Plover" honors early American naturalist Alexander Wilson. Wilson was a contemporary of John James Audubon and is regarded by many as the father of North American Ornithology. No less than 5 bird species in America today bear his name. Loss of habitat from beach development is a significant threat to this species.

Class - **Aves** (birds)

Order - **Charadriiformes** (shorebirds)

Family - **Charadriidae** (plovers)

Snowy Plover *Charadrius nivosus*	Piping Plover *Charadrius melodus*	Semipalmated Plover *Charadrius semipalmatus*

Snowy Plover
Charadrius nivosus

Size: 6.25 inches.

Abundance: Rare.

Migratory Status: Year-round. Peaks in summer.

Presumed range in Florida

Variation: Seasonal plumage variations. Winter birds may be extremely pale gray.

Habitat: Sandy beaches and dunes are the primary habitat in Florida. Inland populations use akaline lake shores.

Breeding: Breeding in Florida occurs on beaches and dunes. Shallow scrap is lined with shells. 3 to 6 eggs is usual.

Natural History: Snowy Plovers can be found in 2 distinct populations in America, an eastern and western population. Both are imperiled by loss of habitat due to development of beach and dune areas along the coast. Western populaitons in California are regarded as federally threatened. Among the eastern populations the Florida Wildlife Commission regards them as a Threatened Species, while birds that nest on the coast of Mississippi and Alabama are considered Endangered. Some will migrate inland to breed on akaline lakes of the west, where human intrusion has less impact than for those that breed on coastal beaches. Their pale color and small size helps nesting birds to blend in with their surroundings. When foraging on open beaches they are more observable, but overall these little plovers are usually overlooked by most beachgoers.

Piping Plover
Charadrius melodus

Size: 7.5 inches.

Abundance: Rare.

Migratory Status: A winter only resident in Florida.

Presumed range in Florida

Variation: Seasonal plumage variations Sexes are alike but winter plumage is paler.

Habitat: Summer habitat is the Great Plains and coastal areas of the northeast. In winter uses southern beaches.

Breeding: Nest is a scrape on sand or gravel, often near a clump of grass in an elevated place on the beach. 4 eggs.

Natural History: The Piping Plover is a federally endangered species that breeds primarily on sandy beaches along America's Atlantic coastline. Widespread coastal development and near complete utilization of beaches by man has made successful nesting in these habitats very problematic for the Piping Plover. In recent years conservation efforts which attempt to mitigate human interferance may be the only hope for the species. Closing of beaches to human activity where nesting occurs along with erecting predator exclusion fences around nests are 2 conservation actions that are regularly taken by conservation teams up and down America's Atlantic coast. Recent political trends aimed at decimating environmental regulations may spell doom for this and many other species facing similar threats across America.

Semipalmated Plover
Charadrius semipalmatus

Size: 7.25 inches.

Abundance: Uncommon.

Migratory Status: A winter resident and seasonal migrant.

Presumed range in Florida

Variation: See photos above. Winter plumage is most likely to be seen in Florida.

Habitat: Winter habitat is along coastlines. Summer habitat is open tundra. Migrants favor mud flats and shorelines.

Breeding: Nests on the ground, usually near water. Nesting grounds are in northern Canada and Alaska. 4 eggs.

Natural History: Most Semipalmated Plovers migrate along the coasts of North America, but a few travel overland and they are regularly seen in New York. Most sightings will likely be along the Atlantic Coast or Great Lakes as they tend to favor shorelines and other open spaces. The food of the Semi-palmated Plover is mostly invertebrate animals plucked from the mud. They hunt these "benthic" organisms along the edges of marshes, lakes, seashores, etc. Aquatic food items include insect larva (especially fly larva), polychaete worms, crustaceans, and small bivalves. On dry land these plovers will eat spiders, flies, and beetles. Most foraging is done along waters edge or in very shallow water or on exposed mudflats. Baby plovers are highly precocial and young Semipalmated Plovers are able to feed themselves immediately.

Class - **Aves** (birds)

Order - **Charadriiformes** (shorebirds)

Family - **Scolopacidae** (sandpipers)

Upland Sandpiper *Bartramia longicauda*	**Whimbrel** *Numenius phaeopus*	**Long-billed Curlew** *Numenius americanus*

Upland Sandpiper — *Bartramia longicauda*

Size: 12 inches.

Abundance: Uncommon.

Presumed range in Florida

Migratory Status: Seasonal migrant. Peaks in August.

Variation: Fall and juvenile plumages paler than breeding adults.

Habitat: An obligate of grasslands and prairies. Migrants will also use pastures and fields.

Breeding: Nest is a shallow scrape on the ground lined with grass. 4 eggs.

Natural History: The bulk of the Upland Sandpiper's summer range is in the northern Great Plains. A few summer very sparsely east of the Mississippi River into the Midwestern US. Unlike most other members of the sandpiper family, the Upland Sandpiper avoids coastal areas in favor of prairies and grasslands well into the interior of the continent. Historically, these birds were much more numerous. Market hunting in the late nineteenth century saw countless numbers of dead Upland Sandpipers shipped by rail from their nesting grounds on the northern plains to markets in the east. At the same time they were being hunted mercilessly on their winter habitats in the Pampas of South America. Even more devastating to their populations was the conversion of the native American prairie to cropland. Amazingly, the species survives. They are an uncommon to rare migrant in Florida.

Whimbrel — *Numenius phaeopus*

Size: 17.5 inches.

Abundance: Uncommon.

Presumed range in Florida

Migratory Status: Winter migrant along both coasts.

Variation: Juveniles have a slightly darker head and neck.

Habitat: Winter habitat in Florida is mostly coastlines. Will also use mudflats and lakeshores.

Breeding: Breeds in the far north. Typically 4 eggs in nest on ground.

Natural History: The likelihood of seeing this species in Florida is not great, but those who do see it will have no trouble recognizing it. Its large size and long, downcurved bill is quite distinctive. On wintering grounds they feed mostly on crabs and the long, crescent-shaped bill is thought to be an adaptation for penetrating the burrows of Fiddler Crabs in marine intertidal zones. On Arctic breeding grounds insects are the major food but some berries are also eaten. Most of these birds migrate along the coastlines of America, but a few travel inland. Most inland migration is through the western Great Plains but some migrate through the Mississippi Flyway or down the Atlantic Coast. Summering and nesting in the Arctic of Alaska and Canada and wintering in South America, this species has been known to make nonstop migratory flights lasting several days and covering over 3,000 miles!

Long-billed Curlew — *Numenius americanus*

Size: 23 inches.

Abundance: Very rare in Florida.

Presumed range in Florida

Migratory Status: Winter migrant or rare winter resident.

Variation: No sexual dimorphism and juveniles resemble adults.

Habitat: Breeding habitat is the short grass and mixed grass prairies of the western Great Plains region.

Breeding: Nest is a shallow bowl or scrape. 4 eggs is usual.

Natural History: Historically these birds were fairly common along the Atlantic Coast of America in migration periods. Today they are extremely rare along the East Coast and most remaining birds are in the Pacific Coast Flyway and the Prairie Flyway populations. All nesting occurs in the northern Great Plains and the intermountain west. The name "Long-billed" Curlew is approriate as this birds bill is so long as to appear to be a liability. In fact it is a specialized tool used to remove crustaceans from their burrows. In Florida this species can be seen only along the coasts. Though records exist for every month of the year, they are most likely to be seen during migration periods or in winter. Their habitat preferences in the state are salt marsh mudflats and exposed tidal areas where they can use their specialized bill to probe for benthic organisms.

Class - **Aves** (birds)

Order - **Charadriiformes** (shorebirds)

Family - **Scolopacidae** (sandpipers)

Marbled Godwit *Limosa fedoa*	**Ruddy Turnstone** *Arenaria interpres*	**Red Knot** *Calidris canutus*

Summer

Summer

Winter

Summer

Size: 18 inches.

Abundance: Uncommon.

Migratory Status: Seasonal migrant and winter resident.

Presumed range in Florida

Size: 9.5 inches.

Abundance: Fairly common.

Migratory Status: Year-round. More common in winter.

Presumed range in Florida

Size: 10.5 inches.

Abundance: Uncommon.

Migratory Status: Seasonal migrant and winter resident.

Presumed range in Florida

Variation: Breeding birds show distinct barring on belly.

Variation: Seasonal plumage variations. See photos above.

Variation: Winter birds are drab gray brown with off white breast and belly.

Habitat: Summer habitat is in the Great Plains. In Florida uses coastal areas. Marshes, intertidal mud flats, etc.

Habitat: Winters on sandy beaches along both coasts. May use lake shores, and mud flats in intertidal areas.

Habitat: Summer habitat is Arctic tundra. Winter and migration habitat is intertidal areas and beaches/coastlines.

Breeding: Breeds in the northern plains of Candad, Dakotas, Montana. Nest is on the ground. 4 eggs.

Breeding: Breeds in the Arctic tundra and coastlines from Siberia and Alaska across Canada to Greenland.

Breeding: Does not nest in Florida. Nest on tundra all the way to the Arctic Ocean. 4 eggs is typical.

Natural History: Although this species is a fairly common migratory and breeding bird on the prairies of America's Great Plains region, it is an uncommon species in Florida. Worms, bivalves, crustaceans, and insects are major food items. Oddly for a shorebird, plant tubers are also included in its diet. Like many of its kin, this species was decimated by overhunting during the late 1800s and it has never fully recovered. Loss of native prairie to agriculture has probably retarded recovery and remains as a major threat to the species. Although it is similar in appearance to the Whimbrel and Long-billed Curlew, it can easily be differentiated from those two large shorebirds by its bill, which is slightly upturned rather than curved downward. It can also be confused with the Upland Sandpiper, which has a much shorter bill.

Natural History: Most Ruddy Turnstones travel up and down America's coastlines during migration, but a few migrate through inland regions of the continent. This is one of the most northerly ranging birds in America, traveling to the northernmost extreme of the continent to breed each summer. Its name comes from its habit of using its beak to overturn pebbles and stones on beaches in search of small invertebrate prey. It also feeds on ocean carrion found on beaches. On the breeding grounds the primary food source is mosquitoes and other dipeteran insects. The unusual genus (*Arenaria*) contains only 2 species and their position in the phylogeny of the shorebirds is unclear. Some will winter as far south as Brazil, but a fair number will spend the winter along Florida's coastlines and a few may linger into the summer.

Natural History: This is North America's largest member of the *Calidris* genus. Like many other Sandpiper species, the Red Knot is a remarkable traveler, with some covering nearly 10,000 miles in a round-trip journey from southern South America to the Arctic and back each year. Some birds may fly nonstop for thousands of miles across great expanses of ocean, mountains and deserts. Nesting is on the most northerly land masses in North America including northern Greenland and Canada's Arctic Archipelago. During the North American winter, some will be enjoying summer in the southern hemisphere as far south as Terra del Fuego on the southern tip of South America. Along the way, these world travelers will sometimes stop for a brief rest somewhere along the coasts of eastern North America.

Class - **Aves** (birds)
Order - **Charadriiformes** (shorebirds)
Family - **Scolopacidae** (sandpipers)

Stilt Sandpiper *Calidris himantopus*	**Sanderling** *Calidris alba*	**Dunlin** *Calidris alpina*

Size: 8.5 inches.

Presumed range in Florida

Abundance: Uncommon.

Migratory Status: Seasonal migrant in spring and fall.

Variation: Winter birds are much paler, more grayish.

Habitat: Ponds, marshes, flooded fields, and lake shorelines. Uses salt marsh and brackish marshes in winter.

Breeding: Nests in lowland areas near the Arctic Ocean. Lays 4 eggs.

Natural History: The Stilt Sandpiper gets its name from its long legs. The long legs are an adaptation that allow it to feed in deeper water than most other *Calidris* sandpipers. Its body shape and habit of feeding in deeper water rather than on mud flats is unusual for its genus and mimics the yellowlegs sandpipers (genus *Tringa*). The migratory routes for this sandpiper are mainly west of the Mississippi River, but many will use the Atlantic coastal flyway. They nest along the northernmost coast of North America and will spend the winter in the interior of the South American continent. As with many other sandpiper species, the Stilt Sandpiper shows a remarkable fidelity to the nest site. After migrating thousands of miles from South America, they often return to the same exact spot on the Arctic coastline to lay their eggs.

Size: 8 inches.

Presumed range in Florida

Abundance: Fairly common.

Migratory Status: Most common in winter spring and fall.

Variation: Significant seasonal variation (see photos above).

Habitat: Shorelines. In winter lives on the beach. During migration frequents lake shores and river bars.

Breeding: Nests on Arctic tundra on bare ground. Lays 4 eggs.

Natural History: Unlike most members of the sandpiper family, which are more likely to be found on mudflats, the Sanderling is commonly found on seashores. Except during migration or when breeding, these birds inhabit sandy beaches throughout the Americas. Any person who has been to the seashore has probably been amused by watching this species running back and forth in front of the waves. On beaches it feeds by running just in front of oncoming wave and chasing right behind receding wave, picking up tiny marine crustaceans, bivalves, and polychaetes. On the breeding ground, it will eat both terrestrial and aquatic invertebrates and insects. Most Sanderlings migrate along the coastlines of America or through the Great Plains. Some can be seen in inland areas however, especially along the shores of the Great Lakes. They are common on Florida beaches in winter.

Size: 8.5 inches.

Presumed range in Florida

Abundance: Failry common.

Migratory Status: Winter resident and seasonal migrant.

Variation: Significant seasonal plumage changes (see photos above).

Habitat: During migration uses flooded agricultural fields, mud flats, and seasonally flooded lowland pastures.

Breeding: Another High Arctic breeder. Lays 4 eggs on ground in open tundra.

Natural History: The Dunlin winters along both coasts of North America where it haunts estuaries and intertidal regions. A few may be seen in winter along northern Atlantic coastlines but most move farther south. In southern Louisiana and gulf coastal Texas it often uses rice fields in winter. Various clams, insects, worms, and amphipods are picked from the mud or plucked from vegetation with its moderately long, probing bill. Like other shorebird species, it is usually seen in flocks, sometimes numbering in the thousands or even tens of thousands. In the early 1800s market hunters killed these birds in enormous numbers. Using cannon-like shotguns known as "punt guns" that were loaded with bird shot, a single blast could kill scores of shorebirds in a closely packed flock. Todays threats include pesticides and other contaminants and loss of wintering habitat.

Class - **Aves** (birds)

Order - **Chariidriformes** (shorebirds)

Family - **Scolopacidae** (sandpipers)

Additional *Calidris* **Sandpipers**

Least Sandpiper *Calidris minutilla*	White-rumped Sandpiper *Calidris fuscicollis*	Semipalmated Sandpiper *Calidris pusilla*

Pectoral Sandpiper *Calidris melanotos*	Presumed combined range in Florida

Size: 6 to 8 inches.

Abundance: Some species like the Least, Pectoral and Semipalmated Sandpipers are commonly seen in Florida during migration. The White-rumped and Western are less common in the state, while the Buff-breasted Sandpiper (not shown) is rare.

Migratory Status: Most species are transient spring and fall migrants in Florida, but some may be seen throughout the year.

Variation: Most of these species exhibit seasonal plumage changes, and are comparably paler in winter than in summer.

Habitat: The name "Mudpiper" would be a more appropriate name for these birds as they favor mud flats and flooded fields over sandy beaches. All can be seen along the coastlines but many migrate through the interior of North America.

Breeding: All nest on the ground in the barren Arctic tundra. 4 eggs is typical.

Natural History: Except for the Pectoral Sandpiper and Buff-breasted Sandpiper (not shown), these species are all similar in their natural history and are confusingly alike in appearance. While serious birders and professional ornithologists take pride in being able to correctly identify any species, most casual observers are satisfied with calling these homogeneous birds simply "peeps." Food habits and feeding methods are also similar in these sandpipers, with mud-dwelling benthic invertebrates making up the bulk of the diet in winter and during migration. Aquatic insect larva and some terrestrial insects are eaten on the breeding grounds. The hordes of mosquitoes for which the Arctic tundra is famous in summer make up a high protein smorgasboard for both the adult birds and the newly hatched young. All the sandpipers are known for their epic migrations. Some species travel non-stop for a thousand miles or more over open ocean. Flights lasting as long as 5 days have been reported. Quite a feat of endurance for birds that can weigh as little as 0.75 to 1.5 ounces! Above are shown five of the more common species observed during migrations through Florida. Two additional species that may also be seen in Florida are the **Western Sandpiper** (*Calidris mauri*) and in the fall the **Buff-breasted Sandpiper** (*Calidris subuficollis*). Recent population declines have been reported for the Least Sandpiper and the Semipalmated Sandpiper, and the Buff-breasted is one of the rarest members of the group. By contrast, the Western Sandpiper is one of the most abundant shorebirds in America with a population estimate of 3.5 million birds.

Class - **Aves** (birds)

Order - **Charadriiformes** (shorebirds)

Family - **Scolopacidae** (sandpipers)

Short-billed Dowitcher *Limnodromus griseus*	Woodcock *Scolopax minor*	Wilson's Snipe *Gallinago delicata*

Size: 11 inches.

Abundance: Fairly common.

Migratory Status: Winter resident and seasonl migrant.

Presumed range in Florida

Variation: See photos above.

Habitat: In inland migrations, dowitchers use mud flats and lake shores. They also use coastal habitats.

Breeding: Breeds in bog and muskeg habitats of northern Canada and Alaska. Both species lay 4 eggs.

Natural History: The nearly identical **Long-billed Dowitcher** (*Limnodromus scolopaceus*-not shown) may also be seen in Florida during winter and in spring and fall migrations. Distinguishing between the 2 in the field is difficult even for experts. The Long-billed is slightly larger at 11.5 inches. It migrates earlier in the spring and later in the fall than the Short-billed. It also is more likely to be seen in inland habitats in Florida while the Short-billed favors coastal areas. Like many shorebirds both species of dowitcher were heavily hunted during the days of market hunting. At that time, it was not known that the 2 similar dowitchers constituted 2 distinct species. The existence of 2 species was not finally confirmed until 1950. Although both species have recovered from the lows experienced during the great slaughter of shorebirds in the late 1800s, their populations are still well below historical numbers.

Size: 11 inches.

Abundance: Uncommon.

Migratory Status: Winter migrant and winter resident.

Presumed range in Florida

Variation: Females are larger.

Habitat: Swamps, regenerative woodlands, thickets, and weedy fields in bottomlands or uplands with moist soils.

Breeding: Nest is on the ground and not concealed. Lays 4 eggs as early as late February.

Natural History: The Woodcock is unique among American sandpipers in that it is strictly an inland species. It is also the only member of its family that breeds widely throughout the Eastern Temperate Forest Level I Ecoregion. Woodcock are known for their elaborate courtship flights that consist of an upward twisting corkscrew accompanied by a twittering call. The long beak is used to probe moist soils for invertebrates. Among its unique features are a flexible upper bill that aids in extracting the favorite food, earthworms, and eyes which are situated far back on the head, allowing for backward vision while feeding. One of the most remarkably cryptic of the sandpipers, Woodcocks are nearly impossible to detect when motionless on the forest floor. Although their nests are often in the open, brooding Woodcock will remain motionless even when closely approached, as their cryptic colors render them invisible.

Size: 10.5 inches

Abundance: Failry common.

Migratory Status: Mostly a winter resident in Florida.

Presumed range in Florida

Variation: No variation.

Habitat: Mudflats, flooded grassy fields, marshes, river bars, water-filled ditches, temporary pools, pond banks.

Breeding: Nest far to the north of Florida in wetlands where it lays 4 eggs on a hummock in marsh or bog.

Natural History: As with other members of the sandpiper family, the beak of the Wilson's Snipe contains sensory pits near the tip which helps to locate invertebrate prey hidden in the mud. It also shares the Woodcock's rearward-positioned eyes for watching behind and above while feeding. This is another highly camouflaged species that is nearly invisible when immobile. It is one of the most common and widespread members of the sandpiper family that often relies on its cryptic coloration when approached. Sitting quietly until nearly trod upon it will burst from the grass with a twisting, erratic flight while emitting a raspy call. Like the Woodcock, the Wilson's Snipe is regarded as a game bird, but few people hunt them. Breeding and nesting occurs in the boreal forests of northern North America from the Great Lakes region all the way to the Arctic Circle of Alaska and northern Canada.

Class - **Aves** (birds)

Order - **Charadriiformes** (shorebirds)

Family - **Scolopacidae** (sandpipers)

Wilson's Phalarope *Phalaropus tricolor*	**Spotted Sandpiper** *Actitis macularia*	**Solitary Sandpiper** *Tringa solitaria*

Size: 9.5 inches.	Presumed range in Florida	**Size:** 7.5 inches.	Presumed range in Florida	**Size:** 8.5 inches.	Presumed range in Florida
Abundance: Rare in Florida.		**Abundance:** Fairly common.		**Abundance:** Uncommon.	
Migratory Status: Mostly a fall migrant in Florida.		**Migratory Status:** Seasonal migrant and winter resident.		**Migratory Status:** Spring and fall migrant in Florida.	

Variation: Sexual, seasonal, and ontogenetic variations. Non-breeding birds are gray above and all white beneath. Juveniles are mottled brown above.	**Variation:** Winter birds lack the spots on the breast and are grayer on the back. Most Spotted Sandpipers seen in Florida will be in summer plumage.	**Variation:** Summer plumage has more distinct white spotting on the back and the back feathers are darker brown than on nonbreeding birds.
Habitat: Uses marshes on breeding range; shallow water habitats along lake shores, ponds, etc. in migration.	**Habitat:** In migration uses edges of ponds, lake shores, stream courses, and river bars.	**Habitat:** Summer habitat is in the boreal regions. In Florida uses ponds, lake shores, and along creeks and rivers.
Breeding: Breeds on inland marshes and wetlands in the west-central US and Canada. Always lays 4 eggs.	**Breeding:** Nests on the ground in grassy situations. Lays 2 to 4 eggs. Does not nest in Florida.	**Breeding:** Uniquely for a sandpiper, it nests in trees and uses old songbird nests. 3 to 5 eggs, usually 4.
Natural History: Phalaropes are known for the unique role reversal of the sexes. In these birds the female is the most vividly colored while the male has drab plumage. Even more unusual, it is the male that incubates the eggs in the nest. These birds are salt lake specialists and during migration they congregate in large flocks around alkaline and highly saline lakes of the interior of North America. The winter habitat is similar saline lakes in the Andes Mountains of South America. Birds seen in Florida are Migrators. The slightly smaller (8-inch) **Red-necked Phalarope** (*P. lobatus*) is a related species that can also be seen in Atlantic waters off the coast of Florida on rare occasions. These birds are migrants moving between northern breeding grounds and wintering areas in tropical seas.	**Natural History:** Unlike most sandpipers that exhibit strong flocking tendencies, the Spotted Sandpiper is always seen singly or in very small groups. This is one of the most widespread sandpipers in America and one of the few that nests in the lower 48. The distinctly spotted breast along with a habit of constantly bobbing up and down makes the Spotted Sandpiper one of the most recognizable members of the Scolapacidae family. Feeds on a wide variety of aquatic and terrestrial invertebrates, especially dipteran (fly) larva. Also eats significant quantities of mayflies, crickets, grasshoppers, caterpillars, beetles, and mollusks, crustaceans, and worms. Many will winter well into the tropics, some as far as South America. Others will spend the winter in the southern US, including Florida.	**Natural History:** As implied by their name, Solitary Sandpipers are nearly always seen alone during migration. In this respect they differ markedly from most other members of their family. They also differ in their nesting habits, as they are the only North American member of the Scolapacidae family that nests in trees. When feeding, it wades in shallows and plucks its food from the surface or beneath the water. Food is mostly invertebrates, both aquatic and terrestrial. Insects make up the bulk of the terrestrial foods. They also take aquatic insects and their larva, small crustaceans, snails, and some vertebrate prey such as small minnows or tadpoles. Due to their solitary habits and the fact that they breed in trees in remote boreal forests, little is known about their population status, but it appears to be stable.

Class - **Aves** (birds)

Order - **Charadriiformes** (shorebirds)

Family - **Scolopacidae** (sandpipers)

Greater Yellowlegs *Tringa melanoleuca*	Lesser Yellowlegs *Tringa flavipes*	Willet *Catoptrophorus semipalmata*

Size: 14 inches.	Presumed range in Florida	**Size:** 10.5 inches.	Presumed range in Florida	**Size:** 15 inches.	Presumed range in Florida
Abundance: Fairly common.		**Abundance:** Fairly common.		**Abundance:** Fairly common.	
Migratory Status: Fall through winter and into spring.		**Migratory Status:** Fall through winter and into spring.		**Migratory Status:** Year-round resident in Florida.	

Variation: Speckled appearance is less prominent on winter adults and young.	**Variation:** Speckled appearance is less prominent on winter adults and young.	**Variation:** Winter plumage lacks brown speckling.

Habitat: Both species are seen in a wide variety of wetland habitats during migration. In winter uses both freshwater and saltwater habitats in Florida.	**Habitat:** Uses variety of wetland habitats. In Florida common on beaches.

Breeding: Greater breeds in northern bogs. Lesser in drier, more upland habitats. Both species nest on the ground and 3 to 4 eggs is the typical clutch size for both.	**Breeding:** Lays 4 eggs in nest on the ground.

Natural History: These 2 related species are sometimes seen together. When seen together they are easily recognized by size. When not found in mixed flocks they are best identified by the shape of the bill. The Greater Yellowleg's bill is longer and ever so slightly upturned at the tip. The Greater Yellowlegs is the least social of the 2, and although it is seen in small flocks it can also be seen singly. Both species were once heavily hunted and during the days of market hunting both species experienced steep population declines. Hunting still occurs in some areas of their migratory range, especially in the Caribbean. Both spend the summer in the boreal regions of Canada and Alaska and winter from the Gulf Coast of the southeastern United States southward into South America. Food items for the Greater include both aquatic and terrestrial invertebrates as well as some small aquatic vertebrates like small frogs or fish. Lesser Yellowleg's food items are mainly invertebrates, both aquatic and terrestrial, but some small fish are also eaten. Both feed mostly by wading in shallows, but the Lesser is a more active feeder, wading rapidly and picking food from both the surface and the water column. It will also feed in this manner in terrestrial habitats such as grassy shorelines or meadow areas. The Greater Yellowleg feeds both diurnally and at night, when it employs a sweeping motion of the bill back and forth through the water, apparently catching food by feel. The major threat to both species today is probably loss of habitat, both on wintering grounds in South America (loss of wetlands) and on summer range in North America, i.e logging in boreal forests (Greater), and loss of wetlands in Alaska (Lesser).

Natural History: The Willet is a true "shorebird" that is quite familiar to those who frequent America's seashores. Both coasts of America are home to Willets during the winter, and some will nest in coastal marshes. Others fly into the interior of North America and nest as far north as the central Canadian prairie. It is these migrants that can be seen in freshwater habitats. Crustaceans, mollusks, insects, small fish, and polycheate worms are listed as food items. Feeds both day and night. In the 1800s they were hunted for food and for their eggs which were also eaten, resulting in a significant decrease in populations. Today, these are fairly common shorebirds whose population appears stable at an estimate of about a quarter of a million birds. They are known to live at least 10 years.

Class - **Aves** (birds)
Order - **Charadriiformes** (shorebirds)
Family - **Laridae** (gulls and terns)

Laughing Gull	Bonapartes Gull	Ringed-billed Gull
Leucophaeus atricilla	*Chroicocephalus philadelphia*	*Larus delawarensis*

Size: 16.5 inches	**Size:** 13.5 inches.	**Size:** 17.5 inches.
Abundance: Common.	**Abundance:** Uncommon.	**Abundance:** Very common.
Migratory Status: Year-round resident in Florida.	**Migratory Status:** Winter resident in Florida.	**Migratory Status:** Mostly a winter resident in Florida.

Presumed range in Florida (all three columns)

Variation: Seasonal plumage variations (see photos above).

Variation: Summer plumage has all black head (not usually seen in FL).

Variation: Juveniles are brownish gray and have greenish legs and bill.

Habitat: These are primarily coastal birds that sometimes wander inland.

Habitat: Frequents large rivers and larger lakes but also coastal habitats.

Habitat: Uses both coastal and inland aquatic habitats. Lakes, rivers, shores.

Breeding: Nests in colonies along the Atlantic and Gulf Coasts. Nests are built on the ground in salt marshes or islands. 3 eggs is typical.

Breeding: The only gull that nests in trees, using conifers bordering remote lakes in Canada and Alaska. Typically lays 3 eggs.

Breeding: Nests in inland areas well to the north and west of Florida. Nest is on the ground on sandbars or rocky beaches. Lays 2 to 4 eggs.

Natural History: Although they are commonly seen in a variety of habitats as much as 60 miles inland, they are quite rare in the interior of the continent. These gulls are much more tied to the coasts and are quite common and familiar along both the Atlantic and Gulf coasts. Following breeding, some birds may follow major river systems well into the continent and a few make it into the interior of the continent. Likewise some will migrate northward along the Atlantic Coast as far as New England in summer. Like many gulls they exhibit seasonal plumage changes as well as age related (ontogenetic) plumage changes. For instance, it takes 3 years for the Laughing Gull to obtain the characteristic black hood worn in summer plumage. These are apparently long-lived birds with a longevity record of 19 years.

Natural History: Many people tend to lump all gull species together and refer to them all as "seagulls." Most species, however, including the Bonaparte's Gull, are often inland birds during the breeding season. Like other gulls, many Bonaparte's Gulls will spend the winter along America's coastlines and sometimes far out to sea. Small to moderately large flocks can be seen on inland rivers and lakes throughout the winter. In Florida they may also be seen around harbors, coastal bays, and beaches. One of our smaller gulls, they feed mostly on small fish such as shad and shiners, but like other gulls they are highly opportunistic feeders and will eat a wide variety of insects and other invertebrates. Unlike other gull species, however, they are not typically seen around towns or dumps.

Natural History: The Ring-billed Gull is one of the most common and widespread gull species in America. Most population estimates put their number in the millions, and they may be increasing. This is the gull commonly seen around inland lakes in summer and along coastal beaches in winter. They are also seen in urban parking lots or hanging around fast food restaurants ready to swoop in and grab a dropped French fry. They are can be common in garbage dumps and may be seen foraging with starlings and other urban birds around dumpsters. These are highly gregarious birds that travel in flocks and nest in colonies. Food is almost anything, from carrion to insects, fish, rodents, earthworms, and human refuse. In Florida, they are most common in winter, but some may be seen in summer.

Class - **Aves** (birds)		
Order - **Charadriiformes** (shorebirds)		
Family - **Laridae** (gulls and terns)		
Herring Gull *Larus argentatus*	**Great Black-backed Gull** *Larus marinus*	**Sooty Tern** *Onychoprion fuscatus*

Size: 25 inches.	**Size:** 30 inches.	**Size:** 16 inches.
Abundance: Uncommon.	**Abundance:** Rare in Florida.	**Abundance:** Rare in Florida.
Migratory Status: Mostly a wintertime resident in Florida.	**Migratory Status:** Winter migrant and rare winter resident.	**Migratory Status:** Summer migrants and summer residents.

Presumed range in Florida

Presumed range in Florida

Presumed range in Florida

Variation: Highly variable as juvenile. Younger birds are dark brownish gray with dark eyes and get lighter with age. Males are larger than females.

Variation: Age-related plumage varition significant. Juveniles are mottled brown on the wings and the back. Adults have jet-black wings and back.

Variation: Juvenile Sooty and Bridled Terns are brownish. Adult Brown Noddy is chocolate brown with white on top of head that is reduced on juvenile.

Habitat: Coastlines, offshore islands, barrier islands, beaches, and shorelines in general. Both salt and freshwater.

Habitat: A gull of the Atlantic coastline from Nova Scotia to Florida. Winter habitat in Florida restricted to northeast coast.

Habitat: Tropical seas and tropical islands. All three species discussed below are worldwide in the tropics.

Breeding: Nest is on the ground in a bowl-shaped scrape lined with vegetation. 2 or 3 eggs are laid.

Breeding: Nests in the far northeastern coastline of North America. 3 eggs is typical. Nest is a scrape on the ground.

Breeding: In Florida these species breed only on the Dry Tortugas. Nest is on the ground and 1 chick is usual.

Natural History: Like the smaller Ring-billed Gull, the Herring Gull is an opportunistic feeder that will eat almost anything, including human garbage. This fact may account in part for their population rebound in recent decades. Like other gull species, they are gregarious and they often nest in large colonies. Only about 50 percent of the young gulls hatched each year reach adulthood, but the species seems to be thriving. Their numbers were drastically reduced during the 1800s but they have recovered completely and may be more numerous now than in historic times. The presence of man-made garbage dumps that serve as a smorgasbord for these birds may explain their recent population expansion. They are widespread in their distribution and are common on both of America's coastlines.

Natural History: At 30 inches in length and with a nearly 5.5-foot wingspan, the Great Black-backed Gull is the largest and heaviest gull in America. By the early 1900s the Great Black-backed Gull had become a very rare bird in America due to egg collecting and feather hunting. Today, the species is recovering and may be expanding its range. Like all gulls, it is an oportunistic feeder and it may have benefited from utilizing human refuse as food source. Another very similar but smaller gull species, the **Lesser Black-backed Gull** (*Larus fuscus*) can also be seen along the coasts of Florida in winter but it is also an uncommon species in the state. The Lesser Black-backed Gull is a much smaller gull at 21 inches in length, but has the same color pattern as the Great Black-backed Gull.

Natural History: The Sooty Tern is one of 3 similar tropical pelagic species that can be seen in the Florida Keys and just offshore in southernmost Florida. The other 2 species are the **Brown Noddy**, *Anous stolidus* and the **Bridled Tern**, *Onychoprion anaethetus.* The Sooty Tern is so well adapted to living at sea that it can stay aloft literally indefinetely and is rarely seen perched except when breeding. Of the 3 species the Sooty Tern is the one that is probably most likely to be seen in Florida, though the Brown Noddy can be briefly common on the Dry Tortugas during breeding season (as can the Sooty Tern). On some tropical islands Sooty Tern breeding colonies can number in the hundreds of thousands. These birds feed by plucking small fish from the surface of the sea.

Class - **Aves** (birds)

Order - **Charadriiformes** (shorebirds)

Family - **Laridae** (gulls and terns)

Black Tern *Chlidonias niger*	Gull-billed Tern *Gelochelidon nilotica*	Caspian Tern *Hydroprogne caspia*

Black Tern — *Chlidonias niger*

Transitional

Size: 9.75 inches.

Abundance: Uncommon.

Migratory Status: Spring, summer, and fall migrant.

Presumed range in Florida

Variation: In winter and in juvenile birds, the dramatic black color of the breast and belly is replaced by white. Transitional birds are blotched.

Habitat: Habitat in is shallow, freshwater marshes, salt marshes, and tidal mud flats.

Breeding: Breeding in New York occurs on protected beaches on Long Island. Nest is a scrape with 2 to 3 eggs.

Natural History: Winters along coastlines from Central America to northern South America. There is a European subspecies that winters in Africa. Like most terns these birds are highly social and usually seen in flocks. Unlike other terns, however, they feed heavily on insects, especially in summer. This is the only inland tern seen in Florida that has a dark breast and belly. Although the number of Black Terns today is estimated to be in the hundreds of thousands, this figure is paltry compared to the size of the population that existed before modern agricultural practices destroyed much of their breeding habitat. These birds are mainly a seasonal migrant in Florida and they will nest far to the north in Northern Plains states, the Great Lakes, and Canada.

Gull-billed Tern — *Gelochelidon nilotica*

Size: 14 inches.

Abundance: Uncommon.

Migratory Status: Mostly a summer resident in Florida.

Presumed range in Florida

Variation: In winter the black head is replaced by white or pale gray and there is a black smudge mark behind the eye. Breeders have solid black cap.

Habitat: Mostly coastal areas. Beaches, marshes, estuaries, etc. Islands are also a heavily used habitat.

Breeding: Colony nester that sometimes nests in mixed species colonies on dunes, barrier islands, etc. 3 eggs.

Natural History: Unlike most terns which are mainly fish eaters, this tern also consumes terrestrial prey like insects and bird eggs. They are known to "hawk" for flying insects that are caught in midair. Although fish is on their diet, they do not "plunge dive" for fish in the manner of many other tern species. Fiddler Crabs are listed as an important food item. Within its North American range this is largely a coastal species, but they may be seen inland at times in Florida. Their worldwide range includes Europe, north Africa, Asia and Australia. As with many shorebirds this species was decimated by the milinary trade in the late 1800s. Today's major threat is coastal development. Sexual maturity is reached at around 3 years of age and they may live as much as 15 years.

Caspian Tern — *Hydroprogne caspia*

Summer

Size: 21 inches.

Abundance: Uncommon.

Migratory Status: Mostly a winter bird in Florida.

Presumed range in Florida

Variation: In winter birds, the black cap becomes mottled with white. Juveniles are similar to winter adults. Sexes are alike.

Habitat: Mainly coastal birds in winter, they use rivers, large lakes, and marshes in migration.

Breeding: North American populations nest on large bodies of water in the interior of the continent. 1 to 3 eggs.

Natural History: The worlds largest tern and also the most widespread. Found all over the world, the Caspian Tern breeds on every continent except Antarctica. Despite its wide range it is not as common in North America as many other terns. Feeds almost entirely on fish. Feeds by hovering and diving. When diving often submerges completely. Food is mostly fish. This is the only large tern regularly seen inland. Nesting occurs on the Great Lakes and on large lakes in Canada. They are found along the southern coastlines and in winter tend to stay along the coasts. They are also seen inland in winter throughout the Florida peninsula. Nesting has been recorded in the northeast on eastern Lake Ontario and northern Lake Champlain. These large terns are known to live up to 26 years.

Class - **Aves** (birds)		
Order - **Charadriiformes** (shorebirds)		
Family - **Laridae** (gulls and terns)		

Least Tern *Sterna antillarum*	**Common Tern** *Sterna hirundo*	**Forster's Tern** *Sterna fosteri*

Size: 9 inches.	Presumed range in Florida 	**Size:** 15 inches.	Presumed range in Florida	**Size:** 14 inches.	Presumed range in Florida
Abundance: Fairly common.		**Abundance:** Uncommon.		**Abundance:** Fairly common.	
Migratory Status: Summer resident in Florida.		**Migratory Status:** Seasonal migrant and winter resident.		**Migratory Status:** Winter resident in Florida.	

Variation: No variation in Florida. Birds that nest on coasts may be a distinct subspecies from inland nesters.	**Variation:** First-year and winter birds have white foreheads and black bill. White on forehead reduced on 2nd year.	**Variation:** Exhibits both seasonal and age-related plumage variations (see photos above).
Habitat: Beaches and dunes are the main habitat, both in summer and winter. Also uses islands on inland rivers. May frequent inland lakes in summer.	**Habitat:** Migrating birds usually associate with major rivers and large lakes. Islands and dunes are frequently used. Also seen on Florida beaches in winter.	**Habitat:** Marshes. Both fresh and salt. Also beaches and coastlines. May also use inland rivers and lakes in Florida in winter.
Breeding: Nest is a scrape on sand with 2 to 3 eggs. May nest near other shorebird species.	**Breeding:** Nests mostly in Canada and along the northern Atlantic coastline. Lays 2 or 3 eggs.	**Breeding:** Breeds mostly on inland marshes in the center of the continent. 1 to 4 eggs in nest of matted vegetation.
Natural History: The Least Tern is as its name implies, our smallest tern species. They are widespread in distribution along America's coastlines and a distinct population also nests inland on major rivers in the middle of the continent. All winter along southeastern coastlines and some as far south as the Caribbean and Central America. In the 1800s, these birds were killed and skinned to adorn womens hats. This birds habitat (sandy beaches and dunes) is also highly valued real estate for humans. Thus coastal development is a major threat to the species today. They are regarded as a Threatened Species in Florida and inland nesting populations are federally endangered. The food is mostly small fishes, usually caught in shallow waters. They will also eat crustaceans and insects.	**Natural History:** The Common Tern is well known to conservationists. They are symbolic of the fight to save many of America's bird species from wanton slaughter. From the early European settlement of North America to the late 1800s, unregulated overhunting of America's wildlife nearly wiped out many species. Millions of herons, egrets, waterfowl, and shorebirds were killed for food and for the millinery trade. At the same time America's large mammal species also suffered dramatic population declines. Today, many wildlife species, including terns, have recovered dramatically, but tern populations are still below historical numbers nationwide. Common Tern nesting colonies situated in coastal areas are in many states now afforded strict protections.	**Natural History:** Forster's Terns can be seen statewide in Florida in winter, usually frequenting the state's major river systems and large impoundments or natural lakes. They are also common on beaches. They are sometimes seen in the company of gulls and other tern species, especially in winter along the coastlines of Florida where gulls and terns can both be common. These medium-sized terns feed almost exclusively on small fish that are captured by diving from above. When "fishing," they fly back and forth over water with the bill pointed downward and plunge headlong into the water. They are graceful fliers that sometimes hover when schools of fish are located. One other medium-sized tern species, the **Roseate Tern**, *Sterna dougalli*, is a regular nester in the Florida Keys.

Class - **Aves** (birds)

Order - **Charadriiformes** (shorebirds)

Family - **Laridae** (gulls and terns)

Royal Tern	Sandwich Tern	Black Skimmer
Thalasseus maximus	*Thalasseus sandvicensis*	*Rychops niger*

Size: 20 inches.	**Size:** 15 inches.	**Size:** 18 inches.
Abundance: Fairly common.	**Abundance:** Uncommon.	**Abundance:** Uncommon.
Migratory Status: Year-round resident in Florida.	**Migratory Status:** Year-round resident in Florida.	**Migratory Status:** Year-round resident in Florida.

Presumed range in Florida

Variation: Forehead turns white in winter and black crest has white speckling. In summer both are solid black.

Variation: Forehead turns white in winter and black crest has white speckling. In summer both are solid black.

Variation: Young birds at hatching have upper and lower mandibles of equal length.

Habitat: A coastal species that can be seen on beaches throughout the state. May move a short way up rivers, creeks.

Habitat: A coastal species that frequents beaches, boat docks, and pilings. Rarely more than a mile from shore.

Habitat: Habitat is bays, salt marsh, and coastal regions. May rarely fly inland to use freshwater lakes.

Breeding: Breeds in large colonies on barrier islands or remote beaches and dunes. Usually lays a single egg.

Breeding: Most nesting is on barrier islands. Nest is a shallow scrape. Colony nester. 1 or 2 eggs is typical.

Breeding: Colony nester on coastal dunes or marsh islands. Nest is a scrape in sand or on mats of vegetation. 4 eggs.

Natural History: This is one of the more commonly seen large terns on Florida beaches. It is surpassed in size only by the very similar appearing Caspian Tern, from which the Royal Tern can be differentiated by its bright orange bill (more reddish in the Caspian Tern). Most food is caught by "plunge diving" from heights of up to 30 feet. Fish and shrimp are 2 of the main foods consumed. Most foraging is done in shallow waters and often in bays or estuaries and tidal areas. Never feeds in freshwater but may travel long distances up and down the coast when feeding. Very large flocks will gather when schools of prey are located. Often these flocks will include pelicans, gulls, and other tern species. Threats include entanglement in fishing line and nets and ingesting of baited hooks or even artificial lures. Lives over 25 years.

Natural History: This is one of the most recognizable of Florida's tern species. Its black bill with a bright yellow tip is unique among Florida's terns. Found throughout Florida's coastline and ranges as far north as the Delmarva Peninsula in summer. Can also be found throughout the Gulf Coast and the Caribbean as well as coastal areas of Central and South America. They are rather rare as a breeding bird in Florida, but several breeding colonies are known to exist in the state. Most breeding colonies are along the western gulf coastal region from Louisiana through Texas. Declined significantly during millinary trade. Severe storms that can destroy ephemeral barrier island breeding sites are a modern threat. The most pressing human threat may be the robbing of eggs from the nest by people in the Caribbean and South America.

Natural History: Another seaside bird with a distinctive bill. The lower mandible is significantly larger than the upper, which allows the Black Skimmer to snatch small fishes from the quite waters of inlets, bays, and especially tidal pools in marshes and intercoastal areas. As they fly just centimeters above the surface with bill slightly agape the longer lower mandible plows the surface and any small fish encountered slides upward on the lower bill to be instantly caught by the upper bill snapping closed. These are highly social birds that nest in colonies and when resting are always seen in large flocks. Nesting colonies are often in the company of nesting terns, and it is possible that some protection from predators may be afforded to the Skimmers by the terns, that can be very aggressive when defending their nests.

Class - **Aves** (birds)		
Order - **Anseriformes** (ducks, geese, and swans)		
Family - **Anatidae**		
Black-bellied Duck *Dendrocygna autumnalis*	**Fulvous Duck** *Dendrocygna bicolor*	**Canada Goose** *Branta candensis*

Size: 21 inches.	Presumed range in Florida	**Size:** 19 inches.	Presumed range in Florida	**Size:** 45 inches.	Presumed range in Florida
Abundance: Uncommon.		**Abundance:** Uncommon.		**Abundance:** Uncommon in FL.	
Migratory Status: Year-round resident in Florida.		**Migratory Status:** Year-round resident in Florida.		**Migratory Status:** Winter migrant and winter resident.	

Variation: Juveniles have dark bills and are uniformly plumage.	**Variation:** Juveniles are less vividly colored than adults.	**Variation:** Subspecies vary significantly in size with light and dark morphs.
Habitat: Wetlands of many types are used including freshwater swamps and marshes, natural lakes, salt, and brackish water marshes and coastal estuaries.	**Habitat:** Tends to favor coastal areas where the main habitat is marshlands. In regions where rice is grown rice fields are an important habitat.	**Habitat:** The habitat includes all types of aquatic situations, from urban parks to remote and inaccessible marshes, swamps, or beaver ponds.
Breeding: Will use natural cavities in trees or sometimes nest on the ground. Breeds throughout the Florida peninsula. Clutch size averages about a dozen.	**Breeding:** The nest is usually constructed on mats of floating vegetation. 12 to 14 eggs is common. Preococial young can swim and dive immediately.	**Breeding:** Nests above the waterline but near water. 4 to 8 eggs is typical. Young will stay with the parents for at least a year.
Natural History: This tropical and semitropical duck has expanded its range in the last century and it appears to be a thriving species. They first began to appear in Florida in the late 1960s and today occupy most of the peninsula, though they are still more common in the southern portion of the state. Black-belled Ducks are fond of perching in trees and in fact the species is sometimes referred to as the "Black-bellied Tree Duck." The Black-bellied Duck is a new world species and is restricted in distribution to the Americas. They can be found from the southern US to Argentina. These ducks are mainly vegetarians and they feed mostly at night. Shallow water habitats are the main habitats used for feeding but they also feed on land.	**Natural History:** Fulvous Ducks have expanded their breeding range in recent decade. The first breeding of Fulvous Ducks in Florida was recorded only about 3 decades ago. They regularly wander north of the area shown on the map above and may expand their breeding range northward in the future. Their current migratory and breeding range in the US includes most of the Gulf Coast region. Rare wanderers have been recorded well to the north along the Atlantic coastline. They feed on plant material in shallow water habitats and in the western gulf (Louisiana and Texas) rice fields are a favorite foraging area. They range from the Gulf Coast of the US to South America and can also be found in Hawaii, East Africa, and parts of Asia.	**Natural History:** This is the most recognized wild goose in America, due in large part to the fact that tame and semi-tame populations are found in parks and on rivers, ponds and lakes in both urban and rural regions. Resident Canada Geese are numerous, but their numbers are swelled dramatically during winter as birds from farther north visit the state for either a brief stopover or a months long stay. The characteristic "V formation" of Canada Geese in flight is a familiar sight and their musical, honking call is to many a symbol of wild America. They are heavily hunted throughout America both for sport and for food. They are long-lived birds and have been known to survive over 40 years. A small species called the **Cackling Goose** (*Branta hutchinsonii*) is the size of a Mallard.

Class - **Aves** (birds)

Order - **Anseriformes** (ducks, geese, and swans)

Family - **Anatidae**

Wood Duck *Aix sponsa*	**Blue-winged Teal** *Spatula discors*	**Shoveler** *Spatula clypeata*

Wood Duck	Blue-winged Teal	Shoveler
Size: 18.5 inches.	**Size:** 15.5 inches.	**Size:** 19 inches.
Abundance: Fairly common.	**Abundance:** Common.	**Abundance:** Fairly common.
Migratory Status: Resident and seasonal migrant in Florida. *Presumed range in Florida*	**Migratory Status:** Mostly a fall through spring resident. *Presumed range in Florida*	**Migratory Status:** Winter resident in Florida. *Presumed range in Florida*
Variation: Significant sexual dimorphism (see photos above).	**Variation:** Significant sexual dimorphism (see photos above).	**Variation:** Significant sexual dimorphism (see photos above).
Habitat: Beaver ponds, swamps, flooded woodlands, and farm ponds are among the favorite habitats in Florida.	**Habitat:** Marshes, beaver ponds, bays, and other shallow water habitats. Uses mostly freshwater wetlands.	**Habitat:** Prefers shallow habitats. Swamps, marshes, flooded fields, and bays. Uses mostly freshwater habitats.
Breeding: Nests in tree hollows and takes readily to artificial nest boxes. Lays about 8 to 12 eggs typically. Nests widely in Florida.	**Breeding:** Nest is concealed in dense vegetation near water but above high waterline. Lays 6 to 12 eggs. Does not nest in Florida.	**Breeding:** Breeds in northern and western United States (including Alaska) and in Canada. Averages 10 to 12 eggs.

Natural History: Male Wood Ducks are one of the most brilliantly colored birds in America. The bulk of the Wood Duck population in America occurs in the forested eastern half of the country. Populations plummeted during the latter half of the nineteenth century as America's forests were felled and swamplands drained. Populations began to recover by the 1950s and today the species is thriving. Wood Ducks are widely hunted and make up a significant number of ducks killed by hunters annually. Although they are a small duck, they are considered by many as highly palatable. Although Wood Ducks are year-round residents in Florida, their numbers are swelled each winter by birds that summered farther to the north and moved south in winter. Some birds seen in Florida in winter may have been hatched in Canada.

Natural History: The food of this species is mostly plant material including algae and aquatic greenery. Many seeds and grains are also eaten, especially in winter when they converge on rice fields and other flooded agricultural areas in America's Lower Coastal Plain. Breeding females will consume large amounts of invertebrates during the breeding season. These ducks are early fall migrators and some of the last to migrate back north in the spring. A few will linger well into late spring or even early summer. Many will winter as far south as South America, but substantial numbers can be seen along the Lower Coastal Plain of North America all winter, including all of Florida. Most breed and spend the summer on the central prairies of the US and Canada and some will nest as far north as Alaska.

Natural History: The Shoveler's name is derived from the unique shape of its bill, which is a highly effective sieve for straining tiny organisms from water. They are often observed swimming along with the bill held under water or skimming the surface. Like several of America's duck species, the Shoveler is Holarctic in distribution and breeds in Europe and Asia as well as North America. Eurasian birds winter southward to north Africa and the Pacific region. All ground nesting birds are vulnerable to mammalian predators and the Shoveler is no exception. Red Foxes and Mink are significant predators on the nesting females, while skunks are a major threat to the eggs. Shovelers nest in North America's "Prairie Pothole" region and during years of drought modern farming practices reduce cover for nesting ducks, increasing nest predation.

Class - **Aves** (birds)

Order - **Anseriformes** (ducks, geese, and swans)

Family - **Anatidae**

Gadwall *Mareca strepera*	American Widgeon *Mareca americana*	Mallard *Anas platyrhychos*

Size: 20 inches.	**Size:** 19 inches.	**Size:** 23 inches.
Abundance: Fairly common.	**Abundance:** Fairly common.	**Abundance:** Fairly common.
Migratory Status: Winter resident in Florida.	**Migratory Status:** Winter resident in Florida.	**Migratory Status:** Winter resident in Florida.

Presumed range in Florida (all three columns)

Variation: Significant sexual dimorphism (see photos above).	**Variation:** Significant sexual dimorphism (see photos above).	**Variation:** Significant sexual dimorphism (see photos above).
Habitat: Marshes and potholes of the Great Plains in summer. Uses all aquatic habitats in winter.	**Habitat:** Winter range includes all types of aquatic habitats in the state (swamps, marshes, lakes, ponds, etc.).	**Habitat:** Found in aquatic situations everywhere, from deserts to tundra to southern swamplands, ponds, lakes, etc.
Breeding: Nests among thick vegetation near water, often on islands in marshes or lakes. Lays 7 to 12 eggs.	**Breeding:** Nests near shallow freshwater wetlands and potholes mostly in the North American prairie. 3 to 12 eggs.	**Breeding:** Nests on the ground in close proximity to water. Lays up to 13 eggs and will renest if nest is destroyed.

Natural History: Gadwalls breed and summer largely in the Great Plains region. In winter they are seen all across the southern half of America, with the greatest numbers wintering along the western Gulf Coast Coastal Plain. Populations of this duck can fluctuate significantly depending upon water levels in the prairies of Canada and the north-central US. Droughts and poor agricultural practices that eliminate habitat can cause populations to plummet. Conversely, good rainfall and good wildlife conservation practices by farmers have shown to be a real boon to this and many other duck species that depend on the marshes and potholes on the Great Plains for nesting habitat. Adult Gadwalls feed mostly on plant material. Ducklings rely heavily upon high protein invertebrates for growth and development.

Natural History: The American Wigeon also goes by the name "Baldpate," a reference to the white crown of the male. This duck has a very similar Old World counter part, the Eurasian Wigeon, which ranges throughout much of Europe and Asia. American birds feed mostly on plant material, but females when breeding opt for a higher protein diet of invertebrates. One of the more northerly ranging members of the "puddle duck" group, some individuals will summer as far north as the Arctic Coastal Plain of Alaska. These ducks may be seen in Florida from November through March, but peak numbers occur in midwinter. Some merely pass through the state headed to tropical regions, but many will stay throughout the winter. As with other puddle ducks, this species is susceptible to population declines during droughts.

Natural History: By far the most familiar duck in America. The Mallard has been widely domesticated but it is also the most common wild duck in the United States. Many parks and public lakes around the country have semi-wild populations that are nonmigratory. Highly adaptable, this is the most successful duck species in America, perhaps in the world. It is the source of all breeds of domestic duck except the Muscovey and they are thus an important food source for humans. They are also a highly regarded game bird and they are hunted throughout North America. They range throughout the northern half of the globe and their range in the western hemisphere closely coincides with the North American continent. Captive Mallards released in the Florida peninsula pose a threat to Mottled Ducks through hybridization.

Class - **Aves** (birds)
Order - **Anseriformes** (ducks, geese, and swans)
Family - **Anatidae**

Black Duck *Anas rubripes*	**Mottled Duck** *Anas fulvigula*	**Pintail** *Anas acuta*

Black Duck
Anas rubripes

Size: 23 inches.

Presumed range in Florida

Abundance: Rare in Florida.

Migratory Status: Winter resident in Florida.

Variation: Sexes are very similar, females have a darker bill than males.

Habitat: Fond of estuaries and coastal marshes. Inland will use other aquatic habitats (lake, marshes, swamps, etc.).

Breeding: For breeding favors coastal marshes and beaver ponds and bogs in boreal forests. Lays up to 14 eggs. Does not breed in Florida.

Natural History: The Black Duck is very similar to the Mallard in size, shape, and voice, and the 2 species are known to hybridize. In appearance and other traits, however, they are quite different. This is one of the few puddle ducks that does not range throughout the continent, being restricted to the eastern half of America. Like many of America's duck species, the Black Duck has been impacted negatively by human related changes to the landscape and environment in America. Drainage of wetlands, urbanization along northeastern coastlines, and deforestation have hit this species harder than most other ducks and the population has declined significantly in the last half century. Interbreeding with the more adaptable Mallard may also be a threat to this uniquely American duck.

Mottled Duck
Anas fulvigula

Size: 22 inches.

Presumed range in Florida

Abundance: Fairly common.

Migratory Status: Year-round resident of Florida.

Variation: Sexual differences are weak. Female has black blotches on bill.

Habitat: Marshes and wet prairies are the primary habitat. Uses man-made waste water treatment wetlands.

Breeding: Nests near water but often in overgrown fields or cattle pastures. Clutch size is 8 to 12 eggs typically. Breeds in Florida.

Natural History: Mottled Ducks are closely related to both the Mallard and the Black Duck. Unlike those two species however the Mottled Duck is totally adapted to life in the Deep South and is the only "puddle duck" species that does not migrate. Unlike most ducks, these birds are not seen in large flocks and are usually seen in pair or in a family group consisting of the female and her brood. It also shows a definite preference for freshwater over saltwater habitats, although it may be found near the coast in freshwater situations. In Florida this species is threatened by hybridization with captive reared Mallards that have been released or escaped. Continued development and subsequent loss of wetland habitat is also a threat. In appearance this species is very similar to the female Mallard.

Pintail
Anas acuta

Size: 25 inches.

Presumed range in Florida

Abundance: Uncommon in FL.

Migratory Status: Winter resident in Florida.

Variation: Significant sexual dimorphism. See photos above.

Habitat: Open country. In Florda uses large wet prairies, salt marshes, estuaries, and bays.

Breeding: Breeds in marshes, potholes, and tundra in the northern and western portions of the continent. 3 to 12 eggs. Does not breed in Florida.

Natural History: Northern Pintail populations are in decline. Modern agricultural practices on the Great Plains of the US and Canada are the greatest threat. They are also highly susceptible to droughts in the prairie regions, which limit breeding habitat. Food is mostly plant material but some aquatic invertebrates are also eaten. On wintering grounds waste grain from farming operations has become an important food source. In recent decades, the species has benefited from a number of conservation efforts by state and federal agencies as well as private organizations, most notably Ducks Unlimited, an organization funded by duck hunters. Conservation efforts that have recently benefited the species are reduced hunter harvest and changing agricultural practices in the Prairie Pothole Region.

Class - **Aves** (birds)
Order - **Anseriformes** (ducks, geese, and swans)
Family - **Anatidae**

Green-winged Teal	Canvasback	Redhead
Anas crecca	*Aythya valisineria*	*Aythya americana*

Size: 14 inches.

Abundance: Fairly common.

Migratory Status: Winter resident in Florida.

Presumed range in Florida

Size: 21 inches.

Abundance: Rare in Florida.

Migratory Status: Winter migrant in Florida.

Presumed range in Florida

Size: 19 inches.

Abundance: Uncommon.

Migratory Status: Winter migrant/resident in Florida.

Presumed range in Florida

Variation: Significant sexual variation. See photos above.

Habitat: Winter range includes all types of aquatic habitats in the state (swamps, marshes, lakes, ponds, etc.). Use both fresh and brackish marshes.

Breeding: Nest is in dense vegetation in wetland habitats of the far north. 6 to 9 eggs are laid as early as May.

Natural History: This is the smallest of America's "puddle ducks," and also one of the more common. They range throughout the northern hemisphere, with a distinct subspecies being found in Eurasia. They are fast and agile fliers and flocks of Green-winged Teal move back and forth across the southern half of the continent all winter in response to weather patterns. Populations of this duck appear stable and may even be increasing. About 90 percent of the population breeds in Canada and Alaska where they favor river deltas and boreal wetlands over the typical "pothole" habitats used by many puddle ducks. Their remote nesting habitats are largely undisturbed by man, which may account in part for this species' abundance. As with many species, the increasing daylight hours of spring triggers migration and breeding instincts.

Variation: Significant sexual variation. See photos above.

Habitat: Primarily a marshland species that alternates between prairie potholes in summer and gulf coastal marshes in winter.

Breeding: The large nest is built from grasses and hidden vegetation. Clutch size averages around 7 or 8.

Natural History: One of the most adept divers of the "Diving Ducks," Canvasbacks have been known to dive to a depth of 30 feet. Feeds mostly on plant material including roots and rhizomes, but will also eat mud-dwelling invertebrates. This is strictly a North American species and is one of the least common duck species in America. They are vulnerable to droughts, habitat loss (mostly from agriculture), and water pollution that can impact the abundance of aquatic food plants. The Canvasback population is closely monitored by the US Fish and Wildlife Service and in years of low numbers hunting of this species may be banned. Even in years when hunting is allowed, the bag limits are typically very low (1 per day). The species name (*valisineria*) is also the genus name for Water Celery, which is one of this duck's favorite foods.

Variation: Significant sexual variation. See photos above.

Habitat: Primarily a marshland species that alternates between prairie potholes and gulf coastal marshes. In migration they will use a variety of habitats.

Breeding: Breeds almost entirely in the "prairie pothole" region. Females often lay their eggs in other ducks nests.

Natural History: An entirely North American species, the Redhead is mostly a vegetarian and feeds heavily on tubers and aquatic vegetation. Most Redhead's congregate in winter on the western Gulf Coast of Louisiana, Texas, and northwest Mexico. In fact hundreds of thousands will concentrate in this region each winter. Here they feed mostly on the roots of shoalgrass. They will also eat some animal matter, mostly aquatic invertebrates. Redheads are easily decoyed and during the days of the market hunting their populations suffered dramatic declines. Recovery in the last few decades has been significant and in a good year the population may reach a million birds. Reproductive success is often tied to weather conditions in the "Prairie Pothole" region fo the Great Plains. Drought years result in poor production.

Class - **Aves** (birds)

Order - **Anseriformes** (ducks, geese, and swans)

Family - **Anatidae**

Ring-necked Duck *Aythya collaris*	**Lesser Scaup** *Aythya affinis*	**Black Scoter** *Melanitta americana*

Size: 17 inches.

Abundance: Fairly common.

Migratory Status: Winter resident in Florida.

Presumed range in Florida

Variation: Sexually dimorphic. See photos above.

Habitat: Open water habitats including shallow bays and flooded river bottoms. Also uses open marshes and large rivers and lakes, where it tends to use mostly shallow-water areas.

Breeding: Nests in Subarctic regions of Canada and the Northern Rockies in the United States. Lays 6 to 14 eggs.

Natural History: Closely related to and very similar in appearance to the scaups, the Ring-necked Duck should be called the Ring-billed duck. Although there is a brownish ring around the neck of the male, it is only visible when the bird is in the hand. The broad white ring near the tip of the bill and the narrow white ring at the base of the bill are both readily discernible on birds in the field. Unlike its relatives the scaups which will feed on crustaceans, insects, and other aquatic invertebrates, the diet of the Ring-necked Duck is mostly vegetarian. Unlike their similar relatives the Scaups, Ring-necked Ducks favor small lakes, ponds and swamps over large rivers and lakes. The Ring-necked Duck is an endemic North American species, but like most waterfowl it is prone to wander off the continent.

Size: 16.5 inches

Abundance: Fairly common.

Migratory Status: Winter resident in Florida.

Presumed range in Florida

Variation: Sexually dimorphic. See photos above.

Habitat: Likes larger bodies of water and deeper water than many other ducks. Regularly uses large lakes and rivers in the state as well as flooded river bottoms.

Breeding: 8 to 10 eggs is typical. Nests in west-central US, Canada and in Alaska.

Natural History: These ducks are the most widespread and common of the "diving ducks." Diving ducks are capable of diving deeper and prefer deeper waters than the "puddle ducks." They are also more clumsy on land and need a running start on the water to get airborne. They thus favor larger lakes and rivers over small ponds and swamplands. They are known for forming large flocks in open water (called "rafts"). These rafts sometimes number in the thousands. A slightly larger version of the Lesser Scaup, known as the **Greater Scaup** (*Athya marila*) can also be seen in the Florida panhandle in winter. The Greater Scaup however is a rare species in Florida. Both species like open water. The Greater Scaup tends to favor coastal areas and salt or brackish marshes.

Size: 19 inches.

Abundance: Very rare in FL.

Migratory Status: Winter migrant in Florida.

Presumed range in Florida

Variation: Sexually dimorphic. See photo above.

Habitat: In fall and winter, Scoters may rarely use large lakes and rivers in inland areas. But in winter they use mostly coastal waters. In summer they are a bird of the boreal forest waters.

Breeding: Scoters nests near shallow inland lakes in the far north, often well into the Arctic Circle. 7 to 12 eggs.

Natural History: There are a total of 3 Scoter species in North America and all 3 have been seen in Florida's coastal waters during winter months. Their tendancy to associate with coastal waters has resulted in them collectively being referred to as "Sea Ducks." They will summer inland in the far north of northern Canada and Alaska. Waterfowl of all species are well-known for wandering widely and sometimes appearing in areas far from their normal habitats. In addition to the the Black Scoter species shown above the **Surf Scoter** (*M. perspicillata*) can also rarely be seen in the state; while the **White-winged Scoter** (*M. fusca*) is the rarest of the 3 in Florida waters. Of the three species the Black Scoter is by far the most likely to be seen in Florida. Its range is restricted to northern FL.

Class - **Aves** (birds)
Order - **Anseriformes** (ducks, geese, and swans)
Family - **Anatidae**

Bufflehead *Bucephal albeola*	**Common Goldeneye** *Bucephala clangula*	**Hooded Merganser** *Lophodytes cucullatus*

Bufflehead	Common Goldeneye	Hooded Merganser
Size: 13.5 inches	**Size:** 18.5 inches.	**Size:** 18 inches.
Abundance: Fairly common.	**Abundance:** Uncommon.	**Abundance:** Fairly common.
Migratory Status: Winter resident/migrant in Florida.  Presumed range in Florida	**Migratory Status:** Winter resident/migrant in Florida.  Presumed range in Florida	**Migratory Status:** Winter resident and migrant in Florida.  Presumed range in Florida
Variation: Sexually dimorphic. See photo above.	**Variation:** Significant sexual variation. See photos above. Juvenile like female.	**Variation:** Significant sexual variation. See photos above.
Habitat: Most winter in saltwater habitats on the coast but a few overwinter on inland lakes and rivers. In summer they use boreal forests and parklands in Canada.	**Habitat:** In winter this species uses large lakes and rivers inland. They are also fairly common in winter in coastal regions. In summer they are a bird of the boreal forests.	**Habitat:** In winter uses swamps, shallow bays of lakes and river floodplains. Less likely to be seen in saltwater habitats but will use brackish estuaries. Often seen in small ponds.
Breeding: Cavity nester. Nest is often an old woodpecker hole. Clutch size ranges from a few to over a dozen eggs.	**Breeding:** Cavity nester that will use artificial nest boxes. May nest over a mile from water. 7 to 12 eggs.	**Breeding:** Cavity nester. Most nest in Great Lakes region. No nesting in Florida. Lays 12 eggs maximum.
Natural History: America's smallest of the diving ducks, the Bufflehead is one of the few duck species that will remain with the same mate year after year. Breeding pairs usually return to the same pond or marsh to breed each year as well. With the exception of some seeds, these ducks are mostly carnivorous, feeding on aquatic insects, crustaceans, and mollusks. Unlike the puddle ducks which often feed on the surface, the Bufflehead finds all its food by diving. Although they are often seen on deep water lakes, they feed in the shallows along the banks or in the backs of bays. Although rarely seen in large flocks, this is one of the few duck species that has actually increased in numbers in the last few decades. Due to their carnivorous feeding habits, they are not highly regarded as a food species.	**Natural History:** As with other diving ducks the Common Goldeneye is an excellent swimmer that feeds by diving beneath the surface. They propel through the water using only the feet, with the wings held tight against the body. They are mostly carnivorous but they do eat some plant material in the form of tubers and seeds. Aquatic invertebrates are the main food and include (in order of importance) crustaceans, insects, and mollusks. Fish constitute only a small portion of the diet. Male Common Goldeneyes engage in a complex courtship display to attract females or reinforce the pair bond. These ducks are Holarctic in distribution, breeding in boreal forests throughout the northern hemisphere. Although widely hunted, they are not regarded as a very palatable duck for eating.	**Natural History:** Unlike our other 2 merganser ducks, both of which are Holarctic in distribution, the Hooded Merganser is strictly a North American duck. Another odd distributional trait is the fact that these birds are rare in the Great Plains region, where many North American duck species are most common. They have a more diverse diet than the larger mergansers, feeding less on fish and more on aquatic invertebrates that are located by means of well-developed underwater vision capability. Winter waterfowl surveys indicate that over 50 percent of the population winters in the Mississippi flyway. Most likely to be seen in Florida in December, January, and February, but records exist for both spring and fall. While still a fairly common species, they are less numerous than in pre-European settlement.

Class - **Aves** (birds)
Order - **Anseriformes** (ducks, geese, and swans)
Family - **Anatidae**

Red-breasted Merganser	Ruddy Duck
Mergus serrator	*Oxyura jamaicensis*

Male

Male

Female

Female

Size: 23 inches.

Abundance: Fairly common in winter.

Migratory Status: May been seen in Florida from November through April.

Variation: Sexual and ontogenetic plumage variations.

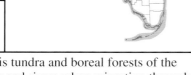
Presumed range in Florida

Size: 15 inches.

Abundance: Uncommon in Florida.

Migratory Status: May been seen in Florida from November through March.

Variation: Significant sexual variation. See photos above.

Presumed range in Florida

Habitat: Summer habitat is tundra and boreal forests of the far north. Uses larger lakes and rivers when migrating through inland areas. Winter habitat in Florida is mainly in coastal areas. Salt marshes, estuaries, etc.

Habitat: Marshes, ponds, lakes, and to a lesser extent, rivers. This is a true "Prairie Pothole" species and nearly 90 percent of nesting occurs in the prairie pothole habitats in the northern plains.

Breeding: Nests on the ground. Nest is well hidden beneath overhanging vegetation or in cavities. 5 to 24 eggs.

Breeding: Nest is usually built in cattails or other aquatic vegetation. 7 or 8 eggs is average.

Natural History: During winter these birds show a preference for coastal regions where they use estuaries and saltwater bays and salt/brackish water marshes. The Red-breasted has a Holarctic distribution and is found in Europe and Asia as well as North America. In summer, this species ranges as far north as the Arctic Ocean and southern Greenland. In winter, they may be seen throughout Florida's coastal regions. Food is mostly small fish that are grasped with the serrated bill. Also eats aquatic invertebrates and amphibians. Feeds both in shallow water and in deep water up to at least 25 feet deep.

Natural History: Ruddy Ducks are primarily western birds that range generally from the Great Plains to the West Coast. Winter range includes most of the western US and a few individuals are regularly seen in the eastern half of the country in winter. The larva of aquatic insects of the order Diptera (flies, mosquitos, midges) are reported to be a primary food of these ducks. Although they are small ducks, their eggs are quite large and are in fact the largest eggs (relative to body size) of any North American duck.

CHAPTER 5

THE CROCODILIANS OF FLORIDA

TABLE 3

—THE ORDERS AND FAMILIES OF FLORIDA CROCODILIANS —

Class - **Eusuchia**

Order - **Crocodylia** (crocodilians)

Family	**Alligatoridae** (alligators and caimans)
Family	**Crocodylidae** (crcodiles)

Class - **Eusuchia**

Order - **Crocodylia** (crocodilians)

Family - **Alligatoridae** (alligators and caimans)		Family - **Crocodylia** (crocodiles)

American Alligator
Alligator mississippiensis

Size: Females are usually under 8 feet. Record for male is 19 feet, 2 inches.	Presumed range in Florida 
Abundance: Common.	

Variation: Young are vividly marked with yellow and black bars on sides and tail. Old adults can be quite dark.

Habitat: Inhabits all freshwater habits in the state (wet prairies, lakes, rivers, canals, and even roadside ditches). Most common in parks and preserves.

Breeding: Female constructs a dome nest from palm fronds, leaves, and other organic detritus. Up to 50 eggs may be laid. Female often guards the nest.

Natural History: No other animal in the state conjures images of "the real Florida" more than the American Alligator. By the 1950s they had been nearly exterminated in most of the state. With the passage of the Endangered Species Act in 1973, they were afforded full protection and began to make a remarkable comeback. Today they are once again a common animal in Florida and are now treated as a game species by the FWC. Controlled harvest through hunting, coupled with a robust "nuisance Alligator" control program, keeps their numbers in check and helps protect the state's human inhabitants from these potentially dangerous crocodilians. Most attacks on humans are the result of Alligators having been fed by humans. A fed Alligator not only loses any natural fear of humans, but worse, comes to associate people with food. That can be a deadly combination in such a large and powerful wild animal.

Spectacled Caiman
Caiman crocodilus

Size: Average is about 6 feet for adult males. Record is 8 feet, 8 inches.	Presumed range in Florida 
Abundance: Rare in Florida.	

Variation: Babies have a distinct pattern of dark brown bands on a greenish background. Adults are dark olive.

Habitat: In Florida, this species is restricted to the southern tip of the state. Vulnerability to freezing temperatures should limit its northward expansion.

Breeding: Female constructs a dome nest from palm fronds, leaves, and other organic detritus. Up to 41 eggs has been recorded from one nest in Florida.

Natural History: The Spectacled Caimen is an exotic species that first became established in Florida as early as the late 1960s. It has since become well established in the southernmost tip of the state. Originally native to Central America and northern South America, Florida populations likely began from escaped or released pet animals. In habits and habitat it is very similar to the American Alligator, but is a more tropical species. They may be seen in the same aquatic habitats as the American Alligator, including in canals and roadside ditches in the Everglades region. Like all crocodilians, they are predators that will eat almost anything they can catch, but fishes, wading birds, and small and medium-sized mammals make up the bulk of the diet for adults. This is one of several caiman species that are native to Central and South America. It is one of the more common crocodilians within its natural range.

American Crocodile
Crocodylus acutus

Size: Females under 10 feet. Males can reach a record length of 23 feet.	Presumed range in Florida 
Abundance: Rare in Florida.	

Variation: Hatchlings are more vividly marked with bold black bars or spots. Males grow twice as large as females.

Habitat: Crocodiles are more likely to be found in salt and brackish water habitats. In Florida, this means mangroves and estuaries in the southern tip of state.

Breeding: Females lay up to 50 eggs in a nest typical of all crocodilians. Eggs hatch in about 3 months into 10-inch-long baby replicas of the adults.

Natural History: This is a tropical species that is widespread throughout the Caribbean, Central America, and northern South America. Southern Florida represents the northernmost distribution of the species, and they are vulnerable to extreme cold snaps this far north. Florida populations are listed as Federally Threatened, and the International Union of Concerned Naturalists lists the overall population as Vulnerable. The current status of population within Everglades National Park is probably stable and may be increasing. But they are vulnerable to increased human alteration of habitat and water management practices elsewhere within their Florida range. As adults, they have no natural enemies, but babies are subject to predation. As with many other crocodilians, the ambient temperature of incubating eggs determines the sex of the offspring. Higher temperatures produces males, lower temperatures females.

CHAPTER 6

THE TURTLES OF FLORIDA

TABLE 4.

— THE ORDERS AND FAMILIES OF FLORIDA TURTLES —

Note: The arrangement below reflects the the order in which the turtless of Florida appear in this chapter. It may not be an accurate reflection of the phylogenetic relationship of the turtles.

Class - **Chelonia** (turtles)

Order - **Cryptodira** (straight necked turtles)

Family	**Kinosternidae** (mud and musk turtles)
Family	**Chelydridae** (snapping turtles)
Family	**Emydidae** (sliders and box turtles)
Family	**Testudinidae** (tortoises)
Family	**Trionychidae** (softshell turtles)
Family	**Cheloniidae** (marine turtles)
Family	**Dermochelyidae** (leatherback)

Class - **Chelonia** (turtles)
Order - **Cryptodira** (straightneck turtles)
Family - **Kinosternidae** (mud and musk turtles)

Eastern Musk Turtle	Loggerhead Musk Turtle
Sternotherus oderatus	*Sternotherus minor*

Size: About 4 inches in carapace length as an adult. Record just under 6 inches.	Presumed range in Florida 	**Size:** 3 to 4.75 inches in carapace length as an adult. Record 5.5 inches.	Presumed range in Florida 
Abundance: Very common.		**Abundance:** Common.	
Variation: In some regions, females are larger than males, but it is not known if that type of sexual dimophism applies in Florida.		**Variation:** There are 2 subspecies of Loggerhead Musk Turtle. Only 1 subspecies (*S.m. minor*) occurs in Florida.	

Habitat: Primarily a stream dweller, but can be found in a variety of aquatic habitats including swamps, oxbows, lakes, wet prairies, etc. They reach their highest densities in waters with abundant aquatic vegetation.	**Habitat:** Found in rivers, creeks, beaver ponds, springs, and other clear water habitats. This species shows a definite preference for flowing water habitats, and also prefers clear or tannin-stained waters over muddy water.
Breeding: Female lays 2 to 5 eggs under leaf litter or sometimes merely on top of the ground. Eggs hatch into tiny turtles that are barely an inch in length.	**Breeding:** 2 to 5 eggs is an average clutch and their may be more than 1 clutch per summer. No real nest is dug but eggs are laid in shallow depressions or beneath litter.
Natural History: Nocturnal and crepuscular and completely aquatic in habits. Unlike most aquatic turtles in America, the Musk Turtle rarely basks, but when it does it may climb several feet up into branches that overhang the water. When disturbed while basking, they will launch themselves clumsily into the safety of the water. Since they seldom leave the water, the carapace is often covered with a thick growth of algae. Their name comes from the presence of musk-producing glands that emit an unpleasant odor when the turtles are handled. This musk also accounts for their other common name "Stinkpot." The Eastern Musk Turtle is widespread throughout the eastern US, being found from the Gulf Coast north to the Great Lakes, but they are absent from most of the higher elevations of the Appalachian Plateau. They do occur statewide in Florida and are one of the most common turtles in the state. They are an omnivorous species that feeds on a variety of aquatic plant and animal matter. Feeds by "bottom walking" under water. Like many turtle species, the Eastern Musk Turtle is a long-lived species and 1 captive zoo specimen lived for 55 years.	**Natural History:** The name "Loggerhead" Musk is derived from the enlarged size of this turtle's head. The males reportedly have larger heads than the females. Individuals living in warm water springs that are common in north Florida may remain active well into the winter. They tend to feed mostly at night or in the early morning and may forage on land near the edge of a stream or river. Many types of aquatic invertebrates are eaten including aquatic insects, fish, crayfish, bivalves, and mollusks. Land prey consumed is mostly insects, spiders, and worms. They will also eat carrion and some plant material such as algea. In fact, they are so varied in their dietary choices that it is safe to say that almost any animal matter that can be swallowed may be consumed. They are easily trapped in minnow traps baited with any type of meat. The ability to absorb oxygen through mucus membranes allows them to withstand submersion for long periods and they have survived being trapped underwater for hours when caught in minnow traps. They can be exceedingly common in springs and spring runs in northern and central Florida. These little turtles may live over 20 years.

Class - **Chelonia** (turtles)
Order - **Cryptodira** (straightneck turtles)
Family - **Kinosternidae** (mud and musk turtles)

Striped Mud Turtle *Kinosternum baurii*	Common Mud Turtle *Kinosternum subrubrum*

Size: Adults range from 3 to 4 inches in carapace length. Record length is 5.5 inches.	Presumed range in Florida 	**Size:** Adults range from 4 to 4.75 inches in carapace length. Record length is 4.875 inches.	Presumed range in Florida 
Abundance: Fairly common.		**Abundance:** Fairly common.	
Variation: No subspecies. The characteristic light stripes on the carapace may be reduced or absent on very old individuals.		**Variation:** There are 3 subspecies. At least 2 are found in Florida but there is very little difference between the subspecies.	

Habitat: Mainly a freshwater species but has been recorded in brackish waters. Typical habitat in Florida is cypress swamps, wet flatwoods, ponds and lakes, flooded ditches, and other shallow, still water habitats.	**Habitat:** Found in a wide variety of aquatic habitats withing its range, but prefers shallow water areas with abundant aquatic vegetation. Common in ponds, swamps, wet prairies, and marshes and wet flatwoods.
Breeding: Lays up to 7 eggs but usually fewer. Young females may produce a single egg but may lay more than 1 clutch per year. Eggs are laid in nest of scraped-up humus.	**Breeding:** Reaches breeding age at about 5 to 7 years old. Breeds in the spring. Females dig a hole and deposit an average of 2 to 4 eggs, sometimes as many as 8.

Natural History: This turtle is endemic to the Florida peninsula and the Atlantic Coastal Plain. Its range extends as far north as the coastal plain of Virginia. A true omnivore that will eat plants and seeds but also consumes large amounts of animal matter. Insects, snails, earthworms, crayfish, and small fishes are known prey items. Like other mud and musk turtles, it feeds mainly by "bottom walking." Although quite aquatic in habits, these little turtles will also forage on land and sometimes are seen far away water. They are known to partially bury themselves in moist soil when inactive on land and they may also aestivate on land during droughts or seaonally dry periods. They are active both day and night but are probably more prone to nocturnal activity. Females are larger than males and both sexes take at least 2 to 3 years to reach sexual maturity. Longevity for this species is believed to exceed 50 years. Young turtles show a lighter color to the carapace which gradually darkens with age. Very old individuals may have a nearly solid black carapace with the characteristic light stripes for which the species is named becoming obscured with age.

Natural History: There are at least 2 subspecies native to Florida. They are the Eastern Mud Turtle (*K. s. subrubrum*-pictured above) and the Florida Mud Turtle (*K.s.steindachneri*). The Eastern Mud occupies most of the panhandle while the Florida Mud is found throughout the peninsula. Some experts suggest that specimens from the westernmost counties in the panhandle may be a third subspecies (*mississippiensis*), the Mississippi Mud Turtle. Although they are very aquatic turtles, they sometimes embark on overland treks, presumably to find new habitats or seek a mate. The mud turtles are easily told from the similar Musk Turtle by the double hinge on the plastron (musk turtles have a single hinge on the front of the plastron). Their diet is omnivorous. A variety of aquatic plants are eaten and animal foods include crustaceans, aquatic insects, mollusks, amphibians, and carrion. They locate much of their food by "bottom walking" under water, but may also feed on land near the water's edge. They can remain under water at least 20 minutes and probably much longer. These small turtles have been known to live up to 40 years and perhaps can survive even longer.

Class - **Chelonia** (turtles)
Order - **Cryptodira** (straightneck turtles)
Family - **Chelydridae** (snapping turtles)

Common Snapping Turtle *Chelydra serpentina*	**Alligator Snapping Turtle** *Macrochelys temminckii*

Size: Maximum carapace length 20 inches. Record weight 86 pounds.

Variation: Specimens found on the Florida peninsula are smaller than those in much of the US, but are not regarded as a distinct subspecies.

Abundance: Very common statewide in Florida.

Presumed range in Florida

Size: Maximum length 31 inches. Record weight 251 pounds.

Variation: Males attain a larger size than females. 3 similar species are recognized in Florida. See Natural History below.

Abundance: Uncommon in Florida.

Presumed range in Florida

Alligator Suwannee
Apalachicola

Habitat: Found in virtually every aquatic environment in the state. Ponds, lakes, rivers, creeks, swamps, and marshes.

Breeding: Eggs are deposited in underground chambers excavated by the female turtle. A typical clutch contains 25 to 50 eggs. Hatchlings are about the size of a quarter.

Natural History: These common turtles can be found in any aquatic habitat in the state, including tiny farm ponds or tributaries narrow enough for a person to step across. They even can exist in waters that are heavily polluted with sewage. Although mainly fresh water, they can sometimes be found in brackish ponds on barrier islands within a few dozen yards of the sea. They will feed on some plant material but are mainly carnivorous and will eat virtually anything they can swallow. Fish, frogs, tadpoles, small mammals, baby ducks, crayfish, and carrion are all listed as food items. Hatchlings turtles often must travel long distances to find a home in a pond or creek, and adults occasionally embark on long overland treks, presumably in search of a more productive habitat after depleting the food source in a small pond or creek. These long hikes overland usually occur in the spring. The ferociousness of a captured snapping turtle is legendary and their sharp, powerful jaws can inflict a serious wound. When cornered on land, they will turn to face an enemy and extend the long neck in a lunging strike that is lighting fast and so energetic that it may cause the entire turtle to move forward several inches. By contrast, when under water they almost never bite.

Habitat: Large rivers and their impoundments. Also oxbow lakes and small tributaries near their confluence with rivers.

Breeding: Adult females leave the water to lay up to 50 eggs in an underground chamber dug by the turtle. The leathery shelled eggs hatch in 3 or 4 months.

Natural History: Alligator Snapping Turtles are the most completely aquatic of any American Turtle. In fact, they never leave the water except for egg-laying excursions by the female. Unlike most aquatic turtles, they do not bask and rarely show more than the tip of the snout when coming up to breath. They spend most of their time "bottom walking" or lying in ambush in the muck or mud. They possess a specialized structure on the tongue that resembles a worm and can be wriggled to effectively lure fish into striking distance. They also eat other turtles, carrion, crayfish, and in fact probably any type of animal matter that can be swallowed. Mussels are reportedly an important food item, the hard shell being no match for the powerful jaws of these huge turtles. The longevity of this turtle in the wild is unknown, but some specimens have been in captivity for over 70 years, suggesting a long life span. These interesting and unique animals have declined significantly throughout their range. There are 3 nearly identical species of Alligator Snapping Turtles recognized today and all occur in Florida. The original Alligator Snapping Turtle (above) is found in the westernmost counties of the panhandle. The **Apalachicola Alligator Snapping Turtle** (*M. apalachicolae*) occupies the lower Apalachicola River watershed, while the **Suwannee Alligator Snapping** (*M. suwanniensis*) lives in the Suwanne River drainages.

Class - **Chelonia** (turtles)
Order - **Cryptodira** (straightneck turtles)
Family - **Emydidae** (water and box turtles)

Pond Slider *Trachemys scripta*	Florida Red-bellied Turtle *Pseudemys nelsoni*	River Cooter *Pseudemys concinna*

Size: Average carapace length is 6 to 8 inches. Record 12 inches. **Abundance:** Common.	**Size:** Average carapace length is 8 to 12 inches. Record 14.75 inches. **Abundance:** Common.	**Size:** Average length is 8 to 12 inches. Record 14.75 inches. **Abundance:** Fairly common.
Variation: Babies have green carapace with yellow markings.	**Variation:** Females are larger. Babies have green carapace with dark markings.	**Variation:** Females are larger. Babies are olive green marked with orange.
Habitat: Most common in large bodies of water but can be found in any aquatic habitat in the state except for very small streams.	**Habitat:** Occupies all types of freshwater habitats within its range. River swamps may be its favorite habitat in Florida.	**Habitat:** Primarily a turtle of large rivers and lakes, but they can also be common in swamps and oxbows that are adjacent to larger streams.
Breeding: Females leave the safety of the water and crawl hundreds of yards to upland areas to deposit their eggs in an underground nest chamber dug with the hind legs. Large females may lay 20 eggs, younger females lay fewer.	**Breeding:** Nest is dug in sandy soil on higher ground or sometimes dug into an Alligator's nest mound. Clutch size may vary considerabley but is probably 1 to 2 doxen in most cases. Baby turtles will hatch in about 3 months.	**Breeding:** Lays about 20 eggs in an underground chamber dug with the female's hind legs. Egg deposition is in late spring or early summer with the eggs hatching in August or September. Babies are slightly larger than a quarter.
Natural History: Highly aquatic but sometimes seen far from water. Omnivorous. Eats a variety of water plants as well as mollusks, minnows, dead fish, aquatic insects, crustaceans, etc. Young are more carnivorous, while mature turtles will consume more plants. Old specimens tend to darken with age and very old specimens may have a black carapace. These are hardy turtles that will emerge from the mud to bask on logs on warm, sunny days throughout the winter. There are 2 subspecies in Florida. The Yellow-bellied Slider (T. *s. scripta*) shown above is native to Florida. The Red-eared Slider (*T. s. elegans*) (inset photo) has been widely introduced in the state and may be seen almost anywhere.	**Natural History:** This is one of Florida's most beautiful turtles. If seen without a growth of algea, the carapace is dark with elongated reddish blotches and the plastron and the bridge is often bright red. Like most other *Pseudemys* turtles they can be difficult to approach closely, but the Red-bellied may be more approachable than many other species. They are conspicuous baskers in rivers and spring runs, and in clear, spring-fed waters they are often visible beneath the surface as they feed on aquatic vegetation. For the most part, this is a Florida endemic, although their range does extend just north of the Florida border into the Okefenokee Swamp of southeastern Georgia. They are diurnal in habits and they may be active year-round.	**Natural History:** Adults primarily eat aquatic plants, including large quantities of algae. Some animal matter is consumed usually in the form of aquatic invertebrates or fish, especially so with younger turtles that need a higher protein diet. In habitats they are strictly diurnal. They spend a good deal of time basking in the open, but they are shy and difficult to approach. Like many other aquatic turtles, they spend the winter buried in the mud at the bottom of a body of water. Their metabolic processes slowed significantly by cold temperatures, they absorb oxygen throught the lining of the cloaca. These large turtles are often utilized as food by humans in other parts of their range, but they are protected in Florida.

Class - **Chelonia** (turtles)		
Order - **Cryptodira** (straightneck turtles)		
Family - **Emydidae** (water and box turtles)		
Southeastern Cooter Turtles - Genus *Psuedemys*		
Suwannee Cooter *Psuedemys suwanniensis*	**Coastal Plain Cooter** *Psuedemys floridana*	**Peninsula Cooter** *Psuedemys peninsularis*

	Presumed range in Florida		Presumed range in Florida		Presumed range in Florida
Size: Averages about a foot in carapace length. Record is 17.25 inches.		**Size:** Averages about a foot in carapace length. Record is just under 16 inches.		**Size:** Averages about a foot in carapace length. Record is just under 16 inches.	
Abundance: Uncommon.		**Abundance:** Common.		**Abundance:** Common.	

Variation: There is little variation among adults in these species. Young turtles are more vividly marked and older turtles tend to have their carapace markings reduced or obscured. Males have longer claws on the front toes and are usually smaller than females.

Habitat: The cooter turtles are all highly aquatic in habits. And collectively the 3 species shown above inhabit just about every freshwater aquatic habitat in the state. Rivers, springs, and spring runs are a primary habitat for all along with lakes, canals, swamps, and marshes. At least 1 species (the Suwannee Cooter) can be seen at times in salt water near the mouth of Suwannee River.

Breeding: Gravid females leave the water and travel overland to suitable nesting localities, which may be very near the water's edge or hundreds of yards away a river bank or lake shore. A flask-shaped cavity is excavated by the female's hind feet and an average of about 20 eggs are laid. Multiple nestings may occur. The young turtles hatch in about 3 months (less if weather is exceptionally warm, longer if exceptionally cool). As with many egg-laying reptiles, chelonians, and crocodilians, ambient temperature in the nest determines the sex of the offspring. The Florida Redbelly Turtle is known to sometimes lay its eggs within the large mound nest of the American Alligator. Predation on nests by mammalian predators like Raccoons and skunks can be very high.

Natural History: All 3 of the species shown on this page are rather similar in appearance and in their natural history. The exact taxonomy of the *Psuedemys* genus has been a nightmare for herpetologists for decades. The above 3 species were all once regarded as subspecies of the River Cooter (P. *concinna*) and some herpetologists still consider that to be the more accurate representation of their taxonomy. Still others will insist that they are all just slightly different geographic populations of the same wide-ranging species. That argument is bolstered by the fact that interbreeding between the species is apparently not uncommon where their ranges meet. Utilization of DNA analysis is adding to the scientific understanding of these turtles, but has still not completely resolved the controversy regarding their phylogeny and proper taxonomy. Life span for these turtles is probably about 20 to 25 years. Historically, cooter turtles were hunted for food by Native Americans and until recently they were still consumed by some people living in Florida. In recent years, all of Florida's cooter turtles have come under the protection of the Florida Fish and Wildlife Conservation Commission. The threats faced by Florida's freshwater turtles today do not stem from their occasional use as food by humans, but from the popularity of many types of rare turtles in the exotic animal trade. State and federal wildlife agencies are attempting to combat the trade in rare species, and Florida's cooter turtles fall under their protection due to the similarities in appearance, habitat, etc. By placing these turtles under protection along with the rarer species, the excuse used by animal traffickers "I thought it was just a cooter," is eliminated as a defense for having in possession any of the several much rarer species.

Class - **Chelonia** (turtles)

Order - **Cryptodira** (straightneck turtles)

Family - **Emydidae** (water and box turtles)

Barbour's Map Turtle *Graptemys barbouri*	**Spotted Turtle** *Clemmys guttata*	**Chicken Turtle** *Deirochelys reticularia*

Size: Females can exceed 10 inches. Males up to 5 inches.	Presumed range in Florida	**Size:** Averages about 4 inches. Record length is 5.6 inches.	Presumed range in Florida 	**Size:** Averages carapace length 6 inches. Record 10 inches.	Presumed range in Florida
Abundance: Uncommon in Florida.		**Abundance:** Very rare in Florida.		**Abundance:** Uncommon to fairly common.	

Variation: Males are much smaller and have longer claws on the front feet.	**Variation:** Yellow spots fade with age. Very old individuals may be solid black.	**Variation:** 2 subspecies occur in Florida. They are very similar.
Habitat: A riverine species. It is found only in the Apalachicola and Chipola river systems.	**Habitat:** Prefers sluggish waters. In Florida inhabits swamps. Sometimes found in wet meadows or wet woods.	**Habitat:** Primarily aquatic. Uses a variety of freshwater habitats with abundant aquatic vegetation.
Breeding: Females are very slow to reach sexual maturity and the clutches are not large (average about 8 to 10). Thus reproduction in this species is limited.	**Breeding:** Female digs a flask-shaped hole and deposits 1 to 8 eggs. Not much is known about the reproductive habits of this turtle in Florida.	**Breeding:** Clutch size varies from 5 to a dozen eggs. 2 clutches per year is not uncommon. Females reach sexual maturity at around 5 or 6 years old.

Natural History: The *Graptemys* turtles are famous for several species which are endemic to 1 or 2 river systems. Species having restricted ranges are highly vulnerable to extinction in today's world and the Barbour's Map Turtle is regarded as an Threatened Species by the Florida Fish and Wildlife Conservation Commission. Map turtles are also known for their food preferences, which for most is mollusks. In addition to bivalves and snails, they also eat crayfish. All these hard-shelled animals are no match for the crushing jaws of large female map turtles. By contrast, the smaller males typically eat more soft-bodied prey like insects. Fish are also eaten on occasion. A similar species known as the **Escambia Map Turtle** (*Graptemys ernsti*) lives in the Escambia River system in the extreme western panhandle of Florida.

Natural History: These handsome little turtles range throughout the Atlantic slope of the eastern United States from southern Maine to northern Florida. A disjunct population is found throughout the Great Lakes region. Many populations are in decline and they are regarded as an Endangered Species by the International Union of Concerned Naturalists. They were probably once much more widespread along the eastern seaboard of the US prior to the draining of wetlands that began with settlement and the advent of modern agricultural practices. The Spotted Turtle is both an omnivore and a scavenger. Aquatic grasses and algea make up the vegetarian diet with insects, crustaceans, snails, amphibian larva, and fish listed as food items. Opportunistic feeding on carrion is also reported. They are shy and docile and rarely attempt to bite when captured.

Natural History: There seems to be some disagreement as to whether the name "Chicken" turtle is a reference to this species' exceedingly long neck or whether it is a reference to the taste of its flesh. During dry seasons or droughts when wetlands dry up, these turtles commonly bury themselves beneath pine straw or leaf mold and enter a period of torpor. Crayfish are a major food item for this species. Large aquatic insects and their larva are also prey items. Although they are widespread throughout the state of Florida, Chicken Turtles don't seem to be as plentiful as the larger cooter turtles. That apparent scarcity may be a reflection of their wariness. They will abandon basking and dive into the water at the first sign of an approaching human. Their long neck and the bright yellow stripes on the hind legs are diagnostic characters.

Class - **Chelonia** (turtles)		
Order - **Cryptodira** (straightneck turtles)		

Family - **Emydidae** (water and box turtles)		Family - **Testudinidae** (tortoises)
Diamondback Terrapin *Malaclemys terrapin*	**Florida Box Turtle** *Terrapene bauri*	**Gopher Tortoise** *Gopherus polyphemus*

Size: Average carapace length 6 to 9 inches for female. Male 4 to 5 inches.	**Size:** Average carapace length is 5 to 6 inches. Record is length is 7.5.	**Size:** Average carapace length 8 to 10 inches. Record is just over 16 inches.
Presumed range in Florida 	Presumed range in Florida	Presumed range in Florida 
Abundance: Uncommon.	**Abundance:** Fairly common.	**Abundance:** Uncommon.

Variation: There are 7 subspecies and 5 occur in Florida. Pictured above is the Gulf Coast subspecies (*ornata*).

Variation: Panhandle populations were once regarded as a distinct subspecies known as the Gulf Coast Box Turtle.

Variation: Like most turtles, mature males have a concave plastron. Hatchlings are dark brown with yellow spots.

Habitat: Diamondback Terrapins are salt marsh specialists. They inhabit salt marshes, intercoastal waterways, and estuaries all along the Florida coastline.

Habitat: Woodlands and ecotone areas where woodlands meet fields or wetlands. Terrestrial but fond of wetland edges and mesic situations.

Habitat: Habitat is regions with upland, sandy soils. Avoids wetlands and low-lying habitats. Prefers Longleaf Pine/Wiregrass and scrub oak sandhills.

Breeding: Eggs are laid in sandy soils above the high tide line. Clutch size ranges from 4 to 18.

Breeding: Lays 2 or 3 (rarely more) eggs in underground chamber. Babies lack a plastron hinge.

Breeding: Eggs are the size and shape of a ping-pong ball. Clutch size averages 6 eggs, often laid in burrow.

Natural History: Diamondback Terrapins have declined significantly in Florida (and elsewhere in America). They have recovered somewhat from the days of market hunting when they were harvested for food in astronomical numbers, but they are much less common today than just a few decades ago. They are probably most common today in undisturbed salt marsh and uninhabited barrier islands along the Gulf Coast of Florida. These turtles are adapted to living in both fresh water and salt water, but their main habitat is salt and brackish water marshes. Salt marsh snails are one their main foods, along with crabs, mussels, marine worms, and some plant material. They possess enlarged and thickened labial regions which is probably an adaptation for crushing hard-shelled prey like snails, mussels, and crabs.

Natural History: Adult box turtles have a hinged plastron and are able to withdraw all 4 legs and the head into the shell and close it tightly. The muscles which close the plastron are remarkably strong and when closed the plastron cannot be pried open. Food is a variety of plant and animal matter as well as fungi. Blackberries are a favorite plant food when in season, with snails and earthworms being a favorite animal food. As with many endemic species in Florida, the Florida Box Turtle has experienced population declines in the last few decades. Populations in the panhandle of Florida are of unresolved taxonomic status and show morphological characteristics that are intermediate between 3 box turtle species (Eastern, Florida, and Three-toed Box Turtles).

Natural History: Gopher Tortoises have been declining throughout their range for several decades. Today, they are a protected species and are regarded as threatened in Florida. The name "Gopher" Tortoise is derived from the fact that these turtles dig an underground burrow, which serves as a permanent home and shelter. The burrow of the Gopher Tortoise is used by many other species in Florida, ranging from spiders to snakes. Thus this turtle is of vital importance to the ecology of Florida and is regarded by wildlife biologists as a "Keystone Species." Among the list of threatened, endangered, and species of concern in Florida are many animals that rely on the burrow of the Gopher Tortoise. Life span is probably at least 60 years.

Class - **Chelonia** (turtles)

Order - **Cryptodira** (straightneck turtles)

Family - **Trionychidae** (softshell turtles)

Florida Softshell Turtle	**Spiny Softshell Turtle**
Apalone ferox	*Apalone spinifera*

Size: Females can reach 26 inches. Male 12 inches.

Presumed range in Florida

Abundance: Common.

Variation: Adult females can be twice the size of males. The pattern of dark blotches and reticulations on the carapace is much brighter in younger specimens.

Size: Female can reach 21 inches. Male 12 inches.

Presumed range in Florida

Abundance: Fairly common.

Variation: Several subspecies occur across America, but there is no significant variation in Florida populations. Adult females can be twice the size of males.

Habitat: Totally aquatic. They can be found in rivers and streams as well as natural ponds and lakes throughout the state. They require permanent waters immune to drought.

Habitat: Occurs in both large and small streams and in impoundments. May also be found in small ponds in some areas. Shows a preference for habitats with sandy substrates.

Breeding: Clutches of large females can exceed 2 dozen eggs. Nest is dug in sandy soil above the high water mark. Multiple clutches per year is common in this turtle.

Breeding: A dozen or more eggs are laid between May and August (most in June or July). Nests are often on sandbars of creeks or rivers.

Natural History: Softshell Turtles are highly aquatic and more at home in the water than any other freshwater turtle in Florida. Of the 4 species of softshells in America, the Florida Softshell is the largest and there is a record of a specimen weighing 71 pounds. The name "softshell" is highly appropriate as the shell of these turtles is soft, pliable, and leathery. These turtles love to bask but are difficult to approach on land. They are active all year in southern Florida and will emerge to bask on warm days in more northerly regions of Florida. In warm water springs, they may also be active in winter. Their soft skin allows for some degree of underwater respiration and they may also exchange gases through mucus membranes. They are thus capable of remaining submerged for long periods. Florida Softshells are sometimes eaten by humans but remain common enough that they can be a nuisance for fishermen using live bait. Unlike most softshell turtles that are loath to leave the water, Florida Softshells are known to embark on overland treks that can take them far from water. Longevity is believed to be at least 25 years.

Natural History: Crayfish, fish, and insects are the primary food items, but dead fish and other carrion can be an important food item, especially in lakes where fishing is common and fish entrails and heads are discarded around boat docks. Spiny Softshells are most active from April to October, but may be seen year-round in Florida if the weather is warm. They hunt both by ambush and by active pursuit. When immobile, they can remain under water or several hours. Because of the soft, permeable shells and skin, softshells are more susceptible to dehydration than other turtle species and thus they seldom stray far from water. These turtles are harvested as food in many parts of their range, and much of this harvest is to date unregulated. Some believe this practice may pose a long-term threat to the species. Like all softshell turtles, the Spiny has a long and flexible neck, which makes handling these turtles without being bitten difficult. Wild adults may bite savagely if handled. They are fond of basking but are always extremely wary and will flee into the water if approached too closely.

Class - **Chelonia** (turtles)
Order - **Cryptodira** (straightneck turtles)
Families - **Cheloniidae and Dermochelyidae** (sea turtles)

Atlantic Ridley Sea Turtle *Lepidochelys kempii*	**Loggerhead Sea Turtle** *Caretta caretta*	**Green Sea Turtle** *Chelonia mydas*
 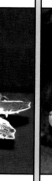	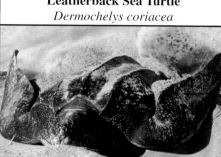	
Hawksbill Sea Turtle *Eretmochely imbricata*	**Leatherback Sea Turtle** *Dermochelys coriacea*	Presumed range in Florida

Size: Atlantic Ridley is Florda's smallest sea turtle with a maximum carapace length of about 30 inches and a record weight of 110 pounds. The Hawksbill reaches 45 inches and 280 pounds. Next is the Loggerhead Sea Turtle at about 4 feet in length and nearly 500 pounds (claims of over 800 pounds exist). The Green Sea Turtle is 60 inches and 835 pounds. The Leatherback is the world's largest living turtle at 8 feet in length and 1,500 pounds.

Abundance: Green Turtle and Loggerhead are fairly common. Others are rare or very rare in Florida waters.

Variation: All exhibit some sexual, size-related dimorphism. In Loggerhead, Leatherback and Atlantic Ridley males are smaller. In Green Sea Turtles, males have a longer carapace. In the Hawksbill the sexes are alike.

Habitat: Warm seas. These turtles are found in tropical oceans around the globe. Some wander north into temperate waters in summer (most noteably the Leatherback). The Atlantic Ridley is most commonly seen in the Gulf of Mexico, while the Hawksbill is more common along the Atlantic Coast. The Green Turtle and the Loggerhead may be seen along the entire coastline of Florida. The Leatherback is an extremely rare turtle in Florida waters.

Breeding: All must come ashore to nest and lay their eggs on sandy beaches above the high tide mark. Nesting by Leatherbacks in Florida was been recorded rarely. Loggerheads and Green Turtles are the two most common nesting species in Florida. All sea turtle nests are subjected to predation by a variety of egg-robbing mammals such as raccoons. Hatchlings run a gauntlet of predators between the nest and the sea, and are then subject to predation by all manner of creatures once in the ocean. Surviving to maturity is a real long shot for a baby sea turtle. Add to that the widespread robbing of eggs for food by humans, the confusion created by artificial lights in developed areas, the hazards of fishing nets, hooks, and pollution, and the outlook for the long-term survival of the world's sea turtle population looks grim.

Natural History: In all sea turtles, the legs and feet are modified into flippers. They are extremely well adapted morphologically and physiologically for a life in the ocean. Except for females coming ashore to nest once every few years, these turtles live their entire lives at sea. Jellyfish are an important food item, especially for the Leatherback. Crustaceans, fish, sponges, and shellfish are also eaten by several species. Green Turtles are mainly vegetarian and feed on eelgrasses. Leatherbacks apparently have the ability to maintain body temperature through metabolic activity even when in cold northern waters. The sea turtles were once an important food source for humans and the Green Turtle's name is derived from the color of its fat. Human exploitation along with beach development has seriously impacted these turtles. Heroic efforts to protect nesting beaches and outlaw exploitation has helped in the effort to conserve these species, but like the ocean ecosystem itself, the future of the world's sea turtles remains in doubt. The Leatherback is quite different from other sea turtles in many respects, but most notably in the fact that it has a leathery shell. It is the sole species of the family Dermochelyidae. All others are in the family Cheloniidae.

CHAPTER 7

THE REPTILES OF FLORIDA

TABLE 5

— THE ORDERS AND FAMILIES OF FLORIDA REPTILES —

Note: The arrangement below reflects the the order in which the reptiles of Florida appear in this chapter. It is not intended to be an accurate reflection of the phylogenetic relationship of reptiles.

Class - **Reptilia** (reptiles)

Order - **Squamata** (lizards and snakes)
Suborder - **Lacertilia** (lizards)

Family	**Anguidae** (glass lizards)
Family	**Eublepharidae, Gekkonidae, Phyllodactylidae, and Sphaerodactylidae**
Family	**Phrynosomatidae** (spiny lizards)
Family	**Corytophanidae** (basilisk)
Family	**Iguanidae** (iguanas)
Family	**Agamidae** (agamid lizards)
Family	**Polychrotidae** (anoles)
Family	**Chamaeleonidae** (chameleons)
Family	**Leiocephalidae** (curly-tailed lizards)
Family	**Scincidae** (skinks)
Family	**Teiidae** (whiptail lizards)

Suborder - **Amphisbaenia** (worm lizards)

Family	**Rhineuridae**

Suborder - **Serpentes** (snakes)

Family	**Colubridae** (harmless egg-laying snakes)
Family	**Dipsadidae** (small rear-fanged snakes)
Family	**Natricidae** (harmless live-bearing snakes)
Family	**Pythonidae** (pythons)
Family	**Boidae** (boas and anacondas)
Family	**Elapidae** (coral snakes and cobras)
Family	**Crotalidae** (pit vipers)

THE REPTILES OF FLORIDA

PART 1: LIZARDS

Class - **Reptilia** (reptiles)

Order - **Squamata** (lizards and snakes)

Family - **Anguidae** (glass lizards)

Eastern Glass Lizard *Ophisuarus ventralis*	**Slender Glass Lizard** *Ophisaurus attenuatus*	**Island Glass Lizard** *Ophisaurus compressus*

Size: Average 2 to 3 feet. Record 43 inches.

Presumed range in Florida

Abundance: Widespread and generally fairly common.

Size: Average 2 to 3 feet. Record 46 inches.

Presumed range in Florida

Abundance: Spottily distributed and absent from many areas.

Size: Averages about 18 inches. Maximum 25.

Presumed range in Florida

Abundance: Uncommon but may be abundant in local areas.

Variation: Young lizards are tan above with dark brown sides. Old adults are black and green.

Variation: Young lizards are tan above with dark brown sides. Old adults often have a "salt and pepper" appearance.

Variation: Young lizards are tan above with lateral stripes. In adults the stripes are broken into stippling anteriorly.

Habitat: Open grassy habitats. Ecotone areas where woods meets fields, grassy areas near canals, and oak or pine woodlands.

Habitat: Favors sandy, friable soils in open or semi-open habitats. Old fields, sandy woodlands, pine/wiregrass uplands. Avoids wetlands.

Habitat: Sand dunes (both along the coast and old, inland dunes), barrier islands, sand pine scrub, and sandy pine flatwoods.

Breeding: Lays as single clutch of eggs in early summer. Average clutch size is about 10 eggs (max 20). Females guards the nest.

Breeding: Lays up to 20 eggs often in a clump of grass. Female stays with eggs during incubation, which lasts up to 2 months.

Breeding: Probably about 10 to 12 eggs are laid. Female attends the eggs during incubation. Little else is known regarding reproduction in this species.

Natural History: These lizards are often confused with snakes due to their lack of limbs. They are easily recognized as lizards, however, by the presence of ear openings and eyelids. When grasped, these lizards will thrash about wildly and break off their tail. The tail is quite long, making up about two-thirds of their total length. The apparent fragility of these lizards and the shiny appearance of their skin has led to the common name "glass lizard." The highly specialized escape mechanism of breaking off the tail is shared with many other lizard species, as is the rare ability to regenerate a new tail, but the glass lizards take this unique defense (known by the scientific term "Autotomy") to an extreme. Regenerated tails grow slowly and never attain the original length.

Natural History: As with the other glass lizards, most of this animal consists of tail. In fact about two-thirds of the glass lizards length is tail. Food is mostly insects and spiders. Difficulty distinguishing this species from other glass lizards and its apparent lack of abundance leaves many questions regarding its exact distribution in Florida. The map above is at best an estimate and it may be more widespread in the state. Likewise, it may not occur in some of the shaded areas shown on the map. The **Mimic Glass Lizard** (*O. mimicus*) is a smaller version of glass lizard that is rather rare and limited in distribution in Florida. It is known to occur in the western panhandle and in a small area of Nassua County in extreme northeastern Florida.

Natural History: This species is poorly understood. Bartlett and Bartlett in *A Field Guide to Reptiles and Amphibians of Florida*, 1999, report finding these lizards in abundance in one locale in southwestern Florida between the hours of 7:30 and 8:30 p.m., but could not find it any at other times of the day. This suggests that they may be more common than generally believed, but are just very secretive or sedentary for much of their lives. The name is presumably a reference to the fact that this species can often be found on offshore islands along the coast. They can be found throughout most of the Florida peninsula but they are absent from most of the panhandle except right along the coast. In addition, they range northward along the coast of Georgia and into coastal South Carolina.

Class - **Reptilia** (reptiles)		
Order - **Squamata** (lizards and snakes)		
Family - **Geckkonidae** (true geckos)		Family - **Sphaerodactylidae**

Madascan Day Gecko *Phelsuma grandis*	**Mediterranean Gecko** *Hemidactylus turcicus*	**Reef Gecko** *Sphaerodactylus notatus*
Indo-Pacific Gecko *Hemidactylus garnoti*	**Tokay Gecko** *Gekko gecko*	Presumed collective range of Geckos in Florida

Size: At 14 inches, the Tokay Gecko is by far the largest. The widespread Mediterranean Gecko and the Indo-Pacific House Gecko can reach 5 and 5.5 inches respectively. Most others are about 4 to 5 inches in length as adults. Florida's only native Gecko, the Reef Gecko, is a small species, reaching only about 2.25 inches in length.

Abundance: The Mediteranean Gecko and the Indo-Pacific House Gecko are probably the most common gecko species in Florida today.

Variation: No less than 15 species from 4 families are represented in Florida today.

Habitat: Most geckos in Florida associate with buildings and man-made structures like fences. Others use trees or shrubs.

Breeding: Many species are capable of multiple clutches per year. A few species are parthenogenetic species that are all female and reproduce without mating.

Natural History: Although there are few species of gecko that are native to the United States, most native North American geckos are found in the southwestern portion of the country. All but 1 gecko species (Reef Gecko) in Florida have been introduced and most are the result of escapees or releases from the exotic pet trade. Some may have arrived as stowaways on cargo. Today, there are no less than 15 species that have become established in Florida (perhaps more). Most are from Asia, Africa, or the Mediterranean. Some are widely distributed throughout the state while others presently are restricted to small populations around specific cities or are restricted to the Everglades and Keys. Most of these lizards possess specialized toes that have tiny bristles which can adhere to the smoothest of surfaces, allowing the geckos to walk upside down on ceilings or vertically up a pane of glass. Many are human commensals that thrive in and around human habitations. One group is known by the nickname "House Geckos." Collectively they range throughout most of the peninsula and at least one can be found in parts of the panhandle.

Class - **Reptilia** (reptiles)

Order - **Squamata** (lizards and snakes)

Family - **Phrynosomatidae** (spiny lizards)		Family - **Corytophanidae** (basilisk)

Eastern fence Lizard
Sceloperus undulatus

Florida Scrub Lizard
Sceloperus woodi

Brown Basilisk
Basiliscus vittatus

Size: Maximum of 7.25 inches.	Presumed range in Florida	**Size:** Maximum of 6 inches.

Size: Maximum of 7.25 inches.

Presumed range in Florida

Abundance: Common.

Variation: Males have bright blue patches on belly.

Habitat: Dry, upland woods and dry pine woodlands. Found in both pure deciduous woods, mixed woodlands, and in pine-dominated woodlands.

Breeding: Egg layer. Deposits 6 to 15 eggs in rotted logs, stumps, etc. 2 clutches per year are common.

Natural History: A woodland species, the Eastern Fence Lizard spends much of its time on tree trunks and fallen logs. Its color and pattern perfectly matches the bark of most trees within its range. This is one of the most common lizards in the eastern US. They are quite arboreal in habits and will regularly climb trees to great heights. Feeds on insects, spiders, etc. Both sexes are often seen perched on rocks, logs, or stumps in wooded areas. Breeding males are especially conspicuous as they attempt to attract females by sitting atop rocks or stumps and methodically raising and lowering their body to show off the bright blue patches on the undersides. Females are similar in appearance but lack blue patches on the belly. The *Sceloperus* genus attains its greatest diversity in the southwestern United States where there are many species. Only 2 species occur east of the Mississippi River and both are found in Florida.

Size: Maximum of 6 inches.

Presumed range in Florida

Abundance: Uncommon.

Variation: Female has dark bars across back.

Habitat: Xeric sandy scrub habitats are favored. Probably most common in the sand pine/scrub oak habitats of the Ocala National Forest.

Breeding: Produces small clutches of only about 4 eggs that are laid in loose soil, often in gopher mounds.

Natural History: The Florida Scrub Lizard is an endemic species. They occur only in Florida. As with so many other Florida endemics, this is an imperiled species. Development and agriculture (primarily citrus groves) along the "Florida Ridge" is the greatest threat. It is still a locally common species where ideal habitat remains intact. These lizards often perch on tree trunks a few feet above the ground and watch for insect prey. They will leap from their post and dart across the ground to capture wandering crickets, grasshoppers, spiders, etc. They are much less arboreal and more terrestrial in habits than their cousin the Fence Lizard, but are similar in many other ways. Where the ranges of the 2 species overlap, hybridization with the Fence Lizard is known to occur. They are most easily told from the similar Fence Lizard by the presence of dark stripes along the side.

Size: Maximum length 27 inches.

Presumed range in Florida

Abundance: Rare in Florida.

Variation: Male larger and has large crest.

Habitat: Tropical forests are the primary habitat in Latin America. In Florida it is usually found along canals in the southern tip of the state.

Breeding: Up to a dozen eggs are laid in a mesic situation. Eggs hatch in about 2 months.

Natural History: Introduced. Basilisk lizards are native to the New World tropics. The Brown Basilisk ranges from central Mexico southward into northern South America. This is the famous "Jesus Lizard," so called by Latin Americans due to its fringed hind toes that allow it to run across the surface of water for a short distance. The male has a large crest on the back of the head and is twice as large as the female (see photos above). Juveniles have a prominent yellowish-white stripes on each side running the length of the body. These are agile and fast-moving lizards that are very difficult to approach closely. When running they often resort to a bipedal stance and run on the hind legs only. These lizards have been established as breeding populations for over a decade and they seem to be rapidly expanding their range in the state. Their northward expansion may be limited by climate.

Class - **Reptilia** (reptiles)

Order - **Squamata** (lizards and snakes)

Family - **Iguanidae** (iguanas)		Family - **Agamidae** (agamid lizards)

Green Iguana
Iguana iguana

Spiny-tailed Iguana
Ctenosaura similis

Introduced Agamid Liards
Various species

Rock Agama

Green Iguana	Spiny-tailed Iguana	Introduced Agamid Liards
Size: Can reach a maximum of 6.5 feet.	**Size:** Can reach a maximum of 4 feet.	**Size:** Peters Rock Agama can reach 12 inches.
Abundance: Locally common in southern Florida and the Keys.	**Abundance:** Locally common in southern Florida and the Keys.	**Abundance:** Still uncommon and restricted in range in Florida.
Variation: Young are solid bright green. Adults vary from green to yellowish with black bars on body. Adult males may be reddish or orange.	**Variation:** Young specimens are more vividly marked with broad, blackish zebra-like strips and the head is often yellowish or light brown.	**Variation:** Currently at least 5 species (probably more) of Agamid lizards representing 4 genera are known to occur in Florida.
Habitat: A tropical species that is mainly restricted to tropical Florida. Very arboreal and will climb high into trees. Favors trees over rivers or canals.	**Habitat:** Strictly a terrestrial species that is rarely seen in trees and avoids aquatic situations. In Florida currently restricted to tropical climates.	**Habitat:** Diverse. Presumably, invasives seek habitats similar to their native range. All are tropical or temperate in climate requirements.
Breeding: Oviparous. Lays up to 35 or 40 eggs in ground or under cover.	**Breeding:** Lays about 20 to 30 eggs that hatch in about 3 months.	**Breeding:** Most Agamidae lizards are oviparous.

Presumed range in Florida

Presumed range in Florida

Presumed range in Florida

Natural History: Introduced. Baby Green Iguanas have been sold in pet stores for decades in spite of the fact that they are a poor choice as a pet animal. Released pets are the origin of Florida's Green Iguana population and the species is quite established along the southern Florida coasts and in the Keys. Green Iguanas are decidely arboreal animals and they spend a great deal of time in trees. As adults they are strict vegetarians feeding on leaves, flowers, and fruits. They are excellent swimmers and in their native habitats in the neotropics they are often seen in tree limbs overhanging rivers. If threatened, they will launch themselves into the water and swim to safety beneath the surface. Their natural range is from southern Mexico through Central America and into southern South America (exclusive of the Andes Mountains).

Natural History: This is a ground-dwelling lizard that digs a burrow which serves as a permanent home. In its native range in Central America, this lizard is most common in upland, savanna-like habitats. It can be common in open fields and pastures and it spends a good deal of time sunning in the open. Favorite sunning perches are often slightly elevated to allow a good view of the surrounding open country. In rural areas they usually flee at the sight of humans, but where they have acclimated to human settlements they can become fairly approachable. Mainly herbivorous, but will also eat small vertebrates and larger invertebrates. The Florida Wildlife Commission website reports the first documentation in Florida dates back to 1978. Since that time they have become increasingly common and have expanded their range considerably.

Natural History: Agamid lizards are non-native, introduced species. This is an Old World family of lizards native to southern Europe, Africa, parts of Asia, and Australia. Some have existed in Florida since the late 1970s and some are newcomers that began to show up in the state in the mid to late 1990s. For the most part, these are small to medium-sized lizards. Their impact on the local ecology and native species is not yet known. The ease with which so many lizards, snakes, birds, and fish are able to establish themselves in Florida is alarming. While the Agamid lizards are not yet known to cause serious problems within native ecosytems, many other invasive species do (and already have)! All Floridians should exercise caution in keeping exotic pets and never, NEVER release non-native animals into the wild!

Class - **Reptilia** (reptiles)
Order - **Squamata** (lizards and snakes)
Family - **Polychrotidae** (anoles)

Carolina Anole *Anolis carolinensis*	**Brown Anole** *Anolis sagri*	**Introduced Anoles** Various *Anolis* species
Brown phase		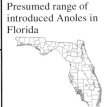Knight Anole

Size: Maximum length 9 inches. Average 4 to 5.	Presumed range in Florida	**Size:** Maximum length 9 inches. Average 4 to 5.	Presumed range in Florida	**Size:** Knight Anole is largest at 19 inches max.	Presumed range of introduced Anoles in Florida
Abundance: Very common throughout the state.		**Abundance:** Common in peninsula, expanding northward.		**Abundance:** Rare or uncommon to locally fairly common.	

Variation: Changes color from bright green to brown. Green in foliage, brown when on bark. Also brown when cold.	**Variation:** Adult males have a ridge along the top of the back that is most apparent anteriorly.	**Variation:** FWC lists a total of 9 species (plus the Brown Anole) as now being found in Florida. Maybe more.
Habitat: Mainly woodlands and woodland edges. Also overgrown fields, swamps, suburban landscape plantings, virtually anywhere there is vegetation.	**Habitat:** Occupies all types of habitats in the state. More terrestrial than the Green Anole and less likely to be seen more than a few feet off the ground.	**Habitat:** Florida's introduced *Anolis* species all hail from the Caribbean. All are from tropical habitats and are currently restricted to southern Florida.
Breeding: Lays only 1 or 2 eggs in late spring or early summer. Eggs hatch in 1 to 2 months. May lay eggs several times throughout the summer.	**Breeding:** The female lays a single egg about every 2 weeks all summer long. Eggs hatch in about a month. Babies reach maturity at about 8 months.	**Breeding:** *Anolis* lizards breed in spring and retain viable sperm throughout the summer. Usually a single egg is deposited every 2 weeks all summer.
Natural History: The Green Anole often goes by name "Chameleon" but that name is properly reserved for Old World lizards of the family Chamaeleonidae. Like true chameleons, this lizard does have the ability to change its colors to match its background. When on bark or soil it is usually brown, changing to green when amid bushes and other vegetation. When cold, the color is also brown, but will change to green when the lizard is exposed to the warming rays of the sun. These little lizards are active diurnal foragers and can be seen leaping from branch to branch in low bushes as they search for tiny insect prey. The males possess a flap of skin on the throat known as a "Dewlap." On breeding males, the dewlap becomes bright red and it is expanded to advertise the male's presence to nearby females.	**Natural History:** Introduced. Native to the Caribbean, these Anoles first appeared in Florida a century ago, but in the last 40 years they have become very common and widespread. Although today they are ubuitous in peninsular Florida, the Brown Anole is an invasive, introduced species and in many areas (especially south Florida), there is evidence that they are out-competing the native Green Anole. The Brown Anole appears to be less arboreal than the Green Anole and it has been suggested that in areas where the 2 species are found together, the Brown Anole commandeers the more terrestrial microhabitat while the Green Anole lives higher up in the bushes and trees. Unlike the native Green Anole, the Brown Anole does not change color from brown to green, but remains consistently brown.	**Natural History:** Florida's non-native Anoles were introduced by either the pet trade or as stowaways on imported ornamental plants. Some are vulnerable to the periodic cold fronts that can cause freezing temperatures to penetrate all the way to the southern tip of Florida. Surviving cold snaps is possible for lizards that are under substantial cover on the ground. Thus while occasional freezes may hit these interlopers hard, enough survive to continue the survival of the population. Most, however, will probably not expand to much farther to the north. One notable exception is the previously mentioned Brown Anole whose natural range is Cuba and the Bahamas, both places that are immune to freezing temperatures. Thus speculation about range expansion in these lizards is presumptious.

Class - **Reptilia** (reptiles)

Order - **Squamata** (lizards and snakes)

Family - **Chamaeleonidae** (chameleons)	Family - **Leiocephalidae** (curly-tailed lizards)	Family - **Scincidae** (skinks)
Veiled Chameleon *Chamaeleo calyptratus*	**Red-sided Curly-tailed Lizard** *Leiocephalus schreibersii*	**Ground Skink** *Scincella laterallus*

Size: Maximum length 24 inches.	**Size:** Maximum length 10 inches.	**Size:** 3 to 5 inches.

Presumed range in Florida  Presumed range in Florida  Presumed range in Florida

Abundance: Generally rare but may be locally fairly common.

Abundance: Rare in Florida but may be locally fairly common in a few places.

Abundance: Common and widespread throughout the state.

Variation: Chameleons are capable of remarkable variability in color and pattern. Not just within the species, but within the individual. The most vivid colors occur in lizards that are breeding or otherwise excited.

Variation: There are 2 species of *Leiocephalus* lizards in Florida. Shown above is the Red-sided Curly-tailed Lizard. The Northern Curly-tailed Lizard is easily recognized by the tail which it curls over the back.

Variation: Color may vary from reddish brown to golden brown or chocolate brown. Color often has a metallic quality. Some individuals may have small dark flecks on the back, most are uniformly brownish above.

Habitat: Chameleons are all warm climate species. But some are subtropical and may be able to survive in northern Florida.

Habitat: In Florida these lizards use successional habitats, agricultural areas, and small towns and suburbs of metropolitan areas.

Habitat: Dry upland woods and pine woodlands. Microhabitat consists of leaf litter and detritus on the forest floor.

Breeding: The Veiled Chameleon can lay large clutches of over 60 eggs.

Breeding: Lays 2 eggs at a time but may lay several times per summer.

Breeding: Small clutches of 3 to 5 eggs is typical. May lay twice per year.

Natural History: Introduced. The Veiled Chameleon's natural range is the Arabian Peninsula. Chameleons have always been popular in the exotic pet trade and that is no doubt how Florida became home to these Old World reptiles. In addition to the Veiled Chameleon, at least 3 other members of the chameleon family have been observed in the wild in Florida. One can be found in a small area of southeastern Florida. The **Oustalet's Chameleon** (*Furcifer oustaleti*) is native to Madagascar. Other chameleon species may become established eventually. All chameleons have remarkable extendable, very sticky tongues that can be thrust forward from the mouth at a blinding speed to ensnare insect prey. Their tongues will extend at least the length of their bodies.

Natural History: Introduced. Native to the West Indies, there are a total of 29 species of Curly-tailed Lizards. At least 2 have become well established in Florida and it is likely that at least 1 other has been introduced. In addition to the Red-sided species shown above, the **Northern Curly-tailed Lizard** (*L. carinatus*) can be found in Florida. It is seen mostly in southeast Florida be also occurs in scattered populations around the peninsula. It may be more common than the Red-sided Curly-tailed Lizard. The Northern was intentionally introduced to control insects in sugarcane fields. The Red-sided is most likely present in Florida as a result of the exotic pet industry. These lizards are very popular as terrarium pets.

Natural History: These tiny ground dwellers dive quickly beneath leaf litter when approached and they are easily overlooked. Often, their presence is revealed by the rustling sound made as they forage through the dry leaves. Despite being rarely observed, they can be quite common in many areas. Foods are tiny insects and other small invertebrates living among the leaf litter on the forest floor. They also go by the name "Little Brown Skink." They are widespread throughout the southeastern half of America and are most common in the Deep South. They are among the smallest native lizards found in Florida.

Class - **Reptilia** (reptiles)

Order - **Squamata** (lizards and snakes)

Family - **Scincidae** (skinks)

Broad-headed Skink *Plestiodon laticeps*	Five-lined Skink *Plestiodon fasciatus*	Southeastern Five-lined Skink *Plestiodon inexpectatus*
	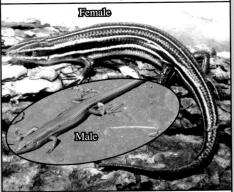	

Broad-headed Skink — *Plestiodon laticeps*

Size: Average 8 inches. Max 13.

Presumed range in Florida

Abundance: Fairly common and may be quite common in ideal habitats.

Variation: Young have blue tails and yellow stripes and resemble Five-lined Skinks. In adults, females have faded, indistinct lines and males are uniformly brown with bright red cheeks.

Habitat: Mesic woodlands, wetland areas, and also dry upland woods with moist microhabitat. May also occur in urban habitats and neighborhoods.

Breeding: Eggs are usually laid on the ground in a hollowed-out depression beneath sheltering log or hollow stump.

Natural History: These very large skinks are quite arboreal and often den in tree hollows many feet above the ground. These arboreal dens are usually used only during summer, and winter hibernation in northern climates takes place underground. In much of the southeast, these lizards are known as "Scorpion Lizards" and some believe the myth that they are dangerously venomous. Although they will bite if handled, they are totally harmless to humans. This is the largest Scincidae lizard species native to the southeast. The largest individuals can barely exceed a foot in length. Insects are the main food but they will also eat small mammals such as baby mice. As with many other skink species, females will remain with their eggs until hatching.

Five-lined Skink — *Plestiodon fasciatus*

Size: Maximum of about 8 inches.

Presumed range in Florida

Abundance: Although common farther north, in Florida this species is rare.

Variation: Young are brightly colored with distinct pale yellow stripes and bright blue tails. Adult females resemble faded young. Adult males are plain brown above with reddish cheek patches.

Habitat: Most common in damp woodlands but also found in swamps and in drier upland areas. Patches of sunlit areas for basking is important.

Breeding: Eggs (6 to 12) are laid in in rotted logs, stumps, sawdust, mulch, or other moisture-retaining material.

Natural History: The young of this species are strikingly colored with bright blue tails and they sometimes are mistaken by laypersons as being another species going by the name "Blue-tailed Skink." These common and well-known lizards are fond of sunning on decks, porches, sidewalks, and patios of homes in rural areas. They can often be found in suburban environments as well, particularly older neighborhoods with abundant large trees and shrubbery. They feed on a wide variety of insects, spiders, and arthropods and they are a useful species in controlling invertebrate pests around the home. Unfortunately, they are highly vulnerable to pesticides and are easily killed by exterminators who commonly spray around the foundation of houses.

Southeastern Five-lined Skink — *Plestiodon inexpectatus*

Size: Averages about 5 inches.

Presumed range in Florida

Abundance: Common and widespread throughout Florida.

Variation: Young are more vividly colored than adults. Adults resemble young but pattern is less vivid on males and older females.

Habitat: This species occurs most frequently in wooded uplands. Prefers pine or mixed woods over pure deciduous forests, but it can be found there.

Breeding: Reproduction is similar to that of the Five-lined Skink. 3 to 10 eggs are laid.

Natural History: The species' scientific name "*inexpectatus*" is an acknowledgment of the fact that until a few decades ago these lizards had remained undiscovered by biologists. They are so similar in appearance, habitat, and distribution to the Five-lined Skink that they managed to go unnoticed until relatively recent times. The only noticable difference has to do with the scales on the underneath side of the tail! They tolerate drier situations than most other skinks. The bulk of their range is in the southeastern US where sandy, well drained soils predominate. Their distribution in Florida is statewide. They tend to retain the juvenile pattern into adulthood much more than our other 2 "five-lined" species (the Broad-headed and Five-lined Skinks).

Class - **Reptilia** (reptiles)

Order - **Squamata** (lizards and snakes)

Family - **Scincidae** (skinks)

Mole Skink	Florida Sand Skink	Coal Skink
Plestiodon egregius	*Plestiodon reynoldsi*	*Plestidon anthrancinus*

Keys Mole Skink

Size: Maximum of 6.25 inches.

Presumed range in Florida

Abundance: Generally uncommon to rare. May be common in ideal habitat.

Variation: There are currently 5 recognized subspecies of the Mole Skink in Florida. The tail color varies from blue to reddish. Shown above is the Florida Keys Mole Skink.

Habitat: Loose, sandy soils that facilitate easy burrowing seems to be the main habitat requirement. These are xeric habitat lizards.

Breeding: Females seek mesic microhabitats to lay about 5 or 6 eggs.

Natural History: The Mole Skink is aptly named as it is a burrowing species that is rarely seen above ground. They are generally regarded as being uncommon or rare, but their abundance is difficult to ascertain due to their secretive habits. Most experts believe they may be much more common than records would indicate in areas of undisturbed habitat. But undisturbed habitat for this species is rapidly disappearing in Florida. These lizards inhabit dry uplands, the same types of habitats favored by developers for building shopping malls, housing developments, etc. At least 1 subspecies of Mole Skink (the Bluetailed Mole Skink, *P. e. lividus*) is now regarded as a threatened species. These skinks have tiny (but functional) legs that are an adaptation for a burrowing lifestyle.

Size: Maximum of 6 inches.

Presumed range in Florida

Abundance: Very rare. A state and federally Threatened Species.

Variation: There is no significant variation in this species. Overall color may vary somewhat from silver to brownish. Pattern of stripes created by lines of dark spots may be vague or prominent.

Habitat: Habitat is ancient sand dunes of central Florida. This is a Florida endemic and its range is restricted to parts of only 7 counties in central Florida.

Breeding: Little is known. Female lays 2 eggs. 1 clutch per year.

Natural History: Sand Skinks are totally adapted for a fossorial lifestyle and have very tiny, vestigial legs with only a single toe on the front feet and 2 toes on the hind feet. They also lack ear openings and this species is in many ways an animal that is morphologically intermediate between the lizard body plan and the snake body plan. It, along with the legless lizards (family anguidae) and the previous species (Mole Skink), provides a living example of the types of evolutionary changes that allowed snakes to evolve from lizard-like ancestors. The range of this species is highly restricted and they occur only in regions that were once coastal sand dunes at a time when sea level was much higher. At that time, central Florida was a chain of islands and the rest of Florida was underwater.

Size: Maximum of 7 inches.

Presumed range in Florida

Abundance: Uncommon to rare in Florida. Restricted to the panhandle.

Variation: There are 2 subspecies of Coal Skink, the Northern and the Southern. Florida's subspecies is the Southern Coal Skink (*P. a. pluvialis*). Young are very dark, nearly black.

Habitat: This species apparently associates with streams and creeks in wooded areas. Favors moist microhabitats such as rotten logs.

Breeding: Female lays 4 to 10 eggs and remains with the clutch.

Natural History: Coal Skinks are one of Florida's least commonly observed skink species. They seem quite secretive and are rather patchily distributed throughout their range. Termites, ant larva and pupae, and earthworms are listed as known food items. Probably feeds on a wide variety of small insects and other tiny invertebrates encountered on leaf litter on the forest floor. In addition to the Coal Skink and the 6 other species of the skinks (Scincidae family) that are native to Florida, there are several similar-looking exotic skink species from the Old World that have become established in isolated pockets here and there on the peninsula of Florida. All the skinks seen in the Florida panhandle are native species.

Class - **Reptilia** (reptiles)

Order - **Squamata** (lizards and snakes)

Family - **Teiidae**

Six-lined Racerunner *Aspidoscelis sexlineatus*	**Giant Ameiva** *Ameiva ameiva*	**Black and White Tegu** *Salvator merianae*

Size: From 6 to 10 inches. Presumed range in Florida	**Size:** Maximum of 25 inches. Presumed range in Florida	**Size:** Maximum of 35 inches. Presumed range in Florida
Abundance: Common. Can be very common in ideal habitats throughout most of Florida.	**Abundance:** Generally rare in Florida. Restricted to small area of southeastern Florida.	**Abundance:** Still relatively rare in most of the state. Increasingly common in south.
Variation: Males and subadults are a bit more vividly colored than mature females. An additional subspecies is found west of the Mississippi River.	**Variation:** Males have blueish gray venter. White or gray venter in females and juveniles. Female retains tan lateral stripes of juveniles.	**Variation:** Juveniles are more brightly marked and light markings tend to be more greenish or brown. Adults as shown above. No sexual dimorphism.
Habitat: Habitat requirements are sandy or gravelly soils in dry upland areas with prolonged exposure to the sun.	**Habitat:** Most common along canal banks and other open areas with access to direct sunlight.	**Habitat:** Xeric and semi-xeric habitats in upland areas seems to be the preferred habitat.
Breeding: Breeds in April or May. 6 or 8 eggs are laid in an underground nest chamber in sandy soil.	**Breeding:** Probably lays 2 to 4 eggs. May produce 2 clutches per year.	**Breeding:** Females will lay up to 35 eggs at a time. Babies are relatively large and have a high survival rate.
Natural History: The *Aspidoscelis* lizards are a common and diverse family in the southwestern United States, but they are represented in the east by this single species. These speedy lizards are aptly named as they can reach a speed of up to 20 mph. They are active at higher temperatures than many reptiles and they will spend the first few minutes of the day basking in the sun to raise their body temperature. At night, they retreat to an underground burrow dug into loose soil. Food is insects and other invertebrates. The *Aspidoscelis* genus is famous among biologists because in some species there are no males and reproduction is accomplished by parthenogenesis (the development of unfertilized eggs into embryos). In most cases, these unisexual species arose from the hybridization of 2 similar species.	**Natural History:** Introduced. The presence of these lizards in Florida is undoubtedly the result of escaped or released animals originating from the exotic pet trade. These lizards are native to tropical South America and there are at least 2 different morphological forms that can be found in southern Florida today. In many respects, the Ameiva lizards are similar to our native Teiidae species, the Six-lined Racerunner. Ameivas are diurnal, fast-moving and active lizards that forage throughout the day in search of a wide variety of invertebrate and small vertebrate prey. They are always alert to any nearby activity and will flee into thick brush or retreat to their nighttime burrow if approached too closely. Like their cousins the racerunners, they are remarkably fast-moving lizards.	**Natural History:** Introduced. Originally native to southern South America, the Black and White Tegu has generated a great deal of interest among wildlife biologists and has received a significant amount of exposure in the local media throughout the state. Although their diet is omnivorous, they they will feed on eggs, small vertebrates, and invertebrates and they are regarded as a potential threat to many of Florida's native species, including some that are already regarded as imperiled. In addition to the areas shown on the range map above, this lizard has been found in several more disjunct populations throughout central Florida. The species is apparently expanding rapidly and the map above may not be an accurate representation of the species range in Florida.

Class - **Reptilia** (reptiles)
Order - **Squamata** (lizards and snakes)
Family - **Rhineuridae** (worm lizards)

Size: Maximum of 11 inches.

Abundance: Very rarely seen but may be more common than sightings would indicate.

Variation: None.

Presumed range in Florida

Habitat: Habitat is probably xeric or semi-xeric soils. Definitely requires friable soil for burrowing and is thus restricted to sandy substrates.

Breeding: Little is known about the biology of this secretive species, and even less is known regarding reproduction. It is an egg layer and 2 or 3 eggs is believed to constitute a clutch.

Natural History: Appropriately named, the Florida Worm Lizard might easily be mistaken for a worm. The body appears segmented by circular annuli which upon very close examination are shown to be scales. Close examination will also reveal the presence of scale-like plates on the wedge-shaped head. The head shape acts to facilitate easier burrowing, and this animal is strictly subterranean in habits. They are sometimes flooded from their burrows during heavy monsoons and that is when most specimens are observed. Except for a very small area in southernmost Georgia, the range of the Florida Worm Lizard is contained entirely in Florida. They are also uncovered beneath palm fronds or leaf mold by people doing yard work. Recent molecular studies indicate that the worm lizards (an unusual group of lizards known to biologists by the name Amphisbaenians) are actually more closely related to snakes than to most lizard species.

THE REPTILES OF FLORIDA

FLORIDA

PART 2: SNAKES

Class - **Reptilia** (reptiles)

Order - **Squamata** (lizards and snakes)

Family - **Colubridae** (harmless egg-laying snakes)

Scarletsnake *Cemophora concinna*	Racer *Coluber constrictor*	Eastern Coachwhip *Masticophis flagellum*

Size: Record length 32.5 inches.

Presumed range in Florida

Abundance: Uncommon.

Variation: 3 subspecies (see Natural History).

Size: Maximum length 6 feet.

Presumed range in Florida

Abundance: Common.

Variation: Young are blotched.

Size: Record 8.5 feet.

Presumed range in Florida

Abundance: Fairly common.

Variation: Variable (see Natural History below).

Habitat: Upland habitats with sandy substrates for burrowing are preferred. Perhaps most common in pine flatwoods (Ashton and Ashton, 1981)

Habitat: Black Racers are habitat generalists that may be found in virtually any habitat. They favor dry upland woods and overgrown fields.

Habitat: Xeric and semi-xeric habitats in upland areas seems to be the preferred habitat. Most common in open woods, overgrown fields, and scrub.

Breeding: Little is known. Lays small clutches of around a half dozen eggs.

Breeding: Females lay about a dozen (from 5 to 20) eggs.

Breeding: Female will deposit up to 2 dozen eggs in moist places.

Natural History: The Scarletsnake is often confused with the venomous Coral Snake, but the Coral Snake has a black snout and the red colors are bordered by yellow. In the Scarletsnake, the red colors are bordered by black. It is a nocturnal, secretive species that spends much time below ground or beneath bark and logs. Feeds mostly on the eggs of other reptiles, but is also known to eat small snakes and young lizards. Although expert herpetologists recognize 2 subspecies in Florida, the differences between the 2 are slight and most people would not be able to tell them apart. The subspecies known as the Northern Scarletsnake (subspecies *copei*) is found in northern Florida and northward to Kentucky, Missouri, and New Jersey. The Florida Scarletsnake (subspecies *concinnea*) is endemic to Florida and found only on the peninsula. A third subspecies (the Texas Scarletsnake, subspecies *lineri*) occurs as a disjunct population along the southern Gulf Coast of Texas.

Natural History: Racers are alert, active snakes that relentlessly prowl in search of almost any type of animal prey that can be swallowed. They will eat insects, amphibians, lizards, other snakes (including the young of venomous species), nestling birds, eggs, and small mammals. They are also adept at catching fish trapped in drying pools of streams and swamps. Unlike many snake species, the Racer is a diurnal animal and may be active even during the heat of the day in midsummer. They are apparently intelligent, curious snakes that will follow livestock and other large animals in hopes of capturing insects and other prey that may be disturbed by the larger animals passing. This is probably how they gained the reputation as aggressive snakes that will chase a human. 3 subspecies occur in Florida but the differences are slight and largely unnoticable to the average person. Their name is appropriate as they are probably one of the fastest snakes in America. They eat almost anything they can swallow.

Natural History: Some Coachwhips in Florida are uniformly light brown or tan in color. Others are darker brown to black anteriorly, gradually fading to lighter brown on the posterior half of the body. Juveniles show a pattern of dark bands or blotches. The Coachwhip is the second longest snake species in Florida, surpassed by only a couple of inches by the Indigo Snake. Most Coachwhips are about 6 feet when grown. Like their relatives the racers, coachwhips are agile snakes and although mainly terrestrial they are excellent climbers and they will not hesitate to dash up into bushes and small trees when hard pressed by a human pursuer. They hunt mainly by sight and are active during the day, retreating beneath cover at night. Any animal small enough to be swallowed can be prey. Like their relatives the racers, these snakes are fierce fighters when captured. In many respects they are a larger, even faster, and more vicious version of the Racer.

Class - **Reptilia** (reptiles)

Order - **Squamata** (lizards and snakes)

Family - **Colubridae** (harmless egg-laying snakes)

Eastern Indigo Snake *Drymarchon couperi*	Mole Kingsnake *Lampropeltis calligaster*	Scarlet Kingsnake *Lampropeltis elapsoides*

Size: Record 8 feet, 7.5 inches.

Presumed range in Florida

Abundance: Uncommon.

Variation: Young has light back markings.

Size: Record 56.25 inches.

Presumed range in Florida

Abundance: Rare in Florida.

Variation: 3 subspecies, 2 in Florida.

Size: Average 18 to 20 inches.

Presumed range in Florida

Abundance: Uncommon.

Variation: No significant variation.

Habitat: Found in a variety of habitats. Most common in habitats that support the Gopher Tortoise or in uplands bordering swamps, marshes, and streams.

Habitat: In Florida this species uses overgrown fields, pastures, pine flatwoods, sandhills, and open woodlands. Common in prairies out west.

Habitat: Prefers flatwoods and wet woodlands where it lives beneath the bark of dead snags. Also rarely in upland woods.

Breeding: Clutch size is reported to be up to 12 eggs, possibly laid in a Gopher Tortoise burrow.

Breeding: Little is known. Females produce about a dozen eggs that are believed to be laid underground.

Breeding: Clutch size is small. Rarely more than 6 eggs, often fewer. Probably breeds in the spring.

Natural History: Nearly eradicated decades ago by habitat loss and over-collecting by the pet trade, in the 1970s the Eastern Indigo Snake became the first snake species in America afforded protection under the newly minted Endangered Species Act. Today populations have recovered somewhat, but they are still regarded as a Threatened Species. These large predators will eat any vertebrate prey they can overpower, including young alligators and young rattlesnakes. The continued development of their habitat in Florida poses a major threat, as do increasing roads and traffic. These large snakes often have large home ranges, and 4-lane highways can be an almost impassable barrier. New road construction continues in the state to accommodate an increasing human population. Coupled with new housing developments, new shopping malls, etc., the future for this magnificent snake in Florida is in doubt in all but large tracts of protected lands.

Natural History: 3 subspecies are found in the southern United States and 2 of those range into Florida (the Mole Kingsnake-*L. c. rhombomaculata*) and the South Florida Mole Kingsnake-*L. c. occiptolineata*). Mole Kingsnakes are a subterranean species that is only rarely seen above ground, usually in early spring. They feed mostly on small mammals which are hunted in their underground burrows. They also eat bird eggs and nestlings, but they are a threat only to those that nest on or near the ground. Despite the fact that this is a fairly common snake in much of the southern US, they are apparently quite rare in Florida and the South Florida subspecies is very rare. Even in the parts of their range where they are common, they are rarely observed due to their burrowing habits. Populations in Florida seem to be disjunct and widely separated from the main population to the north and west.

Natural History: This is another Coral Snake "mimic" that can be identified as harmless by noting the arrangement of the colored bands around the body. On the venomous Coral Snake, red bands are bordered by yellow. On the nonvenomous Scarlet Kingsnake, red bands are border by black. The poem "Red touches yellow, kill a fellow; red touches black, venom lack" is an easy-to-remember phrase used to recall the color sequence. The Scarlet Kingsnake's favorite microhabitat in northern Florida and in the lower Gulf Coastal Plain is beneath the bark of standing dead pine trees or old stumps within wet woodlands. Lizards are the primary prey in the wild but captive specimens will often eat small mice. They seem to be mostly nocturnal in habits and at night they will seek small lizards that sleep beneath the loose bark of dead trees and stumps. The Scarlet Kingsnakes often hide beneath the same bark during the day.

Class - **Reptilia** (reptiles)
Order - **Squamata** (lizards and snakes)
Family - **Colubridae** (harmless egg-laying snakes)

Short-tailed Snake
Lampropeltis extenuata

Eastern Kingsnake
Lampropeltis getulus

Panhandle

Northern Peninsula

Southern Peninsula

Size: Record length 25.75 inches.

Abundance: Rare.

Variation: None.

Presumed range in Florida

Habitat: Lives in xeric habitats in upland regions of the central Florida peninsula. Sandhill scrub, dry oak hammocks, and Longleaf Pine/ Wiregrass habitats. Ocala National Forest in Marion County offers probably the largest tract of undisturbed habitat for this species in Florida today.

Breeding: An egg layer. Practically nothing is known about breeding in this secretive snake. Eggs are probably laid in underground chambers.

Natural History: This unusual snake is an endemic Florida species. Until recently it was the sole member of the genus *Stilosoma*, but it was always thought to be closely related to the kingsnakes. Recent studies have confirmed that it belongs in the genus *Lampropeltis* with other kingsnake species. This is a Threatened species in Florida. The habitat preference for this snake is also highly valued for human use. In Florida, upland habitats are increasingly being converted to suburbs and shopping malls. The impact of an ever increasing human population in Florida has negatively impacted many species whose habitats are being converted to human uses. The common name is derived from the fact that this species has an exceedingly short tail.

Size: Average about 4 feet. Maximum 82 inches.

Abundance: 40 years ago, Eastern Kingsnakes were common in most of Florida. Today they are increasingly rare throughout the state.

Variation: Highly variable. At one time 5 subspecies of Eastern Kingsnake were recognized in Florida. Today, they are all regarded as a single species (though some experts believe subspecific status is still warranted).

Presumed range in Florida

Habitat: Found in nearly all types of habitat in the state except purely aquatic situations. They will uses wetlands such as marshes and wet prairies.

Breeding: An annual breeder that lays 8 to 12 eggs in early summer. Eggs are laid in an moisture-retaining medium, often inside rotted stumps or logs. Eggs hatch in about 60 days. Young Eastern Kingsnakes have a chain-like pattern of white spots.

Natural History: Eastern Kingsnakes are best known for their habit of killing and eating other snakes, including venomous species. These powerful constrictors are immune to the venom of pit vipers and will kill and eat any snake that is small enough to be swallowed whole. They also eat rodents, birds, lizards, and baby turtles. They are mainly terrestrial in habits but have been found inside of standing dead trees several feet off the ground. They may be active both day and night but are mostly crepuscular and during hotter months tend to become more nocturnal. This species is a favorite captive pet of many reptile enthusiasts in America. After some time in captivity, they will become quite tame and rarely bite. When they do bite however, they do so with very strong jaws! The decline of Eastern Kingsnakes in Florida is a mystery. Some blame the introduced fire ant, claiming the ants destroy eggs and kill young snakes. Others believe there could be a potentially more menacing threat such as some form of toxic contaminant in the environment. Certainly there has been significant loss of habitat for the species over the last half century and that is no doubt is another contributing factor.

Class - **Reptilia** (reptiles)

Order - **Squamata** (lizards and snakes)

Family - **Colubridae** (harmless egg-laying snakes)

Rough Green Snake *Opheodrys aestivus*	Crowned Snakes *Tantilla* species	Florida Pine Snake *Pituophis melanoleucus*

Southeastern Crowned Snake

Size: Average 2 to 3 feet. Max 45 inches.	Presumed range in Florida 	**Size:** 8 to 10 inches. Maximum 13 inches.	Presumed range in Florida	**Size:** 4 to 6 feet. Maximum 7.5 feet.	Presumed range in Florida 
Abundance: Fairly common.		**Abundance:** Mostly common.		**Abundance:** Rare, declining.	
Variation: None.		**Variation:** 3 subspecies in FL.		**Variation:** See Natural History.	

Habitat: Open fields, pastures, and edges of woods and fields. Often common in wetlands where there are low bushes and shrubs overhanging water.	**Habitat:** May be found in a variety of habitats but most common in woodland situations. Microhabitat is leaf litter and beneath rocks or logs.	**Habitat:** Dry uplands, especially where there are sandy soils. Open woodlands, overgrown fields and pastures, and Longleaf Pine/Wiregrass.
Breeding: 3 to 12 eggs are laid in late spring or early summer. The babies are slender, miniature replicas of the adult.	**Breeding:** 2 to 5 eggs are laid beneath leaf litter in midsummer. Hatchlings are only about 3 inches long.	**Breeding:** Female Pine Snakes create an underground nest chamber for laying an average of a dozen eggs.

Natural History: Rough Green Snakes live in dense bushes and shrubs where their bright green color renders them invisible. Arthropods of many varieties are their prey. Food includes spiders, caterpillars, crickets, and grasshoppers, to name a few of their favorites. These snakes are sometimes called "grass snakes" in reference to their bright green coloration. These handsome little snakes are rarely observed due to their cryptic coloration. Some people believe they are extremely rare. In fact they are a fairly common snake in Florida and their populations are probably stable. However, they are certainly vulnerable to habitat destruction wrought by modern agricultural practices and development. The widespread use of chemical insecticides poses another likely threat to these and all other insect-eaters. These harmless snakes are extremely docile and they cannot be induced to bite, even when picked up and handled.

Natural History: These tiniest of Florida's serpents are no bigger around than a matchstick. Their name comes from the black-colored "crown" on the top of the head. These are secretive snakes that spend most of their time hiding beneath leaf litter, rocks, bark, or logs. They feed on tiny insect larva, termites, and other miniature invertebrates. Although they may be found in upland woods, their tiny size renders them vulnerable to desiccation and they thus seek mesic conditions as a microhabitat. There are 3 species of *Tantilla* found in Florida and all are extremely similar. They are distinguished from one another by the shape of the black "crown" on the head. Shown above is the **Southeastern Crowned Snake** (*Tantilla coronata*) of the western panhandle. The other 2 species are the **Florida Crowned Snake** (*Tantilla relicta*) from peninsula Florida, and the **Rim Rock Crowned Snake** (*Tantilla oolitica*). The latter is found only in the Florida Keys.

Natural History: In spite of the fact that these are large snakes, they are rarely seen due to their habit of staying in rodent burrows below the ground. When they do emerge their large size and raucus behavior when threatened makes them very conspicuous, which often leads to their death at the hands of humans. They hunt rodents and other burrowing mammals in their subsurface tunnels. They will also consume the eggs and nestling of ground nesting birds. When cornered they will put on an impressive display by hissing loudly and striking savagely. Although widespread in Florida, they are rare and declining and the Florida Wildlife Commission asks that all sightings be reported. Please report any sightings of this snake to https://public.myfwc.com/fwri/raresnakes/, or contact kevin.enge@myfwc.com. They will vary from light gray to dark gray with darker blotches that may be gray, brown, reddish, or nearly black.

Class - **Reptilia** (reptiles)
Order - **Squamata** (lizards and snakes)
Family - **Colubridae** (harmless egg-laying snakes)

Corn Snake *Pantherophis guttata*	**Midland (Gray) Ratsnake** *Pantherophis spiloides*	**Eastern Ratsnake** *Pantherophis alleghaniensis*

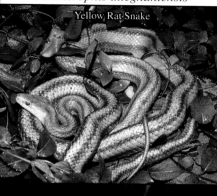
Yellow Rat Snake

Size: Record 6 feet.

Abundance: Fairly common.

Habitat: Found in every habitat except extensive wetlands.

Presumed range in Florida

Size: Maximum just over 8 feet.

Abundance: Fairly common.

Habitat: Woodlands and edge areas bordering woods.

Presumed range in Florida

Variation: Varies slightly in the amount of red and in the brightness of the colors. The color between the blotches ranges from reddish to grayish. Young Corn Snakes are similar to adults but the dorsal blotches are darker and more vivid.

Variation: Body color of adults is always some shade of gray (pale smokey gray to dark gray) with darker blotches on the back. Dorsal blotches may be dark gray, brown, or reddish. Hatchlings are always pale gray with dark gray blotches.

Everglades Rat Snake

Size: Maximum just over 8 feet.

Abundance: Fairly common.

Habitat: Woodlands and edge areas bordering woods. Also in swamps.

Presumed range in Florida

Breeding: Breeds annually in spring and may lay over 2 dozen eggs (averages less). Eggs are laid in a sheltered place with adequate moisture to prevent desiccation. Eggs hatch in late summer.

Breeding: An egg layer that lays up to 20 (average about a dozen) eggs. Eggs are laid in hollow limbs above ground or on the ground in rotted stumps, beneath logs, etc.

Variation: Specimens from the Big Bend region of Florida resemble the Midland (Gray) Rat Snake. Those from northeastern and peninsular Florida are known as Yellow Rat Snakes. Everglades specimens are orange.

Breeding: Essentially the same as the Midland Rat Snake.

Natural History: The Corn Snake is a southern snake that ranges northward as far as Kentucky in the mid-south and as far as New Jersey on the eastern seaboard. They have been recorded from every county in Florida. They are a popular snake in the pet industry and are bred in captivity for the pet trade. Corn Snake breeders in Florida have produced through selective breeding a wide variety of colors and patterns that do not exist in nature. Corn Snakes are good climbers and regularly ascend into trees in search of bird nests. They also eat mice and lizards and young specimens may eat some invertebrates. In Florida these snakes often go by the name "Red Ratsnake," an appropriate reference to their overall coloration.

Natural History: This is the probably most arboreal snake species in Florida and adults spend a great deal of time in trees. They often choose a regular den site in old woodpecker holes or hollows of trees and may be seen sunning with the forepart of the body emerged from a hole. Excellent climbers, they can ascend straight up a tree trunk using only the bark to gain a purchase with their belly scales. They will climb to great heights in search of bird nests. In addition to baby birds and eggs, they will also eat rodents, squirrels, and other small mammals up to the size of a rabbit. The range of this species in Florida is generally west of the Apalachicola River. It and the Eastern Rat Snake were until recently regarded as the same species.

Natural History: Similar to the Midland Rat Snake in habits and food preferences. At one time, all of America's Rat Snakes were regarded as different subspecies of the same wide range and variable species. Many experts reject the idea of full species status for these snakes and interbreeding occurs in areas where the different species meet. Sometimes called "Chicken Snake."

Class - **Reptilia** (reptiles)		

Order - **Squamata** (lizards and snakes)		

Family - **Dipsadidae** (rear-fanged snakes)		

Ringneck Snake *Diadophis punctatus*	**Mud Snake** *Farencia abacura*	**Rainbow Snake** *Farencia erytrogamma*

Size: Average about 14 inches. Maximum 2 feet.

Presumed range in Florida

Abundance: Fairly common.

Variation: No variation in Florida.

Size: Average about 4 feet. Maximum 6 feet

Presumed range in Florida

Abundance: Common.

Variation: 2 subspecies in Florida.

Size: Average about 4 feet. Record 68 inches.

Presumed range in Florida

Abundance: Rare.

Variation: 2 subspecies in Florida.

Habitat: A woodland species that lives in rotted logs, stumps, and beneath rocks and leaf litter on the forest floor.

Habitat: This is a snake of swamps, marshes, and wetland areas. In Florida, they occur statewide in suitable habitats.

Habitat: Inhabits clear spring-fed rivers, springs and spring runs. Associates with dense aquatic vegetation.

Breeding: Lays up to a dozen eggs, usually fewer in rotted logs or other moisture-retaining places. Young are about 5 inches long at hatching.

Breeding: Lays very large clutches of eggs (the record is over 100). Eggs are place in hollows of floating logs or stumps above the waterline.

Breeding: Up to 50 eggs (clutch sizes of 22 to 52 are documented) are laid in moist humus and attended by the female during incubation.

Natural History: Ringneck snakes are still widespread and common in Florida. In fact this is one of the most abundant snake species in the eastern US. But they may be declining. They are often uncovered by humans beneath boards, stones, leaves, or other debris. The distinctive yellow or cream-colored collar around the neck readily identifies them, and even those unfamiliar with reptiles have no trouble recognizing this species. They feed mostly on soft-bodied insects and other invertebrates. Earthworms are a favorite food. When threatened, they will often hold aloft the tightly curled up tip of the underside of their bright yellow tail to distract a predator. This defense mechanism is probably designed to direct an attackers attention away from the vulnerable head to the less vulnerable tail. Despite having enlarged grooved teeth in the rear of the jaw, they are harmless to man.

Natural History: Few people who are not actively seeking this species will ever see one. They live among the tangled mass of vegetation and plant roots in the muck of swamps and marshes, where they prey primarily on several species of aquatic salamanders along with frogs and fish. They are sometimes seen crossing roads at night during periods of heavy rarinfall, but otherwise remain hidden in among aquatic vegetation. The tail of this snake terminates in a stiff, sharp spine that is erroneously believed to be able to sting. Some also believe these snakes to be the mythical "hoop snake," that according to legend can take its tail into its mouth forming a hoop and then roll down hills. This fable also sometimes includes the myth that the spine on the tail is used as a deadly stinger. There are 2 subspecies in Florida but the difference between the 2 is slight. Specimens from the peninsula have more red on the sides.

Natural History: Similar in many respects to the Mud Snake, but much rarer and seems to prefer flowing water rather than the lentic waters inhabited by the Mud Snake. Like the Mud Snake, this species possess a stiff, sharp spine on the tip of the tail. Some have speculated that this spine may be used to prode slimy prey like eels into the throat once they prey has been grasped by the snake. The primary prey of adults is apparently eels, but young snakes are known to take small amphibians. These snakes are extremely docile and neither the Rainbow Snake or its cousin the Mud Snake can be induced to bite even when roughly handled. The multi-colored stripes on the Rainbow Snake are iridescent in sunlight and are responsible for the name. Isolated population near Lake Okeechobee is regarded as a distinct subspecies known as the South Florida Rainbow Snake (subspecies *seminola*).

Class - **Reptilia** (reptiles)

Order - **Squamata** (lizards and snakes)

Family - **Dipsadidae** (rear-fanged snakes)

Eastern Hognose Snake *Heterodon platirhinos*	**Southern Hognose Snake** *Heterodon simus*

Black-morph

Spotted morph - "hooding"

Orange morph

Size: Averages about 2.5 feet. Maximum 45 inches.

Presumed range in Florida

Abundance: Fairly common.

Variation: Highly variable (see photos above). Individuals range from solid black to uniform olive green. Others may be variously spotted or blotched with dark saddles on a yellowish or orange background. The young always exhibit a spotted pattern.

Habitat: Hognose Snakes are most common in habitats with sandy soils which facilitate easy burrowing. They are thus widespread in Florida. They seem to prefer areas with moist soils but can also be found in upland woods and fields.

Breeding: Hognose snakes breed in early spring and lay up to 2 dozen eggs. Nests are probably in an underground chamber in sandy soil. Young snakes are about 8 inches in length and always have a spotted pattern. Babies are grayish brown with well-defined dark gray or black blotches.

Natural History: The Eastern Hognose Snake is famous for the elaborate performance it puts on when threatened. First, they will spread the neck like a cobra (hence the nickname "Spreading Adder"), and with the mouth wide open they will strike repeatedly. They always intentionally miss with the strike and never bite even when picked up and handled. The initial "cobra display" is always accompanied by loud hissing. When their complicated bluff fails to deter the threat, they will roll onto their backs, stick out their tongue and give a convincing impression of being dead. Their primary food is frogs and toads. They possess enlarged teeth in the back of the upper jaw that are used to puncture the bodies of toads that have gulped air and inflated themselves in an attempt to become too large to be swallowed. Herpetologists who have had the skin punctured by the enlarged rear teeth while handling these snakes report a mild to moderately severe burning sensation. Whether it is from the snake's saliva or from toxins secreted from the skin of a recently swallowed toad is unknown. The food of these snakes is almost entirely toads and frogs, making them one of the more specialized feeders among America's snakes. Salamanders are reported to have been found in the stomachs of a few individuals as well. Anecdotal evidence suggests Eastern Hognose Snakes may be declining. Their habit of feeding on toads and frogs almost exclusively may make them vulnerable to insecticides, as frog and toads are primarily insect eaters and poisoning through secondary ingestion is a possibility.

Size: Maximum of 24 inches.

Presumed range in Florida

Abundance: Rare.

Variation: No significant variation.

Habitat: Xeric uplands and sandy soils. Scrub, Sand Pine, and Longleaf Pine-Turkey Oak, xeric hardwood hammocks and sand dunes are also listed as habitats.

Breeding: Breeding can occur from early spring thoughout the summer. Clutch size ranges from 6 to 14 eggs.

Natural History: This completely harmless and interesting little snake has experienced significant population declines throughout is range and its population is currently being monitored in Florida by the Florida Fish and Wildlife Conservation Commission. The cause of its decline is unknown but loss of habitat and other human-related threats such as highways and pesticide use are suspected. The introduced Red Fire Ant may also be a threat by destroying nests. Sightings of this snake should be reported to https://public.myfwc.com/fwri/raresnakes/, or contact kevin.enge@myfwc.com. This species will exhibit the same bluffing behavior as the Eastern Hognose Snake and like that species, it is completely docile and will not bite. It also possesses the enlarged teeth in the rear of the upper jaw which it uses to puncture the inflated bodies of its primary prey of frogs and toads.

Class - **Reptilia** (reptiles)		
Order - **Squamata** (lizards and snakes)		
Family - **Dipsadidae** (rear-fanged snakes)	Family - **Natricidae** (harmless live-bearing snakes)	

Pine Woods Snake
Rhadinaea flavita

Size: Usually about 12 inches. Record 16.	Presumed range in Florida
Abundance: Uncommon.	
Variation: See Natural History.	

Habitat: This snake is a Pine Flatwoods specialist. Their microhabitat is under the bark of rotten logs and stumps and beneath the large sheaths of bark that slough from standing dead pine trees and accumulate at the tree's base.

Breeding: Very little is known about reproduction in this rare and secretive snake. It is thought to lay 2 to 4 eggs. Baby snakes are only about 5 inches long and hide easily beneath the litter on the forest floor. Thus young snakes are almost never seen in the wild.

Natural History: This species is unique among Florida's serpents in that it is the sole representative of its genus in the US. All others are found in tropical America. They range along the Lower Coastal Plain of the southeast from southern North Carolina to eastern Louisiana, but the range is fragmented and disjunct. These snakes have venom glands that produce a mild toxin used to subdue small lizards and amphibians. They are harmless to man and never bite even when handled. If they did bite, it is doubtful the tiny teeth would penetrate deep enough to induce venom, and even if that happened the venom is too weak to affect a human. Exhibits minimal variation, but the color will vary somewhat from tan to reddish brown.

Rough Earth Snake
Haldea striatula

Size: Usually about 10 inches. The record is 15.	Presumed range in Florida
Abundance: Fairly common.	
Variation: No variation in FL.	

Habitat: Mesic woodlands with abundant leaf litter. In Florida can be common in mesic Pine Flatwoods. Microhabitat is beneath the accumulated detritus on the forest floor. Can be found beneath rotted logs, sheaths of bark, etc.

Breeding: Breeding takes place in spring and 3 or 4 young are typically born in late summer or early fall. The largest litters may number as many as 8. Baby snakes are fairly large in comparison to the adult female, and may be as much as 4 inches long.

Natural History: Earth Snakes are fossorial snakes that live beneath leaf litter on the forest floor. They are shallow burrowers, staying within a few inches of the surface and mostly existing in the seam between soil and surface litter. Here they hunt small invertebrates with the favorite food item being earthworms. They can often be found beneath flat objects such as old boards or tin. They have pointed snouts and conical heads for facilitating entry into earthworm burrows. They are sometimes seen on the surface following heavy rains in late summer and fall. They are very similar to the Smooth Earth Snake from which they can be told by their keeled scales. Both species of earth snakes are endemic to the eastern United States.

Smooth Earth Snake
Virginia valeriae

Size: Usually about 10 inches. The record is 15.	Presumed range in Florida
Abundance: Rare in Florida.	
Variation: No variation in FL.	

Habitat: Smooth Earth Snakes are basically a forest species but they can also be found in open fields near forests and around forest edges. Their microhabitat is moist soils beneath leaf litter, logs, stones, etc.

Breeding: These snakes are live-bearers that give birth to 4 to 12 young. The young snakes resemble the adults and measure about 3 inches in length. They are about the girth of a pencil lead and may at first be mistaken for an earthworm.

Natural History: Smooth Earth Snakes are tiny, docile snakes that could not manage to bite a human even if they were so inclined, which they are not. They have tiny heads, even for their size, and thus their food consists of small invertebrates: insects, snails, and, mostly, earthworms. These are secretive little serpents that sometimes emerge to prowl about on the surface after summer rains. Otherwise they are easily overlooked except by herpetologists who know where to find them beneath logs, stones, or amid accumulated humis on the forest floor. As with other small snakes that burrow beneath detritus on the floor of woodlands, these little snakes are occasionally turned up by people raking or doing yard work.

Class - **Reptilia** (reptiles)		
Order - **Squamata** (lizards and snakes)		
Family - **Natricidae** (harmless live-bearing snakes)		

Striped Swamp Snake *Liodytes alleni*	**Black Swamp Snake** *Liodytes pygaea*	**Glossy Swamp Snake** *Liodytes rigida*

Size: Usually about 20 inches. Record nearly 28.	Presumed range in Florida 	**Size:** Usually about 18 inches. Record 22.	Presumed range in Florida	**Size:** Usually about 2 feet. Record 33.	Presumed range in Florida 
Abundance: Common.		**Abundance:** Fairly common.		**Abundance:** Uncommon.	
Variation: No variation in FL.		**Variation:** 2 subspecies in FL.		**Variation:** 2 subspecies in FL.	

Habitat: Aquatic. Found in swamps, marshes, canals, and other lentic waters with abundant vegetation.	**Habitat:** Aquatic. Found in swamps, marshes, wet prairies, and other lentic waters with abundant vegetation.	**Habitat:** Aquatic. Found in waters with abundant vegetation. Swamps, marshes, canals, spagnum bogs, ponds.
Breeding: Gives birth to as many as 10 young. Babies are about 7 to 8 inches.	**Breeding:** Gives birth to up to 11 babies. Young are about 5 inches long.	**Breeding:** Live-bearer. Litter size presumed similar to other *Liodytes*.

Natural History: These snakes are widespread in the Florida peninsula. They can be common among the roots of the Water Hyacinth and amid mats of floating vegetation. They are highly specialized in feeding habits, feeding almost entirely crayfish. Some experts report that they will coil around the crayfish to hold it still while swallowing it (Ashton and Ashton). The members of this genus (*Liodytes*) all have small heads and it is likely that the neonates may consume aquatic insect larva. Until recently all the members of this genus (*Liodytes*) were placed in the genus *Regina,* and they share many morphological characters with that genus. Except for a small disjunct population occurring in southernmost Georgia, the Striped Swamp Snake would be endemic to the Florida peninsula. Mostly nocturnal and crepuscular in activity. This species sometimes leaves the water during periods of heavy rainfall and has been caught crossing roads at night.

Natural History: In most respects the biology of this snake is similar to the preceding species. But this species includes brackish water environments in its habitats. Although mostly nocturnal, it has been seen sunning in the morning during cooler months of the year. As with other members of the genus, they will leave the water on rainy nights and might be seen crossing roadways at that time. Many of their shallow water habitats are susceptible to drying up, and they also sometimes are forced to make overland treks to new habitats during periods of drought. There are currently 3 subspecies of Black Swamp Snake. 1 subspecies inhabits the "low country" of the Carolinas. In Florida, the Northern Florida Black Swamp Snake (*L p. pygaea*) lives in the panhandle and the northern half of the peninsula. It is replaced in the southern half of the peninsula by the Southern Florida Black Swamp Snake (*L. p. cyclas*).

Natural History: The Glossy Swamp Snake ranges throughout the lowlands of the coastal plain from the Carolinas to Texas. There are 3 subspecies, two of which (the Eastern Glossy Swamp Snake-*L.r. rigida* and the Gulf Swamp Snake-*L.r. sinicola*) are found in Florida. The Gulf Swamp Snake inhabits the westernmost counties of the panhandle (generally west of the Apalachicola River), and the Eastern Glossy Swamp Snake lives throughout the rest of the species range in Florida. The natural history of this species is probably similar to the other 2 *Liodytes* species shown on this page. This is a rather secretive species and it is less common in Florida than other members of its genus. Thus its natural history is less well known. They will leave their secretive hideouts amid aquatic vegetation on rainy nights and have been captured crossing roadways at night during heavy rains.

Class - **Reptilia** (reptiles)
Order - **Squamata** (lizards and snakes)
Family - **Natricidae** (harmless live-bearing snakes)

Queen Snake *Regina septemvitta*	**Saltmarsh Snake** *Nerodia clarkii*	**Green Watersnakes** *Nerodia cyclopian* and *Nerodia floridana*

Gulf Saltmarsh Snake

Mississippi Green Watersnake

Size: Average 2 feet. Record 3 feet.	Presumed range in Florida 	**Size:** Maximum length is 3 feet.	Presumed range in Florida 	**Size:** Record 71 inches (Florida Green).	Presumed range in Florida 
Abundance: Rare in Florida.		**Abundance:** Fairly common in coastal areas.		**Abundance:** Rare to common.	
Variation: No variation in Florida.		**Variation:** 3 subspecies. See natural history.		**Variation:** 2 very similar species in Florida.	

| **Habitat:** Found mostly in small, flowing creeks. Its range in Florida is restricted to the panhandle. | **Habitat:** Unique among American snakes in that it lives exclusively in salt/brackish water marshes and estuaries. | **Habitat:** Mississippi Greens are restricted to the lower Escambia River. Florida Greens everywhere else in Florida. |
| **Breeding:** The Queen Snake is a live-bearer that will produce up to a dozen young per litter, a relatively small number for an aquatic snake. | **Breeding:** A live-bearer that produces as many as 22 young per litter. Babies are about 7 to 9 inches in length. Nothing is known about the food of young. | **Breeding:** About 25 young is average for Mississippi Green Watersnakes but litters of 100 have been recorded for the Florida Green Watersnake. |

Natural History: The Queen Snake is a specialized feeder that preys almost exclusively on recently molted, soft-bodied crayfish. In one study, over 95 percent of stomach contents examined contained crayfish (Branson and Baker, 1974). As a result, their distribution is limited to areas where this common crustacean is abundant. Other aquatic vertebrates such as fish, frogs, and salamanders may also be eaten at times. They are often found hiding beneath flat stones in creeks throughout their range. Like other water snakes, they may be seen basking from limbs and branches overhanging water. In morphological characteristics and in its preference for crayfish as a food item, this species closely resembles the swamp snakes of the *Liodytes* genus. In fact those snakes were once classified in the same genus as the Queen Snake.

Natural History: There are 3 subspecies of this snake and all occur in Florida. On the East Coast the Atlantic Salt Marsh Snake (*N. c. taeniata*) is found only in the marshes bordering the intercoastal waterway in Volusia and Indian River Counties. The Mangrove Salt Marsh Snake (*N.c. compressicauda*) inhabits mangroves and marshes from Brevard County southward around the tip of Florida and northward along the Gulf Coast to about the Big Bend region. This is the most colorful of the 3 subspecies and is often deeply reddish. The Gulf Saltmarsh Snake (*N. c. clarkii*) ranges from the Big Bend region all the way to southern Texas. This subspecies is known to hybridize with both the Midland Water Snake and the Southern Water Snake where their ranges meet. All feed on crabs, shrimp, and small fish stranded in tidal pools at low tide.

Natural History: 2 very similar Green Watersnake species are found in Florida. The difference between the 2 pertains to the color and pattern of the belly and the overall adult size (Mississippi Green is much smaller and reaches only 51 inches). They were once regarded as being 2 subspecies of the same snake. Both are primarily nocturnal in habits but in the spring they may be seen sunning by day atop drift, beaver lodges, or branches overhanging water. Mississippi Greens are much more piscivorous than most other water snakes and show a definite preference for large bodies of water. The Florida Green feeds more on frogs and salamanders (as well as fish), and inhabits wet prairies, lakes, ponds, canals, and ditches and especially the vast wetlands of the Everglades. The Mississippi Green Watersnake is rare in Florida. The Florida Green is common.

Class - **Reptilia** (reptiles)
Order - **Squamata** (lizards and snakes)
Family - **Natricidae** (harmless live-bearing snakes)

Plainbelly Watersnake *Nerodia erythrogaster*	Southern Watersnake *Nerodia fasciata*	Midland Watersnake *Nerodia sipedon*

"Yellowbelly" morph

"Florida Watersnake"

	Presumed range in Florida		Presumed range in Florida		Presumed range in Florida
Size: Record 64 inches.		**Size:** Record 62.5 inches.		**Size:** Record is 59 inches.	
Abundance: Common.		**Abundance:** Very common.		**Abundance:** Uncommon.	
Variation: 2 color morphs in FL (see below).		**Variation:** 2 subspecies in Florida.		**Variation:** Males are smaller than females.	

Habitat: Primarily aquatic, but will often wander far from permanent water. They are found in virtually all aquatic habitats throughout their range.

Habitat: Can be found in virtually any aquatic habitat in the state except marine environments. Prefers lentic waters rather than flowing streams.

Habitat: They are very fond of small farm ponds or small streams as habitat, but they can also be found in large lakes and in swamps and marshes.

Breeding: These are among the more prolific of the water snakes and large females will produce litters numbering over 40 babies.

Breeding: Breeds in late winter or early spring and gives birth in late summer to one or two dozen young. Large females can produce over 50 babies.

Breeding: Litters average 2 or 3 dozen, but the largest females may produce nearly 100 babies. Young females may have as few as 6 or 8.

Natural History: These snakes feed primarily on aquatic and semiaquatic vertebrates such as frogs, toads, salamanders, and fish. They are active both day and night in the spring but are more nocturnal or crepuscular during hot weather. Like many other water snakes, they are fierce fighters if caught and will bite and smear the attacker with foul-smelling feces and a pungent musk. As with most water snake species, the female grows considerably larger than the male. They will wander far from water and may even be seen in the driest of habitats atop wooded ridges at higher elevations not usually associated with water snakes. 2 distinct color morphs occur in Florida that were once regarded as distinct subspecies. The "Yellow-bellied" morph is found in the western panhandle and the "Red-bellied" morph occurs elsewhere within the species' range in Florida. Often confused with the venomous Cottonmouth.

Natural History: There are 3 subspecies of this water snake in the southern United States and 2 occur in Florida. The Banded Water Snake (*N.f.fasciata*) is found in the panhandle and the northern third of the peninsula while the Florida Water Snake (*N.f.pictiventris*) lives in the southern two-thirds of Florida. The difference between the 2 subspecies is slight and mostly pertains to the pattern on the belly. The Banded Watersnake shows squarish markings on the belly while the Florida Watersnake has wavy lines across the belly. Food is mostly frogs, but also eats salamanders, fish, and crayfish. Active both day and night but becomes more nocturnal in hot weather. Like all water snakes, it is fond of basking atop floating vegetation, drift, or tree limbs overhanging water. These are very common watersnakes throughout Florida and except for in the Everglades region it may be our most common watersnake species.

Natural History: Midland Water Snakes adapt well to man-made environments like large lake impoundments where they can thrive in the riprap of dams and levees. Frogs and fish are the 2 favorite food items for these snakes. Around man-made impoundments they can become very numerous near boat docks and fishing areas where they scavenge on dead or dying fish and fish heads left behind by fishermen. Like most other watersnake species, they are fond of basking in the sun atop debris and limbs overhanging water. As with other watersnakes, they are commonly confused with the venomous Cottonmouth. Additionally, their dorsal pattern of dark brownish bands on a lighter brown background also causes them to be mistaken for another venomous species, the Copperhead. But Copperheads are terrestrial snakes that only rarely enter water.

Class - **Reptilia** (reptiles)

Order - **Squamata** (lizards and snakes)

Family - **Natricidae** (harmless live-bearing snakes)

Brown Watersnake *Nerodia taxispilota*	**Brown Snakes** *Storeria dekayi and Storeria victa*	**Redbelly Snakes** *Storeria occipitomaculata*

Dekay's Brown Snake

Size: Record 69.5 inches.

Presumed range in Florida

Abundance: Common.

Variation: No color variation. Female is larger.

Habitat: Found in virtually all types of freshwater habitats in the state. May be found in brackish water estuaries but avoids saltwater habitats.

Breeding: Breeds in late winter through spring. 30 to 40 young is a typical litter born in summer or fall. Neonates are up to 11 inches in length.

Natural History: These large watersnakes rival the Florida Green Watersnake in size and they are very heavy bodied, thus large individuals attain an impressive girth. Their food is similar to other watersnake species and consists of a variety of aquatic vertebrates. Young snakes probably also eat invertebrate prey. Like all watersnakes this species is a fierce fighter when captured and will bite viciously with a slashing motion. Large individuals can produce impressive wounds that will bleed profusely but are not deep and despite appearance are never very serious. Although bites from large watersnakes can be painful, infections from nonvenomous snakebites are actually quite rare. These large watersnakes can be quite conspicous in Florida waters as they are found basking on logs and limbs overhanging the water. They are often confused with the venomous Cottonmouth.

Size: Record 20.75 inches.

Presumed range in Florida

Dekay's Brown Snake dark gray
Florida Brown Snake light gray

Abundance: Common.

Variation: 2 similar species, see below.

Habitat: Woodlands, grassy fields, and wetlands. May sometimes be found even in urban areas, especially vacant lots littered with old boards or scrap tin.

Breeding: Gives birth to 5 to 20 young (rarely more, as many as 40). Baby snakes are about 3 inches long with the girth of a toothpick.

Natural History: There are 2 very similar species of Brown Snakes in Florida. Until recently, they were regarded as the same species. The Dekay's Brownsnake is a widespread species but found in Florida only in a small area of the panhandle, while the **Florida Brown Snake** occupies most of the peninsula. These diminutive snakes are often found in vacant lots of large cities and towns, where they hide beneath boards, trash, even small pieces of cardboard. Feeds primarily on earthworms and slugs, but also reportedly eats insects, amphibians' eggs, and tiny fishes. Brown Snakes are known to hibernate communally, an odd behavior for a tiny snake that should have no trouble finding adequate crevices in which to spend the colder months. These snakes are sometimes called "Dekay's Snake," in honor of an early American naturalist. These little snakes make interesting pets and will readily eat earthworms in captivity.

Size: Record 16.5 inches.

Presumed range in Florida

Abundance: Uncommon.

Variation: May be reddish, gray, or brown.

Habitat: Mostly found in wooded areas, in both lowland and uplands. They can also be found in fields around the edges of woods.

Breeding: Live-bearer. Litters number from 5 to 15. Newborn babies are only about 3 inches in length and no bigger around than a matchstick.

Natural History: Redbelly Snakes usually remain hidden by day beneath rocks, logs, etc., and emerge at night to hunt insects and small soft-bodied invertebrates such as earthworms, slugs, beetle larva, isopods, etc. These snakes sometimes exhibit a peculiar behavior when threatened. If voiding of feces and musk fails to discourage a handler, they will curl their upper lip in a ferocious display. It is a purely fallacious action, however, as their tiny teeth could never penetrate human skin. Although these little snakes are widespread across much of the eastern United States, they are less common than many other small snake species. There are 3 subspecies total in America, but only 1 can be found in Florida (The Florida Redbelly Snake-*S.o. obscura*). It ranges throughout the panhandle and into the northern one-third of the peninsula. Its common name comes from the red color of the belly.

Class - **Reptilia** (reptiles)

Order - **Squamata** (lizards and snakes)

Family - **Natricidae** (harmless live-bearing snakes)

Eastern Ribbon Snake
Thamnophis sauritus

Eastern Garter Snake
Thamnophis sirtalis

Family - **Pythonidae** (pythons)

Burmese Python
Python molorus

Eastern Ribbon Snake	Eastern Garter Snake	Burmese Python
Size: 18 to 28 inches. Record 38. **Abundance:** Very common. **Habitat:** Semiaquatic habitats mostly. Edges of streams, wetlands, lakes, etc. Presumed range in Florida	**Size:** Average 2 feet. Max 51 inches. **Abundance:** Very common. **Habitat:** A habitat generalist. Pastures, fields, rural yards, and vacant lots. Presumed range in Florida	**Size:** Record 27 feet. Florida record 17 feet 7 inches. **Abundance:** Uncommon. **Variation:** No variation in FL. Presumed range in Florida
Variation: A total of 4 subspecies are found in the eastern United States and 3 occur in Florida. The color of the light stripes varies (yellow, orange, or blue).	**Variation:** There are 9 subspecies of this widespread snake in the United States. 2 of them can be found in Florida (Eastern and Blue-striped).	**Habitat:** A tropical species native to southern Asia. In Florida, the Burmese Python is found mostly in the Everglades region. There are scattered accounts from father north on the peninsula but it is not known to breed there.
Breeding: Live-bearing. Gives birth to between 10 and 20 young. Births usually occur in August.	**Breeding:** Garter Snakes are live-bearers that give birth to enormous litters of up to 60 babies.	**Breeding:** Large females can lay over 50 eggs. Female coils around eggs and raises her body temperature to incubate.
Natural History: Frogs, toads, fish, and lizards are listed as some of this snake's prey. During certain times of the year, tadpoles and the recently transformed young of frogs and toads are a primary food item. During periods of drought, these snakes will gorge on small fishes trapped in drying pools. Insects and earthworms are also important in the diet. The range of the Eastern Ribbon Snake (subspecies *sauritus*) in Florida is restricted to the western panhandle. The Blue-striped Ribbon Snake (*nitae*) occurs in coastal lowlands of the Big Bend region. The Peninsula Ribbon Snake (*sackenii*) is found through northeast Florida and most of the peninsula. Populations of this subspecies in the Florida Keys are imperiled and protected by Florida Fish and Wildlife Conservation Commission.	**Natural History:** Garter snakes are nonspecialized feeders that will eat insects, earthworms, frogs, toads, salamanders, fish, and rarely small mammals such as baby mice or voles. Their name is derived from their resemblance to the old-fashioned "garters" that were used to hold up men's socks. The name has been widely familiarized to "Garden Snake" in many places. Still appropriate as they are often encountered in people's gardens. They are an ubiquitous species that may be found in both wilderness or urban regions. They are most common in edge habitats and are often found near streams or edges of wetlands. They can also be quite common in suburban areas where they will live among landscape plantings in people's yards. This is one of America's best known snakes and most people recognize them as a harmless species.	**Natural History:** Introduced. The Burmese Python is one of the world's largest snakes and the largest individual known, weighing over 400 pounds. These huge constrictors are capable of killing any other animal native to the Everglades, including small and medium-sized Alligators. Large Alligators often turn the tables on pythons and the pythons become the prey. The threat posed to south Florida's ecosystems is not yet fully known, but they definitely have the potential to negatively impact on virtually all of south Florida's wildlife. The presence of these snakes in Florida is a direct result of the exotic pet trade. Today they can no longer be imported into the state or sold in the pet trade. Another python species, the African Rock Python (*Python sebae*), may also be now established in the southeastern tip of Florida.

Class - **Reptilia** (reptiles)

Order - **Squamata** (lizards and snakes)

Family - **Boidae** (boas)	Family - **Elapidae** (cobra family)	Family - **Crotalidae** (pit vipers)

Boa Constrictor
Boa constrictor

Size: Average about 8 to 10 feet. Max 15 feet.

Abundance: Rare.

Variation: Variable. See Natural History.

Presumed range in Florida

Habitat: In Florida, this species is restricted mainly to tropical habitats in extreme southeastern Florida.

Breeding: Boa Constrictors are live-bearers that can produce large litters of several dozen young.

Natural History: Introduced. This snake is widespread in the neotropics and there are several subspecies. Some are darker with less obvious markings but most specimens from Florida will resemble the photo above. These are highly arboreal snakes that will climb high into trees, but they also hunt small mammals and ground nesting birds on the ground. Their food is mostly warm-blooded prey and they pose a real threat to many of Florida's native mammals and birds. This has been a highly popular snake in the pet trade for many decades and the existance of this snake in Florida is the result of individuals that have escaped or been released in the state over the last 50 years. The first sightings of wild Boa Constrictors in south Florida date back to the 1970s, and they have been confirmed as a self-sustaining breeding population since at least 1994. Individual snakes have been found in scattered locales throughout the state.

Eastern Coral Snake
Micrurus fulvius

Size: Average 2 feet. Max 49 inches.

Abundance: Fairly common.

Variation: No significant variation in Florida.

Presumed range in Florida

Habitat: Inhabits all types of woodland and scrub habitats in Florida. Avoids large expanses of permanent wetlands.

Breeding: Egg layer. Breeds in spring and lays up to a dozen eggs in midsummer. Babies are about 6 to 7 inches.

Natural History: The coral snakes are America's only representatives of the Elapidae family, which includes such famously dangerous snakes as the cobras, mambas, and Australian Death Adder. There are over 70 species of coral snakes in tropical America ranging from Mexico to southern South America. The Eastern Coral is 1 of 3 coral snakes found in the US and is the only species found in Florida. They feed mostly on other snakes and lizards. They can be common in some areas of Florida and sometimes appear in yards or gardens. The venom of the coral snakes is a powerful neurotoxin that kills by blocking nerve impulses to vital organs. Death is usually by suffocation due to paralysis of the diaphragm. Considered on a drop-for-drop basis they have the most toxic venom of any North American serpent. Fortunately, this is an docile species that rarely bites unless handled and there is an effective antivenom for treatment, thus deaths are quite rare.

Copperhead
Agkistrodon controtrix

Size: Average 2 to 3 feet. Record is 58 inches.

Abundance: Rare in Florida.

Variation: No significant variation in Florida.

Presumed range in Florida

Habitat: Primarily woodland animals, but they do wander into overgrown fields, thickets and edge areas.

Breeding: Breeds in spring or in the fall. From 4 to 12 young are born in late August through September.

Natural History: Like most pit vipers, copperheads are primarily nocturnal, especially during hotter months. In early spring and fall, they may be seen abroad during the day. Young snakes eat some invertebrates and small vertebrates such as young frogs, lizards, and small snakes. Larger snakes prey on small mammals (mice and voles), and the young of ground nesting birds. Insects are also taken, especially cicadas and during years when the Periodic Cicada emerges by the millions, they will stuff themselves with these high protein, high fat insects. In Florida these are rare snakes that occur only in a small area of the panhandle. Here they can be fairly common in areas of undisturbed habitat but they are secretive and discreet. They are common and widespread across the eastern US as far north as southern New York and as far west as western Texas. They are responsible for more venomous snakebites than any other US snake.

Class - **Reptilia** (reptiles)

Order - **Squamata** (lizards and snakes)

Family - **Crotalidae** (pit vipers)

Florida Cottonmouth *Agkistrodon conanti*	**Pygmy Rattlesnake** *Sistrurus miliarius*	**Timber (Canebrake) Rattlesnake** *Crotalus horridus*

  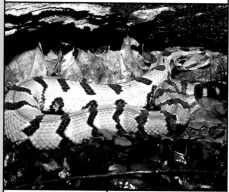

Size: Average 3 feet. Record 6 feet 2 inches.	**Size:** Record 32.5 inches. Average 18 to 20 inches.	**Size:** Averages feet. Record 6 feet, 2 inches.
Presumed range in Florida 	Presumed range in Florida 	Presumed range in Florida 
Abundance: Generally common and very common in ideal habitat.	**Abundance:** Fairly common in most of Florida. Most common in the Everglades.	**Abundance:** Uncommon and declining throughout its range in Florida.

Variation: Adults vary from uniform brown to nearly black. Freshly molted specimens often show a pattern of dark bands on an olive or grayish background. Young have a strongly banded pattern and and resemble their cousin the Copperhead. Like the Copperhead, young Cottonmouths have a bright yellow tail tip used to lure prey.

Variation: There are 3 subspecies of Pygmy Rattlesnakes in the southern US. The Dusky Pygmy Rattlesnake (subspecies- *barbouri*) is found in Florida. Some individuals may be light gray while others are nearly black. A reddish brown middorsal stripe sometimes appears as a series of spots along the midline of the back, or is absent.

Variation: Timber Rattlesnakes can be highly variable in their range across the eastern US. Yellow and brown "light morphs," along with very dark morphs, occur in some areas. In Florida, most will resemble the photo above. The morph seen in Florida is usually called the "Canebrake" Rattlesnake and it was once considered a distinct subspecies.

Habitat: A highly aquatic species, the cottonmouth inhabits mostly swamps and marshes, but they can also be found in creeks, lakes, or ponds.

Habitat: Mesic woodlands, pine flatwoods, tiny islands within swamps, or marshes and upland habitats near water are all used by the Pygmy Rattlesnake.

Habitat: As their name implies, Timber Rattlesnakes are woodland animals. In Florida, they occur mostly in mesic, lowland forests and riparian corridors.

Breeding: Produces 3 to 12 babies in late August or early September. Unlike the copperhead, female cottonmouths may reproduce annually.

Breeding: Breeds in the fall with young being born the following summer in July or August. The tiny babies can coil on a coin the size of a nickel.

Breeding: Young are born in late summer or early fall. Females will produce young only every other year. Average litter is 6 to 12.

Natural History: The name "Cottonmouth" is derived from the habit these snakes have of gaping open the mouth when threatened. The inside of the mouth is white, hence the name. Cottonmouths attain a large size and have powerful venom that is capable of killing a human. But their reputation for being aggressive is hyperbole. Frogs, fish, salamanders, and small mammals are prey. Although mainly found in aquatic situations, they are not dependent upon water and can sometimes seen in upland areas far from water.

Natural History: These tiny rattlesnakes are both secretive and cryptic and are thus easily overlooked. Food items include frogs, lizards, and mice as well as some invertebrates. Their tiny rattle is audible for a distance of only a few feet. They are quick to strike if molested and although they possess virulent venom, their small venom glands do not hold enough volume to kill a healthy adult human. Still the venom is quite powerful and their bite can have serious consequences (gangrene, loss of digits), thus the bite requires medical attention.

Natural History: This is one of the largest rattlesnake species in America and their bite is quite capable of killing a human. Fortunately they are peace-loving animals that only strike as a last resort. They feed mostly on mammals, with squirrels being a favorite food. They are known to lie in ambush beside fallen logs that are frequently traveled by ground foraging squirrels. Almost any type of small mammal can be food and many types of mice and voles are eaten. Mice are probably the main food for the young.

Class - **Reptilia** (reptiles)
Order - **Squamata** (lizards and snakes)
Family - **Crotalidae** (pit vipers)

Eastern Diamondback Rattlesnake
Crotalus adamanteus

Close-up of fangs

Size: Most are fully grown at around 5 to 6 feet. The record length of 8 feet 4 inches is from many decades ago. Today it is rare to see a 6-footer in the wild.	Presumed range in Florida

Abundance: Uncommon and in decline throughout most of its range.

Variation: Very little variation. Some are more brightly colored and patterned.

Habitat: Can be found in pine flatwoods, sandhill scrub, upland pine forest, and coastal dunes and barrier islands. The favorite habitat may be pine/palmetto uplands bordering wet prairies and savannas. They are probably most common today on uninhabited barrier islands or in protected enclaves such as state parks and nature preserves, especially if Gopher Tortoises are present.

Breeding: Live-bearer. A large female can produce litters of up to 2 dozen babies. Most litters will number 12 or 14 baby snakes. Neonates can be 10 inches long at birth and are capable of swallowing a grown mouse within a few days. As is the case with most members of the Crotalidae family, females will typically give birth only every other year. The physiological stresses of producing a litter of young can seriously deplete the fat reserves of the mother snake. For a sedentary animal that may only feed a few times per year, the energy expended during gestatation can leave the female in poor condition following birth. The next year following birth is spent replenishing the female's fat reserves before she will ovulate again.

Natural History: Along with the American Alligator, the Eastern Diamondback is one of Florida's wildlife icons. This is America's largest venomous snake. They possess a highly toxic venom and the gravity of a bite by this species cannot be overstated. A half century ago this was a very common snake thoughout the Sunshine State, and in the days before modern antivenoms it was a feared and dreaded animal to many Floridians. But it is also a magnificent example of a highly specialized creature and a symbol of wild Florida. Sadly, the future for this remarkable rattlesnake is bleak. Continued development and rampant loss of habitat throughout the state has resulted in the Eastern Diamondback being pushed into smaller and smaller enclaves and creating more highly fragmented populations. The primary food for large adults is rabbits, both cottontails and Marsh Rabbits. Remote or protected maritime forests or dune habitats bordering salt marsh with abundant Marsh Rabbit populations can be sanctuaries for this snake. Several such sanctuaries exist around the state, most as state parks. In inland areas, National Forests and Everglades National Park provide expansive habitats. In spite of the many threats presented by modern society, these snakes can still thrive in areas where prime habitat remains protected. The long-term problem is that these protected habitats will become increasingly isolated from one another, producing population "islands" that could be highly vulnerable to disease, natural disasters, and other threats.

CHAPTER 8

THE AMPHIBIANS OF FLORIDA

TABLE 6

— THE ORDERS AND FAMILIES OF FLORIDA AMPHIBIANS —

Note: The arrangement below reflects the the order in which the amphibians of Florida appear in this chapter. It is not intended to be an accurate reflection of the phylogenetic relationship of amphibians.

Class - **Amphibia** (amphibians)

Order - **Anura** (frogs and toads)

Family	**Bufonidae** (true toads)
Family	**Eleutherodactylidae** (rainfrogs)
Family	**Hylidae** (treefrogs)
Family	**Microhylidae** (narrowmouth frog)
Family	**Ranidae** (true frogs)
Family	**Scaphiopodidae** (spadefoots)

Order - **Caudata** (salamanders)

Family	**Ambysotmatidae** (mole salamanders)
Family	**Amphiumidae** (amphiumas)
Family	**Proteida** (mudpuppies)
Family	**Plethodontidae** (lungless salamanders)
Family	**Salamandridae** (newts)
Family	**Sirenidae** (sirens)

THE AMPHIBIANS OF FLORIDA

PART 1: FROGS AND TOADS

Class - **Amphibia** (amphibians)
Order - **Anura** (frogs and toads)
Family - **Bufonidae** (true toads)

Fowler's Toad *Anaxyrus fowleri*	**Oak Toad** *Anaxrus quercicus*	**Southern Toad** *Anaxyrus terrestris*

Size: Average of 2 to 3 inches. Record 3.75.	**Size:** Average 1 inch. Maximum of 1.4 inches.	**Size:** Average 3 inches. Maximum 4.75.
Presumed range in Florida 	Presumed range in Florida 	Presumed range in Florida 
Abundance: Uncommon.	**Abundance:** Fairly common.	**Abundance:** Very common.
Variation: Dark brown, tan, or grayish brown.	**Variation:** Very little variation in this species.	**Variation:** Red, gray, brown, or charcoal.
Habitat: Woodlands, overgrown fields or lawns. In Florida found mostly in bottomland regions.	**Habitat:** Xeric habitats such as Longleaf Pine/Wiregrass, scrub, and upland woods.	**Habitat:** Found in most habitats in the state. Especially common along the shores of lakes and ponds.
Breeding: Breeding is in spring in shallow ponds, ditches, creeks, flooded fields, etc. From 5,000 to 10,000 eggs are laid.	**Breeding:** Eggs are laid in shallow water habitats. Eggs number 250 or less. Eggs hatch in as little as 2 days and tapoles transform in 4 about weeks.	**Breeding:** Eggs are laid in spiraling, gelatinous strands that can contain thousands of eggs. Eggs hatch quickly in warm weather (2 to 3 days).
Natural History: Fowler's Toads breed later in the spring than Southern Toads and young toadlets do not emerge from the tadpole stage until late summer. Like many toads (and many treefrogs), the Fowler's Toad secretes a toxic substance from the skin when threatened. While this toxin can cause irritation to sensitive areas and membranes, the old wives' tale that toads cause warts is a fallacy. Most of this species' range in the eastern US is to the north of Florida, but they can be found in the western panhandle of the state. Mainly nocturnal but sometimes active during the day, especially during rains. All toads are voracious predators of insects, arachnids, and other invertebrates. They should be regarded as a welcome resident in lawns and gardens for this reason. They are also interesting and endearing animals and they are often a child's first encounter with Florida's wildlife.	**Natural History:** This toad is the smallest member of the Bufonidae family. They are active both day and night and are more diurnal in habits than most other toads. Although still fairly common there is some evidence that they are less common today than a few decades ago. These tiny toads feed on very small invertebrates and their small size prevents them from preying on larger insects such as adult grasshoppers and crickets. Their name comes from the fact that they often associate with upland Live Oak hammocks, but in fact they may be more common in pine woodlands or scrub. They range from coastal North Carolina to eastern Louisiana and they can be found throughout the state of Florida. Calling Oak Toads sound like the peeping of newly hatched chickens and when large numbers are calling in chorus, the sound can be quite loud.	**Natural History:** This common toad is familiar to most native Floridians. It is often seen in lawns and gardens throughout the state and is equally at home in the suburbs or wildness. All toads eat a wide variety of insects and other small arthropods. They are adept burrowers and possess hardened spade-like structures on the hind feet that are used for digging. Most will spend the day "backed in" to a shallow burrow in loose soil or sand and will emerge at night to forage. They are especially active in wet weather and may be abroad in daylight during rainstorms. Although toads are less vulnerable to desiccation than most amphibians, they prefer to leave their burrows after dark during hot weather and they may aestivate during periods of drought. On rainy nights, they can be seen in large numbers on rural roads throughout the state.

Class - **Amphibia** (amphibians)

Order - **Anura** (frogs and toads)

Family - **Bufonidae** (true toads)	Family - **Eleutherodactylidae** (rainfrogs)	Family - **Hylidae** (treefrogs)
Cane Toad *Rhinella marina*	**Greenhouse Frog** *Eleutherodactylus planirostris*	**Cricket Frogs** *Acris crepitans and Acris gryllus*

Large South American specimen

Eastern Cricket Frog

Size: Record size 9.25 inches.	Presumed range in Florida	**Size:** Maximum of 1.5 inches.	Presumed range in Florida	**Size:** Maximum 1.4 inches.	Presumed range in Florida

Size: Record size 9.25 inches.

Abundance: Common in Dade and Broward Counties.

Variation: Females are larger.

Presumed range in Florida

Size: Maximum of 1.5 inches.

Abundance: Common and expanding northward.

Variation: Variable. See below.

Presumed range in Florida

Size: Maximum 1.4 inches.

Abundance: Both species are very common within range.

Variation: 2 species in FL.

Presumed range in Florida

Habitat: In Florida the Cane Toad associates with both urban areas and agricultural fields in the southern portion of the peninsula.

Breeding: Breeds in canals and ditches where females may lay as many as 20,000 eggs. The tadpoles are jet black above and whitish below.

Natural History: Introduced. This huge toad also goes by the name "Marine Toad." Although some individuals from the neotropics have exceeded 9 inches in length, in Florida most are under 6 inches at maturity. Apparently these toads were intentionally introduced into south Florida cane fields in the 1950s in the belief that they would control insect pests. In addition to insects they will eat virtually anything they can swallow, and they probably pose a threat to many native small vertebrates in the state. They are also a threat to larger animals due to the toxic secretions from parotoid glands. All toads probably have the ability to secrete "bufotoxins" from these glands, but the large size of the Cane Toad means it can produce prodigious amounts of toxin, enough to kill a raccoon, an opossum, or a dog. They are fairly common today in Dade and Broward Counties.

Habitat: Occupies a wide variety of terrestrial habitat and has expanded its range into northernmost Florida and parts of the panhandle.

Breeding: Unlike most amphibians, these frogs lay their eggs in moist terrestrial environments rather than in water, and the tadpole stage occurs inside the egg.

Natural History: Introduced. Native to the Caribbean, this little frog would seem to be unsuited for life in the subtropical and temperate regions of Florida, but it has become firmly established in most of the state. Its range extends well outside of tropical Florida today and there are scattered records from as far north as southern Georgia. The color of this tiny frog varies from brown or bronze to pinkish. Some individuals have light stripes on each side of the back. This species is capable of breeding throughout most of the year in southern Florida, and from spring through fall in the rest of the state. Another member of this genus, the **Coqui Frog** (*E. coqui*) from Puerto Rico, may have established itself in the Miami area. Coqui Frogs are familiar to tourists who visit Puerto Rico as the tiny, seemingly invisible source of incessant calling throughout the night.

Habitat: Lives along the edges of streams, lakes and ponds. Sometimes wanders away from water, especially in humid weather or rainy weather.

Breeding: Females will deposit up to 200 eggs in small clumps. Eggs will hatch in a few days into tiny tadpoles barely over an inch in length.

Natural History: The 2 cricket frog species found in Florida are the **Eastern Cricket Frog** (*Acris crepitans*) and the **Florida Cricket Frog** (*Acris gryllus*). In appearance and habits they are very similar. The Florida Cricket Frog inhabits the entire state while the Eastern Cricket Frog is restricted to the western panhandle. Where their ranges overlap in the panhandle, they can be told apart by examining the length of the hind leg. In the Florida Cricket Frog, the hind leg is longer than the head/body length. In the Eastern Cricket Frog, the hind leg is equal to head/body/length. These frogs are most common along the shores of ponds and lakes and if threatened they will often jump into the water and then immediately swim back to shore. This may be an "out of the frying pan into the fire" behavior intended to keep them from the jaws of hungry fish.

Class - **Amphibia** (amphibians)
Order - **Anura** (frogs and toads)
Family - **Hylidae** (treefrogs)

Pine Barrens Treefrog	Bird-voiced Treefrog	Cope's Gray Treefrog
Hyla andersonii	*Hyla Hyla avivoca*	*Hyla chrysoscelis*

Size: Maximum of 2 inches.

Abundance: Rare in Florida.

Variation: No significant variation.

Presumed range in Florida

Size: Maximum of 2 inches.

Abundance: Common.

Habitat: Freshwater wetlands or their vicinity.

Presumed range in Florida

Size: Maximum of 2.5 inches.

Abundance: Common.

Variation: See photo above for 3 color morphs.

Presumed range in Florida

Habitat: In Florida this species inhabits riparian wetlands and seepage areas on wooded hillsides.

Variation: Changes color from solid gray with a lichen pattern to gray with a bright green back.

Habitat: Habitat is chiefly woodlands. These treefrogs are more adapted to dry uplands than most Hylidae species.

Breeding: Up to 250 eggs are laid in the shallows of river swamps. Tadpoles are dark olive with pale greenish bellies.

Breeding: Breeds in spring or summer in shallow, vegetated waters of swamps and marshes.

Breeding: Breeds from late spring through summer in small ponds or ditches. Up to 2,000 eggs are laid.

Natural History: The range of the Pine Barrens Treefrog consists of 3 widely separated populations. The northernmost occurs in the Pine Barrens region of New Jersey. There is another population in the sandhill country of the Carolinas, and finally a small area of Florida's western panhandle. The presence of this species in Florida is a bit of a puzzle and it has been suggested that they may have been transplanted here by some unknown herepetology enthusiast many years ago. Because its range in Florida is so small, and many suitable habitats are in unprotected areas, this species is regarded as an imperiled species by the Florida Fish and Wildlife Conservation Commission. This is one of the most beautiful of Florida's frog species. The bright green dorsum is highlighted by a broad lateral stripe that runs from the snout to the groin. The stripe is deep purple in color and bordered top and bottom by white or yellowish white. The groin and belly are spotted with bright yellow.

Natural History: These handsome little treefrogs are easily confused with the Cope's Gray Treefrog. Bird-voiced Treefrogs have a greenish wash on the inner thighs as opposed to the orange or yellow inner thigh seen on the Cope's Gray Treefrog. These are mainly southern animals that reach the northernmost limits of their range in the Upper Coastal Plain region, occurring as far north as southern Illinois. Their range in Florida is restricted to the panhandle region, but they can be quite common there. Their name comes from the sound of the male's breeding call, which resembles the whistling song of a bird. This species survival is dependent upon freshwater wetlands. Loss of wetland habitat in America has been significant since pioneer days and many animals that depend on wetland habitats have seen their ranges diminish. This species needs swamps and marshes to reproduce. Eggs hatch in 3 to 5 days. Metamorphosis of tadpoles occurs in about 4 weeks.

Natural History: These highly arboreal treefrogs are rarely seen on the ground and they often climb high into treetops to forage for insects. They are mainly nocturnal but they may be active by day on cloudy or rainy days or in cooler weather. They shelter by day in small hollows in tree trunks or limbs and have been known to take up residence in small bird nest boxes such as a wren box or bluebird box. They will also live in the rain gutters of house roofs. They can sometimes be seen sitting in the opening of their hiding place with the head and front feet exposed. They possess remarkable camouflage abilities and the gray, lichen-like pattern of their skin will perfectly match the bark of the tree they occupy. They can produce a natural antifreeze in the blood which allows them to hibernate in tree hollows above the ground, or in leaf litter on the forest floor. These frogs range far into the northern states and even into parts of southern Canada.

Class - **Amphibia** (amphibians)

Order - **Anura** (frogs and toads)

Family - **Hylidae** (treefrogs)

Green Treefrog *Hyla cinerea*	Pine Woods Treefrog *Hyla femoralis*	Barking Treefrog *Hyla gratiosa*

Green Treefrog		Pine Woods Treefrog		Barking Treefrog	
Size: Record size 2.5 inches.	Presumed range in Florida 	**Size:** Record size 1.75 inches.	Presumed range in Florida 	**Size:** Record 2.75 inches.	Presumed range in Florida 
Abundance: Very common.		**Abundance:** Common.		**Abundance:** Fairly common.	
Variation: Varies in the amount of yellow spots on the back. May have several or none at all.		**Variation:** Changes color and varies from reddish brown to brown, grayish, or greenish brown.		**Variation:** Varies from green to brown. Sometimes with dark spots or small yellow flecks.	

Habitat: Green Treefrogs are lowland animals that are found in swamps and marshes mostly.

Habitat: Pine woodlands mainly. Also swamps. Can be common around artificial lighting in forests at night.

Habitat: Woodlands in the vicinity of wetlands suitable for breeding seems to be the habitat requirement for this frog.

Breeding: Breeds in early to midsummer. Lays up to 1,500 eggs in shallow waters of swamps or marshes. Multiple clutches may be produced in a summer.

Breeding: Breeds in shallow waters. Temporary pools, small ponds, and roadside ditches. May lay up to 500 eggs in long gelatinous strands.

Breeding: Shallow, fishless ponds are the preferred breeding sites for this species. Breeds from late spring through the summer.

Natural History: Similar to the Barking Treefrog (this page) but has smooth skin and a much slimmer appearance overall. One of this frog's favorite daytime perches are the stems of cattails and sedges where its deep green color renders it almost invisible. Its primary prey consists of caterpillars, spiders, grasshoppers, and other insects. Green Treefrogs are primarily nocturnal in habits but they are sometimes seen during the day, especially during rainy weather. As with most other treefrogs of the genus *Hyla*, this is another mainly southern species. Its range extends northward up the Mississippi Valley through western Kentucky and into southern Illinois where the Gulf Coastal Plain Province reaches its northernmost extension. It is one of Florida's most common treefrog species and it is found statewide.

Natural History: This smallish treefrog can be quite common near human habitations at night where it may be attracted to streetlights and store front lighting which attracts nocturnal insects. Around convenience stores in rural areas they may live under outside ice bins where condensation creates adequate moisture and store lighting attracts insect foods. In more natural habitats in woodlands it is quite arboreal in habits. The Latin species name *femoralis* is a reference to the unique pattern on the inner thigh which helps identify this species from other similar treefrogs, especially the brown morph of the Squirrel Treefrog, which can appear quite similar. This species is endemic to the lower Atlantic and lower Eastern Gulf Coastal Plains. It can be found from Virginia to Louisiana and throughout the state of Florida.

Natural History: This is the largest native treefrog in America. They are both arboreal and terrestrial in habits. Unspotted specimens such as the one shown above closely resemble Green Treefrogs (*H. cinerea*), but the Barking Treefrog has a much stockier appearance and a granular skin rather than smooth. Their name comes from the fact that large breeding congregations when calling produce a sound which from a distance resembles the sound of dogs barking. In cold weather, specimens in northern Florida will retreat beneath leaf litter, large swaths of bark, or into loose soil. At these times, they usually take on a dark brown coloration. The same frog may be bright green with yellow or brownish spots when above ground during warm summer weather.

Class - **Amphibia** (amphibians)
Order - **Anura** (frogs and toads)
Family - **Hylidae** (treefrogs)

Squirrel Treefrog	Cuban Treefrog	Spring Peeper
Hyla squirrella	*Osteopilus septentrionalis*	*Pseudacris crucifer*

Size: Record size 1.75 inches.	**Size:** Record size 6.5 inches.	**Size:** Record size 1.5 inches.
Abundance: Very common.	**Abundance:** Common.	**Abundance:** Very common.
Variation: Can change from brown to green.	**Variation:** Light or dark gray to brownish.	**Variation:** Varies from gray to brown or reddish.

Presumed range in Florida

Presumed range in Florida

Presumed range in Florida

Habitat: Woodlands. Common around home and buildings having dense vegetation. Likes being near water.

Habitat: Mesic woodlands in rural areas and tree-lined suburbs in urban regions. Uses Banana Trees and Palms.

Habitat: Mesic woodlands and successional areas near water. Marshes, swamps, and bogs.

Breeding: Female will lay up to 800 eggs in ponds, canals, or emphemeral waters such as ditches.

Breeding: Lays up to 200 eggs in clumps of 25 to 50. Eggs are deposited in rain water pools, ditches, etc.

Breeding: In Florida breeds in winter. Several hundred eggs are laid in shallow, temporary pools.

Natural History: This little frog can rapidly change its color back and forth from brown to green (and every shade in between) to match a tree trunk or green foliage. These frogs will typically call from their perch in trees during rains and another common name for this species in Florida is "Rain Frog." The name Squirrel Treefrog is derived some the sound of their call, which sounds a little like a Gray Squirrel's call. Although they are quite arboreal they can also be found low to the ground or on the ground and they will take refuge under bark, logs, or withing rotted stumps. In older neighborhoods with large trees, Squirrel Treefrogs are common around the gutters and eaves of houses. Here they are often seen on windows at night as they hunt small insects attracted to lights. They are endemic to the Lower Coastal Plain from Virginia to Texas and they are found throughout the state of Florida.

Natural History: Introduced. Native to the Caribbean. Since being introduced into the Miami area as far back as 1931, this species has gradually extended its range to include most of the Florida peninsula. It is America's largest treefrog species reaching a length of over 6 inches. In addition to insects the Cuban Treefrog will prey on other, smaller treefrogs and there is a concern that it may pose a threat to some native Hylidae species. Many treefrogs have noxious skin secretions that make them less palatable to predators and a large treefrog like this species has enough skin secretions to make it inedible to many carnivores. Thus it probably faces less pressure from predators than the native treefrogs. Weather is probably its worst enemy in Florida and in more northerly regions it can be vulnerable to severe cold snaps. However, populations seem to recover enough to allow it to survive at least as far north as Columbia and Duval Counties.

Natural History: This frog ranges throughout the Eastern Temperate Forest Ecoregion from the Gulf Coast to Canada's Husdson Bay. Its name comes from the fact that it is an early spring breeder in most of it range. The breeding call is a rapidly repeated "peep, peep, peep." Despite being members of the treefrog family, they live mostly on the ground. The species name "*crucifer*" is Latin for "cross bearer" and refers to the x-shaped mark that is always present on this frog's back. These little frogs, along with their cousins the Chorus Frogs, are a true harbinger of spring throughout much of the eastern United States. Its habit of breeding during cool weather means that in Florida it breeds in midwinter rather than very early spring. They may breed in the same flooded field pools with Chorus Frogs or even in the same pool. Feeds on tiny insects and arthropods. A ground dweller, not seen in trees like other treefrogs on this page.

Class - **Amphibia** (amphibians)

Order - **Anura** (frogs and toads)

Family - **Hylidae** (treefrogs)

Family - **Microhylidae** (narrow-mouth frogs)

Little Grass Frog *Pseudacris ocularis*	**Chorus Frogs** - genus *Pseudacris* *P. feriarum, P. nigrita,* and *P. ornata*	**Eastern Narrow-mouthed Toad** *Gastrophryne carolinensis*

Size: Maximum size .875 inches.	Presumed range in Florida
Abundance: Common.	
Variation: Brownish, reddish, or tan.	

Habitat: Moist grassy areas. Grassy banks of ponds, lakes, and ditches.

Breeding: Breeds from late winter into spring. Lays up to 200 eggs in pools, flooded ditches, or permanent water.

Natural History: This is the smallest frog in America and in fact may be the smallest vertebrate on the continent. They are easily overlooked. The best way to spot this little frog is to walk around the edges of ponds or lakes when the water has receded somewhat, leaving a strip of open mud between the grass and the water. Walk in the grass a foot or so from the open strip of mud and look for these tiny frogs as they leap away at your approach. Despite their tiny size, they are capable of leaps of up to a foot. Like most other hylid frogs, the color of this little frog will darken when the frog is cold and is lighter when it is warm. On a cool winter day, their color is very dark brown. Because of its tiny size, some experts in the past have placed this species in the genus *Limnaoedus*. The Little Grass frog is strictly a terrestrial animal and does not climb trees. Another tiny frog species that is today found throughout the peninsula is the introduced **Cuban Flat-headed Frog** (*Eleutherodactylus planirostris*).

Size: Maximum size 1.5 inches.	Presumed range in Florida
Abundance: Very common.	
Variation: 3 species of Chorus Frogs in Florida.	

Habitat: Low wet fields, bottomland woods, swamps, marshes, ponds, and bogs.

Breeding: Breeding activity is triggered by periods of heavy rainfall in late winter or very early spring.

Natural History: The 3 species of chorus frogs found in Florida are the **Upland Chorus Frog** (*P. feriarum*), the **Southern Chours Frog** (*P. nigrita*), and the **Ornate Chorus Frog** (*P. ornata*). At the first signs of spring or in warm rainy weather in winter these frogs appear and gather in large numbers to breed. Breeding may be interrupted several times in north Florida by cold fronts. The name comes from their "chorus" of breeding calls that carries over quite a long distance. Though amazingly common during the brief breeding season, most of the rest of the year they seem to disappear. One species, the Ornate Chorus Frog, is known to burrow beneath the surface and emerge only when foraging in rainy weather or when breeding. Some experts have suggested that these once common frogs may be declining in parts of Florida. The call of these frogs is usually described as mimicking the sound of a fingernail drawn across the teeth of a comb.

Size: Average about an 1 inch.	Presumed range in Florida
Abundance: Common.	
Variation: Dark gray to light gray or rusty brown.	

Habitat: Can be found both in dry upland and in more mesic bottomlands.

Breeding: From 500 to 800 eggs are laid in late spring or summer. Eggs hatch in 2 days.

Natural History: Narrowmouth Toads are confirmed burrowers that are occasionally found hiding beneath flat rocks, boards, etc. Their call is a nasal "baaaa" and sounds like the cry of a young lamb. Ants and termites are recorded as prey and it is likely that other diminutive insects and other arthropods are eaten. The tiny mouth on this frog precludes eating anything larger than the average termite. Despite their name, they are not true toads but are the sole representatives in the eastern United States of a specialized family of anurans known as Microhylidae. Microhylidae frogs are much more common in more tropical regions. Their are over 300 species in the family and they can be found on every major continent except Europe and Antarctica. Development of both the eggs and the tadpoles is very rapid in this frog. Tadpoles transform in 2 to 4 weeks.

Class - **Amphibia** (amphibians)

Order - **Anura** (frogs and toads)

Family -**Ranidae** (true frogs)

Gopher Frog *Lithobates capito*	Bullfrog *Lithobates catesbieanus*	Green (Bronze) Frog *Lithobates clamitans*

Size: Maximum size 4.375 inches.

Presumed range in Florida

Abundance: Uncommon.

Variation: Varies from light to dark gray. Rarely purpleish.

Size: Maximum size 8.5 inches.

Presumed range in Florida

Abundance: Common.

Variation: Females grow larger. Males have larger tympanum.

Size: Maximum size 4.25 inches.

Presumed range in Florida

Abundance: Fairly common.

Variation: Most resemble the specimen shown above.

Habitat: Most common in xeric and sub-xeric uplands including sandhills and upland Long Leaf Pine/Wiregrass habitats.

Habitat: Ponds, lakes, and streams as well as swamps and marshes. May travel overland between ponds or wetland areas during rainy weather.

Habitat: Found in virtually every aquatic habitat within their range, from small ponds and large lakes to streams and wetlands.

Breeding: Breeds in emphemeral pools and shallow ponds that are refilled during heavy rains of late winter and early spring. Masses of several thousand eggs are encased gelatinous material and attached to blades of grass.

Breeding: Breeding and egg laying occurs from late spring through midsummer. Several thousand eggs can be laid and 2 clutches per year is not uncommon. Tadpole metamorphosis does not occur until the following summer.

Breeding: Breeding can begin as early as May and continue until August. Up to 4,000 eggs may be deposited. Male clasp onto female's back and release sperm onto eggs as they are extruded from the female.

Natural History: Usually found in association with the Gopher Tortoise and regularly uses tortoise burrows as a daytime retreat and winter refuge (thus the name "Gopher" Frog). As the Gopher Tortoise has declined in Florida, so to have many species that depend on it for a home and shelter, including the Gopher Frog, which is today regarded as an imperiled species by the FWC. A variety of insects are prey but this frog is also cannibalistic and will readily eat other, smaller frog species. The range of this species in Florida continues to shrink as suitable habitat continues to disappear. Upland areas in central Florida are popular with housing developers and are also prized by the citrus fruit industry. Thus natural uplands are under heavy pressure from Florida's human population.

Natural History: These are the largest frogs in Florida (and in fact in the US). Their hind legs are considered to be a delicacy by many. They are regarded as a game animal and are hunted for food during annual "frog seasons." In some places, they are raised commercially for food and for research or teaching laboratories. They may venture far from water and will travel from pond to pond during rainy weather. Food is almost any animal small enough to be swallowed, including other frogs. Insects are consumed by the young. Adults eat crayfish, fishes, small mammals like mice, and even birds. There is even a record of a large Bullfrog eating a baby rattlesnake! In color they can vary from very dark green to lighter green or brown. Often with a dark mottled pattern.

Natural History: A drive through a wetland on a rainy night in late summer when the tadpoles of *Lithobates clamitans* are emerging onto land will reveal astounding numbers of small frogs crossing the roadway as they disperse into new territories. Adult frogs feed on insects primarily but other arthropods including small crayfish are frequently eaten. Minnows and other small aquatic vertebrates are also potential prey. These frogs are easily confused with the much larger Bullfrog, but are distinguished by the presence of a fold of skin (known as a dorsolateral fold) that runs along each side of the back. Like other aquatic frogs, they sometimes wander away from water on rainy nights to forage for insects in grassy areas. In Florida, this frog goes by the name "Bronze Frog."

Class - **Amphibia** (amphibians)
Order - **Anura** (frogs and toads)
Family - **Ranidae** (true frogs)

Pig Frog
Lithobates grylio

Size: Maximum size 6.5 inches.

Presumed range in Florida

Abundance: Common.

Variation: Greenish or gray to olive brown.

Habitat: Most freshwater habitats are inhabited. Wet prairies and marshes are a favorite habitat.

Breeding: Large masses of up to 8,000 eggs are laid in summer amid aquatic vegetation. Tadpole stage lasts through the winter.

Natural History: Very similar to the Bullfrog and like that species the Pig Frog is hunted for its legs which are regarded as quite tasty. The name comes from its call which sounds a bit like the grunting of a pig. Found throughout the state, this is probably the most common large "true frog" in Florida. This species appears to be in decline in Florida. But it is also known to exhibit a tendency toward cyclical populations. As with many amphibians, severe droughts can drastically reduce the population, while several years of adequate moisture can cause a population boom. These are reportedly highly aquatic frogs that rarely leave the water except during periods of heavy rainfall. Both the Bullfrog and the River Frog overlap the range of the Pig Frog in northern Florida and distinguishing between the 3 species can be challenging. The Pig Frog has a more pointed snout than the Bullfrog.

River Frog
Lithobates heckscheri

Size: Maximum size 6 inches.

Presumed range in Florida

Abundance: Common.

Variation: Gray, greenish gray, or brownish green.

Habitat: Most freshwater habitats are inhabited. River swamps, marshes, lakes, and ponds are all inhabited.

Breeding: Eggs are laid as a film that floats on top of the water and adheres to any object it contacts. Several thousand eggs is typical.

Natural History: Also called the River Swamp Frog in reference to one of its favorite habitats being river swamps. The range of this frog encompasses the lower portions of the eastern Gulf Coastal Plain from Mississippi eastward through northern Florida and southern Georgia, then northward along the Atlantic Coastal Plain to southern North Carolina. In Florida it occurs in the western panhandle from about the Ochlockonee River westward. It is also found in northeastern Florida but is apparently absent from the Big Bend region. In appearance, it closely resembles the Bullfrog. If the frog is in hand, it can be determined to be a River Frog by examining ventral pattern. On the River Frog the belly, gular region, and ventral surface of the legs is heavily marked with dark mottling and their is a light u-shaped marking on the groin area.

Florida Bog Frog
Lithobates okaloosae

Size: Maximum size 2.25 inches.

Presumed range in Florida

Abundance: Rare.

Variation: Brown or brownish green.

Habitat: Spaghnum bogs, seeps, and clear, acidic streams in Florida's western panhandle.

Breeding: Very little information is available on breeding in this species. Apparently breeds from spring through summer and lays several hundred eggs.

Natural History: The Florida Bog Frog was only recently discovered in 1985 by Florida herpetologist Paul Moler. Its name comes from its preference for spaghnum bogs as a habitat. Due to its restricted range and rarity it is regarded as at Threatened Species by FWC. It occurs only in portions of 3 counties in the western panhandle (Walton, Santa Rosa, and Okaloosa). In appearance it closely resembles the Bronze Frog from which it can be distinguished (if in the hand) by the fact that the webbing on the hind toes is much reduced in the Florida Bog Frog. This is the smallest member of the Ranidae family of frogs in Florida. The fact that it was only recently discovered is probably due to its resemblance to the common Bronze Frog, resulting in it being overlooked as a distinct species by most herpetologists.

Class - **Amphibia** (amphibians)
Order - **Anura** (frogs and toads)

Family - **Ranidae** (true frogs)		Family - **Scaphiopodidae** (spadefoots)

Southern Leopard Frog
Lithobates sphenocephalus

Carpenter Frog
Lithobates virgatipes

Eastern Spadefoot
Scaphiopus holbrookii

Size: Maximum size 5 inches.

Presumed range in Florida

Abundance: Very common.

Variation: Green to light tan (see photos above).

Size: Max about 2.75 inches.

Presumed range in Florida

Abundance: Very rare in FL.

Variation: Reddish brown, brown, or olive.

Size: Max about 3 inches.

Presumed range in Florida

Abundance: Fairly common.

Variation: Olive brown to dark brown.

Habitat: Found in virtually all aquatic habitats within its range except salt water. Often wanders into grassy fields far from water.

Habitat: Tannin-stained acidic swamps are the main habitat for this frog in Florida. In Florida found only in the Okeefenokee Swamp and Osceola National Forest.

Habitat: The main habitat requirement is loose, sandy soil that facilitates easy burrowing. Lives in both upland and lowland woods and meadows.

Breeding: Breeds mostly in April and May Breeding localities are ponds, ditches, marshes, and swamps. Lays up to 5,000 eggs in several clumps. Young frogs emerge in midsummer.

Breeding: Eggs are laid in a mass that is often attached to emergent vegetation. As many as 700 eggs can constitute a clutch. The tadpole stage last about a year.

Breeding: Breeds explosively during periods of heavy rainfall from late spring throughout the summer. Up to 5,000 eggs hatch within a few days. Breeding initiated by very heavy rains.

Natural History: Leopard frogs are frequently found some distance from permanent water sources in meadows and overgrown fields. They are one of the most commonly seen frogs in Florida and can even be seen in rural lawns on occasion, especially in late summer. A wide variety of insects, spiders, and other invertebrates are eaten. Like most frogs, during cold weather they will bury themselves in the mud at the bottom of a pond, creek, or other permanent water. In color they are variable from light tan to bright green, but always with a highly visible pattern of dark brown spots from which they derive their name. Until recently there were 2 nearly identical subspecies recognized in Florida. But they were so similar that only experts could tell them apart! Today all Florida Leopard Frogs are properly regarded as being the same frog.

Natural History: Carpenter Frogs are endemic to the Atlantic Coastal Plain and are found as far north as New Jersey. The portion of Georgia's Okeefenokee Swamp that extends into northern Florida represents the southernmost extension of this frog's range. This region of Florida is sparsley populated with limited accessiblity, thus the Carpenter Frog 'may be the least commonly observed frog species in Florida. Their name is derived from the sound of breeding chorus. Their call is best described as "pa-tunk, pa-tunk, pa-tunk," which at a distance sounds very much like the sound produced by a team of carpenters pounding nails as they build a house. They call from spring throughout the summer. They are most likely to be confused with the Bronze Frog, but are differentiated from that species by the lack of a ridge of skin on the upper side known as a "dorsolateral fold."

Natural History: The name "Spadefoot" come from a sickle-shaped horny structure on the hind feet that is used for digging into the ground. They spend much of their lives in burrows only a few inches deep and emerge only on rainy nights. During dry weather, they may spend weeks in the burrow without feeding. They secrete a toxic substance which is highly irritant to mucus membranes, thus making these anurans unpalatable to many potential predators. Touching the face or other sensitive skin after handling a Spadefoot will result in an uncomfortable burning sensation. Although widespread and fairly common across the southeastern US, the Eastern Spadefoot is sporadically distributed and may be absent from many areas shown on the range map above. These frogs are almost never seen except during brief periods of breeding activity.

THE AMPHIBIANS OF FLORIDA

PART 2: SALAMANDERS

Class - **Amphibia** (amphibians)
Order - **Caudata** (salamanders)
Family - **Ambystomatidae** (mole salamanders)

Flatwoods Salamanders *Ambystoma bishopi and Ambystoma cingulatum*	**Mole Salamander** *Ambystoma talpoidium*	**Marbled Salamander** *Ambystoma opacum*

Size: Maximum length 5 inches.

Presumed range in Florida

Abundance: Rare.

Variation: 2 similar species. See below.

Size: Maximum length 5 inches.

Presumed range in Florida

Abundance: Common.

Variation: Variable. See Natural History below.

Size: Record size 5.3125 inches.

Presumed range in Florida

Abundance: Fairly common.

Variation: Sexually dimorphic. See below.

Habitat: Low-lying Pine Flatwoods subject to seasonally flooding are the main habitat for these salamanders.

Habitat: Swamps, marshes, and bottomland woods prone to seasonal flooding. Less commonly in upland woods.

Habitat: Most fond of bottomlands (especially during breeding) but can also be common in upland woods.

Breeding: Breeds in shallow woodland ponds and Cypress Domes. Breeds in the fall and eggs are laid in low areas that will be inundated by coming rains. Makes long overland treks to ponds.

Breeding: Breeding occurs in late fall or early winter and overland treks to breeding areas are made. Eggs are laid in the waters of swamps and marshes. Larva develop in a few months.

Breeding: Breeds in the fall. Eggs are laid on land under rocks, logs, etc. in low-lying areas subject to flooding. Hatching is delayed until eggs are flooded by fall rains.

Natural History: The **Reticulated Flatwoods Salamander** (*A. bishopi*) occurs in the western panhandle while the **Frosted Flatwoods Salamander** (*A. cingulatum*) ranges from the Apalachicola River eastward. These 2 similar species were once regarded as 2 subspecies of the same salamander. They are in decline and the overall range of the Frosted Salamander has apparently receded from its historical range in the central Florida counties of Marion and Alachua. That species is now regarded as a threatened species by the USFWS. Meanwhile, the Reticulated Flatwoods Salamander is a federally endangered species imperiled by timber harvesting and clearing of pine flatwoods. On the map above, the dark gray area is the range of the Frosted Flatwoods Salamander while light gray shows the range of the Reticulated Flatwoods Salamander.

Natural History: This decidedly fossorial salamander is the namesake of the "mole salamander" family. This species is rarely seen above ground except during the breeding season when they will emerge on rainy nights and travel to areas of breeding congregations. They can sometimes be turned up beneath logs or other objects in low, perennially moist areas. These salamanders have a stout-bodied appearance and a large head which distinguishes them from the similarly colored salamanders that share parts of their range. When captured, they will sometimes assume a defensive posture that consists of raising the body off the ground while lowering the head. Some individuals are uniformly dark gray. Others have a varying amount of light gray flecking on the sides. Many *Ambystoma* salamanders can be found in mesic conditions in upland woods, but the Mole Salamander prefers lowlands.

Natural History: This is one of the few salamanders to exhibit sexual dimorphism. The light markings are wider and whiter on the male and narrower and more silver or grayish on the female. Like other members of the "mole salamander" family, Marbled Salamanders are fossorial in habits. In fact, this species may be even more secretive than many of its kin. Thus, though they are fairly common they are not readily observed. They can reportedly produce a noxious secretion from the tail which may help to ward off some predators. Adults probably feed on mostly any small animal they can swallow. Larva have been known to eat the eggs of small frogs. This is a wide-ranging species that can be found as far north as the Great Lakes in the Midwest and as far as Massachusetts along the East Coast. Their range barely extends into northern Florida.

Class - **Amphibia** (amphibians)

Order - **Caudata** (salamanders)

Family - **Ambystomatidae** (mole salamanders)	Family - **Amphiumidae** (amphiumas)	Family - **Proteidae** (mudpuppies)

Eastern Tiger Salamander
Ambystoma tigrinum

Two-toed and One-toed Amphiumas
Amphiuma means and Amphiuma pholeter

Gulf Coast Waterdog
Necturus beyeri

Two-toed Amphiuma

Size: Record size 13 inches.	 Presumed range in Florida	

Abundance: Very rare in FL.

Variation: Variable amount of yellow markings.

Size: See Natural History.

Presumed range in Florida

Abundance: Common.

Variation: 2 species. See Natural History.

Size: Maximum 8.75 inches.

 Presumed range in Florida

Abundance: Fairly common.

Variation: Very little variation in Florida.

Habitat: Woodlands and fields, in both upland and lowland areas. This species is more common farther north of Florida.

Habitat: Swamps, oxbows, flooded roadside ditches, and ponds in low, swampy regions.

Habitat: Blackwater streams and associated wetlands. May inhabit very small streams only a few feet wide.

Breeding: Breeds in small, fishless bodies of water like small ponds, vernal pools, and "borrow pits." Breeding occurs in midwinter.

Breeding: Two-toed lays 200 eggs in depression in the mud. Female remains with the eggs until they hatch. Newly hatched young have external gills.

Breeding: Very little is known about the reproduction of this species since it was recently differentiated as a full species from the Alabama Waterdog.

Natural History: The large size of the Tiger Salamander allows it to feed on much larger prey than most salamander species. Although invertebrates such as earthworms and insect larva are the major foods, small vertebrates may also be eaten and captive specimens will eat baby mice. The apparent decline of this salamander in Florida may be traced to the loss of breeding ponds. Many amphibians require small bodies of water that do not hold significant numbers of aquatic predators such as predaceous fish that will eat amphibian larva. Amphibians are also vulnerable to toxins released into the environment by farming operations where both insecticides and herbicides are widely used. Despite their large size, Tiger Salamanders are rarely seen except during the late winter breeding season when they make their nocturnal overland treks to breeding ponds. At this time they sometimes stumble into basement stairwells, old cisterns, etc. and become trapped.

Natural History: There are a total of 3 species of Amphiuma in the US and 2 can be found in Florida. Identification usually means having the salamander in hand and counting toes. The One-toed is small and reaches a maximum of only 13 inches. The Two-toed can reach a record length of 45.75 inches. These eel-like salamanders are often mistaken for an eel. In fact, they often go by the name "Congo Eel" in parts of the Deep South (especially in Louisiana). Amphiumas are totally aquatic in habits but have lungs for breathing air and they can survive out of water as long as their is enough moisture to prevent desiccation. During droughts they can aestivate in chambers hollowed out in the mud or within crayfish burrows. They forage mostly at night and by day remain hidden in thick mats of aquatic vegetation. They are highly predaceous and will eat almost anything. Insects, fish, frogs, worms, and fish eggs. Specimens in captivity have been fed mice.

Natural History: The Proteidae family of salamanders are a totally aquatic group that breathe through well-developed external gills. The northernmost representative of the group is the widespread Mudpuppy of the northern US. These salamanders are an example of a condition known to biologists as "neotony" (the retaining of juvenile characteristics into adulthood). Many salamanders have larva stages in which the developing salamanders live in water and breathe through gills before transfoming into air-breathing adults. This is exactly the same type of life cycle exhibited by frogs and toads with their well-known "tadpole" stage. In the Proteidae salamanders the animal never metamorphizes into a terrestrial air-breather but instead retains the gills and continues a totally aquatic existence. The Gulf Coast Waterdog is the only member of the Proteidae family that inhabits Florida. They occur generally west of the Ochlockonee River.

Class - **Amphibia** (amphibians)

Order - **Caudata** (salamanders)

Family - **Plethodontidae** (lungless salamanders)

Spotted Dusky Salamander	Southern Two-lined Salamander	Three-lined Salamander
Desmognathus conanti	*Eutycea cirrigera*	*Eurycea guttolineata*

Size: Maximum about 6 inches.

Abundance: Fairly common.

Variation: See Natural History below.

Range of the Southern Dusky

Habitat: Seeps, springs, and spring-fed creeks in wooded areas are the primary habitat for this group of salamanders.

Range of the Spotted (light) and Apalachicola Dusky (dark)

Breeding: The eggs (average 15 to 30) are laid in clusters of individual eggs that are not contained in a gelatinous mass like the mole salamanders and are placed in very wet environments, often bathed by spring waters.

Natural History: There are 3 very similar species of dusky salamanders found in Florida. Even experts have difficulty distinguishing among them in the field and most laypersons must be content with identifying them at the genus level. Pictured above is the Spotted Dusky Salamander. The other 2 species seen in Florida are the **Southern Dusky Salamander** (*D. auriculatus*) and the **Apalachicola Dusky Salamander** (*D. apalachicolae*). The Southern Dusky is the most widespread of the 3 in Florida but has apparently declined in recent decades. Both the Spotted and Apalachicola Duskys are fairly common.

Size: Maximum about 4 inches.

Abundance: Common.

Variation: May be tan, yellow, or orange.

Presumed Range in Florida

Habitat: Streams, wetlands, and seeps. Mostly a lowland animal of riparian woodlands and river swamps but also found in mesic upland environments.

Breeding: To lay her eggs, the female retreats beneath a log or rock in water and attaches her eggs to the underside of the structure and then remains with them.

Natural History: Small and secretive and easily overlooked, the Southern Two-lined Salamander is much more common than most people realize. By day, they hide beneath logs, bark, leaves, or other detritus along the stream bank or sometimes within the stream. They emerge at night to forage for tiny invertebrates. The members of this genus (*Eurycea*) are called the "Brook Salamanders" by biologists. An appropriate name since they love small, flowing waterways. There is a similar but much smaller and much rarer member of the genus that also occurs in Florida known as the **Chamberlain's Dwarf Salamander** (*E. chamberlaini*). It occurs in Florida as a tiny, disjunct population and is an extremely rare species in the state. It can can be found in Florida only in a very small area along the Apalachicola River on the border with Georgia.

Size: Record length 8 inches.

Abundance: Common.

Variation: Very little variation in Florida.

Presumed Range in Florida

Habitat: A lowland species. Swamps, marshes, and wet bottomlands. Especially near springs or seeps. Also found in caves and in riparian woodlands.

Breeding: Breeds from fall through late winter. Lays eggs in hidden areas in aquatic habitats like springs or seeps. Larva transform in a few months.

Natural History: The Three-lined Salamander can be quite common in suitable habitats throughout the southeastern US. Their range in Florida is restricted to the panhandle and they are probably less common here than in other areas just to the north and east. It is one of the only salamanders in Florida that is known to live in the limestone caves of the panhandle. The larva of this species is totally aquatic and has visible external gills, but otherwise has the same color and pattern of the adults. While these salamanders can regularly exceed 6 inches in length, they are mostly tail and are rather slenderly built. Autotomy of the tail in this species is common when they are under attack or if roughly handled. While they will regenerate the tail, the regenerated tail it is not as long as the original.

Class - **Amphibia** (amphibians)

Order - **Caudata** (salamanders)

Family - **Plethodontidae** (lungless salamanders)

Dwarf Salamander *Eurycea quadridigitata*	Mud Salamander *Psuedotriton montanus*	Red Salamander *Psuedotriton rubert*

Size: Maximum about 4 inches.

Abundance: Common.

Variation: Brown, tan, or yellowish.

Presumed range in Florida

Size: Maximum about 8 inches.

Abundance: Uncommon.

Variation: Red, salmon, purpleish, or brown.

Presumed range in Florida

Size: Max about 7 inches.

Abundance: Uncommon.

Variation: Exhibits "ontogenetic melanism"

Presumed range in Florida

Habitat: Low-lying mesic woodlands, ponds, streams, and spaghnum bogs. Sometimes found underwater amid plants such as Water Hyacinth.

Habitat: Mud. Wet, mucky areas in close proximity to seeps and spring runs. Also found beneath leaf litter an accumulated detritus within streams.

Habitat: Found within and in the vicinity of springs and spring-fed brooks. Found both in the water and under moss, logs, etc., near water.

Breeding: Eggs are laid in the water among mats of vegetation or near the shore in wet moss or other detritus. Clutch size can number several dozen.

Breeding: Eggs are laid in fall and winter in spring runs or bogs. About 1 to 2 dozen eggs are laid. Larva are less than 0.75 inches at hatching. They reach up to 3 inches before transforming into adults after 1.5 to 2.5 years.

Breeding: Several dozen eggs are laid in the water in spring-fed streams during late summer/fall. Females will guard the eggs until they hatch in the winter. Totally aquatic larva can take 1 0.5 to 3 years to transform into adults.

Natural History: Aptly named, these tiny salamanders rarely exceed 3 inches in length and they are quite slender. They are often confused with the Southern Two-lined Salamander but that species has 5 toes on the hind foot (Dwarf Salamander has only 4). They usually have a discernible pattern of herringbone-shaped markings on the back. This is the most southerly ranging of the Plethodontidae salamanders in Florida and can be found as far south as the Everglades region. They reportedly are mainly nocturnal. During the day, they shelter in small animal burrows or in mats of floating vegetation if in the water. Spaghnum Moss is also a likely hiding place. They will wander abroad at night, especially during heavy rains, and can sometimes be found on roadways on rainy nights. One other Eurecea salamander can rarely be found caves in Florida's panhandle, the **Georgia Blind Salamander** (*E.wallacei*).

Natural History: In both appearance and life history, the Mud Salamanders are similar to the Red Salamanders (next account). The easiest way to distinguish between the 2 is to note the size and concentration of the black spots. Mud Salamanders have larger, more widely spaced spots and the spots are more perfectly rounded, resulting in something akin to a "polka dot" pattern. Most experts agree that Mud Salamanders are more closely tied to water than the similar Red Salamander. They also are more secretive and less commonly seen than the more terrestrially oriented Red Salamander. There are a total of 4 subspecies of Mud Salamander in the US, all found east of the Mississippi River. Florida's subspecies are the Rusty Mud Salamander (subspecies *floridanus*) and Gulf Coast Mud Salamander (subspecies *flavissimus*) shown above.

Natural History: Adult Red Salamanders will wander away from water and may be found in moist environments a good distance from springs or streams. Young adults are often bright, fire-engine red with scattered black specks throughout the body. As they age, they tend to become darker on the back and very old individuals may be uniformly dark gray or deep purple dorsally. There are 4 subspecies in the eastern US and 1 of those ranges southward into Florida. The Southern Red Salamander (subspecies *viosca*) is probably the least brightly colored subspecies and tends to be more of salmon or pinkish color rather than red. Old adults like the one shown above become darker on the back as they grow older (ontogenetic melanism). Young specimens are a handsome salmon color, especially on the sides and tail.

Class - **Amphibia** (amphibians)
Order - **Caudata** (salamanders)
Family - **Plethodontidae** (lungless salamanders)

Four-toed Salamander *Hemidactylium scutatum*	Southeastern Slimy Salamander *Plethodon grobmani*	Many-lined Salamander *Stereochilus marginatus*

Size: Maximum 4.5 inches.  Presumed range in Florida	**Size:** Maximum about 7 inches.  Presumed range in Florida	**Size:** Record size 4.5 inches.  Presumed range in Florida
Abundance: Very rare in Florida. Found only in 3 counties in the panhandle.	**Abundance:** May be fairly common within its limited range in the state.	**Abundance:** Very rare in Florida. Found only in Okefenokee Swamp region.
Variation: Dorsal ground color varies from light or dark brown to gray or orange. Most specimens have dark speckling on the dorsum but that can vary.	**Variation:** May vary considerably in the amount of spotting or flecking that decorates the all-black body. Light pigments vary from white to silvery.	**Variation:** Olive brown to yellowish brown. The darker brown lateral stripes may be obscure or broken into streaks or spots.
Habitat: Terrestrial but usually near woodland bogs, springs and seeps, or other mesic situations. Spaghnum bogs are a favorite habitat.	**Habitat:** Woodlands. Inhabits both upland woods and the bottoms of ravines or creek bottoms. Requires a damp microhabitat on the forest floor.	**Habitat:** In Florida inhabits spaghnum swamps in the Okefenokee Swamp region of Baker, Columbia, and Nassua counties.
Breeding: Eggs are laid in winter at the edge of streams, ponds, etc. Females remain with the eggs until hatching in about 4 weeks. Aquatic larva stage is short, only 2 to 3 months.	**Breeding:** Terrestrial breeder that deposits eggs in underground nest chambers. As many as 24 eggs are known. Females remain with the eggs until they hatch. No larval stage.	**Breeding:** Female lays up to 50 eggs in hidden spot beneath cover and above the waterline. Female will remain with the eggs for several weeeks until they hatch. Larva are aquatic.
Natural History: The name comes from the fact that they have only 4 toes on the hind foot (most salamanders have 5). There is also an obvious constriction at the base of the tail that is unique to this species. The tail will easily break off when molested. The most readily identifiable characteristic of this species however is its white belly with black spots. No other salamander in Florda is similarly colored and patterned. Although found in scattered, disjunct populations throughout the southeastern US, this salamander is mainly a northern species. Its range occupies a large swath of the northeastern United States as well as parts of upper Midwest.	**Natural History:** Until the advent of DNA technology, there was only 1 ubiquitous species of Slimy Salamander that ranged across most of the eastern United States. There are now over a dozen individual species, nearly all of which are very similar in appearance and all of which show significant variation among local populations. This salamander exudes a thick, sticky mucus from the skin when handled. This material is difficult to wash off and once dried becomes black and crusty. The food of this woodland species is undoubtedly a wide variety of soft-bodied insects, insect larva, annelids, small crustaceans, and other tiny invertebrate life found among the leaf litter on the forest floor.	**Natural History:** Though quite aquatic in habits this salamander may also be found at the water's edge or amid mats of spaghnum moss. When on land they are usually hidden beneath leaf litter or other objects. This is mainly a species of the Atlantic Coastal Plain from southeastern Virginia through the Carolinas and extreme southeastern Georgia into extreme northeastern Florida. The range of this species in Florida encompasses the Okefenokee Swamp region. Very little is known about the natural history of this species in the state, as it is quite rare in Florida. Most studies have been conducted in other regions of its range in the Carolinas and Georgia.

Class - **Amphibia** (amphibians)
Order - **Caudata** (salamanders)
Family - **Salamandridae** (newts)

| **Eastern Newt** *Notopthalmus viridescens* | **Striped Newt** *Notophthalmus perstriatus* |

Adult

Size: Maximum about 4.5 inches.

Presumed range in Florida

Immature "Eft"

Abundance: Less common than Eastern Newt.

Variation: Exhibits the same ontogenetic variation seen in the Eastern Newt. Little variation among adults.

Size: Record length 5.5 inches. Efts are under 4 inches.

Presumed range in Florida

Abundance: Quite common. Although no more abundant than other salamanders, juvenile newts (Efts) tend to be more active above ground and are thus more easily observed.

Variation: There are a total of 4 subspecies of this salamander and 2 subspecies occur in Florida. Exhibits significant ontogenetic variation (see Natural History below).

Habitat: Aquatic situations in or around ponds or small swamps in pine flatwoods of northern Florida. Spottily distributed within its range in Florida.

Habitat: Adults are found in ponds, swamps, or other permanent water. Eft stage is a terrestrial animal of woods.

Breeding: Breeds in winter. Eggs are attached to aquatic vegetation. Larva may skip eft stage during droughts.

Breeding: Breeds in late winter or spring. During breeding, males will clasp the female with their front legs and deposit packages of sperm (called spermatophores) which are then taken up by the female into her cloaca. Thus fertilization occurs internally before eggs are then laid. Eggs are then deposited by the female and stick to twigs or aquatic vegetation. Hatchlings (larva) metamorph into efts in 4 to 5 months.

Natural History: Newts are unique among Florida salamanders in having an extra stage in their life cycle. Following hatching, the young spend the summer as gill-breathing larva then undergo a transformation to an air-breathing semi-adult that lives on land for up to 3 years. Newts in this terrestrial state are called "Efts." Efts actively prowl about on the forest floor foraging for small invertebrate prey. Although they are most active at night, they can sometimes be seen abroad during the day on rainy or cloudy days. After 1 to 3 years as an air-breathing land animal, the eft returns to the water and undergoes another metamorphosis into a totally aquatic adult. After returning to the water the coarse, dessication resitant skin of the eft becomes smooth and permeable and the round tail flattens vertically to become finlike. The remainder of their life is spent as a mainly aquatic salamander that only rarely leaves the water. As aquatic adults, they feed on both small invertebrates and the eggs of fish or other amphibians. Their life span can be up to 15 years. Newts in the eft stage produce a neurotoxin in their skin that protects them from many predators.

Natural History: The Striped Newt is endemic to southern Georgia and northern Florida. This is a species in decline in Florida for unknown reasons, but it is likely that loss of habitat may be blame. In many regards, this newt's life history and biology mirrors that of the Eastern Newt. The fact that the 2 species have ranges that overlap is a little unusual in that they seem to occupy the same ecological niche. But, very little is known about the biology of the Striped Newt and future studies may reveal some unknown factor that allows the 2 species to maintain their integrity. Although the ranges overlap, not enough is known to determine whether they occupy different microhabitat within their overall range. The food of the Striped Newt is also believed to be similar to that of the Eastern Newt.

Class - **Amphibia** (amphibians)
Order - **Caudata** (salamanders)
Family - **Sirenidae** (sirens)
Lesser Siren - *Siren intermedia*

Presumed range in Florida

Size: Maximum length of up to 20 inches.

Abundance: Common in suitable wetland habitats.

Variation: May vary from olive green to brown or very dark brown.

Habitat: Wetlands. Swamps, marshes, oxbows, sloughs, slow-moving streams, and low-lying areas along stream courses.

Breeding: Lays several hundred eggs in a nest hollowed out in the mud. Probably breeds in late winter or early spring.

Natural History: A completely aquatic salamander that breathes through external gills that are easily visible just in front of the forelimbs. Known food items include insects, crustaceans, mollusks, and worms, as well as some plant material such as algea. Capable of surviving drought periods by secreting slime which hardens into a cocoon-like structure, creating a sealed chamber in the mud. Sirens have elongated bodies with very small front legs and lack hind limbs completely. They are often mistaken for eels, but the feathery external gills of the sirens are diagnostic (eels are fish and have internal gills). This is one of the few salamanders that is capable of vocalization. They are reported to communicate with each other using clicking sounds and when captured they sometimes emit a yelping sound.

Greater Siren - *Siren lacertina*

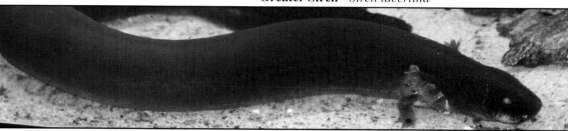

Presumed range in Florida

Size: Record length of 38.5 inches.

Abundance: Common in vegetated aquatic habitats throughout the state.

Variation: May vary from olive green to brown or very dark brown.

Habitat: Ponds, canals, swamps, marshes, oxbows, sloughs, slow-moving streams, and low-lying areas along streams.

Breeding: Very little is known. Several hundred eggs per clutch is possible.

Natural History: Essentially the same as for the Lesser Siren. In most respects a giant version of the Lesser Siren.

Southern Dwarf Siren - *Psuedobranchus axanthus* and **Northern Dwarf Siren** - *Psuedobranchus striatus*

Presumed range in Florida

Size: Maximum length of 8 or 9 inches.

Abundance: Common in suitable wetland habitats.

Variation: Grayish green or olive green. Sometimes with faint lengthwise stripes on body.

Breeding: It is thought these sirens randomly lay their eggs in scattered locations.

Natural History: Little is known about these sirens. Natural history assumed to be similar to the Lesser Siren.

CHAPTER 9

THE RIVERS AND STREAMS OF FLORIDA

As a preface to the next chapter (Chapter 10, The Fishes of Florida), this short chapter is intended to provide a brief introduction into the waterways of Florida, which are home to the state's freshwater fish species. Because Florida is a relatively flat, low-lying state with little elevation variation, the rivers and streams in the state do not have rapidly flowing waters. In Florida, there are no streams that cascade down steep slopes in the manner of streams common in mountainous areas of the country. By contrast, Florida's streams are characterized by slow-moving waters with moderate to slight current and an absence of waterfalls and rapids.

In the panhandle and northern Florida, however, the major rivers often originate well to the north of the state in highland regions. The Apalachicola River for instance begins it journey to the gulf in the Appalachian Mountains of northernmost Georgia. Both the Withlacoochee and the Ochlockonee begin in the Piedmont region of Georgia and the Suwanee drains from southeastern Georgia's mighty Okefenokee Swamp. In the gulf coastal region of the panhandle, the land slopes gently southward toward the Gulf of Mexico and all streams in the panhandle drain into the gulf. The highest elevation in the state occurs in the panhandle in Walton County (345 feet) and some of the streams in this region will have moderately fast flow rates.

On the Florida peninsula, all the state's major rivers have their genesis in the uplands surrounding the Central Florida Ridge, where the maximum elevation is 312 feet. Most of these rivers flow either south to the Everglades region or west to the gulf, but the St. Johns River is a notable exception. Florida's longest river (310 miles), it flows north for most of its length before turning abruptly east and draining into the Atlantic. The mouth of the St. Johns River constitutes the state's largest estuary (over

2,700 square miles) and tidal influence extends upriver for nearly half its length. This slow-moving river has an elevation variance of only about 30 feet from its headwaters to the sea.

In comparison to its neighbors to the north, Florida has few rivers. Florida rivers are also generally shorter than rivers farther inland. The unique shape of the state means that there is no place in Florida that is more than 60 miles from the sea. All rivers ultimately drain to the oceans, and in the case of Florida that often means a relatively short trip for rivers that originate within the state's boundaries. There are just under 26,000 miles of rivers in Florida. By constrast, Georgia has 71,000 miles of rivers and Alabama about 132,000. Figure 9 on the following page shows the major rivers of Florida.

In spite of the overall lack of river miles in Florida compared to other nearby states, the state is by no means impoverished for freshwater habitats. Florida's subtropical climate enjoys ample rainfall, and a myriad of smaller streams ranging in size from tiny brooks to large creeks dissect the state. Additionally, many square miles of the state consist of shallow marshes, swamps, and ponds. The Everglades region alone contains nearly 5,000 square miles of wetland habitats.

There are about 8,000 lakes in Florida with a surface area of 10 acres or more and countless smaller lakes and ponds. There are also more large springs in Florida than perhaps any other comparable size land area in the world. Florida boasts approximately 700 freshwater springs.

Florida's freshwaters are home to at least 222 species of freshwater fishes. Dozens more saltwater species enter fresh and brackish waters at the mouths of rivers, estuaries, and transitional marshes or mangrove swamps along the coasts. A few species specialize in making their home in the transitional zones between fresh and

Figure 9
The Major Rivers of Florida

saltwater. Others may live in salt water most of their lives but return to freshwater rivers to spawn. A few are equally at home in fresh or saltwater and can be found in both environments.

The map above shows the major rivers of Florida. Each of these rivers drains a portion of Florida's land mass. The area of land that is drained by a particular river is known as the river's "watershed." When it comes to the distribution of freshwater fishes, these watersheds can be important factors. Some fish species may be restricted to certain watersheds only.

Some appreciation for these distinct watershed regions is useful when discussing the distribution of Florida's freshwater fishes. A fish of course cannot leave the water and walk overland from one river system to another. To expand its range into another watershed usually means having some aquatic connection between the watersheds. Streams over time can change their course and sometimes connect with one another, then later be separated again by some means such as geological activity. Other means of dispersal of fishes between watersheds may include eggs or living fishes being transported by other animals. For example, an Osprey flying from one stream to another with a live fish in its talons or a heron with viable fish eggs adhered to its feet.

When looking at the range maps shown in the next chapter (Chapter 10, the Fishes of Florida) it is apparent that some species may be restricted to certain river drainages only, while others can be widespread and occur in many or even all the state's drainages. Some appreciation of these drainage basins (or watersheds) can provide insight into the biology of the state's fish species. Of equal importance, conservation organizations can monitor these various watersheds for pollution and other factors that may impact upon the health of fish populations contained within them.

Although Florida still boasts an abundance of freshwater fish species, some species in the state are now regarded as endangered, threatened, or species of concern. Like all other habitat types within the eastern United States, the waterways of Florida have been impacted by man and are vulnerable to degradation caused by direct pollution or indirect contamination from agriculture and urban runoff.

Many of America's aquatic habitats no longer support the population densities and high diversity of fish and other aquatic species that once were abundant. If we regard this fact as a warning sign relating to the health of our aquatic ecosystems, and surely they are just that, then all humans should be acutely concerned about the future of our water and our waterways. We often hear reasonable people argue against stringent protections of our environment. But few things are more important than these protections. Humans can survive for a maximum of 4 minutes without air and maximum of 4 days without water. It follows then that our paramount priorities should be to ensure that we all always have clean air to breath and pure water to drink!

It is an inherent characteristic of watersheds that smaller streams and their watersheds are integrated into larger streams and larger watersheds. With that understanding it becomes apparent that when it comes to water, everything (and everyone) downstream is affected by the quality of the water and the overall environmental health of the water's upstream. The environmental quality of that tiny brook in your backyard or on your farm affects not only the life of organisms living within that stream, but also organisms within the larger streams into which it flows. And ultimately, the wildlife living in our estuaries and coastal marshes, the fishes living in the depths of the Atlantic and the Gulf of Mexico, and the magnificent coral ecosystems of the great reefs of the Caribbean.

Figure 10 on the next page shows the major watersheds of Florida. Missing from this map are some of the state's most beautiful rivers. Florida has many small rivers and "spring runs" that are only a few miles in length. Some are in the interior of the state and originate in huge springs. These "spring-run rivers" usually travel only a few miles before converging with a larger river system or emptying into the sea. The areas shown in white in Figure 10 are areas that are drained by small rivers, spring runs, or creeks and canals that connect directly to the Gulf or the Atlantic.

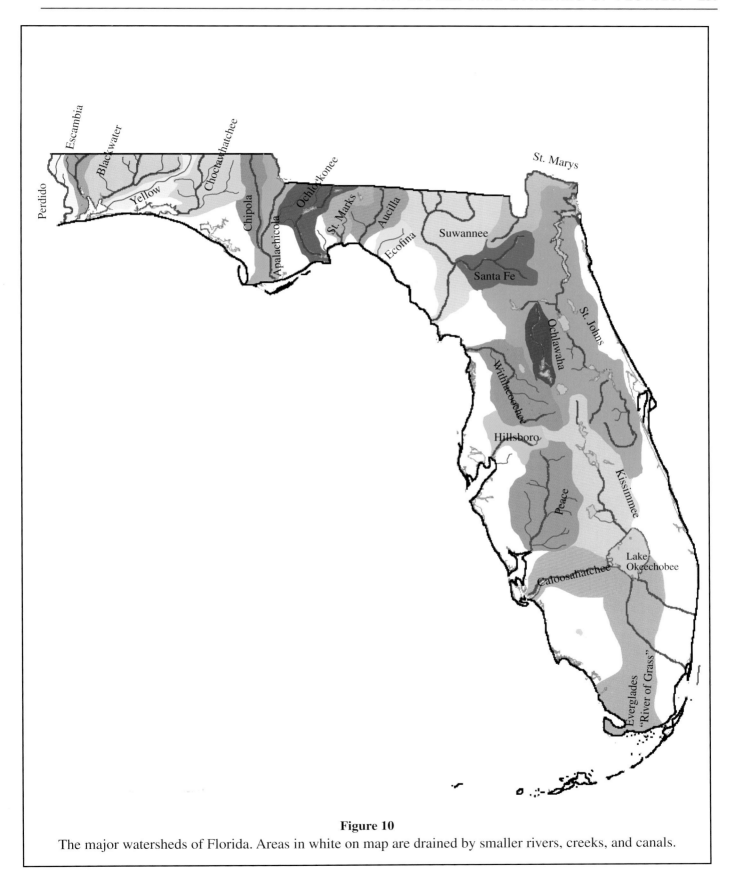

Figure 10
The major watersheds of Florida. Areas in white on map are drained by smaller rivers, creeks, and canals.

CHAPTER 10

THE FISHES OF FLORIDA

Table 7

— THE ORDERS AND FAMILIES OF FLORIDA FISHES —

Note: The arrangement below reflects the order in which the fishes of Florida appear in this chapter. It is not an accurate reflection of the phylogenetic relationship of the fishes.

Class - **Actinopterygii** (ray-finned fishes)

Order - **Perciformes** (typical fishes)

Family	**Centrarchidae** (sunfishes)
Family	**Moronidae** (true basses)
Family	**Elassomatidae** (pygmy sunfishes)
Family	**Scianidae** (drums)
Family	**Percidae** (perches and darters)
Family	**Cichlidae** (cichlids)
Family	**Lutjanidae** (snappers)
Family	**Centropomidae** (snooks)
Family	**Gerriedae** (mojarras)
Family	**Sparidae** (porgies)
Family	**Eleotridae** (sleepers)
Family	**Gobidae** (gobies)
Family	**Chanidae** (snakeheads)

Order - **Plueronectiformes** (flatfish)

Family	**Paralichthyidae** (sand flounders)
Family	**Achiridae** (soles)

Order - **Acipenseriformes** (primitive fishes)

Family	**Acipenseridae** (sturgeons)

Order - **Lepisosteiformes** (gar)

Family	**Lepisosteidae** (gars)

Order - **Salmoniformes**

Family	**Esocidae** (pikes)
Family	**Umbridae** (mudminnows)

Order - **Amiiformes** (bowfin)

Family	**Amiidae** (bowfin)

Order - **Percopsiformes** (pirate perch and cavefish)

Family	**Percopsidae** (pirate perch)

Order - **Mulgiformes** (mullets)

Family	**Mulgilidae**

Order - **Siluriformes** (catfishes)

Family	**Ictaluridae** (American catfishes)
Family	**Ariidae** (saltwater catfishes)
Family	**Callichthyidae** (armored catfish)
Family	**Loricariidae** (suckermouth armored catfish)
Family	**Clariidae** (air-breathing catfish)

Order - **Anguilliformes** (eels)

Family	**Anguillidae** (freshwater eels)
Family	**Ophichthidae** (snake eels)

Order - **Synbranchiformes** (spiny eels)

Family	**Synbrachidae** (swamp eels)
Family	**Mastacembelidae** (spiny eels)

Order - **Atheriniformes**

Family	**Atherinidae** (silversides)

Order - **Beloniformes**

Family	**Belonidae** (needlefish)

Order - **Osteoglossiformes** (bonytongues)

Family	**Notopteridae** (knifefish)

Order - **Elopiformes** (tarpons)

Family	**Elopidae** (ladyfish)
Family	**Megalopidae** (tarpons)

Order - **Clupeiformes** (sardines, herrings, and shads)

Family	**Clupeidae** (herring and shad)
Family	**Engraulidae** (anchovies)

Order - **Cypriniformes** (minnows and suckers)

Family	**Cyprinidae** (minnows)
Family	**Catastomidae** (suckers)
Family	**Cobitidae** (spined loaches)

Order - **Cyprinodontiformes** (topminnows and live-bearers)

Family	**Fundulidae** (topminnows)
Family	**Cyprinodontidae** (pupfish)
Family	**Poeciliidae** (live-bearers)
Family	**Cynolebiidae** (rivulines)

Class - **Actinopterygii** (ray-finned fishes)
Order - **Perciformes** (typical fishes)
Family - **Centrarchidae** (sunfishes)

Flier *Centrarchus macropterus*	**White Croppie** *Pomoxis annularis*	**Black Croppie** *Pomoxis nigromaculatus*

Size: Averages about 6 inches in length. Florida record 1.3 pounds and 12 inches.

Presumed range in Florida

Abundance: Common.

Size: Averages less than 2 pounds. World record is 5 pounds 3 ounces.

Presumed range in Florida

Abundance: Very common.

Size: Florida record 3 pounds, 12 ounces. World record is 5 pounds.

Presumed range in Florida

Abundance: Very common.

Natural History: The Flier is a lowland species that is usually found in natural lakes, oxbows, swamps, or sluggish streams. Most often occurs in waters with mud bottom and abundant aquatic vegetation. This fish has an unusually large anal fin that is as long as the dorsal fin.

Natural History: The Black Croppie likes clearer waters than the White Croppie, though both are often found in the same waters. Popular game fishes, both species have been widely introduced across America. White Croppie is usually much lighter, but not always. Positive ID can be made by counting the stiff spines on the dorsal fin. White Croppie has only 6, Black has 7 or 8. In Florida the Black Croppie is by far the most common and is a well-known game fish species. In Florida it often goes by the name "Speckled Perch." The White Croppie is much less common in the state, being found only in the western panhandle region.

Shadow Bass *Ambloplites ariommus*	**Mud Sunfish** *Acantharcus pomotis*	**Banded Sunfish** *Enneacanthus obesus*

Size: Averages about 5 inches in length. World record is 1 pound 13 ounces.

Presumed range in Florida

Abundance: Uncommon.

Size: Maximum size is 8.75 inches. Average is typically less than 5 inches.

Presumed range in Florida

Abundance: Uncommon.

Size: Maximum size is 3.75 inches. Most are smaller (2 to 3 inches).

Presumed range in Florida

Abundance: Common.

Natural History: An inhabitant of the deep streams of the panhandle where it favors waters with ample vegetation and hiding places such as logs and fallen trees. An agressive, carnivorous little fish that can be taken on hook and line. Feeds on small fish, crayfish, and insects. A relative of the Rock Bass, which is a fish of the cooler waters in the northern United States and Canada.

Natural History: Usually found in waters with a mud substrate. This uncommon fish lives in swamps, backwaters of creeks and rivers, natural ponds, vegetated lakes, and other lentic waters with a heavy growth of aquatic plants. Like most sunfishes is highly predaceous and large individuals may be caught on hook and line by worm fishermen. Rare and limited in distribution in Florida.

Natural History: Lives in shallow waters chocked with vegetation and littered with detritus. Backwaters of rivers and creeks, vegetated lakes, natural ponds, swamps, and pools of small streams. Can persist in tiny creeks and roadside ditches. Endemic to the Atlantic Coastal Plain from New Hampshire to the Florida panhandle. Ranges southward on the peninsula to central Florida.

Class - **Actinopterygii** (ray-finned fishes)
Order - **Perciformes** (typical fishes)
Family - **Centrarchidae** (sunfishes)

Bluespotted Sunfish *Enneacanthus gloriosus*	**Blackbanded Sunfish** *Enneacanthus chaetodon*	**Largemouth Bass** *Micropterus salmonoides*

Size: Averages about 2.5 to 3 inches. Maximum of 3.75 inches.	Presumed range in Florida	**Size:** Averages about 2 to 2.5 inches. Maximum of 3.25 inches.	Presumed range in Florida	**Size:** World record 38 inches and 22 pounds. Florida record 17.25 pounds.	Presumed range in Florida
Abundance: Fairly common.		**Abundance:** Uncommon.		**Abundance:** Very common.	

Natural History: Another lowland specialist that lives in slow-moving streams, natural lakes, and ponds, and small creeks with little current. Mud or sand substrates and abundant aquatic vegetation are characteristic habitats.	**Natural History:** Ranges from New Jersey to Florida in the Atlantic and eastern Gulf Coastal Plains. Distribution in the Atlantic Plain interrupted. Lives in backwaters or creeks and rivers over sand or mud, and in ponds and lakes with ample vegetation. Ranges southward to central Florida.	**Natural History:** This is probably America's most popular freshwater game fish, pursued by anglers throughout the country. Found in virtually any large body of water in the state. Also in smaller streams and small farm ponds. Also called "Black Bass." Florida populations attain a larger size than most.

Shoal Bass *Micropterus cataractae*	**Suwannee Bass** *Micropterus notius*	**Spotted Bass** *Micropterus punctulatus*

Size: World record is 8 pounds and 12 ounces and about 25 inches in length.	Presumed range in Florida	**Size:** Its record size is just under 4 pounds and 14 inches in length.	Presumed range in Florida	**Size:** World record is 10 pounds and 8 ounces. Florida record is 3.75 pounds.	Presumed range in Florida
Abundance: Uncommon in Florida.		**Abundance:** Fairly common in the Suwannee River.		**Abundance:** Uncommon in Florida.	

Natural History: Very similar to the Largemouth Bass and like that species attains a large size. Endemic to the Apalachicola Watershed. The name "Shoal" Bass is a reference to its habitat preference of river shoals (areas of shallow, fast moving waters). Restricted to Apalachicola and Chipola Rivers systems.	**Natural History:** Similar in appearance and in habits to the Shoal Bass, but the Suwannee Bass has blueish wash on throat and breast. It is endemic to the Suwannee and Ochlockonee River watersheds and has been introduced into St. Marks River. Like the Shoal Bass it favors flowing waters and it is often found in spring runs.	**Natural History:** Primarily a fish of clear, flowing waters and streams with gravel or rocky substrates. Tends to avoid the still waters favored by the Largemouth Bass. The very similar **Choctaw Bass**, *Micropterus haiaka,* is a recently described species once considered conspecific with the Spotted Bass. It occurs in the westernmost panhandle.

Class - **Actinopterygii** (ray-finned fishes)

Order - **Perciformes** (typical fishes)

Family - **Centrarchidae** (sunfishes)

Warmouth *Lepomis gulosus*	**Green Sunfish** *Lepomis cyanellus*	**Spotted Sunfish** *Lepomis punctatus*

Size: The world record of 2 pounds and 7 ounces was caught in Florida.

Presumed range in Florida

Abundance: Common.

Natural History: A fish of lowland creeks, swamps, and lakes, the Warmouth is found in suitable habitats throughout the state. Warmouths prefer waters with thick growths of aquatic plants. The name comes from a patch of teeth that are present on the tongue. Maximum length is about 12 inches.

Size: Averages 6 to 8 inches, maximum 12. Record size 2 pounds 2 ounces.

Presumed range in Florida

Abundance: Uncommon in FL.

Natural History: Though it can be found in ponds and lakes, its natural habitat is quite pools of slow-moving streams. It is known to hybridize readily with other *Lepomis* sunfishes, especially the Bluegill. Tolerates warm, low-oxygen, muddy waters better than many other sunfishes.

Size: Average 4 to 5 inches, max of 8 inches. Florida record is just over 0.75 pounds.

Presumed range in Florida

Abundance: Common.

Natural History: The Spotted Sunfish is mostly a fish of the southern lowlands where it inhabits swamps and slow moving streams. Although threatened by draining of wetlands in the more northerly areas of its range, it is still a widespread and fairly common species in Florida. Also called "Stumpknocker."

Bluegill *Lepomis macrochirus*	**Redear Sunfish** *Lepomis microlophus*	**Longear Sunfish** *Lepomis megalotis*

Size: Record of 4 pounds, 12 ounces. Florida record 3 pounds, 15 ounces.

Presumed range in Florida

Abundance: Very common.

Natural History: The Bluegill is America's best known sunfish. It is an important game fish throughout the country. They are regularly stocked in new impoundments and are found in virtually every significant body of water in Florida, including most farm ponds. Typical adult is about 10 inches and weighs about 13 ounces, but can get much larger (see above).

Size: World record 5 pound, 12 ounces. Florida record 4 pounds, 13.75 ounces.

Presumed range in Florida

Abundance: Common.

Natural History: These fish also go by the name "Shellcracker," a reference to their habit of eating small freshwater mollusks such clams and snails. The natural distribution of this fish was originally the southeastern United States. Today it has been widely introduced throughout much of the eastern US. It can be found statewide in Florida in larger rivers and lakes.

Size: Record 1 pound, 12 ounces. No size records available for Florida.

Presumed range in Florida

Abundance: Uncommon in FL.

Natural History: Breeding male Longear Sunfish are one of the most brilliantly colored of the sunfishes. Clear streams with gravelly or sandy substrates are the primary habitat, but they may also be found in impoundments. The name comes from the exceptionally long opercle flap. This species shows a considerable amount of geographic variation.

Class - **Actinopterygii** (ray-finned fishes)

Order - **Perciformes** (typical fishes)

Family - **Centrarchidae** (sunfishes)

Dollar Sunfish	Redbreast Sunfish
Lepomis marginatus	*Lepomis auritus*

Size: Maximum length of about 5 inches. Averages about 3 to 4 inches as adult. No size records available for Florida but presumably the same as for the rest of the population as a whole.

Presumed range in Florida

Abundance: Common.

Natural History: A fish of the Southeastern Coastal Plain, the Dollar Sunfish ranges northward up the Mississppi River Valley into western Kentucky, up the Atlantic Coast to North Carolina, and west to east Texas. It inhabits pristine waters in swamps and unpolluted streams. Unfortunately for this interesting little sunfish, pristine waters are increasingly rare in America.

Size: Florida record of 2 pounds, 1.5 ounces is also apparently the world record. Florida populations are supposedly smaller (Carr and Goin, 1955). Average adult in Florida is probably about 6 inches in length.

Presumed range in Florida

Abundance: Fairly common.

Natural History: The natural range of the Redbreast Sunfish is the Atlantic Slope from Maine to central Florida. Today this species has been widely introduced into much eastern United States This is a popular game fish along the eastern seaboard where it is quite common. Favors streams and rivers with rocky substrates. Breeding males (see above) have bright red breasts.

Family - **Moronidae** (true basses)

White Bass	Striped Bass
Morone chrysops	*Morone saxatilis*

Size: World record 5 pounds, 9 ounces. Florida record is 4 pounds and 11 ounces. Average adult is about a foot in length. 15 inches is regarded as a large individual in Florida.

Presumed range in Florida

Abundance: Uncommon in FL.

Natural History: These important game fish are famous for forcing schools of bait fish to the surface then attacking them in a feeding frenzy. Bait fish leaping from the water create a visible indicator of the presence of feeding bass. Savvy fishermen look for these eruptions of bait fish known as "jumps." Found mostly in the Apalachicola and Ochlockonee Rivers in Florida.

Size: Freshwater world record 78.5 pounds. Florida record is 42 pounds, 4 ounces. Saltwater specimens may exceed 100 pounds. Of course most are much smaller and 10 to 12 pounds is large in Florida.

Presumed range in Florida

Abundance: Fairly common.

Natural History: Striped Bass were originally anadromous fish that lived in salt water but migrated into freshwater rivers to spawn. Now widely stocked in lakes by wildlife agencies, they have adapted to a freshwater existence in many areas. In Florida rivers, it is still mostly an anadromous species. Hybrids between the Striped Bass and the White Bass are known as "Rockfish" or "Sunshine Bass."

Class - **Actinopterygii** (ray-finned fishes)

Order - **Perciformes** (typical fishes)

Family - **Elassomatidae** (pygmy sunfish)

The pygmy sunfish family has a single genus (*Elassoma*) with a total of 7 species. In distribution this family is restricted to the coastal plain of the southeastern United States. 4 species are found in Florida and all are similar in size, appearance, and natural history. Pictured below are 2 of Florida's more common species. The other 2 that are not shown are the **Gulf Coast Pygmy Sunfish** (*E. gilberti*) and the **Okefenokee Pygmy Sunfish** (*E. okefenokee*). Males of all 4 species in Florida are the most colorful with female colors being a more subdued mottled brown.

Banded Pygmy Sunfish *Elassoma zoneatum*	**Everglades Pygmy Sufish** *Elassoma evergladei*

Size: The Banded Pygmy is the largest, reaching a maximum of 1.75 inches. Other species are typically less than 1.25 inches.

Abundance: All are common to fairly common. The Everglades Pygmy is the most common and widespread in Florida.

Natural History: These tiny, secretive fishes are unknown to most Floridians. They are widespread in swamps, small creeks, backwaters, ditches, and sloughs having abundant aquatic vegetation or considerable amounts of debris (limbs, logs, leaves, etc).

Presumed range of Banded Pygmy Sunfish in Florida	Presumed range of Gulf Coast Pygmy Sunfish in Florida	Presumed range of Everglades Pygmy Sunfish in Florida	Presumed range of Okefenokee Pygmy Sunfish in Florida

Family - **Sciaenidae** (drums and croakers)

The Sciaenidae family comprises a total of 290 species worldwide. Most are marine but 1 species lives exclusively in fresh waters across most of North America (but not in Florida). Florida's freshwater representatives are actually mainly marine species that venture into estuaries and river mouths and occasionally well upstream into inland areas. Some are important game fishes. Pictured below are 2 species that commonly invade Florida's freshwater rivers and estuaries. Additional species (not shown) are the **Silver Perch** (*Bairdiella chrysoura*); **Spotted Seatrout** (*Cynoscion nebulosus*).

Red Drum *Scianops ocellatus*	**Spot** *Leiostomus xanthurus*

Size: Record size 94 pounds. Florida record is 52 pounds, 5 ounces.	Presumed range in Florida 	**Size:** Record size 1 pound, 7 ounces. No records for this species in Florida.	Presumed range in Florida 
Abundance: Common.		**Abundance:** Common.	
Natural History: Favors muddy or sandy substrates in coastal areas. Enters estuaries and mouths of rivers. An important game fish in Florida.		**Natural History:** Favors muddy or sandy substrates in coastal areas. Enters estuaries and mouths of rivers. May ascend rivers well inland.	

Class - **Actinopterygii** (ray-finned fishes)

Order - **Perciformes** (typical fishes)

Family - **Percidae** (perch and darters)

Blackbanded Darter *Percina nigrofasciata*	**Saddleback Darter** *Percina vigil*	**Southern Logperch** *Percina austroperca* (not pictured)

Saddleback Darter

Size: Maximum lenght of about 4.5 inches. Averages about 3 to 4 inches as adult.

Presumed range in Florida

Abundance: Fairly common.

Natural History: Inhabits the headwaters of rivers where there is some current. Uses streams with a variety of substrates ranging from mud to sand or gravel. Favors sandy or gravelly bottoms and is probably most common farther to the north in Alabama and Georgia. Food is tiny invertebrates, both insects and crustaceans. Some individuals are nearly solid black above.

Size: One of the smallest of the *Percina* genus, this fish reaches only 3 inches.

Presumed range in Florida

Abundance: Rare in Florida.

Natural History: This fishes range in Florida is restricted to Escambia and Santa Rosa counties in the extreme western panhandle. It is fairly widespread farther to the north and west of Florida. Its habitat is typically sand or gravel-bottomed creeks with moderate current. Uses very shallow waters and riffle areas. Food includes aquatic insect larva and small snails.

Size: Maximum length is given as 6.75 inches. Most adults are about 4 to 5 inches.

Presumed range in Florida

Abundance: Uncommon.

Natural History: The *Percina* genus contains nearly 4 dozen species ranging across the eastern US. The genus is poorly represented in Florida however with only 3 species occuring in the state. The Southern Logperch is found in riffle areas of small to medium rivers in the western panhandle where it is endemic to the Escambia and Choctawhatchee watersheds.

Crystal Darter *Crystallaria asprella*	**Florida Sand Darter** *Ammocrypta bifascia*	**Yellow Perch** *Perca flavescens*

Size: Maximum length is given as 6.25 inches.

Presumed range in Florida

Abundance: Rare in Florida where it is a threatened species

Natural History: The Crystal Darter is found in small and medium-sized clear rivers with sandy substrates. Microhabitat is areas with faster current and fairly deep water. Except for areas having dark pigments, the body of the Crystal Darter is nearly transparent. Seen in FL only in the Escambia River.

Size: Small. Maximum length is only 3 inches.

Presumed range in Florida

Abundance: Fairly common within its limited range.

Natural History: The aptly named sand darters reside in streams with sandy substrates. When not swimming about in search of food or a mate they stay buried in the sand except for the top of head. Their translucent-colored bodies render them effectively invisible under these conditions.

Size: World Record 4 pounds, 3 ounces. Florida 1 pound, 7 ounces.

Presumed range in Florida

Abundance: Very rare in Florida but common elsewhere.

Natural History: The Yellow Perch is a northern fish that is very common and widespread in the northern parts of the continent. The population that occurs in Florida is represents the southernmost population in North America. In the northern US where it is common, it is a highly regarded panfish species.

Class - **Actinopterygii** (ray-finned fishes)

Order - **Perciformes** (typical fishes)

Family - **Percidae** (perch and darters)

<table>
<tr>
<td>

Coastal Darter
Etheostoma colorosum

Size: Maximum length 2.75 inches.

Abundance: Fairly common within its limited range in Florida.

Presumed range in Florida

Natural History: The Coastal Darter is endemic to the western panhandle of Florida and extreme southern Alabama. Its range in Florida is from the entire Choctawhatchee River watershed westward. Inhabits creeks and smaller rivers and favors areas with submerge brush, logs, etc. and sandy or gravelly substrates.

</td>
<td>

Choctawahatchee Darter
Etheostoma davisoni

Size: Maximum length 2.5 inches.

Abundance: Fairly common within its limited range in Florida.

Presumed range in Florida

Natural History: Like the previous species, this darter is endemic to the western panhandle of Florida and extreme southern Alabama. Its range in Florida includes the Escambia, Black, Yellow, and Choctawhatchee Watersheds. It lives in the smaller rivers and creeks of these drainages where it is found in debris-choked pools.

</td>
<td>

Brown Darter
Etheostoma edwini

Size: Very small. Maximum length 2 inches.

Abundance: Probably common in the panhandle.

Presumed range in Florida

Natural History: Lives in shallow riffles and pools in creeks and smaller rivers with fairly swift waters. The population in the Suwanee and St. Johns Rivers is disjunct from main population that occurs in the panhandle and northward into southwestern Alabama and southeastern Georgia. Its color is mottled brown with red spots on fins.

</td>
</tr>
<tr>
<td>

Swamp Darter
Etheostoma fusiforme

Size: Maximum length of 2.25 inches.

Abundance: This is Florida's most common darter.

Presumed range in Florida

Natural History: The name Swamp Darter is a little misleading as this fish can be found in a variety of still water habitats. In additon to swamps it also occupies roadside ditches, canals, and the edges of lakes amid aquatic vegetation. Slow-moving creeks and sluggish rivers are also inhabitated. This is the only darter found statewide.

</td>
<td>

Harlequin Darter
Etheostoma histrio

Size: Maximum length of 3 inches.

Abundance: Very rare in Florida. A Species of Special Concern.

Presumed range in Florida

Natural History: Harlequin Darters range as far north as southern Indiana. They are quite widespread in the Eastern Gulf Coastal Plain from western Kentucky south to the gulf. But in Florida the species is restricted to a single river system, the Escambia River. It inhabits riffle areas with strong currents over sand or gravel.

</td>
<td>

Okaloosa Darter
Etheostoma okaloosae

Size: Maximum length of 2 inches.

Abundance: Very rare. Federally endangered and imperiled.

Presumed range in Florida

Natural History: The Okaloosa Darter is the only darter species that is endemic to the state of Florida. It has a tiny range in Okaloosa and Walton Counties. Fortunately for the Okaloosa Darter, much of this range is protected within the boundaries of Eglin Air Force Base. It inhabits small streams fed by seepage in the lower Choctawhatchee basin.

</td>
</tr>
</table>

Class - **Actinopterygii** (ray-finned fishes)

Order - **Perciformes** (typical fishes)

Family - **Percidae** (perch and darters)

Tessellated Darter *Etheostoma olmstedi*	Goldstripe Darter *Etheostoma parvipinne*	Cypress Darter *Etheostoma proeliare*

Size: Maximum length of 4.5 inches.

Presumed range in Florida

Abundance: Very rare in Florida. A Threatened Species.

Natural History: The population of this darter that occurs in Florida is disjunct from the contiguous range in the Atlantic states. The main body of its range is from southeastern Georgia to eastern Canada. A tiny population exists in Florida in Marion and Putnam Counties.

Size: Maximum length of 2 inches.

Presumed range in Florida

Abundance: Uncommon in the Florida panhandle.

Natural History: Most of the range of the Goldstripe Darter is to the north and west of Florida. They range up the Eastern Gulf Coastal Plain as far as western Kentucky. Their habitat is spring-fed creeks. Their range in Florida is restricted to the panhandle generally west of the Apalachicola River.

Size: Maximum length of 2 inches.

Presumed range in Florida

Abundance: Uncommon in Florida, common elsewhere.

Natural History: Resides in pools and backwaters of small rivers and creeks. Microhabitat is mud-bottomed pools with thick vegetative growth. Another species that is widespread in the Coastal Plain farther north but restricted to the western panhandle region in Florida. Found west of the Choctawhatchee River.

Speckled Darter *Etheostoma stigmaeum*	Gulf Darter *Etheostoma swaini*

 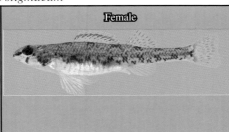

Size: Like most members of their genus these are small fishes with a maximum length of only 2.5 inches. Most are about 2 inches long.

Abundance: Uncommon in Florida. Restricted to the western panhandle. In Florida this species has been recorded from the Escambia and Choctawhatchee River watersheds. It likely also occurs in the Yellow, Blackwater, and Perdido Rivers systems.

Size: Maximum length of 3.5 inches.

Presumed range in Florida

Abundance: Fairly common in the panhandle generally west of Ochlockonee R.

Natural History: As with most other *Etheostoma* darters in Florida, this species is more common farther north in the Eastern Gulf Coastal Plain. It ranges as far north as western Kentucky and southeastern Missouri. Males in breeding season are much more colorful than females, a common trait among most darter species. In addition to all the Etheostoma darters pictured, one other Etheostoma species can be found in the Florida Panhandle. The **Backwater Darter** *Etheostoma zonifer* is a tiny fish with a maximum length of 1.75 inches. It is very rare in Florida with a single isolated population found in the lower Apalachicola River.

Natural History: Widespread in the Eastern Gulf Coastal Plain from western Georgia to Mississippi and north as far as western Kentucky. Favors creeks and small rivers with gravel or sandy substrates where it is found in riffle areas. It often hides in vegetation or small drifts of debris in water only a few inches deep.

Class - **Actinopterygii** (ray-finned fishes)

Order - **Perciformes** (typical fishes)

Family - **Cichlidae** (cichlids and tilapias) **Introduced**

Natural History: In spite of the fact that this family is represented in Florida by at least 20 species, they are an alien group and none are native to the state. Most of Florida's Cichlidae species are native to South America but the family has representatives in the Middle East, Asia, and Africa and some of those can also be found in Florida today. There are 1,700 species worldwide and they range in size from a few inches to nearly 3 feet. Many are popular aquarium fishes and the origin of most of Florida's species was the pet trade. A few species were intentionally introduced as sport fishes and some are well-known commercially farmed species (Tilapias). Since many are tropical in origin their populations may crash with severely cold winter weather, but they rebound quickly. Below are 6 examples of some of the more common cichlids now established in Florida. For a complete list of Florida's alien fish species, visit the Florida Fish and Wildlife Conservation Commission website (myfwc.com).

Oscar *Astronotus ocellatus*	**Rio Grande Cichlid** *Herichthys cyanogutttatus*	**Peacock Bass** *Cichla ocellaris*

Size: Maximum of length of 16 inches. **Abundance:** Common in canals in southeastern Florida. *Presumed range in Florida*	**Size:** Maximum of length of 16 inches. **Abundance:** Most common in Tampa Bay drainages. *Presumed range in Florida*	**Size:** Maximum size 12.5 pounds. **Abundance:** Variably abundant. Vulnerable to cold. *Presumed range in Florida*
Natural History: Introduced. Native range is the Amazon Basin, Orinoco River, and La Plata River in South America.	**Natural History:** Introduced. Native to the Rio Grande River, Texas, and northern Mexico.	**Natural History:** Introduced. Native to the Amazon Basin of South America.
Jaguar Guapote *Cichlasoma managuense*	**Spotted Tilapia** *Tilapia mariae*	**Mayan Cichlid** *Cichlasoma uropthalmus*

Size: Florida record 21 inches and 3.5 pounds. May get larger. **Abundance:** Uncommon but increasing in southeast Florida. *Presumed range in Florida*	**Size:** As much as 13 inches in length and up to 3 pounds in weight. **Abundance:** Common in the southern tip of Florida. *Presumed range in Florida*	**Size:** As much as 15 inches in length and up to 2.5 pounds. **Abundance:** Fairly common in southern tip of Florida. *Presumed range in Florida*
Natural History: Introduced. Native to the Atlantic slope of Central and South America.	**Natural History:** Introduced. Native to West Africa. Introduced in the early 1970s and common in canals in south Florida.	**Natural History:** Introduced. Native to Central and South America. Now regarded as an edible game fish in Florida.

Class - **Actinopterygii** (ray-finned fishes)

Order - **Perciformes** (typical fishes)

Family - **Lutjanidae** (snappers)

Gray (Mangrove) Snapper
Lutjanus griseus

Size: Record size 18 pounds, 10 ounces. Florida record is 17 pounds.

Presumed range in Florida

Abundance: Common.

Natural History: In Florida this species also goes by the name "Mangrove" Snapper and "Black" Snapper. It can be common in salt and brackish water habitats such as mangrove swamps. It will also enter rivers and may travel well inland, especially in the St. Johns River.

Family - **Centropomidae** (snooks)

Common Snook
Centrpomus undecimalis

Size: Can exceed 50 pounds. Florida record is 44 pounds and 3 ounces.

Presumed range in Florida

Abundance: Very common.

Natural History: There are a total of 4 similar Snook species in Florida. The Common Snook is the largest and the one that is most familiar. It is an important game fish. Florida's other Snook species are the **Fat Snook** (*C. parallelus*), **Tarpon Snook** (*C. pectinatus*) and **Swordspine Snook** (*C. ensiferus*). Mainly marine in habitats.

Family - **Gerreidae** (mojarras)

Tidewater Mojarra
Eucinostomus harengulus

Size: May reach a maximum of 6 inches in length.

Presumed range in Florida

Abundance: Very common.

Natural History: There are a total of 3 members of the marine family Gerreidae that frequently enter fresh waters in Florida. The other 2 species are the Striped Mojarra (*Eugerres plumieri*) and the Irish Pompano (*Diapterus auratus*). All favor sandy or muddy substrates and the Tidewater Mojarra may venture quite far inland in larger rivers.

Family - **Sparidae** (porgies)

Sheepshead
Archosargus probatocephalus

Size: Florida record is 15 pounds, 2 ounces. World record 21 pounds, 4 ounces.

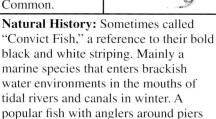
Presumed range in Florida

Abundance: Common.

Natural History: Sometimes called "Convict Fish," a reference to their bold black and white striping. Mainly a marine species that enters brackish water environments in the mouths of tidal rivers and canals in winter. A popular fish with anglers around piers and pilings in saltwater environments.

Pinfish
Lagodon rhomboides

Size: Maximum size is about 16 inches and about 3 pounds. Most are much smaller.

Presumed range in Florida

Abundance: Very common.

Natural History: Primarily a marine species but regularly found in nearshore fresh and brackish water habitats. Likes vegetated waters such as grass beds, mangroves, etc. Often congregates in large schools. Feeds on crustacean, mollusks, and worms. A popular and easily caught gamefish in coastal areas.

Family - **Eleotrida** (sleepers)

Fat Sleeper
Dormitor maculatus

Size: Males may reach 12 inches. Females are a little smaller, reaching 11 inches.

Presumed range in Florida

Abundance: Very common.

Natural History: There are 3 members of the Elotridae family in Florida waters. The Fat Sleeper and the **Bigmouth Sleeper** (*Gobiomorus dormitor*) are brackish and freshwater fish. The **Largescaled Sleeper** (*Eleotris amblyopsis*) is mainly marine but enters fresh and brackish waters on occasion.

Class - **Actinopterygii** (bony fishes)		

Order - **Perciformes** (typical fishes)		

Family - **Gobidae** (gobies)		

Naked Goby *Gobiosoma bosc*		**Crested Goby** *Lophogobius cyprinoides*	

Size: Maximum length is about 2.5 inches.	Presumed range in Florida 	**Size:** Maximum length is about 4 inches.	Presumed range in Florida 
Abundance: Fairly common in streams and canals where it is found in the state.		**Abundance:** Fairly common in southernmost Florida.	

Natural History: The Gobidae family is one of the world's most diverse fish families with about 2,000 species worldwide. 9 can be found in Florida. They range in abundance from fairly common to rare. Most members of this family are marine, but there are some that are freshwater species and some can live in both environments. Most Florida species are seen in coastal environments such as estuaries, tidal streams, brackish bays, etc. Some species, however, are found well inland, especially in the St. Johns River, which is a river that is subjected to tidal influences for many miles upstream. The Freshwater Goby lives mainly in fresh waters but is also found in brackish environments in bays and esturaries. The River Goby inhabits fresh water as an adult but its eggs drift downstream and hatch in salt water. The **Clown Goby** (*Microgobius gulosus*) and the **Naked Goby** (*Gobiosoma bosc*) live in estuaries but can be found well inland in the St. Johns River. Other Florida goby species are: **River Goby** (*Awaous banana*); **Violet Goby** (*Gobioides broussonnetti*); and the **Lyre Goby** (*Evorthodus lyricus*).

Order - **Perciformes** (typical fishes)	Order - **Pleuronectiformes** (flatfishes)	
Family - **Channidae** (snakeheads)	Family - **Paralichthyidae** (sand flounders)	Family - **Achiridae** (soles)
Bullseye Snakehead *Channa marulius*	**Southern Flounder** *Paralichthys lethostigma*	**Hogchoker** *Trinectes maculatus*

Size: Record length is 5 feet, 10 inches. Presumed range in Florida 	**Size:** Can reach a maximum of 30 inches in length. Presumed range in Florida 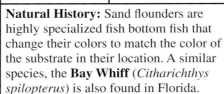	**Size:** Can reach a maximum of 8 inches in length. Presumed range in Florida
Abundance: Rare. Restricted to Broward and Palm Beach County.	**Abundance:** Uncommon in fresh water. Common in marine habitat.	**Abundance:** Fairly common, often well inland.
Natural History. Introduced. Native to Asia, Malaysia, and Indonesia. In Florida can be found in lentic waters such as lakes, ponds, and canals. Favors areas with ample aquatic vegetation. Currently found in southeastern Florida.	**Natural History:** Sand flounders are highly specialized fish bottom fish that change their colors to match the color of the substrate in their location. A similar species, the **Bay Whiff** (*Citharichthys spilopterus*) is also found in Florida.	**Natural History:** Found in both salt and fresh waters in Florida. Ascends rivers well inland and may be more widespread inland than indicated by the map above. Favors clear waters with sandy substrates.

Class - **Actinopterygii** (bony fishes)

Order - **Acipenseriformes** (sturgeon)

Family - **Acipenseridae**

Shortnose Sturgeon *Acipenser brevirostrum*	**Gulf Sturgeon** *Acipenser desotoi*	**Atlantic Sturgeon** *Acipenser oxyrinchus*

Size: Maximum length of about 4 feet and weight of up to 8 pounds.	Presumed range in Florida	**Size:** Maximum length of about 8 feet and weight of 300 pounds.	Presumed range in Florida	**Size:** Can reach 10 feet in length and weigh several hundred pounds.	Presumed range in Florida
Abundance: Rare. An Endangered Species.		**Abundance:** Rare. A Threatened Species.		**Abundance:** Rare. An Endangered Species.	

Natural History: The sturgeons are ancient, primitive fishes characterized by a heterocercal caudal fin, dorso ventrally flattened bodies, and subterminal mouths. They are designed for living a life on the bottoms of the sea, lakes, and rivers. There are 9 species of sturgeon in North America and 3 species that inhabit Florida waters. Nearly all species worldwide are in trouble; all 3 of Florida's species have experienced significant declines and all are regarded as threatened or endangered. Overharvest and dam construction are the greatest threats. All Florida's sturgeons are anadromous fishes. The Shortnose Sturgeon spends most of its time in bays and esturaries and ascends freshwater rivers to spawn. Atlantic Sturgeon and the Gulf Sturgeon spend the winter in brackish or salt water and migrate into freshwater river in the spring.

Order - **Lepisostiformes** (gar)

Family - **Lepisosteidae**

Spotted Gar *Lepisosteus oculatus*	**Longnose Gar** *Lepisosteus osseus*	**Alligator Gar** *Atractosteus spatula*

Size: Spotted Gar can reach 44 inches. Florida Gar 52 inches.	Presumed range in Florida Spotted Gar (dark gray) Florida Gar (light gray)	**Size:** Record 50 pounds (6 feet in length). Florida record 41 pounds.	Presumed range in Florida	**Size:** Record 10 feet and 300 pounds. Florida record 123 pounds.	Presumed range in Florida
Abundance: Both species are common.		**Abundance:** More common in the panhandle.		**Abundance:** Rare and decreasing in Florida.	

Natural History: The **Florida Gar** (*L. platyrhincus*) is very similar to the Spotted Gar and is actually more common and widespread, being found throughout the peninsula. It is nearly identical to the Spotted Gar but somewhat darker. Both inhabit still water environments in creeks, lakes, swamps, and sloughs.

Natural History: The Longnose Gar can be found in both large and medium sized rivers as well as large creeks. Also common in natural lakes and oxbows and in man-made impoundments. Females average larger than males and can live over 20 years. Highly piscivorous, feeding mostly on fishes.

Natural History: Adult Alligator Gars are highly predaceous and known to eat small mammals and birds as well as fish and even carrion. These huge, primitive fish have declined significantly throughout their range and many states (including Florida) now afford them full protection.

Class - **Actinopterygii** (bony fishes)

Order - **Salmoniformes**

Family - **Esocidae** (pikes)

Grass Pickeral *Esox americanus*	

Size: Average 8 to 10 inches. Maximum of 14 inches.	Presumed range in Florida
Abundance: Most common in the panhandle.	

Natural History: Inhabits swamps and streams. In smaller creeks it usually is found in quite pools. This fish likes clear waters and avoids muddy streams. This is the smallest of the "true pikes" family and thus feeds on smaller prey. Minnows and other small fish are the principal prey.

Chain Pickeral *Esox niger*	

Size: Record size 9 pounds 6 ounces. Florida record 8 pounds.	Presumed range in Florida
Abundance: Fairly common in north Florida.	

Natural History: The Chain Pickerel is a fish of clear waters with abundant aquatic vegetation. Like all members of the pike family it is a highly carnivorous ambush predator with a very large mouth. The shape of the jaws is like a duck bill, and the jaws are equipped with rows of sharp, barracuda-like teeth.

Family - **Umbridae** (mudminnows)

Eastern Mudminnow *Umbra pygmae*	

Size: Maximum length of 5.25 inches.	Presumed range in Florida
Abundance: Very common.	

Natural History: The Eastern Mudminnow is the only Florida representative of a very small family of fishes found throughout North America and Europe. They live in swamps and still waters of oxbows or slow-flowing lowland creeks. Endemic to the Atlantic Coastal Plain.

Order - **Amiiformes**

Family - **Amidae** (bowfin)

Bowfin *Amia calva*	

Size: Record size 21.5 pounds. Florida record is 19 pounds.	Presumed range in Florida
Abundance: Fairly common statewide.	

Natural History: The only surviving species of an ancient family of fishes that dates back to the age of the dinosaurs. Found in swamps and oxbow lakes. Capable of gulping air into the swim bladder to breath and burrowing into the mud to survive during droughts.

Order - **Percopsiformes**

Family - **Percopsidae** (pirate perch)

Pirate Perch *Aphredoderus sayanus*	

Size: Maximum length 5.5 inches. Average adult is about 4 inches.	Presumed range in Florida
Abundance: Common to fairly common.	

Natural History: The Pirate Perch is endemic to North America. It lives in swamps and spring-fed wetlands among heavy aquatic vegetation. May also be found in backwaters of large creeks and small rivers. Although they are small fishes, they are quite predaceous.

Order - **Mulgiformes**

Family - **Mugilidae** (mullets)

Striped Mullet *Mugil cephalus*	

Size: Maximum length for Striped Mullet is 20 inches.	Presumed range in Florida
Abundance: Striped Mullet is most common.	

Natural History: Mullet are marine fishes that enter freshwater. There are three species in Florida and the Striped Mullet is by far the most common. Other species are the **White Mullett** (*M. curema*) and the **Mountain Mullet** (*Agonostomus monticola*).

Class - **Actinopterygii** (bony fishes)

Order - **Siluriformes** (catfishes)

Family - **Ictaluridae**

Snail Bullhead *Ameiurus brunneus*	White Catfish *Ameiurus catus*	Yellow Bullhead *Ameiurus natalis*

Size: Maximum length of 11.5 inches. Most adults are 10 inches or less.

Presumed range in Florida

Abundance: Uncommon.

Natural History: 2 populations occur in Florida and 1 is disjunct from the main population that ranges widely from the Apalachicola River of Florida to most of Georgia and the Carolinas. The population in the St. Johns River of Florida is morphologically distinct and is heavily mottled with light spots. Apalachicola form is uniformly olive.

Size: Maximum length of 24 inches. Florida record is just under 18 pounds.

Presumed range in Florida

Abundance: Fairly common.

Natural History: Favors sluggish streams and backwaters. The largest member of its genus but small compared to many other catfishes. Endemic to the Atlantic Coastal Plain of America from southern New England southward into Florida. Though closely related to the Bullheads it resembles the Channel Catfish.

Size: Maximum length of 19 inches. Florida record is just over 5 pounds.

Presumed range in Florida

Abundance: Very common.

Natural History: Widespread, common, and easily caught on hook and line the Yellow Bullhead is a familiar fish to many Floridians. They are often known by the nickname "Mudcat." Ranges from the central Great Plains eastward, including all of Florida. Told from other bullheads by yellow-colored chin barbels.

Brown Bullhead *Ameiurus nebulosus*	Spotted Bullhead *Ameiurus serracanthus*	Blue Catfish *Ictalurus furcatus*

Size: Maximum length 21 inches. Florida record is 6 pounds. May rarely reach 8.

Presumed range in Florida

Abundance: Common.

Natural History: Very similar to the Spotted and Snail Bullheads but is more common. As with other bullheads, the parent fish stay with the eggs until hatching and the newly hatched young swim in schools near the surface with the mother bullhead in attendance. Found in ponds, lakes, sloughs, creeks, and small rivers.

Size: Maximum length of 13.25 inches. No information on Florida record size.

Presumed range in Florida

Abundance: Uncommon.

Natural History: This small catfish favors streams with some current. It inhabits deep pools. Can also persist in stream impoundments. Endemic to several north Florida drainages. Found in the Suwannee/Sante Fe, St. Marks, Ocholochonee, Apalachicola/Chipola, Choctawhatchee and Yellow River watersheds only.

Size: Maximum size 150 pounds and 5 feet in length. Florida record 69.5 pounds.

Presumed range in Florida

Abundance: Rare in Florida.

Natural History: This is America's largest catfish and old reports of specimens in excess of 300 pounds exist, though their reliability is questioned. This is an important game fish and also important commercially. Most common in larger rivers and their impoundments. Only Escambia and Apalachicola rivers in FL. Both a predator and a scavenger.

Class - **Actinopterygii** (bony fishes)

Order - **Siluriformes** (catfishes)

Family - **Ictaluridae**

Channel Catfish *Ictalurus punctatus*	Black Madtom *Noturus funebris*	Tadpole Madtom *Noturus gyrinus*

Size: Maximum of about 65 pounds. Florida record is 44.5 pounds.	Presumed range in Florida 
Abundance: Common.	

Natural History: Perhaps America's best known catfish and a popular game species. Grown commercially as a food fish on fish farms in the south and sold in groceries and restaurants. Specimens in clear water are uniformly dark (as in photo above). Individuals from turbid waters are light gray with black spots.

Size: One of our larger madtoms with a maximum length of almost 6 inches.	Presumed range in Florida 
Abundance: Common.	

Natural History: The Black Madtom has a rather small range in Florida, being restricted to the panhandle from about the Apalachicola River west. Within this limited range, it can be a common species in debris-choked pools and vegetated waters of creeks and small rivers.

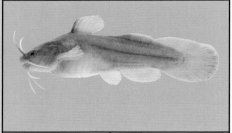

Size: Fairly large for a madtom with a maximum length of about 5 inches.	Presumed range in Florida 
Abundance: Very common.	

Natural History: All Madtoms are secretive and nocturnal, and are thus relatively unknown to the general public. The Tadpole Madtom ranges throughout most of the eastern United States. Like other American catfishes the Madtoms have spiny dorsal and pectoral fins that produce a mild venom.

Speckled Madtom *Noturus leptacanthus*	Flathead Catfish *Pylodictis olivaris*	Family - **Ariidae** (sea catfish)
		Hardhead Catfish and Gafftopsail Catfish *Ariopsis felis and Bargre marinus*

Hardhead Catfish

Size: A typical madtom in size with a maximum length of only 3.5 inches.	Presumed range in Florida 
Abundance: Common.	

Size: Maximum of about 100 pounds. Florida record 63 pounds, 13 ounces.	Presumed range in Florida
Abundance: Uncommon in FL.	

Size: Florida record for Hardhead is 3 pounds, 5 ounces. Gafftopsail 8 pounds, 14 ounces.	Presumed range in Florida 
Abundance: Very common.	

Natural History: All madtoms are predaceous little fishes that feed on a wide variety of aquatic life consisting of both invertebrates and very small fishes. They feed and are active mostly at night, and spend the days hidden beneath overhanging root wads or burrowed into detritus of deep pools. This species likes sandy or gravel-bottomed streams.

Natural History: Second in size only to the Blue Catfish. Found mostly in rivers and in impoundments of larger rivers. Adults are mainly nocturnal and spend the day hidden among submerged structure such as logs or rocks. Often hides in caves in steep banks. More predaceous than our other large catfish. In Florida restricted to Perdido, Escambia, and Apalachicola rivers.

Natural History: These 2 saltwater species sometimes swim inland up muddy rivers. They are similar in appearance but the Gafftopsail Catfish is easily recognized by its elongated "sail-like" dorsal fin. As with many other catfishes the pectoral and dorsal fins are venomous and can cause a painful wound, especially in the Gafftopsail Catfish.

Class - **Actinopterygii** (bony fishes)

Order - **Siluriformes** (catfishes)

Family - **Callichthyidae** (armored catfish)

Brown Hoplo
Hoplosternum littorale

Size: Can reach a maximum of 17 inches.	Presumed range in Florida
Abundance: Fairly common and expanding its range in Florida.	

Natural History: Introduced. Native to South America. This family of armored catfishes is well represented in neotropical America with over 200 species. They are popular in the aquarium trade but so far, only the Brown Hoplo has become established in Florida.

Family - **Loricariidae** (suckermouth armored catfish)

Amazon Sailfin Catfish
Pterygoplichthys pardalis

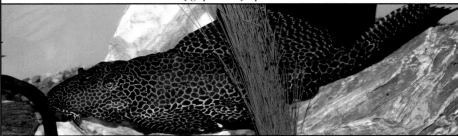

Size: The Amazon Sailfin Catfish can reach a maximum of 30 inches. Other members of the family found in Florida are smaller, reaching only 17 inches.	Presumed range in Florida
Abundance: Several members of this tropical fish family are becoming fairly common in Florida and and expanding their range within the state. Some are restricted to the southern tip of peninsula. Amazon Sailfin is widespread.	

Natural History: Introduced. Native to South America. There are 3 similar species of this exotic catfish family established in Florida. In addition to the Amazon Sailfin Catfish shown above there is also the **Vermiculated Sailfin** (*P. disjunctivus*) and the **Orinoco Sailfin** (*P. multiradiatus*). Another common and well known aquarium species that has become well established in southern Florida is the **Suckermouth Catfish** (*Hypostomus plecostomus*). There are scores of species of this genus (*Hypostomus*) in South America and more than one may occur in Florida.

Family - **Clariidae** (airbreathing catfish)

Walking Catfish
Clarias batrachus

Size: Can reach a maximum of 30 inches.	Presumed range in Florida
Abundance: Fairly common throughout the lower peninsula.	

Natural History: Introduced. Native to Africa and western Asia. In Florida it lives in a wide variety of lentic water environments with muddy substrates. Can live in muddy, low oxygen waters in both fresh and brackish water situations. Known to travel overland on rainy nights using the pectoral fins like legs, hence the name "Walking" Catfish.

Order - **Anguilliformes** (eels)

Family-**Anguillidae** (freshwater eels)

American Eel
Anguilla rostrata

Size: Can reach a maximum of 60 inches.	Presumed range in Florida
Abundance: Can be fairly common. Since all streams ultimately connect to the sea, eels can occur throughout the state. Dams can hinder dispersal and the occurrence of eels in North America today is sporadic. Male eels remain near the sea in estuaries and river mouths while the females move far inland.	

Natural History: Eels have one of the most remarkable life cycles of any fish. After hatching far out in the Atlantic Ocean tiny larva migrate to the coast and swim hundreds of miles upstream in inland rivers. After as many as 15 years adults return to the sea to spawn and die. In addition to the American Eel, 3 other eel species can be seen in Florida. The **Speckled Worm Eel** (*Myrophis punctatus*) is native to North American waters, while the **Spotfin Spiny Eel** (*Macrognathus siamensis*) and the **Asian Swamp Eel** (*Monopterus javanensis*) have both been introduced from Asia. These 3 eel species belong to different fish families and are unrelated to the American Eel, but they are similar in their morphological characters.

Class - **Actinopterygii** (bony fishes)

Order - **Atheriniformes**

Family - **Atherinopsidae** (silversides)

Golden Silverside *Labidesthes vanhyningi*	**Inland Silverside** *Menidia beryllina*

Size: Maximum of 5 inches, average about 4.	Presumed range in Florida
Abundance: Common and widely distributed in Florida.	

Natural History: The Golden Silverside is a freshwater fish that ranges throughout Florida in lakes, ponds, and still water areas of creeks and rivers. Silversides tend to travel in large schools and they are an important food fish for many of Florida's game fish species.

Size: Maximum of 6 inches, most are smaller.	Presumed range in Florida
Abundance: Fairly common in most of the peninsula.	

Natural History: As its name implies the Inland Silverside is a freshwater species that can be found in lakes, ponds, and quiet pools in rivers and streams. Another member of the silverside family that can be seen in Florida is the (**Rough Silverside**, *Membras martinica*).

Order - **Beloniformes**

Family - **Belonidae** (needlefish)

Atlantic Needlefish *Strongylura marina*

Size: Maximum 27 inches, average about 18.	Presumed range in Florida
Abundance: Fairly common and widespread in Florida.	

Natural History: In addition to the Atlantic Needlefish, 2 other needlefish occur in Florida waters. The **Redfin Needlefish** (*S. notata*), and the **Timucu** (*S. timucu*). These 2 species are rather rare in freshwater habitats, but can be found in the mouths of rivers and in canals that connect to the sea.

Order - **Osteoglossiformes** (bonytongues)

Family - **Notopteridae** (knifefishes)

Clown Knifefish *Chitala ornata*

Order - **Elopiformes** (tarpons and tenpounders)

Family - **Elopidae** (tenpounders) | Family - **Megalopidae** (tarpons)

Ladyfish *Elops saurus*	**Tarpon** *Megalops atlanticus*

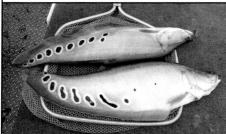

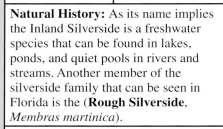

Ladyfish

Size: Florida record is 31 inches and 10 pounds. Maximum length 39 inches.	Presumed range in Florida
Abundance: Rare in Florida.	

Natural History: Introduced. Native to tropical regions of Asia. This species exists in Florida today due to its popularity with aquarium hobbyists. It has become established in a few lakes and canals in southeastern Florida.

Size: Florida record 6 pounds and 4 ounces. Maximum length 36 inches.	Presumed range in Florida
Abundance: Fairly common.	

Natural History: Primarily a marine species, the Ladyfish enters the mouths of rivers. In tidal rivers like the St. Johns it moves far inland. Also enters canals that connect to the sea and may move fairly far inland.

Size: Maximum of 8 feet and 300 pounds. Florida record is 243 pounds.	Presumed range in Florida
Abundance: Very common.	

Natural History: The huge size and specatcular leaping ability of hooked Tarpon have made this species one of the most highly sought game fish in the world. Found in both salt and coastal freshwater environments in Florida.

Class - **Actinopterygii** (bony fishes)		
Order - **Clupeiformes** (herrings and anchovies)		
Family - **Clupiedae** (herrings)		

Skipjack Herring *Alosa chrysochloris*	**Blueback Herring** *Alosa aestivalis*	**American Shad** *Alosa sapidissima*

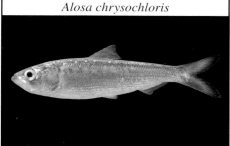  

Size: Averages about 6 inches in length. Florida record 1.3 pounds and 12 inches.	Presumed range in Florida 	**Size:** Can reach about 16 inches. No known size records exist for Florida.	Presumed range in Florida	**Size:** Maximum length is 30 inches. Florida record 5 pounds and 3 ounces.	Presumed range in Florida 
Abundance: Fairly common.		**Abundance:** Uncommon in FL.		**Abundance:** Uncommon in FL.	

Natural History: Most of the 190 species of the Clupiedae family are saltwater fishes. Five species of the *Alosa* genus can be found in Florida's fresh waters. In addition to the 3 shown above, there is also the **Hickory Shad** (*A. mediocris*) and the **Alabama Shad** (*A. alabamae*). Among the freshwater members of the this family are the Skipjack Herring and Alabama Shad. The others are anadromous (American Shad, Blueback Herring, Hickory Shad). Some marine species of this family are commercially important (sadines for instance). In general the freshwater and anadromous species are not highly valued by humans, with the exception being the American Shad which enjoys a robust sport fishery along portions of the Atlantic coast. Most have a habit of traveling in large schools and immatures of many species are important forage fishes for other, more highly valued sport-fish species.

		Family - **Engraulidae** (anchovies)
Gizzard Shad *Dorosoma cepedianum*	**Threadfin Shad** *Dorosoma petenense*	**Bay Anchovy** *Anchoa mitchilli*

Size: Can reach 20 inches and 3.5 pounds. No size records are kept for Florida.	Presumed range in Florida 	**Size:** Averages about 4 to 5 inches. Maximum length of 9 inches.	Presumed range in Florida 	**Size:** Maximum length of about 4 inches. Often less than 3 inches in total length.	Presumed range in Florida
Abundance: Common.		**Abundance:** Fairly common.		**Abundance:** Common.	

Natural History: Gizzard and Threadfin Shad are plankton feeders that filter tiny organisms from the water through specialized gill rakers. These fish occur in major rivers, natural lakes and large impoundments throughout the eastern United States, including most of the larger rivers and streams in Florida. They may also be found in impoundments. The young and immatures are an important forage species for many other fish, including many game species. Even adults of the Threadfin Shad are important prey for larger fish. Both species are popular as bait species. Two other members of the Clupiedae family that can be seen in Florida waters are the **Yellowfin Menhaden** (*Brevoortia smithi*) and **Atlantic Menhaden** (*Brevoortia tyrannus*). Both are mainly marine but will enter river mouths and estuaries.

Natural History: A salt and brackish water species that enters tidal rivers. Usually found in shallow tidal regions along the coast but may be seen well inland in rivers with large amount of tidaly influence such as the St. Johns River. There are 144 species in this family worldwide. Only the Bay Anchovy can be found in fresh waters in North America.

Class - **Actinopterygii** (bony fishes)
Order - **Cypriniformes** (minnows and suckers)
Family - **Cyprinidae** (minnows)

Bluestripe Shiner
Cyprinella callitaenia

Size: A small minnow. Maximum length of 3.5 inches.

Presumed range in Florida

Abundance: Very limited range in Florida.

Natural History: The Bluestripe Shiner is endemic to the Apalachicola River watershed where it inhabits sandy runs of creeks and rivers. Its name is derived from the wide blue-black stripe present along the side, which distinguishes it from the similar Blacktail Shiner.

Bannerfin Shiner
Cyprinella leedsi

Size: Averages about 3 inches. Maximum length of 4 inches.

Presumed range in Florida

Abundance: Fairly common but limited range.

Natural History: The name comes from the enlarged dorsal fin exhibited by breeding males. Very similar to the Bluestriped Shiner but lacks a black spot on the caudal fin base. In Florida, this species inhabits the Suwannee and Ochlockonee River watersheds.

Blacktail Shiner
Cyprinella venusta

Size: Averages about 4 to 5 inches. Maximum length of 7.5 inches.

Presumed range in Florida

Abundance: Common in the panhandle.

Natural History: A fish of lowland streams throughout the Gulf Coastal Plain from western Georgia to central Texas. Usually over sand or gravel substrates in creeks and small rivers. Icthyologists recognize 3 subspecies, only 1 of which occurs in Florida.

Common Carp
Cyprinus carpio

Size: World angling record is 55 pounds. No records available for Florida.

Presumed range in Florida

Abundance: Uncommon in Florida.

Natural History: Many people are surprised to learn that the Common Carp is an invasive species in America. Native to Eurasia, they were first brought to the US in the early 1800s. They are now widespread and common in most aquatic habitats in America. A benthic feeder that "roots" like a hog in muddy bottoms and increases water turbidity. Can negatively impact native species.

Longjaw Minnow
Ericymba amplamala

Size: Averages about 3 inches. Maximum length of just under 4 inches.

Presumed range in Florida

Abundance: Fairly common in panhandle.

Natural History: There are 2 species in this unique genus of minnows. They are characterized by the presence of a row of silver white chambers below the eye on the side of the head. Habitat is clear streams with sandy or gravelly substrates where it can be found in shallow runs. Although widespread in the drainages of the central gulf, in Florida it is restricted to the western panhandle.

Bluehead Chub
Nocomis leptocephalus

Size: Averages about 6 to 8 inches but can reach a maximum of 10.

Presumed range in Florida

Abundance: Very rare in Florida.

Natural History: This is a common fish throughout the Piedmont region and in much of the Gulf Coastal Plain. However, it barely ranges into Florida in the Escambia River in the northern portions of Escambia and Santa Rosa counties. Breeding males develop blueish heads with pronounced tubercles and orange fins.

Class - **Actinopterygii** (bony fishes)

Order - **Cypriniformes** (minnows and suckers)

Family - **Cyprinidae** (minnows)

Striped Shiner *Luxilus chrysocephalus*	**Bandfin Shiner** *Luxilus zonistius*	**Golden Shiner** *Notemigonus crysoleucas*

Striped Shiner

Size: Maximum length 9 inches.

Abundance: Very rare in Florida. Occurs in the Escambia River watershed only.

Presumed range in Florida

Natural History: As with many minnow species, the color and pattern of the Striped Shiner can change with age and significant sexual dimorphism also occurs (shown above is a mature male). Miscellaneous invertebrates including aquatic insect larva are eaten along with algae. Habitat is small creeks with sand or gravel bottoms.

Bandfin Shiner

Size: Maximum length 4 inches.

Abundance: Very rare in Florida. Occurs in the Apalachicola drainage only.

Presumed range in Florida

Natural History: The Bandfin Shiner is endemic to the Apalachicola River and its range extends well into the headwaters in northern Georgias Appalachian Mountains. Here it inhabits rocky pools and riffle areas in clear streams ranging in size from creeks to small rivers. The name comes from distinct black band on the dorsal fin of adults.

Golden Shiner

Size: Maximum size 14.5 inches.

Abundance: Due to being a common baitfish, they are very widespread.

Presumed range in Florida

Natural History: This minnow is well known among fishermen and is sold as a bait fish in many regions of the US. In their natural habitat they are fish of still water pools of streams and backwaters of rivers. They will also thrive in impoundments and small farm ponds. Millions are raised commercially each year to be sold in bait stores.

In addition to the minnows shown in the previous several pages, there are 3 other minnow species that are very rare in Florida and for which not photos were available. Those 3 are listed below. All are found only in the extreme western panhandle of the state.

Pallid Chub *Macrhybopsis pallida*	**Blacktip Shiner** *Lythrurus atrapiculus*	**Cypress Minnow** *Hybognathus hayi*

Pallid Chub

Size: A small fish reaching only about 2.25 inches in total length.

Presumed range in Florida

Abundance: Uncommon in Florida. Western panhandle only.

Natural History: This is a relatively recently described species. It is the only representative of the *Macrhybopsis* genus that can be found in Florida. In Florida it lives in panhandle streams with sand or gravel bottoms from the Choctawhatchee River west to the Escambia River.

Blacktip Shiner

Size: One of Florida's smallest minnows. Maximum length 2.5 inches.

Presumed range in Florida

Abundance: Rare in Florida. Occurs in western panhandle only.

Natural History: Inhabits clear water creeks and small, clear rivers where it occupies pools between shallow runs and riffles. Sandy or gravel bottomed streams are the habitat. Distribution in Florida includes the Yellow and Choctawhatchee River systems. Little information is available about this species in Florida.

Cypress Minnow

Size: Averages about 3 to 4 inches. Maximum length 4.5 inches.

Presumed range in Florida

Abundance: Very rare in Florida. Western panhandle only.

Natural History: This fish ranges across the central Gulf Coastal Plain from Alabama to east Texas and north up the Mississippi Valley to the southern tip of Illinois. In Florida it occurs only in the Escambia and Perdido watersheds. It inhabits stream backwaters or pools in slow moving streasms as well as in swamps. Microhabitat includes mud or detritus substrate.

Class - **Actinopterygii** (bony fishes)
Order - **Cypriniformes** (minnows and suckers)
Family - **Cyprinidae** (minnows)

Rough Shiner *Notropis baileyi*	**Ironcolor Shiner** *Notropis chalybaeus*	**Dusky Shiner** *Notoropis cummingsae*

Size: Maximum 3.5 inches.

Abundance: Very rare in Florida. Occurs in the Escambia River watershed only.

Presumed range in Florida

Natural History: This minnow is widespread in the Tombigbee and Alabama Rivers in Alabama and in the Pascagoula and upper Tombigbee in Mississippi. Its range in Florida is restricted to the northern portions of Santa Rosa and Escambia counties in the Escambia River watershed.

Size: Maximum length 4 inches.

Abundance: This is the one of the most common *Notropis* minnows in Florida.

Presumed range in Florida

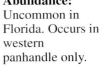

Natural History: Lives in pools and shallows of clear, sandy-bottomed streams with growths of aquatic plants. Food includes both plant and animal matter. Plant material eaten is algaes while tiny insects and small crustaceans make up most of its carnivorous diet. This species thrives in natural, unaltered streams throughout its range.

Size: Maximum length 2.25 inches.

Abundance: Uncommon in Florida. Occurs in western panhandle only.

Presumed range in Florida

Natural History: Females and nonbreeding males are similar to the Ironcolor Shiner (previous). Breeding males (like the one shown above) can be quite colorful. In the sense that most people think of minnows as being small fishes, the members of this genus fit that preconception. Most are under 4 inches as adults and many are less than 3.

Longnose Shiner *Notropis longirostris*	**Taillight Shiner** *Notropis maculatus*

Size: Maximum length 2.5 inches.

Abundance: Fairly common in the panhandle from the Apalachicola west.

Presumed range in Florida

Natural History: The primary habitat for this species is shallow riffle areas over sandy substrates. It can also be found in small pools below riffle areas. The range of the Longnose Shiner includes all of southern Mississippi and Alabama and the entire Apalachicola drainage well into northern Georgia.

Size: Maximum length 3 inches.

Abundance: Widespread and apparently fairly common thoughout Florida.

Natural History: Like other members of its genus it is a short-lived species that probably does not survive beyond 2 years. This is a species of swamps and backwaters of both large and small rivers. It will also inhabit quiet pools in creeks as well as lakes and ponds within its range. There is one other *Notropis* shiner that is found in the state in the western panhandle. That rare species is the **Blackmouth Shiner** (*Notropis melanostomus*). It inhabits slow-moving or still waters of the Yellow and Blackwater Rivers where it is usually found in the presence of aquatic vegetation. No photo is available for that species.

Presumed range in Florida

Class - **Actinopterygii** (bony fishes)
Order - **Cypriniformes** (minnows and suckers)
Family - **Cyprinidae** (minnows)

Coastal Shiner
Notropis petersoni

Size: Reaches 3.25 inches.

Abundance: This is the one of the most common *Notropis* minnows in Florida.

Presumed range in Florida

Natural History: Inhabits coastal plain streams from North Carolina to Mississippi, including all of Florida. The preferred habitat is quiet waters in lakes and pools of creeks and rivers and in the vicinity of springs. Usually found in streams with sandy substrates. Like other *Notropis* minnows it is sometimes collected for use as a bait fish.

Weed Shiner
Notropis texanus

Size: Maximum 3.5 inches.

Abundance: Very common. Especially common in the western panhandle.

Presumed range in Florida

Natural History: Very similar to the preceding species in appearance an in habitat preferences. Found in streams with sandy substrates. Uses shallow riffles and small quiet pools. Overall range includes most of the Gulf Coastal Plain, but it is absent from the Atlantic Coastal Plain. A disjunct population occurs far to the north in the Midwest.

Pugnose Minnow
Opsopoeodus emiliae

Size: Maximum length 2.5 inches.

Abundance: Widespread in distribution in the state and probably common.

Presumed range in Florida

Natural History: This minnow is widespread across the southeast from South Carolina to eastern Texas. It also ranges northward up the Mississippi and Ohio drainages as far as the southern Great Lakes. Habitat is backwaters and pools of low-gradient streams having some aquatic vegetation. Also found in swamps and natural lakes.

Sailfin Shiner
Pteronotopis hypselopterus

Size: Maximum length 2.75 inches.

Abundance: Very common in the panhandle from St. Andrews Bay west.

Presumed range in Florida

Natural History: Found in most streams in the western panhandle. Favors areas with aquatic vegetation in pools and shallows. The **Apalachee Shiner** (*N. grandipinnis*) is a nearly identical species that is endemic to the Apalachicola and Chipola river systems, where it replaces the Sailfin Shiner.

Metallic Shiner
Pteronotopis metallicus

Size: Maximum length 2.5 inches.

Abundance: Probably fairly common. Little information is available.

Presumed range in Florida

Natural History: Very similar to the Sailfin Shiner but found east of the Apalachicola River and well down onto the peninsula. Habitat requirements are the same as for the Sailfin Shiner, i.e., pools and vegetated regions of creeks and small rivers. All members of this genus are endemic to the Coastal Plain.

Flagfin Shiner
Pteronotopis signipinnis

Size: Maximum length 2.75 inches.

Abundance: Very common in the regions where it occurs in Florida.

Presumed range in Florida

Natural History: The Flagfin Shiner has a rather small range in the Lower Coastal Plain of Mississippi, Alabama, and Florida's western panhandle. It ranges inland only about 50 to 60 miles from coast. Its habitat is the same as for other members of its genus: sandy pools and runs of creeks and small rivers.

Class - **Actinopterygii** (bony fishes)

Order - **Cypriniformes** (minnows and suckers)

Family - **Cyprinidae** (minnows)

Bluenose Shiner	Redeye Chub	Dixie Chub
Pteronotropis welaka	*Pteronotropis harperi*	*Semotilus thoreauianus*

Size: Maximum length 2.5 inches.

Presumed range in Florida

Abundance: Probably fairly common in suitable habitats within range.

Natural History: The bulk of this species' range in Florida is in the panhandle but a disjunct population occurs on the peninsula in the middle St. Johns River drainage. It lives in quiet pools in creeks and small rivers and in backwaters of streams. The name comes from the color of the snout on the breeding males, who also have black dorsal fins.

Size: Maximum length 2.25 inches.

Presumed range in Florida

Abundance: Apparently fairly common within its limited range in Florida.

Natural History: This species is easily confused with several of the *Notropis* minnows (see previous pages). In fact, until recently it was classified in that genus. This fish favors springs and spring-fed streams and its range is contained within the region of Florida in which springs are common.

Size: Maximum length 6 inches.

Presumed range in Florida

Abundance: Uncommon in Florida. Occurs in western panhandle only.

Natural History: The Dixie Chub inhabits small rivers and creeks and may be found well up into headwater areas in tiny brooks. Here it is often the top predator in small pools that may be isolated during periods of drought. It is related to the common Creek Chub, which ranges across most of eastern North America.

Family - **Catastomidae** (suckers)

Quillback	Highfin Carpsucker	Lake Chubsucker
Carpoides cyprinus	*Carpoides velifer*	*Erimyzon sucetta*

 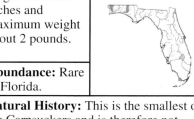

Size: Maximum about 2 feet and 12 pounds. No size records available for Florida.

Presumed range in Florida

Abundance: Uncommon.

Natural History: Feeds on benthic invertebrates sucked from the substrate. Occurs both in rivers and impoundments but may be less tolerant of turbid conditions than its larger cousin the River Carpsucker. In some regions this is a commercial food fish.

Size: Maximum length about 15 inches and maximum weight about 2 pounds.

Presumed range in Florida

Abundance: Rare in Florida.

Natural History: This is the smallest of the Carpsuckers and is therefore not highly valued by commercial fishermen. This species inhabits medium to large rivers and favors clearer waters with some gravel substrates. Siltation and lake impoundments are threats.

Size: Maximum about 15 inches. No size records available for Florida.

Presumed range in Florida

Abundance: Very common.

Natural History: The Lake Chubsucker inhabits natural lakes and slow-moving streams that connect with wetlands. They are very similar to and difficult to distinguish from the Sharpfin Chubsucker (next page), which is found in Florida only in the western panhandle.

Class - **Actinopterygii** (bony fishes)

Order - **Cypriniformes** (minnows and suckers)

Family - **Catastomidae** (suckers)

Sharpfin Chubsucker *Erimyzon tenuis*	Spotted Sucker *Minytrema melanops*	River Redhorse *Mosostoma carinatum*

Size: Maximum length 13 inches.  Presumed range in Florida	**Size:** Maximum 19 inches.  Presumed range in Florida	**Size:** The largest of the *Moxostoma*. Reaches at least 29 inches and 10.5 pounds.  Presumed range in Florida
Abundance: Common within its limited range in western panhandle.	**Abundance:** Probably fairly common. Many records from the panhandle.	**Abundance:** Very rare in Florida.

Natural History: Lives in pools and backwater areas of creeks and small rivers. Found in clear and tannin stained waters usually in the vicinity of aquatic plants. Like most members of the Catastomidae family, the Sharpfin Chubsucker is a bottom feeder. Food is probably all types of benthic organisms that occur in its habitat.	**Natural History:** Lives in pools and slow moving waters of large and small rivers, as well as larger creeks. Moves into smaller creeks in spring to spawn over gravel or rocks. Feeds on small aquatic invertebrates. Although fairly widespread, this is not a common fish and it may be decreasing in much of its range as water quality declines.	**Natural History:** The River Redhorse is a riverine species found in small to large rivers. Their flesh is described as good but bony. Although this large sucker has a wide distribution in the eastern US, they are uncommon in much of their range. In Florida they are restricted to the Escambia River in Santa Rosa and Escambia counties.

Blacktail Redhorse and Apalachicola Redhorse *Moxostoma poecilurum and Moxostoma species*		Family - **Cobitidae** (spined loaches)
		Oriental Weatherfish *Misgurnus anguillicaudatus*

Blacktail Redhorse

Size: Maximum length 20 inches.  Presumed range in Florida	**Size:** Maximum 20.5 inches. Presumed range in Florida	**Size:** Maximum 8.5 inches.  Presumed range in Florida
Abundance: Fairly common within its limited range in the western panhandle.	**Abundance:** Declining but probably still fairly common in its range in Florida.	**Abundance:** No information is available on the abundance of this species in Florida.

Natural History: The Redhorse Suckers are the most diverse group within the sucker family, with 20 species found in North America. The genus ranges across much of the eastern United States but only 3 species range into Florida. The Blacktail Redhorse lives in pools in rivers with a sandy substrate.	**Natural History:** The Apalachicola Redhorse was once considered conspecific with the Blacktail Redhorse, but is now recognized as a distinct (but yet unnamed scientifically) species. It is sometimes referred to as the Grayfin Redhorse. It is endemic to th Apalachicola River drainage. Impoundments are a threat.	**Natural History:** Introduced. Native to southeast Asia. Despite their catfish-like appearance, this fish is in the order Cypriniformes with the minnows and suckers. The can be found today in low oxygen waters of swamps, slow-moving creeks, and backwaters in the vicinity of Tampa Bay.

Class - **Actinopterygii** (bony fishes)

Order - **Cyprinidontiformes** (topminnows and live-bearers)

Family - **Fundulidae** (topminnows)

Lined Topminnow	Banded Topminnow
Fundulus lineolatus	*Fundulus cingulatus*

Size: Maximum 3.25 inches.

Abundance: Common. Ranges from the eastern panhandle to Lake Okeechobee. This is a species of the mainly of the Atlantic Coastal Plain and the peninsula of Florida. It does not range westward very far into the panhandle. It is also absent from the southwestern tip of the peninsula.

Presumed range in Florida

Size: Maximum length 3 inches.

Abundance: Fairly common in the panhandle. Also in Florida Bend drainages.

Presumed range in Florida

Natural History: Range in the Atlantic Coastal Plain runs from southeastern Virginia to peninsula Florida, and westward into the Gulf Coastal Plain of Florida's eastern panhandle. Live in backwaters and pools of streams ranging from small creeks to medium-sizedrivers. Also in natural lakes and ponds. In addition to the *Fundulus* species shown on these pages there is one other rare *Fundulus* species that occurs in Florida only in the Escambia River. That species is the **Western Starhead Topminnow** (*Fundulus blairae*). The name "Topminnow" is derived from the habit members of this genus (*Fundulus*) have of always suspending themselves just below the surface of the water.

Natural History: Habitat is typical for *Fundulus* genus. Lentic waters in swamps, marshes, natural ponds, and stream backwaters. Likes waters with ample aquatic vegetation. Most species of topminnows feed on both aquatic vegetation such as algea but are primarily invertivorous, feeding on tiny aquatic insects, crustaceans, etc.

Russetfin Topminnow	Golden Topminnow	Bayou Topminnow
Fundulus escambiae	*Fundulus chrysotus*	*Fundulus nottii*

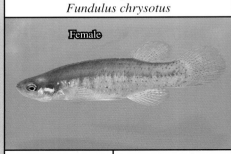

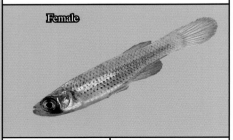

Size: Maximum length 3 inches.

Abundance: Very common in the panhandle. Also in Florida Bend drainages.

Presumed range in Florida

Size: Maximum length 3 inches.

Abundance: Common and widespread. Found throughout the state.

Presumed range in Florida

Size: Maximum 3 inches.

Abundance: Uncommon in Florida. Restricted to western peninsula.

Presumed range in Florida

Natural History: Habitat is typical for *Fundulus* species. Backwaters, swamps, sloughs, etc. Prefers areas with aquatic vegetation but like most other topminnow species it will venture into open areas where it can be easily observed as it swims just below the surface.

Natural History: Lives in backwater pools of creeks and smaller rivers. Also in swamps, sloughs, and tiny streams. Favors areas with abundant aquatic vegetation. Sometimes found in streams where they empty into saltwater estuaries. range extends far to the north up the Mississippi Valley.

Natural History: Very similar to the Russettfin Topminnow and shares much of the same habitat requirements. Adding to the confusion in properly identifying these fishes is the fact that the topminnows exhibit sexual dimorphism and males of one species may resemble females of another species.

Class - **Actinopterygii** (bony fishes)

Order - **Cyprinidontiformes** (topminnows and live-bearers)

Family - **Fundulidae** (topminnows)

Blackspotted Topminnow *Fundulus olivaceus*	**Redface Topminnow** *Fundulus rubrifrons*	**Marsh Killifish** *Fundulus confluentus*

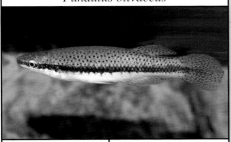 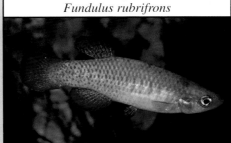 

Size: Maximum 3.75 inches.

Presumed range in Florida

Abundance: Common in the western panhandle of Florida.

Size: Maximum length 4 inches.

Presumed range in Florida

Abundance: Very rare in Florida. Occurs in the Apalachicola drainage only.

Size: Maximum 3.75 inches.

Presumed range in Florida

Abundance: Fairly common in tidal streams and salt and brackish waters near coast.

Natural History: The Blackspotted Topminnow is a stream fish that inhabits quiet pools and slow flowing runs of creeks and rivers. It also thrives in beaver ponds and backwater areas. Prefers sandy or gravelly substrates. As with other topminnows this fish is always seen near the surface and has a bright yellow to whiteish spot on the head.

Natural History: This species is very similar to the Banded Topminnow. Where the ranges of the two species approach one another in the upper Santa Fe River drainage, they can easily be differentiated by noticing the placement of the dorsal fin. In the Redface Topminnow the front of the dorsal fin is behind the front of the anal fin.

Natural History: Mainly a salt marsh species but tolerates fresh water equally well and will be found far inland. Invades the St. John's River system throughout its entire length. In addition to algae will eat a variety of tiny organisms such as insects, crustaceans, snails, and worms. Tiny fish fry are also consumed.

Gulf Killifish *Fundulus grandis*	**Seminole Killifish** *Fundulus seminolus*	**Longnose Killifish** *Fundulus similis*

Size: May reach a maximum of 7 inches in length.

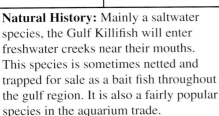
Presumed range in Florida

Abundance: Common along coasts in shallow marine habitats.

Size: May reach a maximum of 6.5 inches.

Presumed range in Florida

Abundance: Common in peninsula Florida. A Florida endemic.

Size: Tiny. Maximum of only 1.5 inches.

Presumed range in Florida

Abundance: Common in tidal influenced waterways.

Natural History: Mainly a saltwater species, the Gulf Killifish will enter freshwater creeks near their mouths. This species is sometimes netted and trapped for sale as a bait fish throughout the gulf region. It is also a fairly popular species in the aquarium trade.

Natural History: Along with the preceding species the Seminole Killifish attains a large size (nearly 7 inches). It and the Gulf Killifish are the giants of this genus of typically very small fishes. As with other members of the genus it is sometimes used as a baitfish.

Natural History: Mainly a marine species that enters creeks and canals that connect to the sea. Mostly lives very shallow marine environments along the coast, especially mangroves and brackish water environments.

Class - **Actinopterygii** (bony fishes)
Order - **Cypriniformes** (minnows and suckers)
Family - **Fundulidae** (topminnows)

Diamond Killifish *Fundulus xenicus*	**Pygmy Killifish** *Leptolucania ommata*	**Bluefin Killifish** *Lucania goodei*

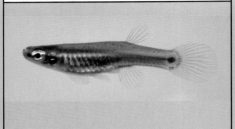

Size: Maximum 1.5 inches.	**Size:** Maximum 1.25 inches.	**Size:** Maximum length 2 inches.
Presumed range in Florida 	Presumed range in Florida	Presumed range in Florida
Abundance: Probably fairly common in suitable coastal habitats.	**Abundance:** Probably fairly common. Many collection records for Florida.	**Abundance:** Common and widspread in most of the state except panhandle.
Natural History: Another mainly marine killifish species that will enter tidal creeks and ditches that connect to the sea. Inhabits very shallow waters along the Gulf Coast from the everglades and keys of southernmost Florida all the way to Texas. Usually found in areas with significant amounts of aquatic vegetation.	**Natural History:** This tiny and handsome little fish rarely exceeds and inch in length. Sometimes called the Lemon Killifish in reference to the bright yellow colors on the breeding male. As with several other members of the topminnow family (Cyprindontiformes), this species is often collected by aquarists and native fish enthusiasts.	**Natural History:** Another tiny but gorgeous little fish that is prized by native fish enthusiasts and aquarists. Found in all types of quiet waters including in backwaters and pools of streams from tiny creeks to medium-sized rivers. Reportedly can be common in springs. Breeding males acquire a rainbow of colors in the dorsal and caudal fins.

Rainwater Killifish *Lucania parva*	Family - **Cyprinodontidae** (pupfishes)	
	Sheepshead Minnow *Cyprinodon variagatus*	**Flagfish** *Jordanella floridae*

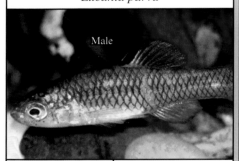

Size: Maximum length 2.75 inches.	**Size:** Maximum length about 3 inches.	**Size:** Maximum length 2.5 inches.
Presumed range in Florida	Presumed range in Florida	Presumed range in Florida
Abundance: Fairly common along the coast. Less so inland.	**Abundance:** Fairly common along the coast. Less so inland.	**Abundance:** Fairly common throughout peninsular Florida.
Natural History: Another mainly marine species that follows rivers and streams well inland into freshwater environments. Lives in vegetated shallows in areas with sand or mud substrates.	**Natural History:** Another mainly marine species that follows rivers and streams well inland into freshwater environments. A purely freshwater subspecies is known from lakes within the St. John's River watershed.	**Natural History:** The Flagish is mostly a freshwater species, although it can tolerate brackish environments and can be found there. Live in sloughs, ponds, lakes, creeks, and small rivers. Endemic to the Florida peninsula.

Class - **Actinopterygii** (bony fishes)

Order - **Cyprinidontiformes** (topminnows and live-bearers)

Family - **Poeciliidae** (live-bearers)

Pike Killifish	Eastern Mosquitofish	Least Killifish
Belanesox belizanus	*Gambusia holbrooki*	*Heterandria formosa*

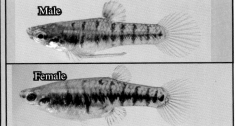

Size: Maximum 2.25 inches.

Presumed range in Florida

Abundance: Uncommon in Florida. Mostly found in the Everglades region.

Natural History: Introduced. Native to Mexico and Central America. The Pike Killifish is the largest member of the Poeciliidae family. So large in fact that other, smaller family members such as the Mosquitofish may be prey! All members of the Poeciliidae family give birth to fully formed young, a reproductive trait that is rare in freshwater fish.

Size: Maximum 2.5 inches.

Presumed range in Florida

Abundance: Very common and widespread. Found throughout the state.

Natural History: True to their name, these tiny fish eat large numbers of mosquito larva. Like other members of their family they give birth to fully formed young. They live in the shallows of swamps and backwaters, where they will forage in water less than an inch deep. They are a close relative of the aquarium Guppy.

Size: Maximum under 1.5 inches.

Presumed range in Florida

Abundance: Common and widespread. Found throughout most of the state.

Natural History: This is one of North America's smallest fish species. It is widespread throughout most of Florida except the northern panhandle. It inhabits quite waters of all types and favors areas with heavy vegetation. Mainly a freshwater species but sometimes can be found in slightly brackish waters.

Sailfin Molly	Green Swordtail	Mangrove Rivulus
Poecilia latipinna	*Xiphophorus hellerii*	*Kleptolebias marmoratus*

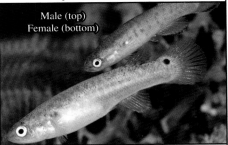

Size: Maximum length 6 inches.

Presumed range in Florida

Abundance: Fairly common everywhere except nothernmost Florida.

Natural History: Named for the exceptionally large dorsal fin of othe male. Inhabits the Lower Coastal Plain from South Carolina to northern Mexico, including all of the Florida peninsula. Lives in still waters. Mainly a freshwater species but also inhabits brackish waters. Can be common near springs.

Size: Maximum 5.75 inches.

Presumed range in Florida

Abundance: Rare in Florida. At least 3 disjunct populations in the state.

Natural History: Introduced. Native to southern Mexico and northern Central America. A popular aquarium fish that has been found in several areas of Florida, likely due to release of captive aquarium specimens. Its preferred habitat is quiet or slow moving waters and abundant plant life.

Size: Maximum 2.5 inches.

Presumed range in Florida

Abundance: Uncommon in brackish and freshwater coastal habitats.

Natural History: A marine species that invades brackish and freshwater habitats along peninsular Floridas southern coasts. Usually found in mangroves but can be seen in canals and ditches that connect to brackish or salt water. These fishes are hermaphorditic and capable of producing both eggs and sperm.

REFERENCES

Chapters 1, 2, and 10

Print

Bailey, Robert G. 2009. *Ecosystem Geography, From Ecoregions to Sites.* Springer Science and Business Media, New York, NY.

Hunt, Charles B. 1974. *Natural Regions of the United States and Canada.* W.H. Freeman and Company, San Francisco, CA.

Ricketts, Taylor, H., Eric Dinerstein, David M. Olson, and ColJ Loucks, et al. 1999. *Terrestrial Ecoregions of North America.* World Wildlife Fund and Island Press. Washington, D.C.

Whitney, Ellie, D Bruce Means, and Anne Rudloe. 2004. *Priceless Florida, Natural Ecosystems and Native Species.* Pineapple Press, Inc., Sarasota, FL.

Florida Natural Areas Inventory and Florida Department of Natural Resources. 1990. *Guide to the Natural Communities of Florida.*

Internet

US Environmental Protection Agency/Ecoregions of North America - www.epa.gov/wed/pages/ecoregions.htm

The Encyclopedia of Earth - www.eoearth.org

USGS - www.usgs/science/geology/regions

Commission for Environmental Cooperation - www.cec.org

Mammal References

Print

Benedict, Russel A., Hugh H. Genoways, and Jerry R. Choate. 2006 *Taxonomy of Short-tailed Shrews (genu-Blarina) in Florida.* Occasional Papers, Museum of Texas Tech University.

Bowers, Nora, Rick Bowers and Kenn Kafuman. 2004. *Mammals of North America.* Houghton Mifflin Company. NY, NY.

Kays, Roland W. and Don. E. Wilson. 2009. *Mammals of North America.* Princeton University Press. Princeton, NJ.

Walker, E.P. 1983. *Walkers Mammals of the World.* The John's Hopkins University Press. Baltimore, MD.

Whitaker, John O. Jr. and W. J. Hamilton Jr. 1998. *Mammals of the Eastern United States.* Cornell University Press. Ithaca, NY.

Wilson, Don E. and Sue Ruff. 1999. *North American Mammals.* Smithsonian Institution.

Trani, Margaret K., Mark Ford and Brian R. Chapman. 2007. *The Land Manager's Guide to Mammals of the South.* The Nature Conservancy, Southeast Region. Durham, NC.

Zinn, Terry L. and W. Wilson Baker. 1979. Seasonal Migration of the Hoary Bat, *Lasiurus cinereus,* through Florida. *Journal of Mammology*; Vol. 60: 334-335.

Internet

American Society of Mammalogists - www.mammology.org

Florida Bat Conservancy - www.floridabats.org

Florida Fish and Wildlife Conservation Commission - www.myfwc.com

Florida Museum of Natural History - www.floridamuseum.ufl.edu

Kentucky Bat Working Group - www.biology.eku.edu/bats

International Union of Concerned Naturalists - www.iucnredlist.org

Nature Serve Explorer - www.natureserve.org

Smithsonian National Museum of Natural History - www.mnh.si.edu

Mammalian Species, American Society of Mammologists species accounts - www.science.smith.edu

US Fish and Wildlife Service - www.fws.gov

Bird References

Print

Clark, William S. and Brian K. Wheeler. 1987. *A Field Guide to Hawks-North America.* Peterson Field Guides, Houghton Mifflin Co. Boston, MA.

DeCalesta, D.S. 1994. Effect of White-tailed Deer on Songbirds Within Managed Forests in Pennslyvania. Journal of Wildlife Management, no. 58 (4): 711-718.

Dunn, John L., Kimball Garret, Thomas Shultz, and Cindy House. *A Field Guide to Warblers of North America.* Peterson Field Guides, Houghton Mifflin Co. Boston, MA.

Farrand, John, Jr. 1998. *An Audubon Handbook, Eastern Birds.* McGraw Hill Book Co. New York, NY.

Floyd, Ted. 2008. *Smithsonian Field Guide to the Birds of North America.* Harper Collins Publishers. New York, NY.

Johnsgard, Paul A. 1988. *North American Owls, Biology and Natural History.* Smithsonian Institution Press, Washington, D.C.

Kaufman, Ken. 2000. *The Birds of North America.* Houghton Mifflin Co., New York, NY.

Peterson, Roger T. 1980. *A Field Guide to the Birds, Eastern Birds.* Houghton Mifflin Co., Boston, MA.

Mengel, Robert M. 1965. *The Birds of Kentucky.* American Ornithologist's Union Monogram, no. 3. The Allen Press, Lawrence, KS.

Stith, B.M., J.W. Fitzpatrick, G.E. Woolfenden, and B. Pranty. 1996. Classification and conservation of metapopulations: a case study of the Florida scrub jay. Pages 187-215 in: McCullough, D.R. (ed.) Metapopulations and wildlife conservation. Island Press; Washington, D.C.

Vanner, Micheal. 2003. *The Encyclopedia of North American Birds.* Parragon Publishing, Bath, UK.

Internet

Audubon Guide to North American Birds - www.audubon.org

Cornell University Lab of Ornithology-Birds of North America Online - http://birds.bna.cornell.edu.bna/species.

Florida Fish and Wildlife Conservation Commission - www.myfwc.com

McGill Bird Observatory - www.migrationresearch.org Environment Canada - www.ec.gc.ca

eBird - www.ebird.org

Waterfowl Hunting Management in North America - www.flyways.us

NatureServe Explorer - www.natureserve.org

US Fish and Wildlife Service - www.fws.gov

Crocodilian References

Print

Ashton, Ray E. Jr. and Patricia Sawyer Ashton. 1985. *Handbook of Reptiles and Amphibians of Florida, Part Two - Lizards, Turtles and Crocodilians.* Windward Publishing, Miami, FL.

Bartlett, R.D. and Patricia Bartlett. 1999. *A Field Guide to Florida Reptiles and Amphibians.* Gulf Publishing Co., Houston, TX.

Conant Roger, and Joseph T. Collins. 1998. *Reptiles and Amphibians of Eastern/Central North America.* Houghton Mifflin Co., Boston-New York.

Collins, Joseph T. and Travis W. Taggart. 2009. *Standard Common and Scientific Names for North American Amphibians, Turtles, Reptiles, and Crocodilians.* The Center for North American Herpetology, Hays, KS.

Internet

Florida Fish and Wildlife Conservation Commission - www.myfwc.com

NatureServe Explorer - www.natureserve.org

International Union of Concerned Naturalists - www.iucnredlist.org

Turtle References

Print

Ashton, Ray E. Jr. and Patricia Sawyer Ashton. 1985. *Handbook of Reptiles and Amphibians of Florida, Part Two - Lizards, Turtles and Crocodilians.* Windward Publishing, Miami, FL.

Bartlett, R.D. and Patricia Bartlett. 1999. *A Field Guide to Florida Reptiles and Amphibians.* Gulf Publishing Co., Houston, TX.

Buhlmann, Kurt. Tracey Tuberville, and Whit Gibbons. 2008. *Turtles of the Southeast.* The University of Georgia Press, Athens, GA.

Carr, Archie and Coleman J. Goin. 1955. *Guide to the Reptiles, Amphibians, and Fresh-Water Fishes of Florida.* University of Florida Press, Gainesville, FL.

Collins, Joseph T. and Travis W. Taggart. 2009. *Standard Common and Scientific Names for North American Amphibians, Turtles, Reptiles, and Crocodilians.* The Center for North American Herpetology, Hays, KS.

Conant Roger, and Joseph T. Collins. 1998. *Reptiles and Amphibians of Eastern/Central North America.* Houghton Mifflin Co., Boston-New York.

Ernst, Carl H., Jeffrey E. Lovich, and Roger W. Barbour. 1994. *Turtles of the United States and Canada.* Smithsonian Institution Press, Washington and London.

Niemiller, Matthew L., R. Graham Reynolds, and Brian T. Miller. 2013. *The Reptiles of Tennessee.* The University of Tennessee Press, Knoxville, TN.

Trauth, Stanley E., Henry W. Robison, and Michael V. Plummer. 2004. *The Amphibians and Reptiles of Arkansas.* The University of Arkansas Press, Fayetteville, AR.

Internet

Center for North American Herpetology - www.naherpetology.org

Florida Fish and Wildlife Conservation Commission - www.myfwc.com
NatureServe Explorer - www.natureserve.org
International Union of Concerned Naturalists - www.iucnredlist.org

Reptile References

Print

Ashton, Ray E. Jr. and Patricia Sawyer Ashton. 1981. *Handbook of Reptiles and Amphibians of Florida, Part One - The Snakes.* Windward Publishing, Miami, FL.

Ashton, Ray E. Jr. and Patricia Sawyer Ashton. 1985. *Handbook of Reptiles and Amphibians of Florida, Part Two - Lizards, Turtles and Crocodilians.* Windward Publishing, Miami, FL.

Bartlett, R.D. and Patricia Bartlett. 1999. *A Field Guide to Florida Reptiles and Amphibians.* Gulf Publishing Co., Houston, TX.

Carr, Archie and Coleman J. Goin. 1955. *Guide to the Reptiles, Amphibians, and Fresh-Water Fishes of Florida.* University of Florida Press, Gainesville, FL.

Collins, Joseph T. and Travis W. Taggart. 2009. *Standard Common and Scientific Names for North American Amphibians, Turtles, Reptiles and Crocodilians.* The Center for North American Herpetology, Hays, KS.

Conant Roger, and Joseph T. Collins. 1998. *Reptiles and Amphibians of Eastern/Central North America.* Houghton Mifflin Co., Boston-New York.

Niemiller, Matthew L., R. Graham Reynolds, and Brian T. Miller. 2013. *The Reptiles of Tennessee.* The University of Tennessee Press, Knoxville, TN.

Shupe, Scott. 2005. *US Guide to Venomous Snakes and Their Mimics.* Skyhorse Publishing, New York, NY.

Shupe, Scott. Editor. 2012. *Venomous Snakes of the World, A Manual for US Amphibious Forces.* Skyhorse Publishing, New York, NY.

Tenant, Alan. 1997. *A Field Guide to The Snakes of Florida.* Gulf Publishing Co., Houston, TX.

Trauth, Stanley E., Henry W. Robison, and Michael V. Plummer. 2004. *The Amphibians and Reptiles of Arkansas.* The University of Arkansas Press, Fayetteville, AR.

Internet

Center for North American Herpetology - www.naherpetology.org
Everglades National Park - www.nps.gov
Florida Fish and Wildlife Conservation Commission - www.myfwc.com
International Union of Concerned Naturalists - www.iucnredlist.org
NatureServe Explorer - www.natureserve.org
Savannah River Ecology Laboratory - www.srelherp.uga.edu
US Fish and Wildlife Service - www.fws.gov

Amphibian References

Print

Ashton, Ray E. Jr. and Patricia Sawyer Ashton. 1988. *Handbook of Reptiles and Amphibians of Florida, Part Three - The Amphibians.* Windward Publishing, Miami, FL.

Bartlett, R.D. and Patricia Bartlett. 1999. *A Field Guide to Florida Reptiles and Amphibians.* Gulf Publishing Co., Houston, TX.

Carr, Archie and Coleman J. Goin. 1955. *Guide to the Reptiles, Amphibians, and Fresh-Water Fishes of Florida.* University of Florida Press, Gainesville, FL.

Collins, Joseph T. and Travis W. Taggart. 2009. *Standard Common and Scientific Names for North American Amphibians, Turtles, Reptiles and Crocodilians.* The Center for North American Herpetology, Hays, KS.

Conant, Roger, and Joseph T. Collins. 1998. *Reptiles and Amphibians of Eastern/Central North America.* Houghton Mifflin Co., Boston-New York.

Niemiller, Matthew L. and R. Graham Reynolds. 2011. *The Amphibians of Tennessee.* University of Tennessee Press, Knoxville, TN.

Trauth, Stanley E., Henry W. Robison, and Michael V. Plummer. 2004. *The Amphibians and Reptiles of Arkansas.* The University of Arkansas Press, Fayetteville, AR.

Dodd, C. Kenneth. 2013. *Frogs of the United States and Canada.* Johns Hopkins University Press, Baltimore, MD.

Internet

Florida Fish and Wildlife Conservation Commission - www.myfwc.com

The Center for North American Herpetology - www.naherpetology.org

International Union of Concerned Naturalists - www.iucnredlist.org

NatureServe Explorer - www.natureserve.org

Fish References

Print

Carr, Archie and Coleman J. Goin. 1955. *Guide to the Reptiles, Amphibians, and Fresh-Water Fishes of Florida.* University of Florida Press, Gainesville, FL.

Eddy, Samuel. 1969. *How to Know the Fresh Water Fishes.* Wm. C. Brown Company Publishers, Dubuque, IA.

Etnier, David A. and Wayne C. Starnes. 1993. *The Fishes of Tennessee.* The University of Tennessee Press, Knoxville, TN.

Goldstein, Robert J. with Rodney Harper and Ridchard Edwards. 2000. *American Aquarium Fishes.* Texas AandM University Press, College Station, TX.

Miller, Rudolph J. 2004. *The Fishes of Oklahoma.* The University of Oklahoma Press, Norman, OK.

Page, Lawrence M. and Brooks M. Burr. 2011. *Peterson Field Guide to Freshwater Fishes of North America North of Mexico.* Houghton Mifflin Harcourt, Boston - New York.

Pflieger, William L. 1975. *The Fishes of Missouri.* Missouri Department of Conservation, Springfield, MO

Robins, Robert H., Lawrence M. Page, James D. Williams, Zachary S. Randall, and Griffin E. Sheehy. 2018. *Fishes in the Fresh Waters of Florida, an Identification Guide and Atlas.* University of Florida Press, Gainesville, FL.

Internet

Encyclopedia of Life - www.eol.org

FishBase - www.fishbase.org

Florida Fish and Wildlife Conservation Commission - www.myfwc.com

Florida Museum of Natural History - www.floridamuseum.ufl.edu

International Union of Concerned Naturalists - www.iucnredlist.org

North American Native Fish Association - www.nanfa.org

National Fish Habitat Action Plan - www.fishhabitat.org

NatureServe Explorer- www.natureserve.org

Outdoor Alabama - www.outdooralabama.com
Roughfish.com - www.roughfish.com
USGS Fact Sheets- www.search.usgs.gov
US Fish and Wildlife Service - www.fws.gov

GLOSSARY

Aestivate/Aestivation	Dormant state of inactivity usually brought on by hot, dry conditions. The opposite of hibernation, which is a wintertime dormancy.
Amphipod	A Crustacean of the order Amphipoda. Includes the freshwater shrimps.
Anadromous	Ascending into freshwater rivers to spawn.
Annelid/Annalida	A class of invertebrate organisms commonly known as worms.
Annuli	Ringlike structures, bands around body.
Anuran	A member of the amphibian order Anura (the frogs and toads).
Arboreal	Pertaining to trees.
Arthropod	A member of the invertebrate phylum Arthropoda.
Aspen Parkland	An open or semi-open area (usually grassland) that is intermingled with groves of Aspen.
Autotomy	Self-amputation of the tail, common in some lizards and salamanders when attacked.
Barbel	A long "whisker-like" appendage orginating near the mouth of fishes, often sensory.
Barrens	Open areas within normally forested or brusy habitats.
Benthic	Pertaining to the bottom of a stream or lake.
Bivalve	An organism of the phylum Molluska (mollusks) or Branchiopoda having a shell consisting of two halves.
Boreal	Northern.
Borrow Pit	Shallow ditches and ponds created by road construction when earth is "borrowed" from a nearby area to build up road beds.
Buteo	A hawk belonging to the genus Buteo. Also known as the "Broad-winged Hawks."
Cache	The act of storing or hiding food for future use.
Carapace	The top half of the shell of a turtle.
Carnivore	A meat eater.
Caudal	Pertaining to the tail.
Chromosone	Long strand of proteins and DNA found within the nucleus of a cell.
Circumpolar	Literally, around the poles. Usually used in reference to the geographic range of an organism, that is found throughout the northern hemisphere.
Cloaca	A common opening for reproductive and excretory functions in an organism. Typical for all animals except mammals.
Congeneric	Belonging to the same genus.
Conspecific	Belonging to the same species.
Contiguous	In contact with or adjoining.
Copepod	A group of tiny crustaceans belonging to the suborder Copapoda. Many are microscopic and aquatic and are important food for tiny fishes and other small aquatic organisms.

CRP	Conservation Reserve Program.
Crustacean	A member of the class Crustacea. A class of Arthropod organisms that includes the crayfish, lobsters, crabs, shrimps, barnacles, copepods, and water fleas.
Cryptic	Pertaining to concealment.
Cypress Dome	A small, rounded cypress swamp in which the trees in the middle are taller than those on the margins, creating a dome-like silhouette when viewed from a distance.
Diploid	Having the normal set of two chromosones.
Detritus	Literally means trash but in most contexts refers to organic material such as leaves, twigs, etc.
Dipteran	An insect of the order Diptera. Includes flies, mosquitos, gnats, and midges.
Disjunct	Not attached to or not adjoining.
Desiccate/Desiccation	Dry out.
Diurnal	Pertaining to day. Being active by day.
Dorsal	The top or back of an organism.
Dorsolateral fold	A ridge of raised skin on the upper side of frog that runs from the tympanum to the groin.
Dorsoventral	The region between the side and the belly of an organism, or along the lower side adjacent to the belly.
Echolocate/echolocation	The use of sound waves to navigate or move about. As in bats.
Ecoregion	A large unit of land or water containing a geographically distinct assemblage of species, natural communities, and environmental conditions.
Ecotone	The region where one or more habitats converge.
Embryo	A young animal that is developing from a fertilized egg. Embryonic stage ends at birth or hatching.
Endemic	Native to a particular area.
Endotherm/Endothermic	A organism that regulates its body tempaerature internally. Warm blooded.
Ephemeral	Fleeting. Temporary.
Estuary/Estuaries	The region where a river or stream meets the sea.
Extirpated	No longer found within a given area.
Extant	Still present. Opposite of extirpated.
Fecund/Fecundity	Capable of producing abundant offspring.
Fin rays	The bony structures that support the membranes of a fishes fin.
Florida Bend	A region along the Gulf Coast of Florida where the coast of the panhandle bends southward toward the peninsula.
Fossorial	Burrowing or living in underground burrows.
FWC	Acronym for Florida Wildlife Commission. Proper name is Florida Fish and Wildlife Conservation Commission.
Gastropod	A class of the animal phylum Molluska. Includes snails and slugs.
Hammock	A woodland dominated by hardwoods such as Live Oak but also often containing other tree species such as Cabbage Palm. Two types occur in Florida, Tropical Hammocks in south Florida and Temperate Hammocks elsewhere in the state.
Herbaceous	A type of flowering plant which does not develop woody tissue.
Hermaphroditic	Possessing both male and female sexual characteristics.

Heterocercal	Pertains to the shape of the caudal fin of a fish in which the upper lobe is longer than the bottom lobe and often has and extension of the spine into the upper lobe of the fin.
Holarctic	The circumpolar region that includes polar regions of North America, Europe, and Asia.
Homogeneous	Of the same kind.
Humus	decayed or decaying plant material.
Insectivorus	Insect eating.
Invertivorous	Feeding on invertebrates.
Intergrade	An organism which possess morphological characteristics that are intermediate between two distinctly different forms.
Irruptive	The sudden movement of animals from one portion of their range to another, often very distant portion of their range. As in when Snowy Owls occasionally move down from the Arctic region into the southern half of North America.
Isopod	An order of Crustaceans that includes the familiar pillbugs.
Keeled Scales	The presence of a small ridge down the middle of the dorsal scales on snakes.
Lentic	Non-flowing bodies of water, lakes, swamps, ponds, etc.
Mandible	The lower jaw of an animal or the bill of a bird.
Marine	Pertaining to living in a saltwater environment.
Mast	Seeds produced by plants in a deciduous forest. Usually means the cumulative production of acorns, nuts, berries, seeds, etc., which are widely utilized by wildlife as food.
Melanistic	A predominance of the dark pigment known as melanin. The opposite of Albinistic.
Mesic	Damp or moist.
Metabolic/Metabolism	The sum of the chemical activity that occurs within a living organism. Usually relates to the digestion of food and utilization of food compounds within the body.
Metamorphose	Change of the body. Usually refers to the change from an immature stage to a more mature stage (as in a tadpole to a frog).
Metamorphosis	Abrupt physical change of body form.
Millinery Trade	The sale of bird feathers.
Molt	The shedding of and renewal (replacement) of skin, hair, or feathers.
Moraine	Large mass of earth, sand, gravels, and rock bulldozed by glacial movement. Moraines usually accumulate along the sides and in the front of glaciers.
Morphology	The study of the body form, shape, and structure of organisms, including colors or patterns.
Muskeg	A Sphagnum bog occuring the boreal (northern) regions of North America.
Neonate	A newborn (or newly hatched) young.
Neotony/Neotenic	The condition of retaining juvenile characteristics into adulthood.
Neotropical	Pertaining to the tropical regions of the western hemisphere.
Nuptial	Pertaining to breeding.
Obligate	In biology means occuring within a restricted environment.
Omnivore	Eats both plant and animal matter.
Ontogenetic	Related to the development or age of an organism.

Opercle flap	The bony structure on the side of a fish's head that covers the gills. Also sometimes called gill cover.
Organism	A living thing.
Orthopteran	A member of the insect order Orthoptera. Includes such well know insects as crickets and grasshoppers.
Ossification	The formation of bone.
Palearctic	The geographic region that includes Europe and northern Asia.
Parotoid Gland	The large lump on each side of the head of toads.
Parthenogenesis	The development of an ovum (egg) without fertilization.
Passage Migrant	Refers to birds that merely migrate through an area without staying any appreciable amount of time.
Pectoral	Pertain to or located in the chest area.
Pelage	Fur.
Pelagic	Pertaining to deep ocean waters far offshore.
Pelvic	Pertaining to or located in the region of the pelvis (hips).
Phylogeny	The evolutionary relationships and/or evolutionary history of organisms.
Physiography	Refers to the natural features of a landscape, i.e. mountians, rivers, plains, etc.
Piscivorous	Fish eating.
Plastron	The ventral (bottom) portion of a turtle's shell.
Plumage	The feathers of a bird.
Polychaete worms	Annelid worms (Phylum Annelida) belonging to the class Polychaeta. Mostly marine but some are fresh water.
Precocious	Having adult (or highly developed) characteristics in the young. Precocial being highly precocious.
Predaceous	Feeding on other animals, being a predator.
Piscivorous	Fish eating.
Puddle Duck	Ducks belonging to the genus *Anas*.
Prehensile	Grasping. As in a prehensile tail that is able to wrap around and grasp a tree limb.
Regenerative	Refers to the ability to repair or replace damage or destroyed tissues or structures.
Riparian	Pertaining to the bank of a stream or river.
Sexual Dimorphism	Morphological differences between the sexes.
Species of Concern	A species or subspecies which might become threatened under continued or increased stress.
Spermatophore	An encapsulated package of sperm deposited in the environment by the male that is then picked up by the female.
Successional woodlands/areas	Landscape areas (usually woodlands) that are undergoing change from an early stage of development to an older stage. As in woodlands regenerating following logging operations.
Sympatric/Sympatrically	A condition where more than one species occurs in the same or overlapping area or habitat.
Taiga	A type of forest occuring in the far north. Usually dominated by dwarfed spruces.
Tannins	Dark-colored compounds that are found in plants. Decaying plant material releases tannins that are responsible for the "tea-colored" waters seen in swamps and "black water" streams.

Tetraploid	possessing four chromosones.
Topography	The configuration of the land surface. Literally, "the lay of the land."
Troglodyte	Cave dwelling. Usually refers to organisms that live in caves.
Torpor	A period of inactivity.
Turbid	Water that is opaque due to the high amount of suspended silt particles.
Tympanum	The circular ear structure on the side of the head of frogs and toads
USFWS	Acronym for the United States Fish and Wildlife Service.
Ventral	Pertaining to the belly or bottom side of and organism.
Vernal	Pertaining to spring. Also frequently used to describe temporary ponds and pools that hold water only during the wet season.
Vestigial	A rudimentary structure. Usually a remnant, degenerative structure that was once (in the evolutionary history of the organism) a fully functioning structure.
Xeric	Dry.
Zygote	A fertilized egg that has not yet begun to divide.

INDEX

PHOTO CREDITS

Florida Fish and Wildlife Conservation Commission

Florida Mouse, Southeastern Shrew, Yellow Bat, Florida Bonneted Bat, White-crowned Pigeon, Leatherback Sea Turtle, Keys Mole Skink, Florida Bog Frog, Striped Newt, Spotted Tilapia, Crested Goby, Bullseye Snakehead, Gulf Sturgeon, Hogchocker, Clown Knifefish, Mayan Cichlid, Brown Hoplo, Pike Killifish, Brazilian Free-tailed Bat

Brian Zimmerman

Swamp Darter, Highfin Carpsucker, Lake Chubsucker, Bannerfin Shiner, Eastern Mudminnow, Lined Topminnow M, Lined Topminnow F, Pygmy Killifish, Rainwater Killifish, Bluefin Killifish, Seminole Killifish, Least Killifish M, Least Killifsh F, Shadow Bass, Snail Bullhead, Speckled Madtom, Inland Silverside

Dr. Edmund Zimmerer

Eastern Glass Lizard, Mediterranean Gecko, Indo-Pacific House Gecko, Florida Scrub Lizard, Striped Swamp Snake, Little Grass Frog, Gopher Frog, River Frog, Frosted Flatwoods Salamander, Southeastern Slimy Salamander

John R. MacGregor

Spotted Skunk, Golden Mouse, Rafinesque's Big-eared Bat, Hoary Bat, Gray Bat, Eastern Red Bat, Four-toed Salamander, Slender Glass Lizard

Matthew R. Thomas

Harlequin Darter, Cypress Darter, Speckled Darter M, Speckled Darter F, Skipjack Herring, Threadfin Shad, Quillback, River Redhorse

Don Martin Bird Photograpy

Least Flycatcher, Ruby-crowned Kinglet, Sedge Wren, Virginia Rail, Henslow's Sparrow, LeConte's Sparrow. Red-cockaded Woodpecker, Gull-billed Tern

Brett Albanese, Georgia DNR

Atlantic Sturgeon, Naked Goby, Southern Flounder, Longnose Shiner, Taillight Shiner, Blacktail Redhorse, Golden Silverside, Bluestripe Shiner, Bandfin Shiner

J. D. Willson

Rainbow Snake, Island Glass Lizard, Coastal Plain Cooter, Florida Reef Gecko, Tokay Gecko, Veiled Chameleon, Walking Catfish

Candy McNamee

Monk Parakeet, Smooth-billed Ani, Rufeous Hummingbird, Nanday Parakeet, Magnificnet Frigatebird, Sooty Tern

Jake Scott
Mud Salamander, Many-lined Salamander, Florida Worm Lizard, Giant Ameiva, Spectacled Caimen

David Speiser, www.lilibirds.com
Connecticut Warbler, Saltmarsh Sparrow, Black Scoter M, Black Scoter F

James Kiser
Evening Bat, Southeastern Bat, Seminole Bat, Oak Toad, Pine Barrens Treefrog

Alan Cressler
Greenhouse Frog, Knight Anole, Brown Darter

Konrad Schmidt
Crystal Darter, Marsh Killifish, Russetfin Topminnow

Corey Raimond
Dwarf Salamander, Northern Dwarf Siren, Rough Earth Snake

Noel Burkhead and Howard Jelks, USGS
Florida Sand Darter, Chocktawahatchee Darter, Dixie Chub, Banded Topminnow

Noel Burkhead, USGS
Coastal Darter, Okaloosa Darter, Black Madtom, Oriental Weatherfish

W. Mike Howell
Bay Anchovy, Longjaw Minnow

NOAH Library and SEFSC Pacagoula Laboratory; collection of Brandi Noble
Pinfish, Atlantic Needlefish

U.S, Fish and Wildlife Service
Oldfield Mouse, Hawksbille Turtle

Dan Scolaro
Black-whiskered Vireo, Short-tailed Hawk

Fishingwithpole
Blueback Herring, American Shad

Howard Jelks, USGS
Red Eye Chub

Cheryl Tanner
Eastern Harvest Mouse

Jeffrey Offermann
Long-tailed Weasel

John Williams
Eastern Woodrat

Chris Crippen
Shornose Sturgeon

Aubrey Pawlikowski
Southeastern Pocket Gopher

Sandeep Gangadharan
Red-whiskered Bulbul

Tim Johnson
Feral Hog

Victor G. Ferenzi
Round-tailed Muskrat

T. Travis Brown
Striped Mullet

Greg Schechter
Southern Short-tailed Shrew

Jules Wyman
Florida Sand Skink

Dr. Adam Kaeser
Suwannee Bass

Frans Vermeullen, www.itrainsfishes.net
Mangrove Rivulus

Anthony Terceira
Red-faced Topminnow

ABOUT THE AUTHOR

Naturalist Scott Shupe began his professional career in 1971 at the famed Ross Allen Reptile Institute and Venom Laboratory in Silver Springs, FL. He later worked at the St. Augustine Alligator Farm in St. Augustine, FL, and worked under contract with Reptile Gardens in Rapid City, SD. From 1992 to 2002, he partnered with the Knight and Hale Game Call company in Cadiz, KY, where he served as director of The Woods and Wetlands Wildlife Center, a private zoo/nature center. He is the founder and original owner of the Natural History Educational Company, an organization of professional naturalists that provided live-animal wildlife education programs to thousands of schools throughout

the United States. From 2005 to 2017, he enjoyed an association with the Kentucky Reptile Zoo and Venom Laboratory in Slade, KY, traveling to schools and libraries with his World of Reptiles program.

He has served as a host and narrator for wildlife-related television programming (In the Wild, Outdoor Channel), produced educational life science videos, and has appeared as a guest naturalist on a number of public television programs and satellite networks. He has been recognized for his contributions to conservation education by the US Fish and Wildlife Service, named naturalist of the year by the Kentucky Society of Naturalists, awarded the Jesse Stuart Media Award by the Kentucky School Library Association on two occasions, and received the Environmental Stewardship Award from the Kentucky Environmental Quality Commission. From 1987 to 2018, he contracted annually with the Kentucky Department of Parks to provide naturalist programming in state parks across Kentucky.

He has written for outdoor and nature periodicals and scientific journals and his wildlife photographs have appeared in dozens of nature magazines and books. This is the fifth book in as series of wildlife encyclopedia being produced for Skyhorse Publishing. He has also authored for the same publisher wildlife encyclopedias for the states of Kentucky, Ohio, New York, and Illinois, as well as authoring *US Guide to Venomous Snakes and their Mimics* and editing *Venomous Snakes of the World, A Handbook for Use by US Amphibious Forces*. A freelance naturalist with nearly forty years experience in a wide array of nature interpretation, wildlife tourism, education, zoological exhibits administration, writing, and wildlife photography and videography, he currently describes himself as a dedicated wanderer who roams the continent in search of new species to photograph.

Contact Scott Shupe at: kscottshupe@gmail.com.